C000076282

ALLIES IN WAR

ALLIES IN WAR

BRITAIN AND AMERICA AGAINST THE AXIS POWERS
1940–1945

MARK A. STOLER

A MEMBER OF THE HODDER HEADLINE GROUP

MORAY COUNCIL LIBRARIES & INFO.SERVICES	
20 20 29 50	
Askews	
940.54012	

First published in Great Britain in 2005 by
Hodder Education, a member of the Hodder Headline Group,
338 Euston Road, London NW1 3BH

Paperback edition published 2007

www.hoddereducation.com

Distributed in the United States of America by
Oxford University Press Inc.
198 Madison Avenue, New York, NY 10016

© 2005 Mark A. Stoler

All rights reserved. No part of this publication may be reproduced or
transmitted in any form or by any means, electronically or mechanically,
including photocopying, recording or any information storage or retrieval
system, without either prior permission in writing from the publisher or a
licence permitting restricted copying. In the United Kingdom such licences
are issued by the Copyright Licensing Agency: Saffron House, 6–10 Kirby Street,
London EC1N 8TS.

The advice and information in this book are believed to be true and
accurate at the date of going to press, but neither the author nor the publisher
can accept any legal responsibility or liability for any errors or omissions.

British Library Cataloguing in Publication Data
A catalogue record for this book is available from the British Library

Library of Congress Cataloging-in-Publication Data
A catalog record for this book is available from the Library of Congress

ISBN: 978-0-340-72027-1

1 2 3 4 5 6 7 8 9 10

Typeset in 10.5/12.5 Apollo MT by Servis Filmsetting Ltd, Manchester
Printed and bound in the UK by CPI Bath

What do you think about this book? Or any other
Hodder Education title? Please send your comments to
the feedback section on www.hoddereducation.com.

For Eben, Tara and David
with love

CONTENTS

LIST OF ILLUSTRATIONS

LIST OF MAPS

ABBREVIATIONS

AAF	US Army Air Forces
ABDA	American-British-Dutch-Australian combined command in Southeast Asia/Pacific
AMTRAC	amphibious tractor landing craft
ASDIC	sonar
CBI	US China-Burma-India theatre
CCS	Anglo-American Combined Chiefs of Staff
CIA	US Central Intelligence Agency
CIGS	British Chief of the Imperial General Staff
CNO	US Chief of Naval Operations
COS	British Chiefs of Staff Committee
COSSAC	Chief of Staff, Supreme Allied Commander (Designate)
ETO	US European Theater of Operation
FUSAG	fraudulent First US Army Group
GATT	General Agreements on Tariff and Trade
HF/DF	High Frequency Direction Finding
JCS	US Joint Chiefs of Staff
KMT	Chinese *Kuomintang* Party
LOC	lines of communication
LST	landing ship tank
METOX	German U-boat device to detect airborne radar
MI5 and MI6	British Intelligence Divisions
NAFTA	North American Free Trade Agreement
NATO	North Atlantic Treaty Organization
OPD	Operations Division, US Army General Staff
OSRD	US Office of Scientific Research and Development
OSS	US Office of Strategic Services
POA	Pacific Ocean Areas
POW	prisoner of war
RAF	Royal Air Force
SACO	Sino-American Co-operative Organization
SEAC	Southeast Asia Command
SHAEF	Supreme Headquarters, Allied Expeditionary Forces
SOE	British Special Operations Executive
SWPA	Southwest Pacific Area
USSTAF	US Strategic Air Forces in Europe
WTO	World Trade Organization

CODE NAMES

ABC-1	Anglo-American 'Germany-first' strategic agreement of March 1941
ACCOLADE	Plan for capture of Rhodes, 1943–44
ANAKIM	Plan for reconquest of Burma, 1943
ANVIL/DRAGOON	1944 invasion of Southern France
ARCADIA	Anglo-American summit conference in Washington, DC, December 1941–January 1942
ARGONAUT	Anglo-American-Soviet summit conference in Yalta, USSR, February 1945
AUTUMN FOG	German Ardennes offensive, December 1944
AVALANCHE	Invasion of Salerno, Italy, September 1943
BARBAROSSA	1941 German invasion of the Soviet Union
BATTLEAXE	Failed British offensive against Rommel in Libya, June 1941
BAYTOWN	Invasion of 'toe' of Italy, September 1943
BODYGUARD	Deception plan for 1944 cross-Channel attack
BOLERO	Plan for build-up of forces in Britain in preparation for a cross-Channel assault
BREVITY	Failed British offensive against Rommel in Libya, May 1941
BUCCANEER	Plan for amphibious assault in Bay of Bengal, 1943–44
CARTWHEEL	Plan to take or isolate the major Japanese base at Rabaul on New Britain in the Bismarck Archipelago, 1943–44
CHAMPION	Late 1943 plan for major offensive in northern Burma
COBRA	Breakout from Normandy at Saint Lo, July 1944
CROSSBOW	Intelligence and air campaign against German V-1 and V-2 weapons site at Peenemunde
CRUSADER	Late 1941 British offensive against Rommel in Libya
DRACULA	1945 attack on Rangoon
DRAGOON	See ANVIL
ENIGMA	German cipher machine
EUREKA	Anglo-Soviet-American summit conference in Teheran, November 1943
FORTITUDE	Final version of BODYGUARD

FORTITUDE NORTH	Deception plan to convince Germans 1944 invasion of Europe would include a diversionary attack against Norway
FORTITUDE SOUTH	Deception plan to convince Germans 1944 cross-Channel attack would occur at Calais
GALAHAD	American long-range penetration groups in Burma
GOODWOOD	British offensive against Caen in Normandy beachhead, July 1944
GYMNAST	Plan for 1941–42 invasion of French North Africa
HABBAKUK	Special aircraft carriers to be made out of shatterproof, non-melting ice
HADRIAN	Plan for August 1943 cross-Channel attack
HERCULES	Axis plan for 1942 conquest of Malta
HUSKY	Invasion of Sicily, July 1943
ICHIGO	1944 Japanese offensive in China
JUPITER	Plan for invasion of Norway
LIGHTFOOT	El Alamein offensive against Rommel in Egypt, October 1942
MAGIC	Deciphered Japanese diplomatic and military communications
MAGNET	US replacement of British troops in Northern Ireland, 1941–42
MANHATTAN	Atomic bomb project
MARKET GARDEN	Failed attempt to cross Rhine River in the Netherlands with airborne and ground forces, September 1944
MINCEMEAT	Allied deception plan prior to invasion of Sicily 1943
MULBERRIES	Artificial harbours for 1944 Normandy invasion
NEPTUNE	Amphibious assault at Normandy, 6 June 1944
OCTAGON	Anglo-American summit conference at Quebec, September 1944
OLYMPIC	Planned November 1945 invasion of Kyushu
ORANGE	Pre-World War II US plan for war against Japan
OVERLORD	1944 invasion of France
PLUTO	Underwater oil pipeline for 1944 Normandy invasion
POINTBLANK	Combined bomber offensive against Germany
PURPLE	Japanese cipher and machine
QUADRANT	Anglo-American summit conference in Quebec, August 1943
RAINBOW	1939–41 US contingency plans for war against the Axis powers
RANKIN	Plans to land major Anglo-American forces in

	Europe should Germany weaken or collapse before OVERLORD, 1943–44
RED	Pre-World War II US plan for war against Japan
ROUNDUP	Plan for 1943 cross-Channel assault
S-1	Atomic bomb project
SEA LION	German plan for invasion of Great Britain, 1940
SEXTANT	Anglo-American-Chinese and Anglo-American summit conferences in Cairo, November and December 1943
SHINGLE	Amphibious assault at Anzio, Italy, January 1944
SLAPSTICK	Invasion of inside 'heel' of Italy, September 1943
SLEDGEHAMMER	Plan for September 1942 cross-Channel assault
TERMINAL	Anglo-Soviet-American summit conference at Potsdam, July 1945
TOLSTOY	Anglo-Soviet summit conference in Moscow, October 1944
TORCH	November 1942 invasion of French North Africa
TRIDENT	Anglo-American summit conference in Washington, DC, May 1943
TUBE ALLOYS	Atomic bomb project
ULTRA	Deciphered German communications
WATCHTOWER	Guadalcanal-Tulagi invasion and campaign, 1942–43

GENERAL EDITOR'S PREFACE

Today's armies – certainly those of Britain and America – regard their principal function to be the fighting of major wars. But, 60 years after the end of the Second World War, they are losing their grip on what a major war might be. In 1945, the definition, if not precise, could at least command some common elements. For armies, it implied the conscription of manpower and operations at corps level or bigger; for their home societies, it required the conversion of industry to war production and consequently carried the risk that they themselves would be attacked. 'Total war' was the phrase that best encapsulated these themes. It is one employed, with historical precision because it was so used at the time, by Mark Stoler in *Allies in War*.

As Mark Stoler shows in his concluding chapter, the aftermath of the Second World War, the Cold War, proved to be a 'long peace'. But it was the Cold War that kept alive concepts of total war, not least because nuclear weapons threatened levels of destruction that dwarfed even those suffered in 1939–45. The success of deterrence was such that the armies of Britain and America were able to abandon conscription, and thought about corps operations without ever conducting them. They readied themselves for a major conventional battle, even while nuclear weapons made such a battle improbable. They studied the failure of 'Operation Goodwood', Montgomery's attempt to break out of the Normandy beachhead in July 1944, in order to learn from the Germans how to conduct a defensive battle in the event of a Soviet invasion on Europe's central front. And their political masters referred (and still refer) to the British appeasement of Hitler in the 1930s and to the success of the Japanese surprise attack on Pearl Harbor in December 1941 in order to justify robustness in foreign policy.

However, it is not just the lack of alternative and more recent examples that explains the long reach of the Second World War in shaping our understanding of modern war. It is also the reality of infantry combat. This is war at its sharp end, the aspect of war where it is easiest to garner evidence to support the argument that war's character is unchanging. The attack on Monte Cassino; the Battle of the Bulge; the capture of Iwo Jima – no battle fought by either army since 1945 has matched these for their intensity as well as their scale. American forces suffered 40 per cent casualties in September 1944 when capturing Peleliu, one of the Palau islands in the Pacific. Mark Stoler tells us that the Japanese had created deep defensive systems to negate the effectiveness of American bombers and naval guns. Small-unit, close-quarter action made it a struggle of individual resolve. This too was the face of major war, even if worked out through minor tactics.

Only a minority of those Britons and Americans involved in the waging of the Second World War saw it as infantry soldiers. By the end of the war in Europe less than a quarter of the US Army's manpower was serving in combat divisions. Most of the British Army spent most of the war at home, in the United Kingdom, rather than abroad. As Mark Stoler is at pains to point out, the bulk of the German army after 1941 was committed to the Russian Front, and therefore the primary land component in the so-called 'Grand Alliance' was provided not by Britain or America, but by the Red Army. It is a theme of *Allies in War* that the Anglo-American coalition was built not on land power but on sea power. Both in the Pacific and in Europe, its armies depended on the sea for their deployment and supply. Amphibious operations, whether 'island-hopping' in the Pacific or in the sequence that ran from 'Operation Torch' in North Africa to D-Day itself, became their characteristic contribution to modern warfare. Moreover, those landings themselves depended on prior victories at sea and in the air.

The controversy about launching the so-called 'second front' in Europe too often misses the point. In 1942 and 1943, in bitter debates which Mark Stoler discusses in depth, the Americans were wont to see the British as enamoured of a peripheral strategy, reluctant to take on the German Army in its European heartland, and preferring to attack Italy or to take the war to the Balkans. In reality, the Allies would have only one bite at this particular cherry: defeat on the Normandy beaches in 1943 would have been a far worse outcome than were the consequences of delay until 1944. And that delay was predicated less on British strategic predilections and much more on the harsh realities of the battle of the Atlantic. Until that was won, there could be no American build-up in Britain. Until the U-boats were crushed, there could be no cross-Channel armada. The battle of the Atlantic was to the western Allies what Stalingrad was to the Soviet Union, and it went on far longer, from 1940 to 1943: indeed, it challenges our use of the word 'battle', which implies a short, contained action rather than a campaign lasting years.

Victory at sea, like victory on land, rested on victory in the air. Here were controversies which cut across services rather than nations. The Royal Air Force was committed to an independent strategic bombing offensive, which became a surrogate second front in 1942, but which in the process leeched air assets from the battle of the Atlantic. The United States Army Air Force joined it in the campaign over Germany, but in doing so stuck to its own philosophy of precision bombing, even if that was more rhetoric than reality. Both air forces engaged in a battle whose primary direct effects were on German cities and their occupants. The moral justification for what they did rests on the strategic outcome, and that was indirect. The German Air Force was pulled back from its support of its army's ground operations for the purposes of home defence. This gave the Allies' armies an immediate operational advantage whose pay-off was evident on all fronts, and above all on D-Day. Furthermore, in 1944–45, the Luftwaffe itself was broken in the battle in the skies over Germany: Mark Stoler tells us that 98 per cent of German fighter pilots were killed or wounded in the Second World War.

Strategic bombing's denouement was the dropping of the atomic bombs on Hiroshima and Nagasaki. Confronted with the employment of weapons of mass destruction by two liberal powers, historians have sought explanations that rest on racism, on the one hand, and the incipient needs of the Cold War, on the other. The image of the Japanese was transformed by the conduct of the war in the Pacific into one of sub-human fanatics, especially in the eyes of the American people. For the American Government, the war against Japan presented an opportunity to warn Stalin and the Soviet Union of the awesome power which the United States now possessed. Stoler, while not denying these elements in the decision to use the atomic bombs, also stresses its antecedents. The development and procurement of nuclear weapons were driven by the needs of the war in Europe before those of the war in the Far East. Moreover, the notion that civilians and cities were proper targets was already one to which the war in both theatres had accustomed the Allies. Mark Stoler is in no doubt that atomic bombs would have been used against Germany if the opportunity had presented itself.

That link between the war in Europe and the war in the Pacific is precisely what makes *Allies in War* both important and original. Historians have tended to be expert in one or the other, or to treat the two in separate compartments. The dysfunctional aspects of the Axis may make that an acceptable approach for Germany or Japan. The decision-making of each took scant regard of the other. But it does not make sense for Britain and America. Each of them individually, and both collectively, lived with the need to attend to the two theatres and to each other on a daily basis. The decision to prioritize Europe over the Pacific did not mean that Japan did not continue to create demands on the Allies' war efforts. Juggling between the two was the staple of Allied grand strategy between 1941 and 1945.

Indeed, the consequent need to think globally was what gave birth to grand strategy itself. Compromise is a word with connotations of weakness and even failure. It is a word which Mark Stoler has to use a great deal, as it is what the Allies did. But compromise gave strength to the alliance. The Chiefs of Staff in Britain and the Joint Chiefs of Staff in the United States thrashed out deals which they then carried forward to their common planning body, the Combined Chiefs of Staff. War was bureaucratized, and, while its conduct could therefore seem ponderous and unimaginative, there was no other way to harmonize the massive resources of the United States with the servicing of so many competing needs.

It is tempting to conclude that, because *Allies in War* is concerned with strategy as an exercise in management, modern war itself should be seen in this light. The more substantive point is that modern war has been, to an extraordinary extent, coalition warfare. No alliance has fought as effectively as did the Anglo-American alliance of 1941–45, a point Mark Stoler is at pains to stress. It had its trials and tribulations; its chiefs of staff frequently went 'off the record' to vent their anger and frustration. But crucially they continued to talk to each other: this was a glass half full rather than a glass half empty.

Ultimately, however, as well as ironically, its heart-beat was personal, not managerial. The two parties used the same language, albeit in different ways, and subscribed to the same core ideologies, expressed by Woodrow Wilson in his 'Fourteen Points', enunciated in an earlier war in 1918, and reaffirmed though the 'Four Freedoms' which found their way into the Atlantic Charter of 1941. Personality prevailed over personality: the most charismatic and egotistical of each nation's generals, Bernard Montgomery and George Patton, could barely be in the same room together, but Dwight D. Eisenhower was able to harness both in the same theatre of war. And over the generals – and admirals and air marshals – presided two individuals, Winston Spencer Churchill and Franklin Delano Roosevelt, whose friendship set the tone for those serving beneath them. They embodied the 'special relationship' and lived it out, through meetings, through letters, through leg-pulling. Perhaps this was the most distinctive feature of this war in relation to earlier wars: its waging was symbolized less by the feats of great commanders and generals and more by the direction of great statesmen. It was a war too important to be left to generals.

Hew Strachan
Chichele Professor of the History of War,
All Souls College,
University of Oxford

PREFACE

'History will bear me out,' Winston Churchill once boasted, 'particularly as I shall write that history myself.' He did, albeit in an extraordinary memoir often mistaken for a history. The two are not the same. 'This is not history,' he once admitted in that regard; 'this is my case.'[1]

That is true of all memoirs. But Churchill's memoirs were so special as to lead people to treat them as history instead of what they actually were. They were published between 1948 and 1953 in the USA (1954 in the UK), before most of the other memoirs by important World War II figures, and in six lengthy volumes that dwarfed in size and depth what any other World War II figure could or would write. They were also the only memoirs written by the head of government of a major Allied power in World War II, and they contained a gold mine of highly classified documents that otherwise would not have been available to historians for decades. As if all of that were not enough, they were beautifully written by one of the great masters of the English language – who also happened to be one of the most famous and admired men in the world.[2]

As a result of all of these factors, Churchill's memoirs were for many years considered *the* great history of World War II, and his organization, interpretations and conclusions – indeed, even his subtitles[3] – became (at least in Great Britain and the United States) the standard approach to the war for decades. In many ways they still are.

The problem, of course, was that the six volumes were indeed a memoir rather than a history. As such, they were at least partially designed to explain and justify the controversial decisions Churchill had made and the positions he had taken during the war years. To make matters worse, political factors in the years 1948–53 led Churchill to avoid comments that might alienate his Cold War American ally – especially in light of the major European crises of those years, the fact that he remained an active politician who would become prime minister again in 1951, and the fact that Dwight D. Eisenhower, the World War II Allied commander in Europe with whom he had often disagreed, was elected US president in 1952.[4]

Holes in the Churchill version of the war, and the Churchill legend, first appeared in the late 1950s when the memoirs of his high-level military advisers began to be published; most notably the combined biography-diary-memoir of Lord Alanbrooke, the acerbic wartime Chief of the Imperial General Staff, who often disparaged the strategic ideas of Churchill as well as his American counterparts.[5] It was not until the major declassification in both Britain and the United States of the full World War II documentary record during the 1970s, however, that a full-scale assault upon the Churchill version of the war could be launched. Historians using those records, both military and political/ diplomatic, soon made discoveries requiring not only revision of the Churchill version of the war, but indeed all previous wartime histories. Most famous and notable in this regard were revelations regarding the so-called 'Ultra Secret' and other Allied intelligence breakthroughs that had remained classified and unavailable for over 30 years, revelations that have led to a major and ongoing reassessment of all Allied military campaigns.[6] But equally important were the diplomatic reassessments of the Anglo-American wartime alliance, which Churchill had labelled the 'special relationship' and sought to maintain into the post-war world. That relationship, numerous scholars noted throughout the late 1970s and the 1980s, had been marked by disagreements regarding both wartime strategy and post-war policies much sharper and more bitter than Churchill had led his readers to believe – so sharp and bitter as to lead British historian Christopher Thorne to entitle his masterful and pathbreaking 1978 history of Anglo-American relations in the war against Japan *Allies of a Kind*.[7] Equally forceful and important reassessments of the Anglo-American alliance during and immediately after the war, based on extensive archival research, were published throughout the last quarter of the twentieth century by numerous other scholars, such as David Reynolds, Warren Kimball, William Roger Louis, Robert Hathaway, Terry Anderson, Alan Dobson, Fraser Harbutt, John Sbrega and Randall Woods. Many of them also noted and analysed the extensive conflicts within each government that had taken place regarding appropriate policies toward its wartime ally.[8]

This volume, a combined diplomatic-military history of the Anglo-American alliance and war against the Axis powers, relies extensively on the works of these other scholars. It is also an effort to provide an overall and up-to-date assessment of that alliance and war in light of the most recent scholarship. As such, it is a synthesis more than a piece of original research, though my own scholarship on these subjects over the past three decades also informs much of the text.[9]

That text, it must be emphasized, is a history of only a part of World War II. Indeed, this fact cannot be overemphasized. As a study of only the Anglo-American war, it all but ignores what in retrospect was clearly the largest and most important component of Allied victory over Nazi Germany: the Soviet Union. The enormous Russo-German War of 1941–45 is properly the subject of an entirely separate volume in this series by Evan Mawdsley.[10] One should constantly keep in mind when reading this volume, however, that the German Army was primarily defeated on the Eastern Front, where it suffered the overwhelming bulk of its combat casualties. Whether the Soviet Union could have defeated Nazi Germany without its Anglo-American allies is, admittedly, questionable; but whether those allies could have defeated Nazi Germany without the Soviet Union as a continental ally, and with Hitler consequently in control of all the resources and manpower of Europe, is far more questionable.

That, of course, is not the impression one gets from reading Churchill's memoirs – or, indeed, most Anglo-American memoirs and histories of the war.

Over the past few decades, British and American historians such as John Erickson and David Glantz have tried to correct this distortion,[11] unfortunately with only a limited impact on public perceptions. Most audiences to whom I lecture on World War II are still shocked to hear the incredible statistics of German and Russian casualties on the Eastern Front as compared to German, British and American casualties on the Western Front during that conflict. This paragraph and the preceding one are included here in the hopes that reading this volume will not reinforce this distorted Anglo-American perception of the war.

The idea of publishing a volume with such an Anglo-American focus, and another volume focusing on the Russo-German War, was not mine. It properly belongs to series editor Hew Strachan, who first contacted me a decade ago with the proposal and an enquiry as to whether I would be interested in writing the Anglo-American volume. I almost declined before I even completed reading his letter, for I was at that time buried under numerous other commitments. I also thought at first that he was suggesting separate volumes in this series on the war against Germany and the war against Japan – a standard division done so frequently in the past as to make it boring and non-appealing to me – and probably to readers as well. But he then explained that 'Our intention is to go in a somewhat different direction', with one volume written from a Soviet/Central European perspective and its 'partner' volume, 'Atlantic in outlook', focusing on the Anglo-American relationship in *both* Europe *and* the Pacific.[12] That approach piqued my interest. To my knowledge, it had never been done before. He also made it clear that my prior commitments, and a subsequent need to have a completion date far in the future, were not insurmountable problems.

What sealed my decision to write this volume was an ensuing telephone conversation with Warren Kimball, editor of the Churchill–Roosevelt wartime correspondence and author of excellent recent works on Roosevelt and the Churchill–Roosevelt relationship.[13] Had the Anglo-American global approach Hew Strachan was suggesting, I asked, ever been taken before in a World War II volume? No, he answered, and for good reason: it could not be done.

That reply was not, appearances to the contrary, a recommendation to reject the proposal as unworkable – at least not to me. Warren Kimball and I had both grown up in New York City, where in our childhoods and adolescence such a comment was usually a dare rather than a warning. That is how I interpreted his words, whether or not he intended them to be interpreted in that way. Consequently I accepted Hew Strachan's offer, for a dare is seldom turned down on the streets of New York!

Over the ensuing years I often regretted what I had come to consider that rash decision. The prior commitments proved to be even more time-consuming than I had anticipated, delaying even further completion of this work. So did unexpected illness. And in attempting to write such a comprehensive volume, I became deeply aware of how much I did not know about the Anglo-American relationship and war effort, despite all my previous research and scholarship.

Furthermore, while Warren Kimball may have overstated when he told me that such a volume could not be written, how to organize a combined diplomatic-military history covering the entire globe presented extraordinarily difficult problems. Indeed, years passed before the reviewers, editors, publishers and I could all agree on appropriate organization and coverage.

That organization is primarily chronological from chapter to chapter, with the numerous Anglo-American conferences and the issues discussed at each of these used as focal points within each chapter. Each chapter therefore also contains sections on both the war against Germany and the war against Japan. Separating these two wars may make comprehension of each of them easier in hindsight, but only by introducing a fundamental distortion. Neither Churchill, nor Roosevelt, nor their military chiefs, had the luxury of ignoring one war while pursuing the other. The two were closely related, constantly competed for resources, and had to be considered in conjunction – often on a daily basis. Historian Waldo Heinrichs' superb study of Franklin D. Roosevelt's diplomatic and military policies during 1941 makes that abundantly clear. Indeed, Heinrichs designed his volume at least partially to explain and emphasize that often-ignored fact.[14] This volume similarly attempts through its organization to make clear the global nature of the Anglo-American war effort, and the subsequent inseparability of events in Europe, Asia and the Pacific.

Acknowledgements

The dawning realization of my own ignorance regarding numerous aspects of the Anglo-American global war effort led me not only back to the documents and the works of other historians, but also to pestering those I knew with telephone calls and e-mails. For their willingness to respond to my incessant queries over the past year, I would like to thank in particular Warren Kimball, Theodore Wilson, Larry Bland and Conrad Crane. I would also like to thank the numerous others I have pestered and relied upon during the many preceding years that I have worked on this project: J. Garry Clifford, Alexander Cochran, Alex Danchev, Lloyd Gardner, Waldo Heinrichs, Walter LaFeber, Melvyn Leffler, Timothy Nenninger, Thomas Paterson, David Reynolds, Ronald Spector, as well as my colleagues at the University of Vermont.

In addition to detailed information, my other key prerequisite for completion of this volume was time to write. That was provided first by the University of Vermont via a sabbatical leave in 2001–02, during which I completed the first rough draft of more than half of this manuscript, and then by the US Army Military History Institute in Carlisle, Pennsylvania, which awarded me its Harold K. Johnson Visiting Chair in Military History for 2004–05. With that chair came the time, space and resources to complete the first draft as well as two revised drafts.

In his Pulitzer Prize-winning *An Army at Dawn*, Rick Atkinson described the Military History Institute (MHI) as 'a national treasure beyond value'.[15]

Preface

I wholeheartedly concur in that judgement. Holding extensive manuscript collections, oral histories and unit histories as well as a superb library of published primary and secondary sources, and possessing an outstanding and exceptionally helpful staff, the Institute proved to be the best possible environment in which to complete this volume. Previously it had been housed in Upton Hall adjacent to the Army War College at Carlisle Barracks. In 2004 it moved to a new, state-of-the-art facility a very short distance from the walls of the barracks and became part of the new Army Heritage and Educational Center (AHEC). I am deeply indebted and grateful to the entire Institute and Center staffs for their invaluable assistance, but in particular to Institute Director Dr Conrad C. Crane and Center Director Colonel Robert J. Dalessandro. An excellent historian in his own right, Dr Crane was a constant source of historical information and lively discussion as well as guidance in my new environment; he also provided invaluable assistance in reviewing and revising sections of this manuscript. Colonel Dalessandro was an incredible 'problem solver' and treated me as 'part of the family'. The same held true for his operations officer, Major Michael Lynch – a budding historian in his own right. Archivists Dr Richard Sommers and David Keough constantly brought to my attention relevant items from the Institute's collections, as they had during my previous but much briefer visits to Carlisle. Janet Jacobs kept the Institute office functioning smoothly, and helped me with my often complicated travel arrangements. Jan Shafer and Terry Myers rescued me all too frequently from my computer illiteracy and ensuing problems. Luis Mora, Tommy Shird and Melinda Torres similarly saved me from numerous administrative woes, while Tom Hendrix provided invaluable assistance in my War College class. At the War College itself, I profited enormously from conversations with members of the faculty, most notably Dr Tami Biddle, who also helped me revise sections of this manuscript, and Rick Atkinson who held the visiting Omar N. Bradley chair for 2004–05, as well as Dr Jerry Comello, and foreign service officers Dr Louis Nigro and Michael Malinoski. All of them, and indeed the entire MHI/AHEC and War College staffs, made my year-long stay a joy.

I have done my best to ensure ranks of military officers are correct at the chronological moment when they are introduced, but, as a scholar based in the USA with limited archive access to British records, this has not always been easy to determine.

At Hodder Arnold I am particularly grateful for the assistance provided by Christopher Wheeler, Michael Strang, Jamilah Ahmed, Tiara Misquitta, Amanda Bradley and Yuen Ching Lam.

The assistance provided by all the individuals listed in the above paragraphs was invaluable in the completion of this volume. Responsibility for its contents and quality, however, rests solely with the author.

Burlington and Starksboro, Vermont
Carlisle, Pennsylvania

1

AXIS THREAT AND ALLIANCE FORMING

Given their superiority in both human and material resources, the Allied victory over the Axis powers in World War II appears inevitable in hindsight. So does the unique Anglo-American wartime alliance, the 'special relationship' in the words of wartime British Prime Minister Winston S. Churchill, which played so important a role in that victory. In reality, however, neither the Allied victory nor the Anglo-American alliance was inevitable. To the contrary, each appeared highly unlikely in the opening stages of World War II.

Anglo-American antagonisms

Many immigrants had originally come to the United States to escape Europe's numerous alliances and wars, not to participate in them. Indeed, in its entire history prior to World War II, the United States had signed only one formal alliance with a European power. Moreover, that alliance with France in 1778 had been based on desperate need during the American War for Independence and had led to numerous problems, culminating in an undeclared naval war between the two nations, before it was terminated in 1800. This only reinforced the general American antipathy towards any political involvement with Europe, an antipathy that came to be known as 'isolationism' and that harked back to the warnings against alliances that President George Washington had supposedly enunciated in his 1796 Farewell Address.

There was admittedly more myth than reality to such claims. What Washington primarily warned against in 1796 were not 'entangling alliances', words that do not even appear in the address, but permanent alliances and, more importantly, emotional attachments and antipathies in foreign affairs as well as domestic factionalism. Furthermore, the United States was not at that time and never would be economically isolated from the rest of the world. Nevertheless, there was indeed an old and general American dislike of Europe and a desire to steer clear of its alliances and wars. President Thomas Jefferson aptly summarized these feelings in his 1801 inaugural address when he referred to the United States as 'kindly separated by nature and a wide ocean' from a Europe he labelled 'the exterminating havoc of one quarter of the globe'.[1]

If Americans disliked and shunned European politics and nations in general, they had a history of disliking Great Britain more than the others. Supposedly, Americans and Britons shared a common heritage and language. But, as George Bernard Shaw once quipped, the two peoples were separated rather than joined by that common language – a fact illustrated by their very negative reactions to each other's accents and pronunciations (to Americans, the British sounded haughty and prissy; to the British, the Americans sounded barbaric). They were also separated by their supposed common heritage. Admittedly, the United States had originated as English colonies in the seventeenth century, and by the twentieth century the two nations possessed similar liberal democratic political institutions and values. But the two nations nevertheless differed dramatically in their political cultures as well as their histories.[2] Indeed, the American nation had officially been born in a bitter, bloody and lengthy eighteenth-century war for independence against what it considered and publicly labelled a tyrannical England.

That war, which began in 1775, eventually became a world war and lasted until 1783, when London finally admitted defeat and recognized American independence. But relations between the former colonies and their mother country remained very poor over most of the next three decades, with constant conflicts over trade, boundaries and neutral rights culminating in a second war from 1812 to 1815. A third Anglo-American war was only narrowly averted in the 1830s and 1840s, and again during the American Civil War of 1861–65. And throughout much of this time England remained in American eyes the antithesis, rather than a beacon, of liberty. Relations did improve substantially during the late nineteenth and early twentieth centuries as Britain recognized the dominant US position in the western hemisphere and sought informal understanding with the United States, as well as numerous other nations, in light of its imperial overcommitments and the new threat posed by an aggressive Germany. Nevertheless, numerous Anglo-American tensions remained, along with a legacy of hostility and suspicion, when World War I began in 1914.

The World War I and post-war experiences

The United States eventually entered World War I on the side of Britain and its allies, but only in April of 1917, nearly three years after the war had begun. Furthermore, Washington declared war on Germany primarily as a result of Berlin's renewed and unrestricted submarine warfare against US shipping, and only after a series of bitter conflicts with Britain in the preceding years over neutral rights. As a result of those conflicts, its continued distrust of Great Britain, and its continuing antipathy regarding alliances in general, the United States fought World War I not in formal alliance with Britain and the other Allied nations, but instead as a separate 'Associated' power.

Such distrust was exacerbated during the war by numerous conflicts, most notably (but far from exclusively) over Anglo-French efforts to amalgamate fresh US forces into existing Allied units. These efforts the Americans resisted fiercely, demanding instead an independent American army in an American theatre of operations on the Western Front. Distrust was further exacerbated during the ensuing Paris Peace Conference of 1919 by a host of conflicts between US President Woodrow Wilson, on one side and the British, French and Italian Prime Ministers (David Lloyd George, Georges Clemenceau and Vittorio Orlando) on the other, over the appropriate treatment for a defeated Germany and the shape of the post-war world. The four leaders did manage to compromise their differences in the Treaty of Versailles, but the US Senate refused to accept the compromise and did not ratify the Treaty or join the League of Nations embedded within it, thereby crippling efforts to create a stable post-war world. To the British, the United States had proven to be an untrustworthy and fickle ally. To the Americans, 'perfidious Albion' had manipulated the United States into a senseless war and poisoned the peace.

Such bitter feelings continued during the inter-war years as the two nations collided over a host of economic and strategic issues. Indeed, Anglophobia remained a potent force in the United States during this period, and US military planners concluded that commercial rivalry could easily result in formal hostilities with a Great Britain they considered a persistent, perfidious and deadly rival. Consequently, they developed war plans for just such a contingency.[3] On the other side of the Atlantic, conflicts over the size of the two navies as well as trade led even Churchill to warn in 1927 that war between the two nations was not 'unthinkable'.[4] The onset of the Great Depression further deepened the bitter feelings between the two nations, especially after newly elected US President Franklin D. Roosevelt rejected British plans for international currency stabilization at the London Economic Conference of 1933 and was subsequently blamed in Britain for the failure of the conference. Still valid was the warning Woodrow Wilson had given the British 15 years earlier:

> You must not speak of us who come over here as cousins, still less as brothers; we are neither. Neither must you think of us as Anglo-Saxons, for that term can no longer be rightly applied to the people of the United States. Nor must too much importance in this connection be attached to the fact that English is our common language. . . . No, there are only two things which can establish and maintain closer relations between your country and mine; they are community of ideals and of interests.[5]

Rise of the Axis threat and the outbreak of war

The Great Depression also led to the rise of highly aggressive dictatorships around the world. Particularly noteworthy were those established in Germany and Japan, as well as the one that had existed in Italy since 1922. Espousing a militaristic ideology known as Fascism, these three dictatorships rejected the results of World War I (even though two of the three had been victors in that war, they were grossly dissatisfied with the rewards they had received) and were determined to overthrow the existing international order by force. Acting on their own, officers in Japan's Kwantung Army took over the north-ernmost Chinese province of Manchuria in 1931–32 and created the puppet state of Manchukuo; when the League of Nations condemned such behaviour, Japan withdrew from the League and continued its aggression. In 1933, Adolf Hitler and his Nazi movement came to power in Germany determined to over-throw the limits placed upon it in the Versailles Treaty and make Germany the master of Europe; within a few years he had withdrawn from the League and begun to rearm. In 1935, the Italian dictator Benito Mussolini invaded and conquered the African kingdom of Ethiopia, and in 1936 Hitler reoccu-pied the demilitarized Rhineland in violation of the Versailles Treaty. In that same year, a Fascist movement in Spain led by General Francisco Franco revolted against the Spanish Republican Government and received large-scale military assistance from Germany and Italy in the civil war that ensued. Simultaneously, the Japanese armed forces took over the government in Tokyo, announced their intention to create a 'New Order' for an Asia that they would rule, and in 1937 invaded China proper, conquering much of the coastal area and forcing the government of Chiang Kai-shek to abandon its capitol of Nanking and retreat to the interior. By that time Germany, Italy and Japan had also aligned in the so-called Rome–Berlin–Tokyo Axis. Officially the alliance was known as the Anti-Comintern Pact and was directed against Communist Russia (the Soviet Union); in reality, it was directed against the entire existing international order and its defenders, most notably France, Great Britain and the United States.

In their goals, methods and ideologies, these Axis powers constituted a mortal threat to the democratic nations. Yet as war clouds gathered in Asia and Europe, more and more Americans concluded that their entry into World War I had been a tragic error caused in part by British manipulation, and that the United States both could and should avoid being dragged into another war on Britain's side. Partially, such conclusions stemmed from the obvious failure of World War I to ensure a democratic and peaceful world, as Woodrow Wilson had promised it would. Partially, they stemmed from historical and journalis-tic revelations regarding the role of arms manufacturers and bankers – the so-called 'merchants of death' – as well as British propaganda and the pro-Allied sympathies of Wilson and his advisers, in leading the United States into the war. Most noteworthy in this regard were the highly publicized findings of the Senate investigating committee headed by Senator Gerald P. Nye. Responding to these revelations, the US Congress passed a series of Neutrality Acts between 1935 and 1937 outlawing the 1914–17 activities with Britain and France that Americans now believed had been primary causes of their entry into World War I. Specifically, these acts prohibited American travel on belligerent ships, loans to belligerents, any trade in armaments, and any other trade in US ships. If Britain and France wished to purchase non-military items they could do so, but only via 'cash and carry' – i.e., by paying cash for the items and providing their own transport.

The Neutrality Acts only reinforced both the British belief that the United States was untrustworthy and London's tendency to avoid another war at all costs, most notably via its policy of appeasement of the Axis powers. Although usually associated with British Prime Minister Neville Chamberlain and universally condemned in historical hindsight, appeasement of Germany had also been practised by Chamberlain's predecessors and possessed a long and successful history in European diplomacy. Its practice at this time was based on the understandable, if incorrect, beliefs that anything would be better than another world war and that Hitler could be appeased. It was also based upon perceived Anglo-French military unpreparedness and distrust of the Soviet Union as well as the United States.

Chamberlain personified such distrust. In regard to the United States, he believed that 'it is always best and safest to count on *nothing* from Americans except words'. Roosevelt aptly concluded that 'fundamentally' Chamberlain 'thoroughly dislikes Americans'.[6]

Anglo-French appeasement reached its apogee, or nadir, in 1938, when Britain and France acquiesced in German absorption, first, of Austria in violation of the Versailles Treaty, and then the western portion of Czechoslovakia known as the Sudetenland at the notorious Munich Conference. But when Hitler in early 1939 violated his previous pledges by taking over the remainder of Czechoslovakia and making territorial demands on Poland, Britain and France reached the limits of their willingness to appease and guaranteed Polish territory. Hitler quickly countered on 23 August by signing a non-aggression pact with the Soviet Union, despite his ideological antipathy towards the Communist state. This deprived Britain and France of a critical potential ally and, Hitler believed, would consequently force them to back down and to acquiesce in his planned military conquest of Poland. One week later, on 1 September, his armies invaded that country. But contrary to his expectations, Britain and France responded on 3 September with formal declarations of war. A second twentieth-century general war in Europe had formally begun.

Unlike Woodrow Wilson at the beginning of World War I, President Franklin D. Roosevelt did not ask Americans in September of 1939 to remain neutral in thought as well as action. Most of them found Fascist ideology and behaviour repulsive and threatening, and despite previous antipathy they clearly favoured Britain and France. Reflecting such opinion, the US Congress in November of 1939 agreed to Roosevelt's request for a repeal of the arms embargo, thereby allowing Britain and France to purchase war supplies as well as other goods on a 'cash and carry' basis. Congress remained adamantly opposed to any military intervention in the conflict, however, and convinced that such intervention could be avoided. Consequently, it retained all other provisions of the Neutrality Acts. Better to sit on the sidelines and let the two sides batter each other to exhaustion as they had done in World War I, with eventual Allied victory as the likely result. Many Britons had no problem with this approach in 1939. 'God protect us from a German victory and an American peace,' American radio commentator Edward R. Murrow remembered hearing in England at that time; 'Britain and her Allies propose to win this one alone.'[7]

World War II was not to be a military replay of World War I, however. This fact became crystal clear in the first, stunning year of the war.

The revolution in warfare and the German conquest of Europe

In 1914 each of the major European powers had gone to war with an offensive plan designed to provide quick and decisive victory. All of these plans had failed completely. The result had been four years of bloody stalemate, often in the form of hideous trench warfare, that took 10 million lives and wounded another 20 million.

A major cause of this unprecedented carnage was the Industrial Revolution of the late nineteenth century, which had enabled the great powers to create and mass produce a host of new and extraordinarily lethal weapons, such as the rifled musket, the machine gun, long-range heavy artillery and poison gas. These increased enormously both the distance over which soldiers could be killed and the number that could be killed in a given period of time. Moreover, many of these weapons – the machine gun, for example – could be used more effectively by the defence than by an attacking force. The transportation revolution of the late nineteenth century similarly gave an enormous advantage to the defence. Although railroads could bring large attacking or defending armies to the front, once the battle began, they could continue to supply and reinforce only the latter; attacking armies could not build railroad lines as they advanced, and would thus have to move and be supplied/reinforced by foot or horse.

In effect, those attacking armies still advanced on foot and by horse as they had done a hundred years earlier during the Napoleonic Wars, but now through a killing field far larger than the one that had then existed and against an enemy armed with weapons of mass destruction and consistently supplied as well as reinforced by rail. The result was an appallingly bloody stalemate on the Western Front, with both sides creating trench systems running from the Swiss Alps to the English Channel and both attempting unsuccessfully to break their opponent's lines. The war turned into a huge campaign of human and material attrition, in which Germany and its allies finally collapsed from exhaustion before the Allies did.

In the final stages of the war, however, both sides began to experiment with new weapons and tactics designed to break the trench deadlock. These would be further developed during the inter-war years, and would succeed during World War II in destroying many of the advantages that the defence had held during World War I.

The key invention in this military revolution was the internal combustion engine, which spawned and powered not only automobiles and trucks, but also military aircraft and armoured vehicles such as the tank. These could be used as incredibly powerful offensive weapons. Many of them actually pre-dated World War I and had been used in that conflict. But they were still in their technological infancy and were largely used on a limited, experimental basis and without any clear doctrine for their military use. That gap was filled during the inter-war years.

During those years, airpower theorists such as Guilio Douhet in Italy, Hugh Trenchard in Great Britain and William B. 'Billy' Mitchell in the United States, argued that fleets of independent bombers could be used to deter an enemy from attacking and, if such deterrence failed, to win any ensuing war quickly and decisively without heavy casualties by attacking enemy cities. Such attacks would quickly destroy the industrial capacity of the enemy and/or the civilian will to resist, both of which were essential to successful warmaking in the modern era. No defence against these bombers was possible, the theorists maintained, and their existence would render existing armies and navies obsolete and irrelevant.

This doctrine, which came to be known as 'strategic bombing', quite obviously aroused the ire of army and navy officers, who attacked it as unproven, if not totally false, and as a bureaucratic rationalization to justify an independent air force. It would also extend war to the civilian populace, and indeed virtually end the concept of civilians. Nevertheless, it was embraced by many in the democratic nations (especially in Great Britain where an independent air force had been established in 1918) because it offered both a deterrent against future war and a promise of quick victory with a minimal number of casualties should such a war occur.[8]

Not all inter-war airpower theorists embraced strategic bombing, however. Many saw aircraft primarily as tactical rather than strategic weapons, to be used primarily to support naval vessels or ground armies and to prevent an enemy from achieving similar support by attacking its aircraft. Such concepts would lead to the development of aircraft carriers within the world's major navies during the 1920s. In army circles these concepts would become part of a new doctrine of mobile warfare based upon armoured and motorized vehicles.

As with the airplane, such vehicles had been used during World War I but only on a limited and experimental basis, and without any doctrine or understanding of their effectiveness. The British, for example, achieved a breakthrough during their successful experiment with a massed tank attack at Cambrai in late 1917, but they had not developed the tactics to exploit that breakthrough. Ironically, however, the Germans were at that very moment successfully developing such exploitation tactics with their pre-existing weapons.

Evolving from 1915 onwards, these new tactics focused on surprise and quick movement. Instead of the standard huge artillery barrages lasting days, which had both warned the enemy of an attack and turned the battlefield into an impassable quagmire, they substituted a brief 'rolling' barrage, followed by the immediate advance of specially trained shock troops. These would break through the first enemy line and bypass strong points in order to keep moving directly behind the artillery barrage that would itself then advance to the next enemy line and eventually into the enemy rear, creating communication breakdown and chaos as well as breaking up enemy forces into small pockets that could then be tackled by mopping-up troops. Used in 1917 against the Russians at Riga and then against the Italians with devastating results at the battle of Caporetto, these tactics were applied to the Western Front during the Germans' spring offensive of 1918 and brought them to the edge of victory in front of Paris before they were finally halted.

During the inter-war years, military innovators combined these German tactics with the new weapons resulting from the internal combustion engine to create a new doctrine of mobile, mechanized warfare with combined arms. Aircraft would coordinate with massed tanks as well as artillery to blast holes in enemy lines, through which the tanks followed by infantry in armoured personnel carriers, and trucks carrying supplies, would then pour, to destroy enemy command and control, and to fragment and isolate enemy resistance into pockets that follow-up ground troops could force into surrender. They would be aided by airborne troops, who would be dropped behind enemy lines via special aircraft and parachutes to further disrupt the enemy and to seize in advance such key points as airfields and bridges. These tactics, the innovators maintained, would restore mobility to the battlefield and result in short, decisive and relatively low-casualty wars.

Proponents of this type of warfare existed in the Allied countries as well as Germany during the inter-war years. Indeed, J.F.C. Fuller and B.H. Liddell Hart in England, as well as J.B.E. Estienne and Charles de Gaulle in France, pioneered its development. The ideas were fully accepted only in Germany, however, where officers such as Heinz Guderian were able to develop them and win approval for their use. The eventual resulting doctrine became known as *Blitzkrieg*, or 'lightning war'.

German acceptance of these ideas was partially and ironically due to the strict limitations placed upon the size of their army by the Treaty of Versailles, which required them to make more efficient use of the few troops they were allowed, and to the fact that Germany had lost the previous war. Defeat often encourages military soul-searching as to what had 'gone wrong' and thus leads to an openness to new ideas, whereas victory often leads to the further institutionalization of old ideas that had supposedly 'worked', and thereby creates a powerful block against military innovation. This was particularly true in France, where the continued dominance of defensive and firepower doctrines led to the building of an enormous fortification system known as the Maginot Line along the entire border with Germany. Moreover, in favouring attack, mobile warfare appeared to favour aggression, and thus found little support in democratic countries. It appealed strongly to Hitler, however, and it perfectly matched his plans for a series of short, decisive wars.[9]

These new air and ground war doctrines would in the end prove to be far less decisive than the inter-war theorists maintained. Otherwise World War II would not have lasted as long as it did or resulted in so many deaths. From 1939–41, however, *Blitzkrieg* as practised by the Germans was extraordinarily successful and resulted in their quick conquest of most of Europe.

Contrary to popular belief at the time and later, this was *not* the result of massively superior German armour, aircraft and manpower – a myth created by German propaganda to cow their opponents into submission. The British and French, in fact, possessed greater numbers of tanks, planes and soldiers. Moreover, only a small percentage (10–15 per cent) of the German Army was fully mechanized and motorized; the rest still relied primarily upon horse-drawn vehicles. But that small percentage had been integrated and organized into a small number of armoured (*Panzer*) divisions possessing enormous offensive capabilities and a clear doctrine as to how they should be used. The German Air Force, or *Luftwaffe*, was also designed for tactical support of these divisions via both its training and its aircraft. Particularly notable in this regard was the Stuka divebomber, which added psychological warfare to the air war via a siren designed to terrify the enemy, and a doctrine of terror-bombing civilians as well as enemy troops so as to create panic and clogged roads behind enemy lines.

The results in 1939–40 were staggering. In successful surprise attacks the *Luftwaffe* destroyed most of the Polish Air Force on the ground in the first four days of September 1939 while the German Army broke through Polish lines and, with large pincer movements, destroyed the Polish Army in less than a month. So rapid was the German advance that the Soviet Union invaded eastern Poland on 17 September to claim the territory it had secretly been promised in the recently signed non-aggression pact before German forces occupied the entire country. Shackled by a defensive strategy, the British and French did nothing, which led to jokes that while *Blitzkrieg* took place in Eastern Europe, *Sitzkrieg*, or 'sitting war', took place in the West.

That ended on 9 April 1940, when the German Army overran Denmark in a few hours while the German Navy successfully landed troops to occupy all Norwegian ports and the capitol of Oslo, the far superior British fleet notwith-standing. This led to the fall of the British and French Governments in early May, just as the German armed forces (*Wehrmacht*) launched their long-awaited assault on France and the Low Countries (the Netherlands, Belgium, Luxembourg) on 10 May. Aided by airborne troops who captured numerous critical bridges in the Netherlands and the key Belgian fortress of Eben Emael with only 85 men (the fortress contained nine times that number), German Army Group B, under General Fedor von Bock, was able to force the surrender of the Netherlands in only five days and to drive deep into Belgium.

Although this attack appeared to be essentially a repeat of the German line of advance in 1914, whereby the bulk of the German Army had attempted to take Paris via the invasion of Belgium, it was actually a ruse that used only 30 of Germany's 136 divisions on the Western Front and that was designed to

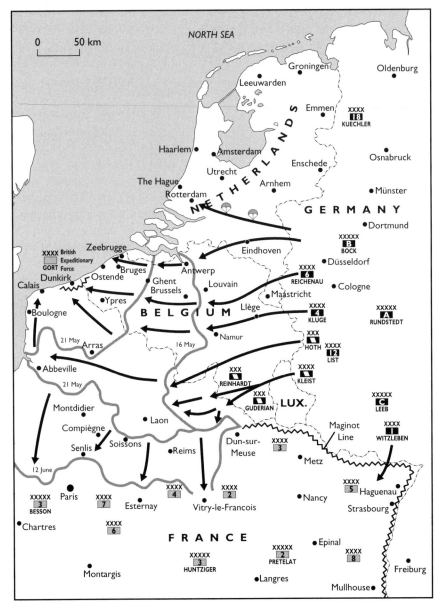

1 The German invasion and breakthrough in the West, May 1940.
Note in particular German breakthrough by Army Group A to Abbeville, British evacuation at Dunkirk; German outflanking of Maginot Line; and attack on remainder of French Army.

lure Anglo-French forces away from the true focal point of the German attack. That focal point was further south, along the Belgian-Luxembourg-French border. Here 45 divisions, under General Gerd von Rundstedt, including 1800 tanks organized into seven *Panzer* divisions along with three motorized divisions, had been concentrated for an attack through the supposedly impassable and thus weakly defended Ardennes Forest. Between 10 and 13 May they succeeded in breaking through the forest and crossing the Meuse River in northern France, creating a breach in the Allied lines 50 miles wide that split the British and French armies while simultaneously outflanking the Maginot Line to the south. Within a week von Rundstedt's forces had reached the English Channel, thereby trapping the British and part of the French Army between them and von Bock's Army Group B in Belgium.

Aided by a temporary and highly controversial 'halt' to the German ground advance ordered by Hitler, some 338,000 of these Allied forces were able to escape to England via a dramatic seaborne rescue at the port of Dunkirk in late May and early June, despite the 28 May surrender of Belgium. But they left behind all their heavy weapons and equipment. They also abandoned the remainder of the French Army south of the German breakthrough, an army now outnumbered by the Germans, forced out of its outflanked Maginot Line and onto open terrain, and thoroughly demoralized. Italy joined in the ensuing attack by declaring war against France and Britain on 10 June. Paris fell on 14 June. On 24–25 June the French signed an armistice whereby Germany would occupy the northern two-thirds of the country, including Paris and the entire Atlantic and Channel coasts, while a collaborationist French Government under World War I hero Marshal Henri Pétain would rule the rump of the country and the overseas empire from the small resort city of Vichy. What the German Kaiser Wilhelm II had failed to do in four years of bloody fighting that had cost millions of lives from 1914–18, Hitler had done in less than two months at a total cost of fewer than 30,000 German dead and 163,000 total casualties. Only a crippled and isolated Britain now stood between the German dictator and total victory.

The Battle of Britain

Militarily, the British situation appeared so hopeless as to necessitate acceptance of virtually any German peace offer, let alone the apparently generous one that the new British Government under Winston Churchill received during the summer: continued possession of their sovereignty and overseas empire on condition that they agree to return Germany's pre-World War I colonies, abandon their traditional balance-of-power policy in Europe, and instead acquiesce in German hegemony on the Continent. Contrary to popular mythology, the British War Cabinet had seriously discussed negotiating with Hitler during the dark days of late May. But Churchill had insisted that any agreement would doom Britain to subservience as what he bluntly labelled 'a slave state' run by a puppet government, and that even a request for negotiations would be deadly to British morale.[10] Such logic led to the rejection of the German offer and determination to continue the war. That determination was reinforced by the British belief that their military situation was not as hopeless as it looked, and that they might be able to use their navy and air force to preclude a successful German invasion. It would not be easy. With his extraordinary rhetoric, Churchill rallied his countrymen, offering his 'blood, toil, tears and sweat' and calling upon them for an effort that history would label 'their finest hour'.[11]

The Germans believed that a successful invasion of Britain, code-named Operation SEA LION, would necessitate the prior destruction of the Royal Air Force by the *Luftwaffe* so as to achieve the air supremacy necessary to preclude successful British air or naval attacks on the German fleet and troop transports crossing the English Channel. They were unable to achieve this objective during their ensuing summer air campaign, which became known as the Battle of Britain, despite their apparently superior numbers in aircraft and trained pilots.[12] Major reasons for this failure included serious German deficiencies and errors, as well as numerous hidden British advantages.

As previously explained, the *Luftwaffe* had been designed to support the German Army in *Blitzkrieg* warfare, and it had done so brilliantly in Poland and during the spring campaigns of 1940. But it lacked any clear doctrine or idea as to how to achieve this new and different overall objective in the summer of 1940, as well as forces properly balanced for such a campaign. The Germans also shifted their specific objectives during the campaign, focusing first on shipping and ports, then in mid-August on British fighter command bases (aerodromes), and then in early September on London. Although supposedly designed with the same overall objective – the destruction of the Royal Air Force (RAF) through attrition – the focus on London in effect constituted a shift to 'strategic' bombing for which the *Luftwaffe* was neither designed nor prepared.

The British, meanwhile, possessed a superb new fighter aircraft, the Spitfire, which was superior to the German fighters and which, together with the more numerous Hurricane fighters, quickly disproved the inter-war theorists' contention that there was no effective defence against bombers. They also possessed newly developed and deployed radar, along with ground control, an observation corps, and an emerging ability to read German codes,[13] which enabled them to know in advance when, where and with what strength the Germans would be attacking. These could not compensate totally for the superior German numbers, of course, but the critical British decision never to commit the bulk of their fighters to any single battle meant that the Germans simply could not destroy the RAF in one decisive blow. Furthermore, and contrary to the predictions of pre-war advocates of strategic bombing, the attacks on London only strengthened civilian morale while diverting the *Luftwaffe* from the fighter command bases and radar installations that should have remained its primary targets. Simultaneously, the RAF dramatically increased the number of fighter pilots available, while British factories outproduced the Germans in fighter plane replacements. By late September the

German air campaign had clearly failed and Hitler was forced to postpone the invasion. But the toll on the RAF pilots had been enormous. In Churchill's ringing words, 'Never in the field of human conflict was so much owed by so many to so few.'[14]

Despite this victory, Britain's long-term situation still appeared quite grim. It did not possess the resources to defend its enormous overseas empire against Axis attacks, or to defeat the German Army on the European Continent. Even worse, Britain itself was not self-sufficient in food and thus was vulnerable to the German submarines that had launched a highly successful campaign against British shipping. Britain would need allies simply to survive, a fact Churchill clearly realized and made the centrepiece of his foreign policy. And in the second half of 1940 virtually all his efforts in this regard focused on the United States.

The United States agrees to aid Britain

Given the extraordinary German military victories of 1940, only two nations with sufficient potential power remained unconquered and possible future allies of Britain: the Soviet Union and the United States. But the 1939 Nazi-Soviet Pact had made Russia a virtual ally of the Germans, an ally whose conquest of Eastern Poland and the Baltic States as well as its aggressive 1939–40 war against Finland had further alienated western public opinion. Furthermore, Soviet dictator Josef Stalin deeply distrusted the British in general, and Churchill in particular. The feeling was mutual. Britain had a long history of conflict with Russia, while Churchill had a long personal history of opposition to the Soviet Union and its Communist ideology. The United States was far more promising, despite the previously cited history of Anglo-American antagonism. Moreover, Churchill's mother had been American and he was a strong believer in close Anglo-American ties. In 1940 he clearly pinned his hopes on obtaining US aid and eventually bringing the United States into the war. As he informed Parliament on 4 June, he intended to fight on no matter how desperate the situation until 'the New World, with all its power and might, steps forth to the rescue and the liberation of the Old'.[15]

Churchill found the United States far more receptive to such rescue in the summer and autumn of 1940 than it had been in 1939. The German victories had come as a tremendous shock to the American people, and had destroyed one of the cornerstones of their neutrality legislation: the belief that the war would be a long and bloody stalemate similar to World War I. Now instead they faced a militarily triumphant and ideologically fanatical Germany bent on global conquest and able to mobilize for war the resources of the entire European Continent. In response, Congress quickly began in the spring and summer of 1940 to appropriate enormous sums to build up the American armed forces, including the first peacetime draft in US history and a 500 per cent increase in defence spending to fund increased arms production, a greatly expanded army and air force, and a two-ocean navy. But even with such a build-up, could the United States successfully maintain itself against a German invasion if Britain fell?

Some Americans answered yes, arguing that the Atlantic Ocean still provided 3,000 miles of security and that the nation therefore could and should maintain its traditional aloofness from European politics and wars. But others insisted that this was a dated and deeply flawed view, one that ignored the revolution in modern warfare as well as the nature of the Nazi menace and that misunderstood the geopolitical basis of American security. The range of modern aircraft, they argued, negated much of the security previously supplied by the Atlantic. Moreover, that ocean was only 1,600 miles wide between West Africa and the eastern 'bulge' of South America, a continent dangerously open to German penetration.

More fundamentally, they argued, security against European attack had actually depended for more than 125 years not on the Atlantic Ocean per se, but on the British fleet controlling it and on the European balance of power that fleet and British diplomacy had maintained so as to preclude the rise of any hegemonic power on the European continent. Britain thus constituted the first and most important line of American defence and must be assisted so it could survive and eventually triumph. It also constituted the only other major and undefeated democratic power in the world, and its fall would leave the United States ideologically isolated and incapable of survival, save as a militarized garrison state. Those who supported this view were often labelled 'internationalists' or 'interventionists', and would organize such groups as the Committee to Defend America By Aiding the Allies, while their anti-interventionist opponents would respond with the America First Committee. The result would be a major public debate that lasted until December 1941.

President Roosevelt agreed wholeheartedly with the internationalist analysis and conclusions, enunciating many of its key points in public addresses and providing the movement with key leadership. As early as September 1939 he had also initiated a private correspondence with Churchill, then First Lord of the Admiralty, that would now expand and develop into an extraordinary partnership and friendship. In response to Churchill's pleas for help, especially the prime minister's 15 May warning that 'the voice and force of the United States may count for nothing if they are withheld too long',[16] the president in the spring and summer of 1940 enunciated strong and public support for material aid to Britain.

Deeply fearful of Nazi Germany, and impressed by British courage during the Battle of Britain, as reported by Edward R. Murrow on the radio and by numerous journalists in their published articles, an overwhelming majority of the American people (some 80 per cent) supported such aid. Yet an even larger majority (82 per cent) opposed formal US entry into the war. It is unclear whether Roosevelt shared such conflicting beliefs or simply realized he had to work within them if he wished to retain office – especially in light of the fact that he would be seeking an unprecedented third term as president in the fall of 1940. Either way, he trod cautiously in terms of the actual material support he was willing to offer Britain, limiting himself throughout the spring and summer of 1940 to the release of military supplies for sale and justifying such sales as a way for the United States to remain out of war by allowing the British to continue to hold back the Germans.

Roosevelt also sent military observers to England to assess the situation and meet their British colleagues. Their ensuing positive reports regarding the chances of British survival reinforced his own beliefs and willingness to provide limited military assistance. Simultaneously he moved to preclude a partisan political division over aid to Britain and American rearmament by appointing two leading internationalists from the opposition Republican Party to his cabinet as Secretary of War and Secretary of the Navy: former Secretary of State (1929–33) and Secretary of War (1909–13) Henry L. Stimson, and former vice-presidential candidate (1936) Frank Knox.

Fearing that the sale of military equipment to England was actually a step toward entry into rather than avoidance of war, anti-interventionists in both parties strongly opposed it. So did leaders of the US armed forces, who doubted Britain's ability to survive and who desperately needed the scarce supplies then available for their own build-up. As one army officer warned in June, 'If we were required to mobilize after having released guns necessary for this mobilization and were found to be short in artillery materiel . . . everyone who was a party to the deal might hope to be found hanging from a lamp post.' Consequently, US Army Chief of Staff General George C. Marshall and Chief of Naval Operations Admiral Harold R. Stark recommended what British historian David Reynolds has aptly described as 'a virtual ban on further arms sales to Britain'.[17]

Undeterred by such warnings, or by congressional legislation prohibiting further sale of military supplies unless they were certified as non-essential by the heads of the armed forces, Roosevelt pressed ahead. In September of 1940 he took an additional and major step. In belated response to a series of pleas by Churchill for naval assistance dating back to 15 May,[18] he now agreed via executive decree to trade 50 over-age US naval destroyers, which Britain desperately needed for defence against German submarines, in return for 99-year leases on eight British bases in the western hemisphere and a public pledge by Churchill never to surrender or scuttle the British fleet – something the American president greatly feared. The proud Churchill at first baulked at what he considered humiliating terms, arguing that 'Empires just don't bargain.' 'Republics do,' US Attorney General Robert Jackson responded, thereby illustrating a conflict that would emerge numerous times during the war.[19] The desperate Churchill bowed and agreed to the terms. Naval chief Admiral Stark then certified that the bases constituted a net strategic gain for the United States, thereby allowing the administration to bypass the congressional ban on the sale of essential military items. Republican presidential nominee Wendell Willkie supported the trade. So did 70 per cent of the public.

The destroyer–bases deal was clearly an unneutral act that aligned the United States informally with Great Britain, a Britain that Americans were coming to consider the first line of their defence. In that sense, the agreement was highly significant diplomatically for future Anglo-American relations – and for the Axis response that would soon follow.[20] It was also significant in US history for its expansion of executive power at the expense of Congress. But militarily the 50 over-age US destroyers were far from sufficient, quantitatively or qualitatively, to resolve Britain's shipping crisis. Nor did they in any way address London's looming financial crisis.

Far Eastern problems and the issues joined

To make matters worse, Japan decided to take advantage of Hitler's military victories by pressuring the Europeans holding colonial empires in Southeast Asia. By the autumn of 1940 Tokyo had forced the Dutch Government, now in exile in England, to grant trade concessions in its East Indies colonies (present-day Indonesia). The Japanese also forced the British and French to close supply routes to China through Burma and Indochina (present-day Vietnam, Cambodia and Laos), with Japanese troops stationed in the northern part of that French colony. Roosevelt responded with an embargo on iron and scrap steel and by moving the US fleet 3,000 miles westward, from its California base to Pearl Harbor in Hawaii.

In late September, Germany, Japan and Italy responded to these presidential moves and the destroyer–bases deal by signing a new military alliance, the Tripartite Pact. By its terms each nation promised to come to the aid of any one of them who might be attacked by a presently neutral country, excluding the Soviet Union. That could only mean the United States. Should Roosevelt continue to aid Britain and try to halt Japan, he would face a war on two fronts.

In reality, this pact was nothing more than a diplomatic bluff designed to scare the United States into inaction. Although they were unified by a common ideology, the three Fascist powers did not trust each other and, as will be shown, they never effectively coordinated their military operations. These facts were not known to the American people, however, who concluded that the three Axis nations were truly united against them. But rather than scare Americans and their government into inaction, the perceived Axis threat soon led them to favour increased opposition to Axis aggression. While loans were extended to China, Roosevelt ordered the fleet he had originally sent to Pearl Harbor on a temporary basis to remain there indefinitely as a deterrent against further Japanese aggression.

The Atlantic was the critical theatre in 1940, however. Yet FDR remained unwilling to go further in aiding Britain than the destroyer–bases deal until he had successfully won re-election. Churchill clearly understood and accepted this political fact of life. With Roosevelt's re-election accomplished in early November, however, the British Prime Minister decided to press for much greater American assistance – assistance that amounted to US involvement in the war as an unofficial ally of Great Britain.

At virtually the same moment, US Naval Chief Admiral Stark was informing the president that the United States would eventually become a belligerent and that the situation called for a fundamental reorientation of US strategic thinking as well as military coordination with the British.[21] Limited military aid, both Churchill and Stark emphasized in their messages to the president, was not enough to defeat Germany, or even to maintain Britain in the war. If Hitler was indeed a menace to the United States, and Britain its first line of defence against that menace, then much greater US assistance, amounting to an informal alliance, would now be necessary. That alliance would be formed in 1941.

2

THE ALLIANCE FORMED
AND THE GLOBALIZATION OF THE WAR,
1940–1941

During the 12 months from December of 1940 to December of 1941, the United States gradually moved from limited to unlimited support of Great Britain and creation of a de facto military alliance. Included in this alliance by the spring of 1941 were extensive US military supplies for England at no charge, and combined strategic planning. A Churchill–Roosevelt summit meeting and a public statement of combined war aims followed in August. By November, the emerging coalition also included the shipment of supplies in armed and escorted US merchant vessels, and an undeclared American naval war against German submarines. Formal war and formal Anglo-American alliance came a month later, but as a result of events in the Pacific rather than the Atlantic.

Lend-Lease

With Roosevelt re-elected in November, on 8 December Churchill sent the president a lengthy and very carefully drafted letter that he later described as 'one of the most important I ever wrote'. In it he warned that Britain was running out of funds to purchase war supplies as well as the shipping to get those supplies safely across the submarine-infested Atlantic. Desperately needed, according to the prime minister, were American loans, merchant ships and naval escorts as well as war materiel.[1]

Fulfilling Churchill's requests directly would require a congressional repeal of the Neutrality Acts and acceptance of full-scale hostilities against Germany. Congress was far from ready to take such drastic action. Nor was Roosevelt. Instead the president made use of novel, indirect methods to achieve the same results.

Roosevelt first decided to focus on the financial problems Churchill had mentioned in his 8 December letter. Instead of requesting a repeal of the ban on loans contained in the Neutrality Acts, however, the president instead proposed that the United States get rid of what he labelled at a 17 December press conference 'the silly, foolish old dollar sign' by agreeing to lend or lease war material to Britain. In a famous analogy, he argued that one did not request payment if a neighbour's house was on fire and he asked to borrow your garden hose; instead you loaned him the hose to protect your own home as well as his, and he returned it or replaced it after the fire was out. Similarly, the president argued in his 29 December 'fireside chat' radio address to the American people, the United States should in its own interest agree to lend Britain war supplies and in the process become 'the great arsenal of democracy' against the Axis powers. By doing so it could keep Britain in the war as America's first line of defence and thereby avoid direct military involvement.[2] In his annual message to Congress a week later, on 6 January, Roosevelt further asserted an American goal of creating a world based upon 'four essential human freedoms' which constituted 'the very antithesis of the so-called new order of tyranny which the dictators seek to create with the crash of a bomb': 'freedom of speech and expression'; 'freedom of every person to worship God in his own way'; 'freedom from want'; and 'freedom from fear'.[3]

Anti-interventionists disagreed vehemently with Roosevelt's claim that Lend-Lease could keep the United States out of the war, and they countered that such a belligerent act would actually lead to direct military involvement – and to numerous American deaths. As the New Deal's Agricultural Adjustment Act had ploughed under every fourth acre, Senator Burton Wheeler of Montana sardonically warned, so Lend-Lease would plough under every fourth American boy. Lending military equipment, Senator Robert Taft of Ohio added, was like lending chewing gum; after it was used, you really did not want it back. Despite such caustic opposition, the Lend-Lease Bill had extensive public support and easily passed both houses of Congress in March, with a vote of 60 to 31 in the Senate and 317 to 71 in the House of Representatives. Under its terms the president was given the power to sell, transfer, exchange, lease or lend war material to any nation whose defence he deemed vital to the defence of the United States. The initial appropriation was for $7 billion, but by the war's end it would total more than $50 billion, approximately 60 per cent of which went to Britain.[4]

Although Churchill would label Lend-Lease 'the most unsordid act in the history of any nation',[5] it was not motivated by altruism. Rather, it was based on a clear recognition by the president and a majority of the American Congress and people that Germany constituted a threat to them as well as to Britain, that Britain's continued survival in the war and victory over Germany were therefore in American interests, and that the United States both could and should aid Great Britain with all aid short of war as a means of achieving these objectives, without actually entering the war. Furthermore, all aid short of war was far from the full-scale US participation that Churchill desired, and it made little material difference to the British war effort in 1941 (Lend-Lease accounted for only 1 per cent of British munitions in 1941, previous cash contracts another 7 per cent).[6] Lend-Lease also carried a price tag that would become clear later in the war as the immediate crisis receded, old American suspicions of Britain resurfaced, and important policy differences emerged.[7]

Nevertheless, Lend-Lease would eventually be of critical importance to Britain's overall war effort, and in early 1941 it clearly made the United States an ally – albeit an unofficial and limited one. It also constituted throughout the war one of America's most important contributions to the entire Allied war effort, as the United States eventually supplied all the anti-Axis powers and fulfilled Roosevelt's call to become 'the great arsenal of democracy'. It was able to do so because of its enormous productive capacity, which had been underutilized during the Great Depression of the 1930s and was now available and being harnessed to a war effort, and because throughout the war the United States remained the only major belligerent not to experience major enemy air or ground attack.[8]

Plan Dog and ABC-1

The emerging unofficial alliance between London and Washington was not limited to material aid. At the same time that Congress was debating and passing the Lend-Lease Bill, presidential adviser and confidant Harry Hopkins was meeting Churchill and his advisers in England in order to discuss a host of war-related issues. Simultaneously, high-level British and American military officers were secretly meeting in Washington to develop a combined strategic plan, should the United States and Britain find themselves formally allied in a war against the Axis powers.

These military meetings had resulted from a November recommendation by Chief of Naval Operations Admiral Harold R. Stark, that they take place and that American strategic priorities be revised in light of the situation. Those priorities had been in a state of flux since late 1938/early 1939, when US military planners had realized that their existing contingency war plans, each for war with a specific country identified by a colour (i.e., ORANGE for Japan, RED for Great Britain, etc.), were dated and needed to be replaced by plans for war against the entire Axis coalition, perhaps with and perhaps without allies. The resulting directive had called for the creation of five so-called RAINBOW plans (to signify a combination of the colours), with the military events of 1940 leading to a defensive focus on RAINBOW 1 and RAINBOW 4 for unilateral continental and hemispheric defence, respectively. British survival and Roosevelt's policies called into question the continuation of such a focus. So did British requests for a revival of naval staff talks that had first taken place in 1938 and 1939, and, as in those previous talks, for US naval assistance at Singapore.

Stark would concur with the former request for revived staff talks, but not with the latter one regarding Singapore, in his pivotal November memorandum. Fully accepting the internationalist argument, the US naval chief in effect maintained that American security had previously and still depended upon a strong British navy and empire to maintain the balance of power and preclude the emergence of a hegemonic European power. Support of Great Britain against Germany was thus a vital policy for US defence. If Britain fell, Stark warned, the United States would not only lack the protection of the British fleet, but would also find itself 'alone, and at war with the world'. Going further, he pointed out that Britain did not possess the military power to defeat Nazi Germany by itself. Victory would in all likelihood require land offensives against Germany that would necessitate US ground as well as naval forces and material.

Given these facts, Stark rejected three pre-existing strategic options for the United States: (1) a continued emphasis on hemispheric defence and avoidance of war as long as possible (Plan A); (2) offensive operations against Japan (Plan B); (3) and maximum military assistance to potential allies in both the Pacific and the Atlantic (Plan C). Instead he proposed in Plan D, or 'Dog' in naval parlance, that the United States should assume the strategic defensive against Japan in the Pacific and focus, in conjunction with Great Britain, for combined offensive action in the Atlantic/European theatre against the more dangerous German foe. Stark further recommended that high-level staff conversations with the British be initiated, as London had requested, but so as to achieve agreement on this strategy – which would be fully implemented when the United States officially entered the war.[9]

Both the army and the president concurred, and in mid-January the staff talks secretly began in Washington. Numerous problems soon emerged, most notably the British preference for a continued US naval focus on the Pacific so as to aid in the defence of Singapore in the event of war while London took care of the Atlantic. To the Americans, this was yet another example of British deviousness. Once again London was attempting to get others to defend its overextended empire, thereby fulfilling a pre-conference military warning to the American negotiating officers that British proposals would probably 'have been drawn up with chief regard for the support of the British Commonwealth. Never absent from British minds are their post-war interests, commercial and military.'[10] The British stance was also an example, from the American perspective, of their shortsightedness in ignoring the real threat to both countries – Germany – and the fact that they were no longer capable of defending the Atlantic by themselves.

Desperately desirous of additional agreements that could lead the United States closer to actual participation in the war, Churchill ordered his envoys to abandon their call for US assistance at Singapore and accede to American strategic plans. The British delegates therefore concurred in the US proposal to concentrate jointly against Germany in the Atlantic and assume a defensive stance in the Pacific should both nations find themselves at war with all the Axis powers, with no mention of US naval assistance for Singapore. The United States would for the present keep its main fleet in the Pacific to deter Japan, but it would shift specific ships to the Atlantic – which would in turn allow the British to shift their own ships to the defence of Singapore instead of relying on assistance that the United States remained unwilling to provide.[11]

The resulting agreement, known as ABC-1, was signed in March, the same month Congress passed the Lend-Lease Bill. It became the strategic basis of the eventual, formal alliance between the two nations, and indeed for their joint conduct of the war. In the following month US military strategists similarly revamped American war plans, with a revised RAINBOW 5 plan for a Europe-first strategy in conjunction with Britain and a defensive effort in the Pacific being approved as the national complement to the bilateral ABC-1 and replacing the RAINBOW 1 and 4 plans for unilateral continental and hemispheric defence (RAINBOWS 2 and 3 had proposed offensive operations in the Pacific).[12]

The spring crisis

Neither Lend-Lease nor ABC-1 and RAINBOW 5 would do anything for Britain's shipping crisis, however, or for the military crisis that erupted during the spring of 1941. While air attacks on British cities increased with better weather, and the German battleship *Bismarck* broke out into the Atlantic to add a potent surface weapon to Hitler's U-boat fleet, the British suffered stunning military defeats in Libya, Greece and Crete that once again called into question their ability to continue the war alone.

These defeats followed a series of military victories against the Italians that had previously buoyed British and American hopes. In the summer and autumn of 1940, Mussolini had invaded Greece and Egypt, as well as British Somaliland in East Africa. In an extraordinary gamble, Churchill had sent major armoured reinforcements to Egypt, in the midst of the Battle of Britain, in order to halt the Italian threat to the Suez Canal. The forces under Middle East commander General Sir Archibald Wavell and his field commander, Lieutenant General Sir Richard O'Connor, comprising Indian, Australian and New Zealand as well as British troops, did much more than that; in late 1940 and early 1941 they totally routed the Italians under Marshal Rodolfo Graziani, throwing them out of Egypt, conquering eastern Libya from Bardia all the way to El Agheila, and capturing 130,000 prisoners at the cost of 2,000 casualties. ('Never,' quipped British Foreign Secretary Anthony Eden in a satiric rephrasing of Churchill's famous tribute to the Royal Air Force during the Battle of Britain, 'has so much been surrendered by so many to so few.'[13]) Simultaneously, Wavell's forces retook British Somaliland and conquered the entire Italian Empire in East Africa, while the Greek Army defeated the invading Italians and threw them back into Albania. And in the Mediterranean itself, the British Navy scored stunning victories against the Italian fleet, first in a naval air attack against the Taranto naval base on 11 June 1940 (with Swordfish biplanes, no less), and then in a surface night attack at Cape Matapan off the Greek coast on 28 March 1941.

In mid-February, however, Churchill ordered a halt to Wavell's Libyan offensive so that British forces could be diverted to aid the Greeks. A month later a coup in neighbouring Yugoslavia overthrew its pro-German government.

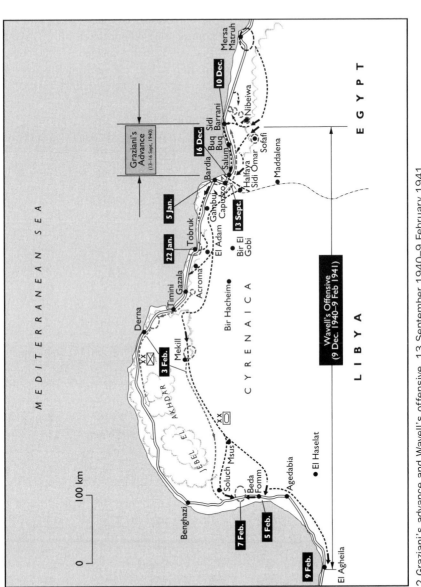

2 Graziani's advance and Wavell's offensive, 13 September 1940–9 February 1941

Within the figure:

MEDITERRANEAN SEA

EGYPT

LIBYA

CYRENAICA

JEBEL EL AKHDAR

Mersa Matruh
Nibeiwa
Buq Buq
Sidi Barrani
Salum
Sofafi
Maddalena
Sidi Omar
Halfaya
Capuzzo
Bardia
Gambut
El Adam
Tobruk
Bir El Gobi
Gazala
Acroma
Timini
Bir Hacheim
Derna
Mekill
Soluch Msus
Beda Fomm
Benghazi
Agedabia
El Haselat
El Agheila

Graziani's Advance (13–16 Sept. 1940)

Wavell's Offensive (9 Dec. 1940–9 Feb 1941)

Date labels: 10 Dec. | 16 Dec. | 5 Jan. | 22 Jan. | 13 Sept. | 3 Feb. | 7 Feb. | 5 Feb. | 9 Feb.

0   100 km

An infuriated Hitler quickly moved to reassert his control over the Balkans as well as save his beleaguered Italian ally by sending two understrength German divisions under General Erwin Rommel to Libya in February, and by launching a massive invasion of Yugoslavia and Greece in April.

The tactically brilliant Rommel and his Afrika Korps stunned the weakened British with an unexpected and highly successful German-Italian counter-offensive in March that captured O'Connor and reconquered all of eastern Libya save for Tobruk, a critical port that the British managed to hold, while the *Wehrmacht* (along with Hungarian and Italian troops) quickly overran Yugoslavia and Greece during April in another stunning *Blitzkrieg* campaign, throwing the British off the European continent for a second time. German airborne troops then attacked the retreating British on Crete, capturing the island and its defenders in May. Although they suffered casualties so heavy that they never attempted another major airborne assault during the war, they had inflicted upon London yet another devastating and humiliating defeat. To make matters worse, a revolt in Iraq by the pro-Nazi Rashid Ali with German air support from Syrian airfields succeeded in April, while British counter-attacks against Rommel in May and June (Operations BREVITY and BATTLEAXE) failed. A major pincer movement against the Suez Canal from North Africa and the Balkans/eastern Mediterranean now seemed likely, with at least tacit support from Rashid Ali in Iraq and the Vichy French in Lebanon and Syria. Such a movement would threaten the entire British position in the Middle East and the Mediterranean lifeline to India, at the same time their Atlantic lifeline to North America was being threatened by the German underwater and surface fleets.

This pincer movement never took place, however, for Hitler's invasions of Yugoslavia, Greece and Crete had all been preliminaries not to the conquest of the Middle East, but to his long-desired invasion of the Soviet Union. Code-named Operation BARBAROSSA and launched on 22 June with over $3\frac{1}{2}$ million men, 3,600 tanks and 2,500 combat aircraft, it constituted the largest invasion in history and precluded any major German activity in the Mediterranean or Middle East for the time being. Consequently British, Australian, Indian, Arab Legion and Free French troops were able to successfully invade and take over Iraq, Syria and Lebanon between May and July. The British Navy also succeeded in sinking the German battleship *Bismarck* on 27 May, thereby lessening the surface menace to British convoys in the Atlantic. The submarine menace remained, however, with increased sinkings resulting in a very serious and growing shortage of merchant ships and naval escorts.

Churchill and Roosevelt both quickly welcomed Soviet dictator Josef Stalin as a new ally and promised him military assistance, despite the previous Nazi-Soviet Pact and Churchill's well-known anti-Communism. If Hitler invaded Hell, the prime minister said in explaining his welcome of Stalin, he 'would at least make a favourable reference to the Devil!'.[14] Roosevelt concurred by making military supplies available to the Soviets. In August,

3 The war in the Balkans, the Mediterranean and North Africa, September 1940–June 1941.

White arrows in North Africa show British counteroffensive against Italians and sending of forces to Greece, September 1940–February 1941. Black arrows show arrival and successes of Rommel and his Afrika Korps in Libya, February–March 1941; and successful German invasions of Yugoslavia, Greece and Crete, April–June, 1941.

British and Soviet troops invaded Iran, forcing the abdication of the pro-German Shah in favour of his son and securing an important supply route. In November, Roosevelt extended Lend-Lease assistance to Moscow. But desperately needed shipping and naval assistance to the British was another matter, for FDR was in the spring and summer of 1941 still unwilling to risk a congressional battle over repeal of the 'cash and carry' provision of the Neutrality Acts that precluded the use of American merchant ships, let alone try to win congressional support for use of the American Navy against the German U-boats.

Throughout this time, however, Roosevelt did use his executive authority as commander-in-chief of the US armed forces to provide Britain with some additional if still limited assistance. In March, he ordered the seizure of all Axis ships in US ports, and, in early April, he extended the previously announced hemispheric defence line, within which warfare was supposedly prohibited, eastward so as to include Greenland. Here US air bases would be constructed. Roosevelt also transferred warships from the Pacific to the Atlantic and ordered the beefed-up Atlantic fleet under Admiral Ernest J. King to patrol west of Greenland, trail German submarines, and report their positions to the British. Later in April he expanded by executive action previous defence agreements with Canada. In May, he proclaimed a state of unlimited national emergency and in early July he redefined the western hemisphere once again by extending the defence line, this time to Iceland, where US troops replaced British troops. Simultaneously he began to toy with the idea of sending an expeditionary force to French Northwest Africa or the Cape Verde and Azores islands in the South Atlantic so as to preclude any German occupation and possible movement into Brazil. But, still afraid of isolationist sentiment, Roosevelt would not order the navy to convoy British ships within the new hemispheric defence line or ask Congress to allow US merchant ships to carry goods to England.

The Atlantic Conference and Charter

In August, Roosevelt went a step further by meeting Churchill, along with their key civilian and military advisers, in Placentia Bay, off the coast of Newfoundland. This was the first of what would be their numerous wartime summit meetings. Here the two leaders began the warm personal relationship that would be so important to the effective functioning of the wartime alliance and that both much desired ('I wonder if he will like me?' Churchill had asked presidential representative W. Averell Harriman before the meeting, a query that shifted to the present tense once the conference began).[15] Here too they agreed to a broad public statement of war aims, many taken from Woodrow Wilson's 14 Points of World War I and Roosevelt's more recent Four Freedoms, even though the United States was not officially in the war. Known as the Atlantic Charter, this statement pledged both nations to a post-war settlement based on a series of fundamental principles: no territorial aggrandizement for themselves; no territorial changes for others without their consent; national self-determination and self-government; equal access for all to trade and raw materials; future economic collaboration; freedom from want and fear; freedom of the seas; disarmament of the aggressor nations and the establishment of a new League of Nations. Along with this document came the extraordinary symbolism, captured by photographs displayed in the newspapers of both countries, of the two democratic leaders not only meeting but also attending with their military chiefs and servicemen a mixed Sunday morning religious service aboard the British warship *Prince of Wales*.[16]

Churchill left the meeting disappointed, however, for he had crossed the Atlantic in hopes of obtaining formal US belligerency. He did not do so. Roosevelt remained fearful of isolationist opinion, apparently with good reason: in the midst of the meeting, Congress agreed by only one vote, 203 to 202, to an extension of the term of service for the more than one million men who had been drafted in 1940. Public opinion polls still showed 80 per cent opposing a declaration of war, though more than 60 per cent now felt that defeating Hitler was more important than staying out of war.[17] The prime minister's disappointment increased when Roosevelt allowed the State Department to water down the tough warning to Japan against further aggression that the two leaders had agreed to send, and did not act on his promise to institute US naval escorts for convoys west of Iceland.

Moreover, beneath the symbolic unity of the Sunday religious service and the Atlantic Charter, serious differences between the two nations simmered just below the surface – and occasionally above it. Particularly noteworthy for the future was disagreement over four issues: (1) post-war territorial agreements; (2) post-war trade policy; (3) the future of colonial empires; and (4) combined military strategy in the event of US entry into the war.

On the first issue, Roosevelt and his advisers feared territorial accords between Britain and its new Soviet ally regarding post-war Eastern Europe and the Balkans that would alienate American public opinion, much as the World War I 'secret treaties' had done when they became known. Particularly worrisome in this regard was the future status of the three Baltic states of Estonia, Latvia and Lithuania, eastern Poland, and the Romanian provinces of Bessarabia and Bukovina – most of which had been part of the Czarist Russian Empire before World War I, lost from 1918–39, and then retaken by Stalin in 1939–40 via the Nazi-Soviet Pact.

On the second issue, the Americans desired British acceptance of their traditional 'Open Door' policy of free trade and therefore opposed the tariffs that Britain had adopted during the early 1930s, as well as the Imperial Preference System embodied in the Ottawa Agreements of those same years that had granted special privileges to members of the British Commonwealth. Some of Roosevelt's State Department advisers proposed that Lend-Lease be used as a club to force British abandonment of those tariffs and agreements (British economist Sir John Maynard Keynes would refer to these during a 1941 visit to Washington as 'the lunatic proposals of Mr. Hull'). Continued conflict over this issue precluded the signing of any Master Lend-Lease accord in 1941.[18]

Similarly, and related, the Americans maintained their traditional opposition to European colonialism, which the British of course supported. Roosevelt and his advisers saw the national self-determination principles of the Atlantic Charter applying to all peoples, including the people of India and other European colonies, whereas Churchill and his advisers clearly did not.

On all three issues the Americans expressed their differences with the British before as well as during the conference. Compromise wording in the Atlantic Charter papered over these differences for the time being, but it did not resolve them.

On the issue of military strategy too, strong disagreement existed beneath the surface accord. As previously noted, British and American officers had agreed in the ABC-1 accord of March 1941 to a global strategy focusing on the defeat of Germany first, with a defensive effort against Japan, should the two nations be formally aligned in a war against the Axis Powers.[19] ABC-1 did not address in any detail, however, the question of exactly how Germany was to be defeated. During the conference, the British military Chiefs of Staff (COS) had explained to their American colleagues their peripheral strategy for this purpose, a strategy that emphasized strategic bombing and naval blockade rather than direct confrontation with the German army on the European continent. A month later, in September, US Army and Navy Chiefs Marshall and Stark, as well as their planners, made clear their fundamental disagreement with this strategic approach,[20] both in formal response to the British chiefs and, more forcefully, in their response to a previous presidential request for an estimate of US production requirements needed to defeat the Axis. In that response, known as the 'Victory Program', they boldly asserted that US participation in the war would be necessary to defeat the Axis and that 'naval and air forces seldom, if ever, win important wars. It should be recognized as an almost invariable rule that only land armies can finally win wars.' Following up on this conclusion, army planners called for the creation of a huge US army of 8 million men, comprising 215 divisions as well as a very large air force, for a massive confrontation with the German army in Central Europe no later than July of 1943.[21] Clearly, US and British strategists disagreed sharply over the proper way to defeat Germany, their earlier agreement to do so before dealing with Japan notwithstanding.

Just as clearly, General Marshall and his advisers disagreed with their president over this issue. Although Roosevelt had strongly supported and often led the 1940–41 drive to rearm, he had previously focused and now continued to focus on naval and air power, apparently due to both agreement with the British strategic approach and recognition of the limits public opinion placed upon the military action he could undertake. Indeed, in the autumn of 1941 he was considering an actual reduction in army size and he sharply rejected the army's proposals, informing Secretary of War Stimson in late September that he was displeased with the army conclusion 'that we must invade and crush Germany' and that it would elicit a 'very bad reaction' from the public if it became known – which it did via a press leak on 4 December.[22]

The undeclared war in the Atlantic

'American mothers don't want their boys to become soldiers,' Roosevelt had told diplomat Robert Murphy, though they 'don't seem to mind their boys becoming sailors'.[23] With this fact obviously in mind, Roosevelt had by the autumn begun to give Churchill some of what he wanted in the Atlantic, though again via indirect and, in all honesty, duplicitous methods. As he had informed the prime minister during the Atlantic Conference, he intended 'to wage war, but not declare it,' and to 'force an "incident". . . which would justify him in opening hostilities'.[24]

That 'incident' occurred in early September, with the president announcing that a German U-boat had attacked the American destroyer USS *Greer* in the Atlantic. What he did not mention was that the destroyer had been stalking the submarine and reporting its position back to British aircraft, which had also attacked the German U-boat. The submarine had thus turned on the *Greer* in self-defence, and without knowledge of its American nationality. Ignoring these facts, the president portrayed the sub's behaviour as unprovoked aggression and used his authority as commander-in-chief to order the navy in response to 'shoot on sight' if it spotted German U-boats. Simultaneously he now further ordered the navy to escort all merchant ships within the newly defined hemispheric security zone, i.e., as far as Iceland, thereby establishing a de facto convoy system.[25]

Then, in October, Roosevelt requested from Congress an end to what he labelled the 'crippling provisions' of the Neutrality Acts so that US merchant ships could be armed and could transport war supplies to Great Britain. Later that month German U-boats attacked the US destroyer *Kearny* and sank another destroyer, the *Reuben James*, resulting in the deaths of 11 and 115 US sailors, respectively. Congress then agreed by close votes of 212 to 194 in the House of Representatives and 50 to 37 in the Senate to repeal the arms embargo and to allow both the arming of US merchant ships and their use in sending military supplies to Great Britain. Simultaneously, the president returned to the possibility of sending an American expeditionary force into Vichy-controlled French West Africa to preclude any German move into the area and the ensuing threat to South America.

By November the United States was thus not only an unofficial ally of Great Britain but also engaged in an undeclared naval war with Germany, one that pitted armed US merchant vessels and navy warships against German submarines. Still the majority of the American people did not support a formal declaration of war. Ironically, formal war and formal alliance with Great Britain would come in December as a result of events in the Pacific, not the Atlantic.

The road to Pearl Harbor and global war

In April of 1941, US Secretary of State Hull and the new Japanese Ambassador Nomura Kichisaburo had begun a series of high-level negotiations in a major effort to resolve the growing crisis between their two nations. These negotiations quickly deadlocked, however, as the demands of the two nations appeared irreconcilable. Nomura called for a full restoration of trade and an end to US aid to Chinese leader Chiang Kai-shek, while Hull insisted on complete Japanese military withdrawal from China and French Indochina, respect for the Open Door policy, disavowal of the Tripartite Pact, and recognition of Chiang Kai-shek's government. In July, Japanese troops landed in southern Indochina. Washington responded by halting the negotiations and freezing all Japanese funds in the United States. As interpreted and implemented in Washington, that freeze created a de facto total embargo on trade with Japan.[26] Possessing enough oil only for 12–18 months, the Japanese government decided to continue negotiations but simultaneously to plan for war against the United States and Great Britain if those negotiations failed. A second Japanese envoy, Kurusu Saburo, was sent to join Nomura with new and final Japanese proposals. Along with those proposals was a warning to the Japanese emissaries that if agreement was not reached by late November, 'things are automatically going to happen'.[27]

That of course meant war, and the American negotiators knew it. They also knew the final Japanese proposals before those proposals had even been officially presented, for US cryptographers had broken the Japanese diplomatic code (MAGIC), and were reading the instructions being sent from Tokyo to Washington. Hull found the final Japanese proposal unacceptable, but the United States was unprepared for war in the Pacific as well as already engaged in a shooting war against the Germans in the Atlantic. Consequently, Army Chief Marshall and Navy Chief Stark, who had previously requested a change in Far Eastern policy so as to avoid a two-front war, now requested at least temporary agreement so as to allow them sufficient time to send reinforcements to the Philippines.

Most important in this regard was the new B-17 bomber, known as the 'Flying Fortress'. Prior to its availability, the Philippines, a US possession promised future independence, had been considered indefensible against a Japanese attack due to its size, geography and location (7,000 islands spread over 1,000 miles of ocean and 5,000 miles distant from Pearl Harbor). Military opinion shifted dramatically with the production of this long-range bomber, for the armed forces believed it possessed so much destructive power over so wide an area that it could deter a Japanese attack or, failing that, so wound the Japanese as to preclude a successful invasion of the Philippines. During the summer of 1941, former Army Chief of Staff and now Philippine Field Marshal Douglas MacArthur had been recalled to active duty and placed in charge of US forces in the Philippines. To provide him with additional time to prepare his forces as well as receive B-17s,

Marshall and Stark requested a temporary agreement based on Japan's final proposal.

Hull at first agreed and prepared a 90-day *modus vivendi* whereby the United States would agree to a limited sale of oil and resumption of trade in return for Japanese concessions that included withdrawal from Indochina and renunciation of the Tripartite Pact. But Chiang Kai-shek objected vehemently to what appeared to be abandonment of his cause and virtually threatened a separate peace, while America's British, Australian and Dutch allies in the area were far from enthusiastic. The president thus had to fear the negative diplomatic consequences of proceeding with the *modus vivendi*, which could include the weakening, if not the destruction, of the developing coalition of nations against Japan. He also had to fear the domestic political consequences. For nearly two years now he had been attacking isolationism and appeasement in regard to Europe and leading the country into both war and alliance with Great Britain; how could he simultaneously expect the public to accept additional appeasement of Japanese aggression?

New strategic considerations also affected Roosevelt's reaction to the final Japanese offer. Defying almost all expert military opinion in Britain and the United States, the Soviet Union had not collapsed within six weeks of the massive German invasion, and in November it still stood as an active belligerent against Hitler. The Soviets had admittedly suffered frightful casualties and enormous territorial losses since June, but in return they had inflicted and continued to inflict enormous losses upon the Germans, losses greater than the *Wehrmacht* had suffered in all its previous campaigns combined.[28]

Roosevelt had been one of the first to recognize the significance of these events. Indeed, as early as 26 June, he had commented that if Russia survived the German assault, it would eventually mean 'the liberation of Europe from Nazi domination'.[29] In July, he had sent Hopkins to meet Stalin in Moscow as well as Churchill in London, and throughout the summer he demanded that his dubious military advisers make scarce military supplies available to the Soviet Union. By September, continued and fierce Soviet resistance had led those advisers to change their position and agree that providing such supplies was 'one of the most important moves that could be made by the enemies of Germany'. The Russian front, they now believed, offered 'by far the best opportunity for a land offensive against Germany, because only Russia possesses adequate manpower situated in favorable proximity to the center of the German military citadel'.[30] Roosevelt agreed. As the historian Waldo Heinrichs has emphasized, maintenance of the Russian front had by this time become the 'centrepiece' of FDR's global strategy because its survival was 'essential' to defeat Germany.[31] By October/November, the president realized that any temporary agreement with Tokyo would free Japanese forces for an attack on the Soviet rear in Siberia, at the very moment he was extending Lend-Lease aid to the Soviets and Stalin was transferring crack Siberian troops for the defence of Moscow against Germany's final and furious assault of 1941.[32]

Hull thus responded to the final Japanese proposal not with a 90-day *modus vivendi* offer, but instead with a ten-point statement of American principles on 26 November that reiterated US insistence on complete Japanese withdrawal from China and Indochina as well as recognition of Chiang and renunciation of the Tripartite Pact in return for a resumption of US trade. He knew this meant war, for as he told Stimson, 'I have washed my hands of it, and it is now in the hands of you and Knox, the Army and the Navy.'[33]

What neither Hull nor any other American knew was where or how that war would begin. Japan clearly had to obtain a new source for oil and other critical resources in light of the US embargo, and that meant attacking the Dutch East Indies (present-day Indonesia) and British Malaya. It also meant an attack on the Philippine Islands that lay between these resource-rich colonies and Japan in order to preclude an American counter-attack on Japanese supply lines. Japanese troop transports and naval forces had been spotted heading south, reinforcing the belief that this was Tokyo's plan. But American intelligence officials missed another key Japanese target, Pearl Harbor, and severely underestimated Japanese capabilities.

In Japanese eyes, the US Pacific Fleet at Pearl Harbor constituted a second and far more dangerous threat to their southern advance than the meagre US forces in the Philippines. Admiral Yamamoto Isoruku, commander-in-chief of the Combined Japanese Fleet, insisted that this US fleet could and indeed must be eliminated if Japan was to have any chance of winning a war against the vastly superior United States. Roosevelt had placed the fleet at Pearl Harbor in 1940 to serve as a deterrent, but an effective deterrent is also by definition a target. And Yamamoto believed that it was a vulnerable target. A surprise attack launched by Japanese planes taking off from aircraft carriers, he insisted, could succeed in destroying this threat.

An attack on Pearl Harbor thus became a key part of the Japanese war plan. Simultaneous invasions of British, Dutch and US possessions in Southeast Asia and the western Pacific would secure for Japan the oil and other resources it needed for economic self-sufficiency and further war, as well as complete the isolation and eventual defeat of Chiang Kai-shek in China, while the destruction of the US fleet would preclude any counter-attack by the only force capable of stopping the Japanese in the near future. Yamamoto and other Japanese leaders were well aware of the fact that the attack on Pearl Harbor could give them only a temporary advantage, for Japan did not possess the human or material resources to invade the United States or defeat it in a lengthy and unlimited war. But they believed a successful attack would provide sufficient time to complete their conquests and establish a strong defensive perimeter in the east and the south. Facing the enormous cost of breaching that defensive perimeter, and preoccupied with Germany, the United States would be forced to agree to a negotiated peace that would recognize Japan's conquests and future control over all of Asia.

The first part of the plan worked perfectly as a Japanese naval task force was able secretly to travel 3,500 miles, approach Hawaii undetected from the

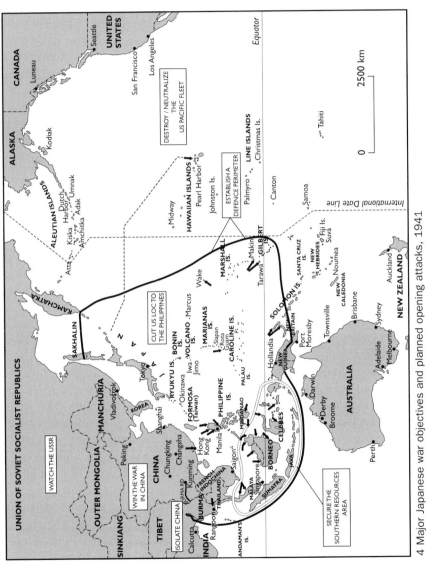

4 Major Japanese war objectives and planned opening attacks, 1941

north, and on 7 December launch two devastating early-morning air strikes with torpedo and dive bombers that destroyed both American ground-based aircraft and much of the US Pacific fleet. At a cost of only 29 planes destroyed and 70 damaged, they sank 4 battleships and 3 destroyers as well as numerous smaller vessels, severely damaged the other 3 battleships and 3 light cruisers in the harbour, destroyed 160 aircraft, disabled 128 more, and killed more than 2,400 Americans. Simultaneously, and on the next day, Japanese forces attacked British Malaya, Hong Kong, Guam, Wake and the Philippines. Referring to 7 December as 'a date which will live in infamy', Roosevelt on 8 December requested and received from the US Congress a declaration that war existed by act of Japan.

Britain also declared war on Japan on 8 December. Indeed, upon hearing radio reports of the Pearl Harbor attack on the evening of 7 December, Churchill had immediately telephoned Roosevelt. 'It's quite true,' the president told him. 'They have attacked us at Pearl Harbor. We are all in the same boat now.'[34]

Despite the losses inflicted on the Americans and the defeats that were certain to come, Churchill was overjoyed. On that same day he had also received news that Hitler's last offensive against Moscow had failed and that the Soviets had launched a massive counter-offensive in minus 40 degree weather. Russia had survived and the United States was fully in the war 'up to the neck and in to the death,' he wrote in his memoirs. 'So we had won after all!', he concluded. Despite all the defeats of 1939–41, eventual victory was now assured. 'United we could subdue everybody else in the world,' he wrote. That night, 'saturated and satiated with emotion and sensation', the prime minister later wrote, he 'went to bed and slept the sleep of the saved and thankful'.[35]

The Roosevelt and Churchill statements were somewhat premature, for Germany and the United States were not yet officially at war. Indeed, the president now faced the problem of being officially at war only with Japan, while the approved American war plan called for action, in conjunction with Great Britain, against Germany. Hitler resolved that problem for Roosevelt a few days later, on 11 December, by declaring war on the United States. Congress reciprocated, thereby completing the globalization of the regional wars that already existed in Asia and Europe.

How could the Pearl Harbor attack have come as a total surprise, especially in light of the MAGIC decryptions of Japanese messages? Critics after the war argued that actually it did not come as a surprise, that, indeed, Roosevelt had known about plans for the attack beforehand and had actually provoked the Japanese strike as a 'back door' to the full-scale war against Hitler that the American Congress and people were still unwilling to accept – and that the German dictator had been unwilling to provide.[36] Supposed evidence for such a conspiracy includes not only the existence of MAGIC, but also the fact that no US aircraft carriers, the decisive naval weapon in the Pacific war, were in Pearl Harbor on 7 December. But MAGIC was deciphering primarily Japanese *diplomatic*, not military, messages; the key Japanese naval code would not be broken until early 1942. Similarly, the primacy of aircraft carriers was not yet established; indeed, it was only the Japanese success at Pearl Harbor, and the naval battles of early 1942, that made clear the superiority of these new vessels over battleships. Moreover, such a conspiracy would have required the connivance of Roosevelt's entire cabinet as well as his key military advisers – individuals who had consistently advised him to avoid war with Japan. It would also have required a belief that Hitler would keep a treaty for the first time in his life and actually come to Japan's assistance, even though the Tripartite Pact as a defensive alliance did not even require him to do so, along with a belief that a US president who had been an assistant secretary of the navy in World War I and loved the service would choose to start a war by allowing his fleet to be destroyed.

The truth of the matter is that the Japanese achieved surprise because the Americans expected an attack elsewhere, because they were overwhelmed with a flood of intelligence data and could not separate the truly relevant material from this intelligence 'noise', because their intelligence agencies were under-staffed and uncoordinated, and because they severely underestimated Japanese capabilities.[37] Yet the conspiracy thesis refuses to die. It reemerges with 'new evidence' in every generation, sometimes with Churchill as a co-conspirator, only to be discredited by scholars and then to reemerge once again.

One reason for the continued popularity of the conspiracy theory is that the attack on Pearl Harbor appears so predictable in hindsight. But hindsight dis-torts this particular past event, as it does many others, because those of us looking back on the events preceding the specific event under study know what eventually did happen. Roosevelt and his advisers did not have such knowledge of Pearl Harbor beforehand. They did commit numerous blunders, both diplomatically and militarily. But such blunders often appear as incom-prehensible in hindsight as being caught by surprise does, and essentially for the same, just-cited reason. The result is conspiracy theories – about Pearl Harbor, and about numerous other events in history. In truth, most such the-ories actually tell us much more about their authors, and about the societies and time periods that accept them, than they tell us about what actually occurred.

The Japanese attack was also far less successful than it originally appeared to be. Three US aircraft carriers as well as seven heavy cruisers were else-where, and all but two of the battleships sunk or damaged at Pearl Harbor (all of which were of World War I vintage) would soon be repaired and sent into battle. This was partially because US repair and maintenance facilities at Pearl Harbor remained intact; so did the submarine base and crucial fuel storage tanks. The Japanese had incorrectly ignored these targets.

They had also grossly miscalculated the American response to their attack. That attack admittedly did virtually guarantee them success in the limited war for colonial empire that they had planned. But it also and ironically gua-ranteed them an unlimited war against the United States, one they could not win, by ending the fierce isolationist-interventionist debate within the country and uniting the American people in a desire for revenge and total victory. The Japanese incorrectly believed that the Americans were too 'soft' and too preoccupied with Germany to pursue such a war. They were wrong. So was Hitler in believing that the United States would for some time remain preoccupied with the Pacific, and that he could therefore add the Americans to his list of formal enemies without serious negative consequences.[38]

Such contradictory perceptions vividly illustrate how shallow the German-Japanese alliance truly was. The same was not to be true of the Anglo-American alliance. Over the previous two years the two nations had overcome their historic antagonisms and suspicions to forge an effective if limited and informal coalition. This had been primarily the result of their clear if belated recognition of the common threat posed by Nazi Germany and Japan, and the initiatives of Churchill and Roosevelt to overcome their differences and mutual suspicions in order to face the common threat together. Now the informal alliance they had forged was to become formal. It was also to become far more extensive than anyone had previously thought possible.

3

THE ANGLO-AMERICAN MUSTER AGAINST THE AXIS

Churchill's elation on the evening of 7 December was a bit premature, militarily as well as diplomatically. Victory was far from assured, despite the entry of the United States into the war and the survival of the Soviet Union. Indeed, the Axis powers held the initiative in virtually every theatre and were on the verge of a series of military successes that would bring their opponents to the brink of defeat. Axis offensives would have to be halted to prevent such defeat, and successful Allied counter-offensives launched. And that would require unprecedented Allied cooperation.

The Grand Alliance: unity and discord

As previously noted, British and American military representatives had theoretically agreed in March to a combined global war plan – ABC-1 – in the event the two nations found themselves allied in war against Japan as well as Germany. By its terms the two would assume the strategic defensive in the Pacific and concentrate their forces in the Atlantic for offensive operations against the more dangerous German foe.[1] ABC-1 had not foreseen the destruction of the US fleet at Pearl Harbor, however. Worried that the Americans might abandon the Germany-first approach in light of this event, Churchill decided on 8 December to travel to the United States in order to meet Roosevelt. FDR quickly agreed, thereby setting the stage for a second Anglo-American wartime summit conference.

Code-named ARCADIA, this conference in Washington remains one of the lesser known of the numerous Churchill–Roosevelt wartime meetings. Yet it was clearly the longest, lasting three weeks from 22 December through to 14 January, and arguably the most important in the formation of the Anglo-American wartime coalition. For it was at the ARCADIA Conference that the British and Americans actually created their formal alliance and clearly established their global strategy, the essential principles for their conduct of the war, and many of the combined Anglo-American bodies that would make possible their eventual victory. It was also during this conference that Churchill and Roosevelt truly established their close personal relationship, with

Churchill staying at the White House as the president's personal guest. The result would be an alliance of unprecedented closeness leading to total victory, though one marked by numerous conflicts and problems.

The formal alliance was proclaimed to the world on New Year's Day, 1942. Entitled at Roosevelt's suggestion the Declaration by the United Nations, it announced the subscription of all signatories to the principles enunciated in the Churchill–Roosevelt Atlantic Charter of August 1941. It further pledged each of them to employment of full resources against the Axis power(s) with which each was at war, cooperation with other signatories, and no separate armistice or peace. Originally signed by the governments of 26 nations, it was open to new adherents and eventually encompassed 45 countries. It also gave its official name to the post-war international organization that its members created in 1944–45 – the United Nations. Unofficially, however, the coalition became known by the name Churchill gave it: the Grand Alliance.[2]

Despite the large number of signatories, the Grand Alliance was from its inception dominated by its three most militarily powerful and active members: Great Britain, the Soviet Union and the United States. Together these three clearly possessed the material and human resources needed to defeat the Axis, but only if they remained united, survived the 1942 Axis onslaught and coordinated their war efforts. Each of those necessities was highly problematic in late 1941/early 1942.

Militarily the Axis held the initiative in all theatres. In Asia and the Pacific, Japanese forces swept through British, Dutch and American possessions in the aftermath of Pearl Harbor and appeared unstoppable. In the Atlantic, German U-boats, now freed from the restrictions placed upon them before Hitler's 11 December declaration of war, feasted on US as well as British shipping. In North Africa, Rommel was preparing for a major offensive. Only in Russia had the Germans been stopped, and that halt appeared to be temporary as Soviet counter-attacks achieved very limited success and the Germans prepared for another major offensive in 1942.[3] Checking the Axis in any of these theatres would be extremely difficult. Failure to do so could easily spell total defeat.

Keeping the three major allies unified and coordinating their war efforts would not be easy either. The three were geographically separated from and highly suspicious of each other. They also possessed very different concepts of how to win the war and how to create a stable and secure post-war peace. All three did agree that Germany needed to be defeated before Japan (the Soviet Union was not even at war with Japan at this time) and that the victors needed to make sure that such aggressor nations would never arise again. But they disagreed sharply as to how to accomplish these goals.

As the oldest belligerent, Britain had the most clearly articulated military proposals. Strategically the British continued to favour the peripheral approach to Europe previously enunciated to the Americans in the summer of 1941, an approach that sought to avoid the frightful casualties they had suffered in the World War I trenches by emphasizing a host of alternatives to direct continental confrontation with the German armies. These included naval blockade, military supplies to the Soviets, strategic bombing, commando raids, and support for European resistance movements against the Nazis. Proposed Anglo-American ground campaigns for the coming year were to take place not on the European continent but in North Africa and the Mediterranean against Germany's weak Italian ally in order to, in Churchill's words, 'close the ring' around Germany and eventually force its collapse. On the long ocean voyage to Washington, Churchill composed a lengthy strategic memorandum forcefully explaining this approach in detail for the Americans while reasserting the primacy of the European theatre over the Pacific. In the process he specifically called for major US forces to undertake numerous peripheral operations in the European theatre: occupation of northern Ireland (Operation MAGNET) so as to release British forces for a new offensive that had recently begun against Rommel in Libya (Operation CRUSADER); a combined bomber offensive against Germany; and a 1942 invasion of French North Africa (Operation GYMNAST).[4] As he explained to his military chiefs of staff prior to departure, the previous, cautious approach used with the Americans before Pearl Harbor was now dated. 'Oh! That is the way we talked to her while we were wooing her,' he told them 'with a wicked leer in his eye', 'now that she is in the harem, we talk to her quite differently!'[5] As for what the world would look like after the Axis defeat, Churchill's government essentially desired a return to the status quo that had existed before the 1930s, both in Europe and around the world.

Such British strategic and post-war plans were anathema to the Soviet Union. Facing over 90 per cent of the German *Wehrmacht* and suffering frightful losses of men and territory, Stalin desired, and throughout the second half of 1941 had been demanding, not merely the sending of military supplies, but also the establishment of a major 'second front' against Hitler in northern France so as to divert German forces from Russia and force Berlin into a two-front war. As for the post-war era, the old status quo that Britain desired to resurrect had, in Stalin's eyes, kept the Soviet Union an isolated outcast and allowed German aggression to take place. Consequently, he rejected British policy and instead demanded a post-war framework based upon wartime agreement both to keep Germany weak and to divide Europe into Soviet and British spheres of influence. Indeed, while Churchill was travelling to Washington, Stalin was laying out for visiting British Foreign Secretary Anthony Eden in Moscow a treaty proposal incorporating these points. By that proposal, Britain would recognize Soviet territorial acquisitions in Eastern Europe that had resulted from the 1939 Nazi-Soviet Pact and agree to a post-war division of Germany, as well as Soviet bases in Eastern Europe, in return for Soviet agreement to similar British bases in Western Europe, European confederations that London desired, and a council of victorious powers. Without such wartime agreement regarding war aims in post-war Europe, Stalin warned Eden, 'there would be no alliance'.[6]

Roosevelt and the US State Department disagreed vehemently. Even before its official entry into the war, the United States had adamantly opposed such territorial settlements on the grounds that they would violate the Atlantic Charter, reward previous Soviet aggression, and create both diplomatic and public opinion problems similar to those that had been created by the secret Allied territorial treaties during World War I. Pearl Harbor in no way altered this opposition. Churchill was also opposed at this time to the territorial treaty Stalin was proposing, both out of hostility to Communism and to sanctioning past Soviet aggression, and out of fear of alienating the United States at this crucial juncture.[7]

US and British post-war goals and policies clashed sharply in other areas, however. Most notable were the conflicts over European colonialism, which the Americans strongly opposed while Churchill fiercely defended and indeed symbolized; and over post-war economic policies, which the Americans wished to be based on free trade as opposed to such protectionism as the British Imperial Preference System. Moreover, on strategic issues, the American armed forces agreed with the Soviets regarding the need to create a second front in northern France instead of continuing with a peripheral campaign that they believed could not lead to German defeat. Only a direct, massive confrontation with the German *Wehrmacht*, they maintained, leading to its destruction, could force a German surrender.

This fundamental difference in strategic approach would bedevil the Anglo-American alliance throughout the war. Indeed, it pre-dated World War II, and it reflected the different histories, traditions and experiences as well as the present positions of the two powers.

Britain's precarious position in 1940–41 had left it with no option save to adopt a peripheral strategy, for under no circumstances after the fall of France and its own defeats could it hope to successfully face Germany in a direct continental confrontation. Throughout much of its history, however, London had often relied upon a similar indirect approach, especially when it found itself lacking a Channel ally,[8] so as to make use of its great assets of seapower and geographic separation from the European continent while minimizing the weakness of its relatively small population and army. Such a strategy had in the past enabled it not only to defend itself successfully against more powerful European enemies, but simultaneously to defend and even expand its extensive overseas empire. In World War I, however, a direct continental strategy had been pursued in conjunction with France and had resulted in casualties so enormous as to constitute the decimation of an entire generation. Avoiding any repetition of this carnage was a major if unstated British goal in World War II. Furthermore, the British had concluded that their eventual success in World War I had resulted from the collapse of the German economy and will, and that a peripheral strategy could create a second such collapse. Airpower theories greatly reinforced such beliefs. So did a misreading of the German economic situation (leading to an incorrect belief that the German economy was already stretched to breaking point)[9] and the need to defend a far-flung overseas empire. Furthermore, Churchill was a strong proponent of the peripheral strategy. Indeed, he had planned the ill-fated Gallipoli expedition in World War I and believed that its failure had been the result of poor implementation rather than a defective approach.

The Americans, on the other hand, had throughout their history seldom put much faith in peripheral strategies designed to destroy the enemy will. Instead they had favoured a direct approach designed to destroy the enemy *capacity* to resist, most notably (but far from exclusively) during the Civil War of 1861–65.[10] Their experiences during World War I had only reinforced this approach, for they had not entered the war until 1917 and had thus seen their first direct offensives in 1918 succeed in obtaining German surrender. In the process they had suffered only relatively light casualties. Also unlike the British, the Americans possessed the abundance of manpower and industrial capacity needed for a direct approach, and they had not suffered the humiliating defeats at the hands of the Germans that they claimed made their British allies overly cautious. As a result of these factors, they thought the British approach was seriously defective militarily. Continued British adherence to that approach, they argued, was a politically inspired attempt by Churchill to prove his World War I ideas correct and to place US as well as British forces in areas of imperial interest, a political goal antithetical to their own, rather than win the war as quickly and decisively as possible.

Such military and political differences were nothing new in the history of coalition warfare. Indeed, conflicting strategies and policies had seriously weakened past wartime alliances and had often led to defeat. Napoleon had once quipped that he would never lose if left to fight coalitions, and Marshal Ferdinand Foch had admitted to having less respect for Napoleon's abilities after having led a coalition command in World War I. But without the others, none of the three major allies could hope to defeat the Axis powers alone. As Benjamin Franklin supposedly said regarding the signing of the US Declaration of Independence in 1776, the signatories needed to 'all hang together, or most assuredly we shall all hang separately'. Churchill said the same thing in different words when he quipped during the war that 'There is only one thing worse than fighting with allies, and that is fighting without them!'[11] His trip to Washington was clear recognition of this fact, a recognition shared by his allies but not by his Axis enemies.

The ARCADIA Conference and the structure of Anglo-American cooperation

Despite Pearl Harbor, Churchill upon arrival in Washington found that Roosevelt and his military advisers remained committed to the Germany-first approach of ABC-1. They were most concerned with immediate defensive moves in both oceans, however: in the Pacific to halt the Japanese advance and in the Atlantic to maintain the Lend-Lease lifeline to Britain as well as preclude any German move on Latin America via French West Africa. This latter possibility had deeply concerned them even before Pearl Harbor, and had led them to develop plans for an expeditionary force to one or both of these areas, plans that now took on a new urgency. Just before Churchill's arrival, Roosevelt and his military chiefs had agreed to make West Africa the 'foremost' area to be considered for an expeditionary force. Consequently, they voiced no major objections at this time to the overall British approach to European strategy or to their participation in Operation GYMNAST. Roosevelt was particularly attracted to this operation, and it became a topic of discussion during his first meeting with Churchill on the evening of 22 December. Indeed, Churchill later noted that 'the discussion was not *whether*, but *how*'.[12]

In this defensive mode of thinking, and still reeling from the Japanese attack, the American armed forces did not challenge at this time the overall British approach. Indeed, by 31 December the British and American Chiefs of Staff had further agreed to a broad peripheral strategy in the European theatre for 1942 that would focus on three general goals: (1) maintenance of sea communications between the allies; (2) closing and strengthening the ring around Germany; and (3) wearing down German resistance. Specific 1942 activities would include blockade, material assistance to Russia, the strategic bombing of Germany, increasing strength in the Middle East, gaining possession of the entire North African coast, and organizing resistance movements within German-occupied Europe. In the Far East, defensive efforts would focus on maintaining the security of Australia, New Zealand and India, supporting the Chinese war effort, and trying to maintain a supply route to China through Burma as well as holding Hawaii, Alaska, Singapore, the Dutch East Indies and the Philippines.

To accomplish these goals, US Army Chief of Staff General George C. Marshall made a startling proposal during a Christmas Day meeting of the British and American Chiefs of Staff. Firmly convinced from his World War I experiences of the importance of both inter-service and inter-allied military cooperation, he suggested, under the innocuous-sounding military principle of 'unity of command', that the two nations and their allies in Southeast Asia and the Southwest Pacific agree to place all their army, navy and air forces under a single commander. 'We cannot manage,' he warned, by mere 'cooperation'; full-scale and binding military coordination would be required.[13]

Such military coordination would be unprecedented on both national and service levels, and for good reason. As Marshall himself noted, 'Human frailties are such that there would be emphatic unwillingness to place portions of troops under another service', be it of the same or of a different nation. As Churchill bluntly asked, clearly in opposition to the proposal, what could an army officer possibly know about handling a ship? 'What the devil does a naval officer know about handling a tank?', Marshall shot back. His purpose was not to enlist sailors or tank drivers, but to achieve unified control at the highest levels of Allied forces facing the Japanese. If they failed to do so, he warned, 'we were finished in the war'.[14]

Marshall succeeded in winning approval for his proposal from the US Navy, the president, the British Chiefs of Staff and their prime minister via such logic and warnings – and via his willingness to make a British field marshal and former commander-in-chief in the Middle East and in India, Sir Archibald Wavell, the Allied commander in the area. That particular combined command – dubbed ABDA for American-British-Dutch-Australian forces – would end in disastrous defeat,[15] but it clearly established the precedent that Marshall had desired for unity of command in other theatres. Henceforth all British, American and other Allied ground, naval and air forces in a single theatre would serve under a single commander – a coordination unprecedented for major powers in military history.

Equally unprecedented was the Anglo-American body created at ARCADIA to direct these commanders around the world. During the Christmas Day meeting Marshall had noted the importance of such a body, stating that he favoured 'one man in control' of ABDA, 'but operating under a controlled directive from here'.[16] Roosevelt had concurred and pressed for the establishment of an inter-Allied Supreme War Council in Washington, but Churchill baulked at the proposed multilateral nature of the body as well as the location, preferring instead a bilateral Anglo-American organization with branches in London as well as Washington. By 31 December he had shifted on the latter point and agreed to the single US location, while Roosevelt agreed to keep the body bilateral rather than make it multilateral.[17] The result was the creation of a Combined Anglo-American Chiefs of Staff (CCS), composed of the US and British Army, Navy and Air Chiefs and meeting in continuous session in Washington. The chiefs would meet in person at the numerous Allied wartime summit conferences. At all other times the British chiefs would be represented by a Joint Staff Mission in Washington, headed by the recently relieved former Chief of the Imperial General Staff, Field Marshal Sir John Dill. The CCS as a whole would be responsible and report directly to Churchill and Roosevelt.

Creation of the Combined Chiefs of Staff required a reorganization of the American high command so as to parallel the British system. The latter was headed by a Chiefs of Staff Committee (COS), composed of four individuals: the Chief of the Imperial General Staff, General Sir Alan Brooke; the First Sea Lord, Admiral Sir Dudley Pound; the Chief of the Royal Air Force, Sir Charles Portal; and Churchill's representative, Chief of Staff to the Defence Minister, Major General Sir Hastings Ismay (Churchill was defence minister as well as prime minister). The Americans possessed no such organization. During and immediately after the ARCADIA Conference they in effect created one entitled the Joint Chiefs of Staff (JCS), the forerunner of the contemporary body with that name. It was originally composed of Army Chief of Staff General Marshall, Chief of Naval Operations (CNO) Admiral Harold R. Stark, Army Air Forces (AAF) Chief General Henry H. 'Hap' Arnold, and Commander-in-Chief of the Fleet Admiral Ernest J. King. In March, however, Stark was sent to England as commander of US naval forces in Europe, and King assumed the combined positions of naval chief and commander of the fleet. Four months later, Roosevelt appointed former CNO and Ambassador to Vichy France Admiral William D. Leahy to the JCS as 'Chief of Staff to the Commander in

1 US Joint Chiefs of Staff – seated (left to right): Army Chief of Staff General George C. Marshall; Army Air Forces Chief General Henry H. Arnold; JCS Secretary Brig. Gen. John R. Deane; Chief of Naval Operations and Commander-in-Chief of the US Fleet Admiral Ernest J. King; and Chief of Staff to the Commander-in-Chief Admiral William D. Leahy – with their aides, gather around a conference table at Quebec to map out the war strategy, 23 August 1943 © Bettmann/CORBIS

2 British Chiefs of Staff. Seated (left to right): Chief of Air Staff Sir Charles Portal; Chief of Imperial General Staff Sir Alan Brooke; Winston Churchill; First Sea Lord and Chief of Naval Staff Sir Andrew Cunningham. Standing: Maj.-Gen. L.C. Hollis, Sec. to Chiefs of Staff Committee, and Gen. Hasting Ismay, Chief of Staff to the Defence Minister, 8 May 1945 © Bettmann/CORBIS

Chief', a position similar to Ismay's on the COS and one that evolved after the war into the present-day chairman of the US Joint Chiefs of Staff. These four would remain the US Joint Chiefs for the duration of the war. Brooke, Portal and Ismay would similarly remain on the COS for the rest of the war, though Admiral Sir Andrew B. Cunningham would become First Sea Lord when Pound died in 1943, and Combined Operations Chief Admiral Lord Louis Mountbatten would become a de facto member in 1942.

The British and Americans further agreed during and soon after ARCADIA to the creation of separate theatres around the world in which unity of command would be practised, with command and direction going to the predominant military partner in that area. The Pacific would thus be under an American commander reporting to the JCS, while the Middle East, Indian Ocean and South Asia would be under British commanders reporting to the COS. The primary European theatre would be one of shared responsibility, with the commander reporting to the CCS. Stalin and Chiang along with their military staffs and commanders would of course be in charge of the Soviet and China theatres, respectively, but they would not be part of the CCS – a body that would remain purely Anglo-American.

Unity of command would be violated in some theatres. No unified Anglo-American naval command existed for the entire Atlantic, for example, which was instead divided into British eastern and American western zones. Moreover, the Americans would on their own divide the Pacific theatre into two commands: the Pacific Ocean Areas (POA) under Admiral Chester W. Nimitz and the Southwest Pacific Area (SWPA) under General Douglas MacArthur. Although this division could be justified on the grounds of the enormous size of the Pacific, the world's largest ocean, it had more to do with inter-service conflicts focusing on the impossibility of placing the very senior MacArthur under the relatively junior Nimitz and the navy's refusal to place its capital ships under an army officer. Furthermore, there was seldom any meshing of British and American forces on the lower levels of organization. Each nation maintained its own army divisions and corps and its own naval and air fleets. But in most theatres these were unified at the highest levels under a single commander with an Anglo-American and/or inter-service staff. In itself such unification was unprecedented.

It also stood in sharp contrast to the almost total lack of Axis military co-ordination. Despite their common Fascist ideology and official alliance, the three powers essentially did not trust each other sufficiently to coordinate their military efforts, and unlike the Allies they did not believe in 1941–42 that they needed to do so. Had they done so, they might very well have won the war – via a combined German-Japanese attack on the Soviet Union that would have precluded Stalin's shift of Siberian troops to the defence of Moscow and that Roosevelt had sought to avoid in late 1941, for example, or via a major Japanese movement westward into the Indian Ocean in early 1942 instead of south or eastward, in order to link up with German forces coming down from the Caucasus and Rommel moving eastward across the Middle

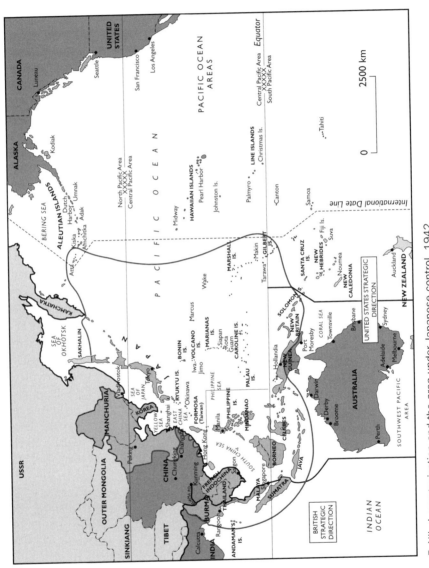

5 Allied reorganization and the area under Japanese control, 1942

East — a possibility that terrified Allied planners in that it would not only have connected Axis forces but also given them control of the Middle East oil reserves.

Based on the COS model, a series of pivotal joint and combined committees were also created during and after the ARCADIA Conference to advise and report to the JCS and the CCS on such matters as intelligence, war plans and logistics (all Anglo-American committees during the war were known as 'combined', whereas all British or American inter-service committees were known as 'joint'). Both nations also agreed at ARCADIA to the establishment of a Munitions Board under the CCS to allocate munitions production, and to the creation of a Combined Raw Materials Board and a Shipping Adjustment Board.

These latter bodies were in turn part of a broad effort at economic coordination during the war, based upon Lend-Lease and other 1941 agreements but now expanded. By mid-1942 they also included reciprocal aid in the form of raw materials by Britain (so-called 'Reverse Lend-Lease'), a Combined Food Board, and a Combined Production and Resources Board. Even more than in the military sphere, however, such coordination remained limited to planning and never reached the level of systematic combination of production. Moreover, much of the economic cooperation that did take place bypassed the combined boards and occurred via the Lend-Lease organization and direct agency negotiations. Nevertheless that cooperation was effective overall and enabled the two powers, and the alliance as a whole, to make efficient use of their economic resources.[18]

Most notable in this regard was, of course, American Lend-Lease. The United States possessed an enormous productive capacity, far beyond that of any other belligerent and, once harnessed to the war effort, American industry would produce enough war materiel to supply both its allies and its own substantial forces — and in effect to bury its Axis opponents under an unbelievable mass of American steel. The statistics for American war production in this regard are staggering: 297,000 aircraft, 193,000 artillery pieces, 86,000 tanks, 2.4 million army trucks and jeeps; 1,200 combat vessels and 8,800 total naval vessels; 87,000 landing craft; 3,300 merchant ships and tankers; 14 million shoulder weapons; 2 million army trucks. As historian Richard Overy has noted, this constituted nearly two-thirds of all Allied military equipment produced during the war. The percentage of US Gross National Product devoted to defence and the war effort rose from 2 in 1939 to 42 in 1945, with military spending increasing 8,000 per cent.[19]

US military forces were also quite extensive, totalling more than 12 million in uniform in 1945. Nevertheless they constituted only 25 per cent of the Allied total. British military forces, taken from a smaller population base, were far smaller than the Americans in both numbers and percentage of the Allied total; but Commonwealth and Empire military forces, including 2.4 million Indian troops, raised those numbers and percentages substantially.[20]

Lend-Lease eventually totalled $50 billion and by the war's end had been distributed to 38 different countries, with approximately 60 per cent going to

Great Britain. This not only helped to supply the British but also covered more than 50 per cent of their balance of payments deficit, thereby enabling the British economy to focus on war production instead of exports that would otherwise have been needed to cover this deficit. Lend-Lease was not a one-way street, however. 'Reverse Lend-Lease' was substantial, consuming a percentage of British domestic output similar to the percentage of US domestic output devoted to Lend-Lease, and it included not only natural resources from the empire but also imperial commodities, supplies for US troops stationed in England and the empire, and oil for US forces in the Mediterranean.[21]

At least as important as Lend-Lease and other forms of inter-allied economic cooperation was the fact that each of the three major allies mobilized its economic resources for a long, total war with much greater efficiency than their Axis opponents did. Indeed, Germany, Italy and Japan all planned originally for short, decisive wars and did not prepare adequately for the lengthy conflict that did take place. Their early victories merely reinforced this tendency, whereas Allied defeats in 1940–42 led them in the opposite direction. As early as the summer of 1940 Britain was producing far more replacement aircraft than Germany, and by 1943 American aircraft production was more than twice the combined production of Germany and Japan. The figures on naval craft are even more staggering, with the United States commissioning 104 new aircraft carriers during the war to 14 for Japan. As early as the end of 1942, American war production was already greater than that of all the Axis nations combined. It was also more efficient, with productivity per capita far greater than German or Japanese workers.[22]

Throughout 1942 the British and the Americans also expanded upon technical ties that had been established in 1940–41. Indeed, as historian Theodore Wilson has aptly noted, as early as mid-1941, 'an elaborate network of personal and organizational communication linked British and American officials', and these links were now expanded massively in a host of areas. Just the British Army Staff in North America, which originated in a series of small and specific 1940–41 technical missions, would now grow to exceed 1,500 personnel at 45 locations in North America.[23]

This staff and other British organizations would now deal with a host of war-related issues. These included the trading and sharing of major weapons inventions, such as radar, and of scientific research designed to produce new weapons. Most notable in this latter regard would be the effort to develop an atomic bomb, an effort that had been initiated in each country independently as early as 1939–40. It was only in mid-1941, however, that American scientists came to agree with their British counterparts on the MAUD Committee that wartime development of such a weapon was indeed feasible and that a major effort should be undertaken.[24] Roosevelt was informed of this in early October of 1941 and quickly proposed to Churchill that they 'correspond or converse' on this matter so that 'any extended efforts' by the MAUD Committee and the recently established US Office of Scientific Research and Development (OSRD) under Dr Vannevar Bush 'may be coordinated or even

48

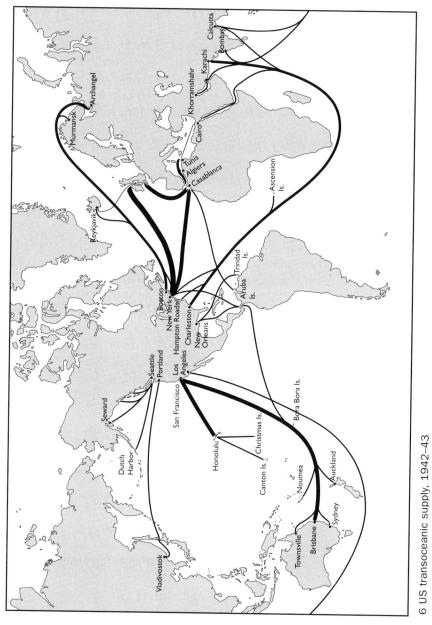

6 US transoceanic supply, 1942–43

jointly conducted'.[25] According to Churchill, the two discussed the matter during the ARCADIA Conference and again at their next US meeting in June, verbally agreeing to a combined Anglo-American effort with full sharing of information and results. Mutual suspicions delayed any formalization of this agreement, however, until August of 1943 and September of 1944 at the two Quebec Conferences.[26]

The British and Americans would also expand in 1942 upon the intelligence ties that had similarly been established in 1941.[27] Most notable in this regard was the sharing that took place in regard to the new and extraordinary cryptographic intelligence that was enabling both nations to break the highest codes of their Axis enemies. At Bletchley Park in England, British cryptologists had, in an operation known as the ULTRA SECRET, since 1940 been deciphering encrypted German radio signals sent and received via a machine code-named ENIGMA. The longest and best-kept Anglo-American secret during World War II, it was revealed to the world only in 1974 and has led to major reassessments of numerous battles and campaigns as well as the virtual creation of a new sub-field in World War II history. Of equal importance was the American MAGIC, the deciphering of Japanese cryptographic radio messages sent via the PURPLE machine. Throughout 1941 the Americans had been able to break and read the diplomatic codes, and by 1942 they would be successful in breaking the key Japanese naval code, with decisive results at the Battle of Midway. Furthermore, the MAGIC diplomatic messages would often provide extremely valuable information on German plans and capabilities as relayed to Tokyo by the Japanese ambassador in Berlin, Count Oshima Hiroshi. Indeed, General Marshall in 1944 called Oshima the 'main basis of information regarding Hitler's intentions in Europe'.[28]

The British and Americans continued to maintain separate intelligence operations, but gradually agreed to share some of their results. At ARCADIA they established a Combined Intelligence Committee for the CCS, and in June 1942 American codebreakers joined the British at Bletchley Park. Then in late 1942/early 1943 the two nations agreed to a fuller sharing of results, and of personnel, one unprecedented in modern history. 'Never before', historian Bradley F. Smith concluded, 'had two countries agreed to share the most profound secrets they possessed about their enemies. Even more significant, no governments previously had obligated themselves to carry out an exchange of personnel within such sensitive and secret operations.' Indeed, Smith maintains that it virtually guaranteed post-war continuation of the Anglo-American alliance, since any end to it would compromise the security of both nations.[29]

The result of all these organizations and sharing was the creation, both during and soon after the ARCADIA Conference, of a very special Anglo-American alliance within the larger and now-formal Grand Alliance. Despite the very real limits on their collaboration, never before had two nations even attempted such a level of coordination and meshing of their military, economic, scientific and intelligence forces and efforts. The fact that such an effort largely succeeded, despite pre-existing and continued conflicts and suspicions, was primarily due to the military and political leadership in both countries.

Numerous Anglo-American strategic conflicts would erupt within the CCS throughout the war, sometimes so violently as to necessitate 'off the record' conversations that almost turned into brawls. Particularly noteworthy in this regard were the conflicts between the caustic and opinionated British General Brooke and the highly irascible and Anglophobic US Admiral King, whose supposed motto was 'When they get into trouble they send for the sons-of-bitches.' ('He is one of the most even-tempered men in the world', one of his daughters once claimed. 'He is always in a rage.')[30] Nevertheless the two did not come to blows. Rather, they and the other British and American chiefs of staff were consistently able to see the 'big picture', to compromise their differences and thereby to achieve unprecedented cooperation. General Marshall and Field Marshal Sir John Dill, the former Chief of the Imperial General Staff appointed head of the British Joint Staff Mission in Washington during the ARCADIA Conference, were particularly noteworthy in this effort, and the development of a very strong friendship between the two was of crucial importance in the smooth functioning of the Anglo-American war effort. (So strong was that friendship that when Dill tragically died in 1944, Marshall had him buried in Arlington National Cemetery – the only non-American so honoured.) Equally if not more crucial to the smooth functioning of the Anglo-American war effort was the exceptional friendship that also emerged at ARCADIA between Churchill and Roosevelt.

Churchill and Roosevelt: the personal equation[31]

Churchill and Roosevelt had got along well during their first meeting the previous August off the coast of Newfoundland, but it was at ARCADIA that their friendship truly blossomed. Throughout the three weeks of the conference Churchill was Roosevelt's personal guest at the White House, where informality ruled.[32] On one occasion, according to a famous story, the invalid Roosevelt wheeled himself unannounced into Churchill's room, only to find the prime minister recently out of the bathtub and naked. Excusing himself, Roosevelt began to leave, only to be told by Churchill to stay as he had absolutely 'nothing to conceal' from the President of the United States![33]

That was a humorous but gross overstatement, for each leader hid a great deal from the other throughout the war. They also had fundamental disagreements, particularly over the colonialism that Churchill strongly supported and that Roosevelt opposed and hoped to dismantle. Closer to the truth was Roosevelt's comment in a late January telegram to Churchill: 'It is fun to be in the same decade with you.'[34] Simply stated, the two men enjoyed each other's company enormously, and indeed often behaved like little boys when together. Such behaviour often drove their advisers to distraction. So did many of their individual personal habits. Most notable in this regard were Roosevelt's chaotic administrative procedures and Churchill's late-night sessions and notorious consumption of alcohol, which today would classify him as an alcoholic. C.P. Snow once humorously challenged that description on the grounds that no alcoholic could drink as much as Churchill did! (Nevertheless, even Churchill found it difficult to stomach the vile concoctions of gin with both dry and sweet vermouth that Roosevelt insisted on mixing and serving before dinner as a 'martini' – and that Churchill quickly learned to secretly toss into the nearest bathroom or flower pot.[35])

The close personal relationship between Churchill and Roosevelt enabled the two leaders to conduct an enormous quantity of business through personal messages and meetings. From 1939–45 they would correspond with each other more than 1,700 times on a gamut of war-related topics. After Pearl Harbor they would also meet each other, along with their military advisers, on ten separate occasions, totalling 120 days. To a great extent, Anglo-American strategy for the war was determined at these meetings.

Churchill and Roosevelt shared a similar strategic outlook, focusing on air and naval over ground forces, as well as an incessant optimism regarding what could be accomplished militarily, and a belief that their strategic abilities and insights were at least as good as, if not superior to, the abilities and insights of their military chiefs. Consequently, they pressed throughout the war for operations those chiefs considered unwise, if not impossible. Indeed, strategic disagreements just as often pitted Churchill and Roosevelt against the CCS as they pitted British against American concepts.

To say this upset the chiefs of staff would be an understatement, and in both London and Washington they complained bitterly about what they considered the wrongheaded if not insane strategic proposals of their leaders. When Churchill and Roosevelt were together, as at the ARCADIA Conference, it only compounded the problems. On one occasion at the next summit conference in Washington six months later, Marshall lost his temper when called into one of their late-evening sessions and walked out with the comment that he refused even to discuss their strategic proposal at that hour. Brooke's daily frustrations with Churchill in this regard were preserved in his diary, along with his utter rage over what he called the prime minister's strategic 'absurdities' and 'nonsense' that made him 'a public menace'. Even before he had to deal with Churchill, US General Dwight D. Eisenhower humorously commented, after listening to civilian strategic advice, that there were 'only two professions in the world in which the amateur excels the professional: one, military strategy and, two, prostitution'.[36]

The generals and admirals were not always correct in this perpetual tug-of-war. Churchill and Roosevelt often succeeded in prodding their conservative military chiefs into successful actions those chiefs would otherwise not have undertaken.[37] But the chiefs similarly succeeded on numerous occasions in talking Churchill and Roosevelt out of military schemes that would in all likelihood have ended disastrously. Consequently, the number of major Anglo-American military blunders was relatively small in comparison with those committed by the Axis powers. Indeed, the entire Anglo-American coalition effort stood in stark contrast to the Axis coalition effort.

Axis vs Allied conflict and cooperation

As previously noted in Chapter 1, the Tripartite Pact of 1940 was essentially a diplomatic bluff designed to scare the United States, via the threat of a two-front war, into not assisting Britain or China or in any other way opposing Axis aggression. In that it totally failed. It also failed as a military alliance. With a few Italo-German exceptions, the three powers never coordinated their military forces or operations. Indeed, so great was their level of mutual distrust, despite their common ideology, that they seldom made war in common. Mussolini, for example, did not join Hitler in war against France and England until France was all but defeated. Japan did not join in the 1941 invasion of Russia, and did not go to war with the latter until Moscow declared war in August of 1945. Nor did Germany, Italy and Japan keep each other informed of their projected military operations. The 1940 Italian invasion of Greece, the 1941 German invasion of Russia and the Japanese attack on Pearl Harbor were each launched unilaterally and secretly. As a result, the three Axis powers fought separate wars. Indeed, their distrust of each other often placed their diplomatic and military moves at cross-purposes. Unaware of Hitler's plans to attack Russia in June of 1941, for example, the Japanese signed a non-aggression treaty with the Soviets in April so as to protect their flank while they moved east and south against the Americans and the British – a decision in turn influenced by what they considered Hitler's betrayal of their anti-Comintern Pact via his 1939 Non-Aggression Pact with Stalin. Had Germany and Japan joined in the attack on Russia in 1941, or had they coordinated their 1942 offensives so as to attempt a triple junction in the Indian Ocean, the war might have ended differently.

Their Allied opponents fought a far more effective coalition war. On an absolute basis the Grand Alliance was far from the most efficient coalition possible. On a relative basis, however, both historically and in comparison with the Axis, the Allied coalition was superb. Indeed, it stands as a model of successful coalition warmaking, while the Axis alliance is a classic case study of how not to conduct a coalition war. As David Reynolds has aptly concluded, while American perceptions of 'a cohesive totalitarian plot' helped bring the United States into the war in 1941, 'the reality of Axis divergence helped ensure eventual Allied victory'.[38]

All was not rosy within the Grand Alliance, however. The simmering Anglo-American strategic debate had been temporarily buried amidst the defensive necessities and organizational arrangements at ARCADIA, but it would re-emerge during the spring and summer in particularly virulent form. And post-war differences reared their head even during the conference in the form of Stalin's continued demands for a territorial treaty recognizing his conquests in Eastern Europe. On 8 January Churchill informed Eden that he and

Roosevelt strongly opposed those demands. He also asserted his belief that postponement of such matters would serve Anglo-American interests, for at war's end Britain and the United States would constitute 'the most powerfully armed and economic *bloc* the world has ever seen, and . . . the Soviet Union will need our aid for reconstruction far more than we shall then need theirs'.[39]

Nor were Anglo-American relations free of discord. Suspicions as well as sharp differences of opinion remained on both sides, and they surfaced in hard bargaining in 1941 and 1942 over the specific terms of the destroyer–bases deal and terms for a Master Lend-Lease agreement.

Partially that hard bargaining stemmed from the belief of many American officials that the two nations had been and would continue to be trade rivals, and that tough negotiations were therefore appropriate. The British, fighting alone for their lives in 1940–41, disagreed. 'These people are gangsters', former Prime Minister David Lloyd George had told the Foreign Office when he heard American terms for the destroyer–bases deal in early 1941.[40] But the hard bargaining also stemmed from very different national conceptions of appropriate trade policies.

Throughout much of their history, Americans had claimed that trade restrictions led to depression and war, while so-called 'free trade', or 'Open Door', led to economic prosperity, interdependence and peace. Britain had concurred in the mid-nineteenth century when it was economically strong, but clearly recognized that such a system rewarded the strong and penalized the weak – and that, indeed, it was the 'imperialism of the strong'. This was something the Americans refused to admit. Nor would they admit to their own violations of their principles within their high tariffs.

In its 1930s economic weakness Britain had reverted to high tariffs and the institution of an Imperial Preference System, also known as the Ottawa Agreement, whereby members of the British Commonwealth and Empire received preferential trade treatment. US Secretary of State Cordell Hull, an avid free trader to the point of obsession, called this system 'the greatest injury, in a commercial way, that has been inflicted on this country since I have been in public life'.[41] He and his State Department representatives consequently demanded that London agree to dismantle the system as the price for Lend-Lease. This disagreement had forced postponement of a Master Lend-Lease accord in mid-1941. Whether or not Churchill and Roosevelt actually argued over this issue at their first meeting, as FDR's son Elliot later claimed, the clearly existing disagreement was papered over via compromise wording in the Atlantic Charter article on future trade, which promoted free trade as the Americans insisted, but with 'due respect for existing obligations' as the British insisted. And although Roosevelt told Churchill on 11 February 1942 that asking Britain 'to trade the principle of imperial preference as a consideration for Lend-Lease', was 'the furthest thing from my mind', that is exactly what Hull and his associates demanded and now forced the British to agree to, at least in principle, within the Master Lend-Lease agreement. Signed on 23 February, that document called for 'the elimination of all forms of discriminatory treatment in international commerce'. Its stringent terms also prohibited the exportation of British goods that used any raw materials supplied by Lend-Lease or the inclusion of US civilian goods, which the British had to pay for with hard currency while selling all their American assets.[42]

Equally if not more serious disagreements divided the two allies on the issue of colonialism. Born in one of the first anti-colonial revolts of modern history, Americans viewed the British Empire and other European colonial empires as classic examples of oppression, as another cause of war and as anachronisms that should be dismantled. The British of course felt differently. They also found the American position more than a little hypocritical in light of US continental and overseas expansion during the nineteenth century. As Eden caustically quipped, whereas Soviet policy was amoral, US policy was 'exaggeratedly moral, at least where non-American interests are concerned'. Furthermore, Churchill was one of the strongest of all defenders of British imperialism, and had publicly stated in 1941 that the Atlantic Charter self-determination pledge applied only to Axis conquests and not the British Empire. Roosevelt, however, would state in early 1942 that it applied to the whole world.[43] He would also raise the issue of independence for India during the ARCADIA Conference. Churchill's response was so explosive that the president never raised the issue directly with the prime minister again. Later in 1942, Churchill would bluntly and publicly assert that he had not become prime minister to preside over the liquidation of the British Empire.

Despite these conflicts, harmony dominated throughout most of the ARCADIA Conference. Furthermore, Churchill played a very important public role during the conference as a critical symbol to the American people of British resistance, determination and friendship. At the Christmas Eve tree lighting ceremony he spoke from the White House balcony of 'the common cause of great peoples who speak the same language, who kneel at the same altars, and, to a very large extent, pursue the same ideals'. On Christmas Day he and Roosevelt attended church together, and on the following day he addressed a joint session of Congress, joking that had his father been American and his mother British rather than vice versa, 'I might have gotten here on my own.' He received his loudest applause, however, when he asked, regarding the Japanese attack, 'What sort of people do they think we are?'[44]

Such brave words were sorely needed at this time, for both during and immediately after the ARCADIA Conference, the Axis powers launched a series of awesome offensives that brought them to the verge of victory.

4

MILITARY DISASTERS AND DISPUTES OVER GRAND STRATEGY, DECEMBER 1941–JULY/AUGUST 1942

The ARCADIA Conference coincided with a series of Anglo-American military disasters in both the Pacific and the Atlantic. Additional disasters followed within the next six months in Libya, Egypt, the Mediterranean, South Asia and Russia, bringing the Axis powers to the verge of total victory. This in turn precipitated a major crisis within the Grand Alliance over the appropriate strategic response. The strategic decisions made at this time, and the ensuing major battles and military campaigns, would have enormous consequences for the course of the war. They would also have equally enormous consequences for Allied relations and the post-war world.

Japan runs amok

The attack on Pearl Harbor was but one part of a massive and simultaneous Japanese offensive designed to conquer all of Southeast Asia and the western Pacific, complete the isolation of China, achieve economic self-sufficiency and create an impregnable defensive barrier against Anglo-American counter-attacks. The first part of the plan worked almost perfectly, far beyond the Pearl Harbor attack itself, as Japanese air, naval and ground forces succeeded in conquering Wake, Guam and the Philippines from the Americans, and Hong Kong, Malaya, Singapore and Burma from the British, as well as the Dutch East Indies (Indonesia). They thereby created one of the largest empires in history within the space of only a few months, and they did so with an extraordinarily small number of forces. Indeed, throughout this campaign, and the entire war, the bulk of the Japanese Army remained in China; ground troops used in the 1942 offensive totalled no more than 11 divisions, none of them armoured.

Japanese success was partially the result of the surprise they achieved in all their attacks on 7 and 8 December. It was also the result of the superior training and skill of their forces, gross Allied underestimation of Japanese capabilities, and some extraordinary Allied blunders.

The attack on Pearl Harbor removed the greatest threat to Japanese naval supremacy in the western and southern Pacific. It also enabled the Japanese quickly to isolate and conquer the US island of Guam in the Marianas, which fell in two days, and the island of Wake, which fell on 23 December after its 500 defenders put up surprisingly strong resistance. British-controlled Hong Kong fell three days later. Extensive Allied forces remained in the other areas, however, especially in the Philippines, British Malaya and Singapore.

The Japanese launched two main and virtually simultaneous thrusts against these targets on 7/8 December – one against the Philippines and the other against Malaya and Singapore. Both offensives succeeded despite being out-numbered, and paved the way for the successful Japanese conquest of Burma and the Dutch East Indies a few months later.

Singapore was a supposedly impregnable island fortress and naval base, protected on the south by its fleet and guns and on the north by the impass-able jungles and mountains of Malaya as well as British airfields and an army of nearly 90,000 men under Lieutenant General Arthur Percival. In reality, however, those jungles and mountains were not impassable, and there were no fortifications in northern Malaya to stop a Japanese invasion. Moreover, the airfields did not possess adequate aircraft, quantitatively or qualitatively. Nor did the naval base possess adequate capital ships, for Europe and the Middle East both had higher priority in British strategic planning than the Far East. To make matters worse, Percival's army was a combined British-Australian-Indian-local force, inadequately trained and lacking appropriate weapons.

The British were thus unable to prevent a successful landing on 8 December by 17,000 Japanese troops under General Yamashita Tomoyuki along the north coast of Malaya. Two days later the Japanese obtained total naval control when their aircraft attacked and sank the two capital ships of the British Singapore squadron that had sallied forth without air cover, HMS *Prince of Wales* (which had carried Churchill to his August 1941 meeting with Roosevelt) and HMS *Repulse*, killing 800 British seamen – including squadron commander Admiral Sir Tom Phillips – and decisively illustrating along with Pearl Harbor the vulnerability of battleships to aircraft. Yamashita's reinforced troops then quickly moved through the jungles and mountains of Malaya, capturing and turning against the British the airfields the latter had built to defend Singapore and consistently outmanoeuvring their befuddled British opponents. By the end of January, Yamashita had conquered all of Malaya and forced the remaining 85,000 British defenders into Singapore itself. He then successfully invaded the island with 40,000 men and captured its main water supply. On 15 February, Percival surrendered Singapore to a force half the size of his own. Japanese casualties in the entire campaign totalled only 9,800, compared to more than 138,000 for the British, most of them (approximately 130,000) captured. It was one of the most staggering and humiliating defeats in British history, and it dealt a severe blow to British imperial prestige in Asia.

A similar if somewhat lengthier débâcle occurred in the Philippines, which were defended by 31,000 US and Filipino regular troops and the 102,000-man Filipino Army that former Army Chief of Staff General Douglas MacArthur had been hired to train during the 1930s. In mid-1941 Washington had recalled MacArthur to active duty and placed him in charge of US forces on the islands as well. Reversing previous army plans, MacArthur as well as the army general staff in Washington now insisted that the Philippines could and would be successfully defended, primarily via air-power. Yet despite the previous assault on Pearl Harbor, MacArthur's air forces were decimated by a successful Japanese surprise attack on 8 December and a series of ensuing air raids over the next ten days. Those raids also crippled naval installations at Manila Bay and forced much of the small US Asiatic Fleet to retreat southward. Combined with Pearl Harbor, the result was the naval and air isolation of the Philippines. This doomed MacArthur's forces, notwithstanding the general's incorrect insistence that relief forces both could and would be sent.

Successful small-scale Japanese landings on Luzon began in the north on 10 December, followed by a larger landing of two divisions under General Homma Mashaharu on 22 December at Lingayen Gulf, on the west coast of Luzon. Rejecting the pre-war plan to withdraw to defensive positions on the Bataan peninsula, MacArthur instead attempted, unsuccessfully, to repel the invaders on the beaches. After this failure he did withdraw to Bataan, but he now had to do so without needed supplies because they had been lost on the beaches. His forces were then decimated by disease and lack of food as well as Japanese thrusts. They were able to stabilize their lines and success-fully repel Japanese attacks for four months, however, longer than any other Allied force facing the Japanese onslaught. They thereby turned what had to end as a humiliating defeat into a partial psychological victory for the American people, who responded by turning MacArthur into a hero rather than a goat, as happened to Lieutenant General Walter Short and Admiral Husband Kimmel, the army and navy commanders at Pearl Harbor. Instead, Roosevelt and Marshall recommended MacArthur for the Congressional Medal of Honor and on 12 March ordered him to leave the Philippines for Australia, where he was to take command of all Allied forces in the Southwest Pacific Area. He was succeeded in the Philippines by Lieutenant General Jonathan Wainright, who was forced to abandon Bataan on 9 April but con-tinued resistance from the fortified island of Corregidor in Manila Bay until 5 May, when that fortress was invaded and forced to surrender.

In both the Philippine and the Malayan/Singapore campaigns, the Japanese Army followed its victories with atrocities against Allied prisoners of war (POWs) and civilians. The most infamous of these atrocities was the 'Bataan Death March' in the Philippines, during which 100,000 US and Filipino POWs, many already weakened, ill and malnourished from the fighting on Bataan, were forced to undertake a 55-mile march to a railhead. Some 7,000 would die en route. Partially this resulted from the large number of prisoners, four times what the Japanese had expected, and an ensuing breakdown in Japanese logistics. But it also resulted from a Japanese contempt for surrender, which was considered dishonourable by their *Bushido* warrior code, an equal contempt for other peoples based upon a belief in their own racial superiority, and the brutality of their own lives as soldiers. Not all Japanese units committed such atrocities, but this was far from the first or last time the Japanese Army would behave in such a manner. (During the notorious 'Rape of Nanking' in 1937–38, for example, the Japanese soldiers may have massacred as many as 300,000 civilians.) In this particular case, the Bataan Death March would infuriate Americans and harden their own racist attitudes against the Japanese. When combined with Japanese racist attitudes and belief that death in combat or via suicide was preferable to dishonourable surrender, the result would be a race war in the Pacific, just as grim as the race war in Eastern Europe, in which no quarter was asked, expected or given on either side. It was, as historian John Dower has analysed, a 'War Without Mercy'.[1]

Although the Malayan/Singapore and Philippine campaigns were far from over in January, the Japanese felt sufficiently confident in their progress to begin the invasion of the Dutch East Indies on the 11th of that month. Within less than two months they had conquered Borneo, Celebes and Sumatra. An ABDA fleet attempting to intercept the invasion force heading for Java was instead sunk in the Battles of the Java Sea on 27 February and Sundra Strait on 29 February. By 8 March, Java too had been conquered.

The invasion of Burma, then a British colony, took a bit longer but was equally successful. It began on 10 December with an attack by Japanese troops from neighbouring Thailand. A month later, on 19–20 January, a much larger invasion force attacked farther north. It captured Rangoon in early March and chased the British, Indian, Chinese and US defenders first into the three river valleys in the northern part of the country and then all the way into India. In doing so, the Japanese cut the supply line to Chiang Kai-shek's armies in China and once again humiliated the British and the Americans. 'I claim we got a hell of a beating,' US Lieutenant General Joseph Stilwell bluntly admitted to the press. 'We got run out of Burma and it is humiliating as hell.'[2]

While this campaign was in progress, a large Japanese naval task force steamed into the Indian Ocean and attacked the island of Ceylon (Sri Lanka) in hopes of destroying the large British naval force there and taking the island, thereby further crippling Allied sea communications and naval strength. The bulk of the British fleet was able to escape, but it had to retreat as far as the East African coast.

Throughout all these campaigns, Allied forces had consistently been outmanoeuvred, outfought and defeated by the quantitatively inferior but qualitatively superior Japanese. As a result, Japan's high command by May of 1942 had accomplished all of its objectives and now possessed an enormous empire, its diameter equivalent to half the circumference of the entire globe, with all the resources necessary for the economic self-sufficiency it desired. In the process of conquering that empire the Japanese had also dealt western imperialism a blow from which it would never recover. They had shattered the myth of white invincibility in Asia, and with it the willingness of Asians to submit to white rule.

The German high tide

While the Japanese were scoring their impressive victories in the Pacific and Asia, German submarines were enjoying one of their best seasons against Allied shipping and threatening once again to starve Britain into surrender. American entry into the war had removed all the restrictions the U-boats had previously faced and enabled them to attack US ships at will. Consequently, German submarine commander Admiral Karl Dönitz sent additional submarines into American waters, where they were extraordinarily successful. Their success was due to a combination of insufficient US escort vessels, a change in the ENIGMA cipher that stymied British cryptologists, and a lack of proper American precautions. Particularly noteworthy in this latter regard was the lack of a blackout for east coast cities, which meant that coastal merchant ships were silhouetted at night for the U-boat attackers. Whereas German submarines had sunk an average of only 180,000 tons per month in 1941, they averaged nearly 500,000 tons a month in early 1942, 600,000 tons in May, and in June more than 700,000 tons – the figure Dönitz believed necessary for victory.

At the same time, the Japanese onslaught in Southeast Asia led the British to shift forces away from their offensive against Rommel in Libya (Operation CRUSADER), which had begun on 18 November. New British Middle East commander General Claude Auchinleck had by early December been able to force Rommel to retreat and had relieved the siege of Tobruk. But the ensuing shift in British forces to the Far East, as well as a German air fleet that neutralized the British base at Malta, and fresh supplies for Axis forces, allowed Rommel to counter-attack successfully in January of 1942, taking Benghazi and forcing the British back to Gazala, only 35 miles west of Tobruk. Then in late May–early June, the German commander first attacked and then lured British Major General Neil Ritchie into attacks at Gazala in which the latter lost more than 90 per cent of his tanks. Rommel then successfully counter-attacked, this time taking on 21 June the fortress of Tobruk that had eluded him in 1941, with 35,000 British prisoners, and advancing into Egypt to within 60 miles of Alexandria. His forces now directly threatened the Suez Canal as well as the Middle East oilfields. At the same time, German forces launched their second major offensive in Russia, this time turning south toward Stalingrad on the Volga River and the Caucasus oilfields.[3] In horrified Allied minds loomed the prospect of a triple junction between these forces moving south, Rommel advancing eastward through Suez, and the Japanese moving west through the Indian Ocean.

Allied strategic options

As in most of its previous wars, the island nation of Great Britain was primarily dependent upon sea power during World War II. Little known is the fact that, despite its continental size, so was the United States.[4] Without control of the world's oceans, Lend-Lease supplies could not be sent to Britain or Russia, thereby calling into question their continued survival. Nor could the large American army then training be successfully transported overseas to fight Axis forces anywhere. Indeed, the Allied defeats of early 1942 had by March forced the cancellation of Operation GYMNAST, the proposed invasion of French North Africa, and no ground offensive appeared possible in any theatre until control of the seas had been re-established. Halting the Japanese Navy in the Pacific and the German U-boats in the Atlantic thus constituted the first Anglo-American priorities.

By the previous ABC-1 accord of March 1941, the Atlantic clearly took precedence over the Pacific. ABC-1 had not anticipated either the destruction of the US fleet at Pearl Harbor or the ensuing Japanese conquests, however, and throughout the early months of 1942, new US naval chief Admiral Ernest J. King insisted that halting the Japanese would require a major alteration in previously agreed-upon global strategy. Sending air and ground forces to garrison islands in the Pacific while concentrating major naval forces for offensive operations was the only way to halt that sweep, King argued, before it encompassed Australia and New Zealand – something intolerable both strategically and politically. Strategically, the fall of these nations would deprive the Allies of their new and only remaining major base in the South Pacific. Politically, King informed Roosevelt, it would mean Japanese conquest and occupation of 'white man's countries', which had to be avoided because of the 'repercussions ... among the non-white races of the world'. Moreover, King maintained, a static defence in the Pacific was simply not possible. Instead he proposed an immediate 'defensive offensive', a strategy to 'hold what you've got and hit them where you can, the hitting to be done not only in seizing opportunities but by making them'.[5]

US Army planners at first agreed to send reinforcements to the Pacific in a desperate effort to stem the Japanese sweep after Pearl Harbor. With the obvious failure of such efforts by February, however, they began to object strongly to any further dispersion of their forces to the supposedly secondary Pacific. They also began to voice once again their opposition to Britain's peripheral strategy, with its focus on North Africa and the Mediterranean. The then-little-known head of the Army General Staff's War Plans Division, Brigadier General Dwight D. Eisenhower, derisively noted that additional army garrisons in the Pacific would give the navy 'a safe place to sail its vessels' but little more. 'We've got to get to Europe and fight!' he privately noted in late January, 'and we've got to quit wasting resources all over the world – and still worse – wasting time.' The sending of reinforcements to any peripheral areas, be it those desired by the US Navy or by the British, had to cease and be replaced by a proper concentration of Anglo-American resources and armed forces to seize the strategic initiative from the Axis powers.[6]

Such an effort, Eisenhower and his staff in the new Operations Division (OPD) insisted by March,[7] should focus on a cross-Channel invasion of northern France from England. Beyond the assumed safety of the continental United States, Hawaii, the Caribbean and South America above the Brazilian 'bulge', they argued, only three military tasks were truly 'necessary': securing the British Isles and the Atlantic sea lanes; holding India and the Middle East so as to prevent a German-Japanese junction; and retaining the Soviet Union in the war as an active belligerent. Everything else, even the defence of Alaska, Australia, New Zealand and the remainder of South America, was 'merely desirable' in the present crisis. And of those three 'necessary' tasks, only retaining Russia in the war presently required offensive as opposed to defensive action, in the form of cross-Channel operations, to divert portions of the German Army from the Eastern Front.

The focus on Russia was directly related to its surprising survival in 1941, and to the fact that it was engaging the overwhelming bulk of the German army. When Hitler's forces had first invaded Russia in June of 1941, Anglo-American military opinion had been almost unanimous in concluding that they would cut through the Red Army 'like a hot knife through butter' and force a Soviet surrender within six weeks.[8] At first, such predictions appeared accurate, as the Germans advanced very rapidly and inflicted massive casualties on the Red Army; but Soviet resistance stiffened throughout the summer and autumn, and by year's end the Russians had halted the Germans in front of Moscow. In the process they had inflicted more casualties on the *Wehrmacht* than in all its previous campaigns combined. Now in the spring of 1942, Hitler was preparing a second major offensive in Russia. Should that offensive succeed and Russia be knocked out of the war, he would be able to exploit the human and material resources of all Eurasia and overwhelm the British and the Americans. Should he fail, however, he would be seriously weakened and vulnerable to Anglo-American operations on the European continent.

Continued Russian survival thus meant eventual victory, while Russian defeat would preclude the possibility of such a victory by Anglo-American forces alone. Ensuring that survival was thus a critical Anglo-American task, one that required, according to Eisenhower and his OPD staff, a cross-Channel invasion of northern France and establishment of a 'second front' to divert German forces from the East and force Hitler into a two-front war that he could not win. It was also an operation that could succeed because the Germans were presently preoccupied in Russia. As Eisenhower realized, the strategic logic was circular: only a second front could keep the Soviets in the war, and only their continuation in the war could enable Anglo-American forces to successfully establish such a front.[9]

Neither the American public nor the US Navy would accept further losses in the Pacific, however, and in March US Army planners bowed to political

necessity by modifying their cross-Channel proposals so as to include maintenance of presently held positions in the Pacific as a vital defensive task. All
forces remaining after these and other critical defensive positions had been
secured, however, were to be concentrated in England for an Anglo-American
cross-Channel attack in 1942 or 1943.

The US Joint Chiefs of Staff concurred in these conclusions. So did President
Roosevelt, who sent his close adviser Harry Hopkins and General Marshall to
London in early April to obtain British agreement. Churchill and the British
Chiefs of Staff were anything but impressed by the American proposals.
Brooke found them nothing more than politically inspired but militarily
absurd 'castles in the air', and he concluded that Marshall was a strategic fool
and 'a very dangerous man' even to propose them.[10]

Yet the British Chiefs of Staff and government formally agreed to the US proposals at this time for fear that the Americans would turn completely to the
Pacific if they were rejected. Consequently, the two nations agreed to the
immediate concentration of all available forces in the United Kingdom
(Operation BOLERO) for cross-Channel operations in 1942 or 1943. The 1943
operation, code-named ROUNDUP, would involve 48 divisions (18 British and
30 American) and 5,800 aircraft. The 1942 operation, code-named SLEDGE-
HAMMER, would be launched in September with whatever divisions were
then available if Russia appeared to be on the verge of collapse. In that even-
tuality, according to the Americans, the operation might well have to be considered a 'sacrifice for the common good' – i.e., a doomed venture but one that
would save the Russians by diverting German forces to the west.

The British, however, had no intention of creating another Dunkirk or
worse – especially since the forces to be sacrificed would be overwhelmingly
their own; the Americans could transport only 2½ divisions by September.[11]
Indeed, getting even this small number of US troops to Europe would not be
possible without a prior halt to the U-boat offensive. Furthermore, Admiral
King remained preoccupied with the Pacific. Partially as a result of that preoccupation, and partially as a result of Japanese actions, Allied success came
first in the Pacific, not the Atlantic, in 1942.

Coral Sea and Midway

Altering their original war plans, Japanese leaders in the spring of 1942
decided to further expand their empire rather than focus on fortifying what
they had already conquered. They disagreed, however, as to which direction
that expansion should take. The army favoured breaking off the offensive in
the Pacific and attacking the Soviet Union in conjunction with the new
German offensive. Naval leaders rejected this proposal but disagreed among
themselves as to whether to expand south to Australia and New Zealand; or
east to the island of Midway to destroy the remnants of the US fleet.

In retrospect, a fourth and better option existed: a movement west through
the Indian Ocean for a possible link-up with the Germans. But this option had

no major advocates within the Japanese High Command – a clear sign of the hollowness of the Axis Alliance. Instead the debate centred on a southern vs an eastern advance, with Pearl Harbor commander Admiral Nagumo Chuichi favouring the former and the architect of the attack, Admiral Yamamoto Isoroku, the latter. The eventual Japanese decision was to undertake Yamamoto's Midway operation, along with a feint northward that would include invasion of the Western Aleutian Islands, but only on condition that Australia be sealed off first via the taking of Port Moresby on the southeastern coast of New Guinea and the islands of New Caldeonia, Fiji and Samoa, as well as Tulagi in the Solomon chain.

In effect, the Japanese leaders had by this plan foolishly decided to undertake *both* a southern *and* an eastern offensive, and to do so simultaneously. They had fallen victim to 'victory fever' and overextension, and they would pay the price in two ensuing naval battles: Coral Sea and Midway.

Unbeknown to the Japanese, American cryptologists had by April broken a key Japanese naval code and thus knew of the Japanese plans. New US Pacific Fleet Commander Admiral Chester W. Nimitz, who had replaced Admiral Kimmel in Hawaii, first responded by sending a naval task force under Rear Admiral Frank Jack Fletcher to halt any amphibious Japanese attack on Port Moresby. Facing Fletcher were two Japanese fleets under Admiral Inouye Shigeyoshi, who had taken Guam and Wake in December. In the ensuing Battle of the Coral Sea on 7–8 May, US and Japanese naval aircraft inflicted heavy damage on each other's ships from great distances. Indeed, for the first time in the history of naval warfare, the two fleets did not even see each other. Tactically the battle was a draw, as each side lost one aircraft carrier (the *Shoho* and the *Lexington*) and had another severely damaged (the *Shokaku* and the *Yorktown*). But strategically it was a US victory because Inouye called off the amphibious assault on Port Moresby and withdrew. Moreover, two of his carriers returned to Japan for repairs, planes and pilots, and were thus unavailable for the Battle of Midway that took place a month later.

Midway was Yamamoto's brainchild and primarily the result of his insistence on destroying the remainder of the US fleet, most importantly the four US aircraft carriers than had not been in Pearl Harbor on 7 December (three after the destruction of the *Lexington* in the Battle of the Coral Sea). That insistence was only reinforced by the daring air raid conducted against Tokyo and other Japanese cities on 18 April by 16 US Army Air Force (AAF) B-25 bombers, commanded by Colonel James Doolittle and launched from the US aircraft carrier *Hornet* 700 miles southeast of Japan. The raid itself did very little damage and was quite costly in terms of lost planes, all of which either crash-landed or had their crews bail out. But it buoyed American spirits and lent added weight to Yamamoto's insistence on the need to destroy the US carriers and expand the Japanese defensive perimeter. While President Roosevelt joked that the bombers had come from 'Shangri-La', a humorous reference to both a mythical paradise in the Himalayas popularized in the novel *Lost Horizon* and the presidential retreat in Pennsylvania that he gave the same name (now Camp David), Yamamoto was well aware that they could have come only from US carriers in the Pacific.

Yamamoto planned a trap for those carriers and their escorts that focused on the small island of Midway but covered an enormous area in the Pacific. Japanese forces would invade the Aleutian Islands of Attu and Kiska in the far north, west of the Alaskan mainland, so as to divert US forces to this area while a Japanese naval and amphibious force bombed and invaded Midway. When the US fleet returned and tried to retake the island, it would be destroyed by an enormous Japanese naval force of 4 heavy carriers from the Pearl Harbor attack, 2 light carriers, 7 battleships, 15 cruisers and 44 destroyers. Leading the naval air strike force was Pearl Harbor commander Admiral Nagumo, followed by the 'main body' under Yamamoto himself.

US Navy cryptologists had figured out the plan from intercepted Japanese messages and thus would not fall for the ruse in the Aleutians. Nevertheless the US task was formidable, as Nimitz had only two undamaged aircraft carriers, the *Enterprise* and the *Hornet*, along with the badly damaged *Yorktown* from the Battle of the Coral Sea, and their escorts, to counter Yamamoto's enormous fleet.

That the Americans were able to defeat the Japanese despite these odds resulted from some extraordinary courage and luck, as well as numerous Japanese blunders. First, Yamamoto unwisely split his huge force in three – one group north to the Aleutians, a second under Nagumo in the lead toward Midway, and his own 'main body' substantially behind. He also made three critical assumptions: that the *Yorktown* had been sunk at the Battle of Coral Sea and that he would therefore face only two US carriers; that the Americans knew nothing of his plans and location, and would be lured up to the Aleutians, thereby enabling him to conquer Midway before they returned; and that he could find out their location through the use of advance submarines. All three assumptions proved incorrect. As a result, it was the Americans, not the Japanese, who possessed the element of surprise in the form of two undetected task forces east of Midway: one centred on the *Enterprise* and *Hornet* under Rear Admiral Raymond Spruance, and a second around the just-repaired *Yorktown* under Fletcher.

On 4 June Nagumo's aircraft attacked Midway. They achieved only limited success and suffered serious losses. Furthermore, the Japanese carriers faced counter-attacks from Midway's land-based aircraft. Consequently Nagumo decided to shift the ordnance on his reserve aircraft, from armour-piercing to high explosive, for a second strike against the island. But while doing so his scout planes belatedly discovered the US fleet, causing him to order a second shift back to anti-carrier ordnance. Before that shift could be completed, and while his original strike force was returning for rearming and refuelling, US torpedo bombers attacked his carriers. Most were destroyed by Japanese anti-aircraft fire and 'Zero' fighter aircraft, but that in turn left the Zeros dispersed and at sea level when American dive bombers from the *Enterprise* and *Yorktown* appeared overhead. They quickly scored direct hits, and with the planes, fuel and ordnance on the Japanese decks, three of the heavy carriers (the *Soryu*, *Akagi* and *Kaga)* were destroyed in 15 minutes. Planes from the fourth Japanese heavy carrier, the *Hiryu*, found and crippled the *Yorktown*, and two days later it was sunk by a Japanese submarine. But in return Spruance's dive bombers sank the *Hiryu*. Informed of the catastrophe to his carrier fleet, Yamamoto now steamed forward with his main body in hopes of destroying the Americans via a night-time surface engagement. But Spruance wisely withdrew eastward, forcing Yamamoto to return home.

Midway was one of the decisive naval battles of the war, and indeed of all modern naval history. US dive bombers had destroyed four Japanese heavy carriers along with 253 aircraft and their pilots. Not having planned for a lengthy war and possessing limited industrial capacity, the Japanese could not make up for these losses. The United States could and would quickly make up for its own losses, both here and at Pearl Harbor. In effect, the Japanese were now forced to surrender the naval strategic initiative.

They had already occupied Tulagi and Guadalcanal in the Solomon Islands, however, thereby threatening US communications with Australia and New Zealand. And although they would no longer attempt an amphibious assault on Port Moresby, they had landed an army on the northern coast of New Guinea that was advancing by land on this strategically important site on the island's southern coast. Consequently, both General MacArthur in Australia and Admiral King in Washington pressed for a counter-offensive to halt the Japanese advance, evict them from the Solomons and New Guinea, and seize the initiative in the South Pacific.

The Allied strategic dispute

US Army planners in Washington objected strongly to the King and MacArthur proposals. So did Churchill and his advisers. But simultaneously the British also voiced opposition to launching Operation SLEDGEHAMMER, the proposed 1942 cross-Channel attack that they had approved 'in principle' only a few months earlier and which Roosevelt had subsequently 'promised' the Russians. London now believed that this operation would definitely end in disaster. Instead Churchill proposed to Roosevelt a return to GYMNAST, the plan to invade French North Africa, and in late June he came to Washington with his advisers for another conference and in hopes of convincing the president.

The diplomatic background to Roosevelt's second front 'promise' to the Russians and the ensuing controversy was quite complex. As previously noted, Churchill had in December–January joined Roosevelt in opposing the territorial agreement that Stalin demanded while the war was in progress and had informed Foreign Secretary Anthony Eden of this fact.[12] Eden had disagreed with Churchill's position and reasoning, and by March he had convinced the prime minister to reverse his position and agree to negotiate such a treaty with Soviet Foreign Minister Vyacheslav Molotov in London, continued

American opposition notwithstanding. Roosevelt had countered by offering Stalin a 1942 second front instead, and indeed as a substitute for the treaty, and by inviting Molotov to visit Washington as well as London. At the White House, the president on 30 May authorized the Soviet foreign minister to inform Stalin 'that we expect the formation of a second front this year', and a few days later he agreed to a public communiqué stating that 'full understanding' had been reached during Molotov's visit 'with regard to the urgent tasks of creating a Second Front in Europe in 1942'.[13]

Churchill then countered by informing Molotov on his return to London in early June that Britain, which would have to provide the bulk of the forces for any cross-Channel attack that year, could not and would not give any promises regarding a 1942 second front. The British Prime Minister also informed Roosevelt of the problems with SLEDGEHAMMER and pressed for its replacement with one of his pet alternatives: an invasion of Norway (Operation JUPITER) or North Africa (Operation GYMNAST). As he had reminded Roosevelt in late May, 'We must never let "GYMNAST" pass from our minds.'[14] At that time he had sent Admiral Mountbatten, head of British Combined Operations, to explain to Roosevelt SLEDGEHAMMER's numerous problems. Now the prime minister made plans to come to Washington himself in order to convince FDR to agree to a strategic shift back to North Africa.

The ensuing summit conference began on 19 June amidst a bleak military outlook. That outlook became even bleaker on 21 June when Churchill and Roosevelt, returning to Washington from the president's home in Hyde Park, New York, were informed that Tobruk had just fallen to Rommel. The news visibly shook Churchill. ('Defeat is one thing,' he later wrote of this episode; 'disgrace is another.') 'What can we do to help?' Roosevelt immediately asked. 'Give us as many Sherman tanks as you can spare,' Churchill replied, 'and ship them to the Middle East as quickly as possible.' Marshall quickly agreed to send 300 new tanks along with 100 105mm guns, even though they had just been issued to his own armoured forces.[15]

The US Army chief would not budge, however, in his opposition to GYMNAST. Carefully examining the grim military situation around the globe as well as in Egypt, Marshall and all his US and British colleagues on the Combined Chiefs of Staff (CCS) had been able to agree even before the fall of Tobruk that while the BOLERO build-up of US forces in the United Kingdom should continue, no offensive operations should be launched in the European theatre in 1942 save in case of 'necessity' (i.e., imminent Russian collapse) or 'an exceptionally favourable opportunity' (severe German weakening or collapse). They had further agreed that in either case an invasion of northern France, Norway or the Channel Islands was preferable to North Africa.[16] This accord suited the British Chiefs of Staff (COS) because it enabled them to focus on the defence of Suez in light of the threat posed by Rommel's advance. It also suited the American Joint Chiefs (JCS) because it blocked GYMNAST while maintaining the BOLERO build-up in Britain and the possibility of future action.

It in no way suited Churchill or Roosevelt, however, who bluntly vetoed the CCS agreement on 21 June (which the official British military history consequently referred to as the 'Day of Dupes') and insisted that some 1942 European offensive was 'essential' – for domestic public opinion and for the Russians, who had been publicly and privately promised such assistance by Roosevelt just a few weeks earlier. Churchill and Roosevelt also made clear that if a successful SLEDGEHAMMER appeared 'improbable', their alternative choice was GYMNAST, their military advisers' objections notwithstanding.[17] Soon after his return to London from Washington, Churchill in early July informed Roosevelt that the British considered a successful SLEDGE-HAMMER quite improbable and suggested formal agreement to GYMNAST instead. 'This has all along been in harmony with your ideas,' the prime minister noted. 'In fact it is your commanding idea. Here is the true second front of 1942.'[18]

Such stroking of the president's ego was far from accidental. As Churchill would state a few years after the war ended, in regard to this matter, 'No lover ever studied every whim of his mistress as I did those of President Roosevelt.'[19]

The US Joint Chiefs were furious over Churchill's behaviour. They also disagreed vehemently with his conclusion that a North African invasion could be 'the true second front of 1942'. From their perspective, GYMNAST was a politically inspired and militarily worthless plan that would not aid the Russians in the slightest. Indeed, it would so disperse Anglo-American forces as to preclude any cross-Channel operations until 1944. It would also heavily drain US resources and jeopardize the entire American naval position in the Pacific. On 10 July Marshall and King informed Roosevelt of these conclusions and consequently proposed formal abandonment of the entire Germany-first strategy if Britain insisted on GYMNAST. In the face of such insistence, they argued, the United States should 'assume a defensive attitude against Germany' in order to 'turn to the Pacific and strike decisively against Japan'.[20]

Was this startling proposal merely a bluff, as some of its proponents later claimed? Clearly it contained an element of bluff designed to scare the British into renewed support of SLEDGEHAMMER. Simultaneously, however, Marshall and King were deadly serious in the event that the threat failed. Giving up on cross-Channel operations until 1944 in their minds equalled giving up on the Russian front, since GYMNAST would not aid the Russians in the slightest, and thus giving up on any hope of decisive victory over Germany. Better in that situation to turn against Japan. Furthermore, if Russia could perchance survive the 1942 German onslaught without an Anglo-American second front, a Pacific offensive would, in US assessments, at least provide limited aid to the Soviets by precluding a Japanese attack on Siberia. GYMNAST, on the other hand, would in no way aid the Soviets.[21]

Roosevelt, however, flatly rejected this direct attack on the Europe-first strategy, stating that it was 'exactly what Germany hoped the United States would do' and calling it equivalent to 'taking up your dishes and going away' as well as 'something of a red herring, the purpose for which he thoroughly understood'.[22] Instead he ordered Marshall, King and Hopkins back to London in mid-July to reach agreement with the British on some combined 1942 offensive operation in the European theatre. SLEDGEHAMMER remained his first choice, but if Britain refused to cross the Channel, his envoys would have to agree to GYMNAST or a Middle East operation. During the ensuing London meetings the British maintained their objections to SLEDGEHAMMER as an operation that, due to its small size, could neither maintain itself nor divert any German forces from the Eastern Front. That stand, combined with Roosevelt's instructions, forced Marshall and King to agree to the North African invasion, GYMNAST, now renamed TORCH.

The American JCS and their planners considered TORCH a politically inspired and militarily counter-productive operation that they had been forced to accept by their commander-in-chief because of Churchill's manipulation and public opinion. Marshall later stated in regard to the latter factor that one of the most important lessons he had learned in the war was that a democracy required a successful offensive every year. 'We failed to see,' he told his official biographer, 'that the leader in a democracy has to keep the people entertained. That may sound like the wrong word, but it conveys the thought ... People demand action.'[23] That was true, but only a partially correct assessment of Roosevelt's motives in this episode. The president needed and demanded an Anglo-American offensive in the European theatre in 1942 not only to keep the American people 'entertained', but also to shift their focus from the Japanese, whom the majority in public opinion polls considered their primary enemy, to their true primary and far more dangerous enemy – the Germans. Japanese defeat would do nothing to aid in the defeat of Germany, he reminded his military advisers, whereas German defeat 'means the defeat of Japan, probably without firing a shot or losing a life'.[24] A focus on Japan would also wreck the Grand Alliance, whose lowest common denominator was agreement to the Germany-first strategy.

Roosevelt also insisted on North Africa because of his previous promise of a second front to the Soviets. Even though his military advisers warned him that TORCH would not divert any German forces from the eastern front, the president apparently believed that it could serve as a psychological boost to the Soviets by showing them *some* 1942 Anglo-American action in the European theatre. In that sense it was far superior to the inaction or Pacific-first strategy that his military advisers favoured.

Churchill concurred, and during his ensuing mid-August visit to Moscow to inform Stalin personally that there would be no cross-Channel attack in 1942 (a task he later compared to 'carrying a large lump of ice to the North Pole'), he explained and defended TORCH as an alternative second front for 1942 that could effectively attack the 'soft [under]belly' of the Axis 'crocodile' in the Mediterranean as well as its 'hard snout' in northern France, a snout that would be directly attacked in 'a very great operation' in 1943.[25] Despite some initial receptivity, Stalin was not convinced by such metaphors. Instead he bitterly attacked the TORCH decision both during and after the conference, while continuing to demand a cross-Channel attack capable of actually diverting numerous German forces from the East.

Yet TORCH was not the only politically inspired and diversionary front that would be approved at this time and established in 1942. The continued Japanese advance in New Guinea and the Solomon Islands seriously worried US Army and Navy leaders, who in June had agreed that an Allied counteroffensive was both necessary and possible. Consequently, in early July, they agreed to a campaign to retake the islands of Guadalcanal and Tulagi in the Solomons during August. Now in England a few weeks later, Marshall and King demanded that, in return for their agreement to TORCH, the COS agree to a combined document transferring 15 air groups and additional shipping to the Pacific as well as stating that TORCH rendered a 1943 ROUNDUP 'impracticable of successful execution' and that the Allies had therefore 'definitely accepted a defensive, encircling line of action for the Continental European Theater, except as to air operations'. The British disagreed vehemently, for they viewed TORCH as part of an extensive and aggressive Middle East and Mediterranean campaign. But they apparently concluded that they had pressed the Americans as far as they could at this time, and that their signatures on this document – CCS 94 – constituted a small price to pay for agreement to launch TORCH.[26]

Those signatures loomed large in August, however, as the military chiefs argued over the actual size, date and objectives of the North African invasion. For the COS those objectives included the quick conquest of Tunisia and, in conjunction with the British Eighth Army in Egypt, the complete ejection or destruction of Rommel's forces. Consequently they pressed for large-scale landings as far east as Algiers or Bone. The Americans countered that this was far from the limited, defensive operation outlined in CCS 94, and that it ignored the dangers of Vichy French resistance and a German move through Spain that could cut off the Allied landing forces. Consequently they proposed that the landings include Casablanca in French Morocco on the west coast of northern Africa as a precaution against such a German move and go no farther east than Oran in western Algeria. The resulting debate became known as the 'transatlantic essay contest' and was resolved only in early September when Churchill and Roosevelt agreed to a compromise whereby there would be a landing of reduced size at Casablanca in order to project forces as far east as Algiers as well as Oran. 'Hurrah!' Roosevelt cabled Churchill on 5 September; 'Okay full blast,' the prime minister replied.[27]

By that time US forces had already landed on Guadalcanal and had begun what would turn out to be an unexpectedly bloody and long six-month campaign in the South Pacific. TORCH would also be quite bloody and last an unexpected six months, British plans for quick victory notwithstanding. So would the campaign for Stalingrad and the Caucasus on the Eastern Front.

The successful completion of these three campaigns would mark the great 'turning point' in the Allied war effort. Together with the just-described strategic debate of 1942, however, they would also sow the seeds for bitter Allied recriminations and future disagreements over grand strategy. From London's perspective, both Washington and Moscow had proposed potentially disastrous operations in the European theatre and had thankfully been stopped by British strategic prudence and wisdom. The Americans, however, had responded by continuing their efforts since Pearl Harbor to overthrow the Germany-first strategy and still needed to be halted from such a disastrous course of action. From Moscow's perspective, both the North African and the Pacific campaigns illustrated that their supposed allies had abandoned them in 1942 and left them with nothing but vague promises for 1943. And from the perspective of the JCS in Washington, even those promises could not be fulfilled because the duplicitous British had first pledged themselves to cross-Channel operations they had had no intention of undertaking and had then manipulated President Roosevelt into substituting a politically inspired and militarily worthless operation in North Africa that would preclude a 1943 as well as a 1942 second front. Inter-allied suspicions of each other were thus heightened during 1942, and the stage was set for serious additional recriminations that would in 1943 threaten the very existence of the Grand Alliance – and with it Allied victory.

5

TURNING THE TIDE,
JULY/AUGUST 1942–JANUARY 1943

In the early summer of 1942 the Axis Powers held the initiative in virtually every theatre of the war and appeared to be on the brink of total victory. By early 1943, however, the Allies had successfully halted Axis offensives in the Middle East, Russia and the South Pacific, and had seized the strategic initiative in a series of critical military victories: El Alamein, North Africa, Stalingrad, Guadalcanal and Papua. These are commonly described as the great 'turning point' campaigns that determined the eventual outcome of the war.

Such a description is accurate, but simultaneously misleading. Allied successes in the second half of 1942 precluded total Axis victory. They did not, however, make total Axis defeat inevitable. That would require two and a half more years of bloody warfare as well as much greater Allied coordination and effort.

El Alamein

By the end of June Rommel's successful offensive in Libya and Egypt had reached El Alamein, only 60 miles west of Alexandria. Determined to halt the Germans at this natural defensive site flanked by the Mediterranean in the north and the impassable Quattara Depression in the south, British Middle East Commander General Claude Auchinleck relieved the defeated Major General Neil Ritchie and took over personal command of the British 8th Army. In early July, in what became known as the First Battle of El Alamein, his forces successfully repelled an attempted German breakthrough along this 36-mile front. Although ensuing British counter-attacks failed, this battle, far less known that the famous Second Battle of El Alamein in October, nevertheless halted Rommel and in retrospect was the true turning point of the North African campaign.

That was not apparent to Churchill, however, and it did not result in any honours for Auchinleck. To the contrary, he was blamed for Ritchie's prior defeats as well as the failed counter-attack, and consequently removed from both 8th Army and overall Middle East Command. In his place, Churchill in August appointed General Sir Harold Alexander as Middle East

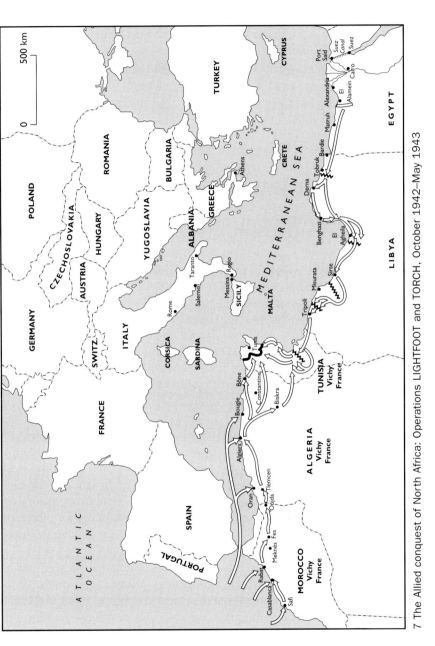

7 The Allied conquest of North Africa: Operations LIGHTFOOT and TORCH, October 1942–May 1943

Commander and Lieutenant General Bernard L. Montgomery as 8th Army Commander.

Operating largely on his own, Montgomery, or 'Monty' as he would become known to the public, would in October provide Britain with its first major victory in the war at El Alamein and become the most famous and highly decorated of Britain's wartime generals. In the process, however, his enormous ego and arrogance would infuriate his American allies as well as numerous British colleagues. As two American historians have recently and aptly stated, 'He was not a nice person [and in that sense was the opposite of Alexander]; dogged, conceited, vain, completely sure of his own abilities, and incapable of understanding other human beings, Montgomery also possessed the attributes of a great general.' These included rigorousness, enthusiasm, flexibility, training ability, and an understanding of 'the mind and stomach of the common soldier'.[1] But others have suggested that his military defects outweighed his assets.

Perhaps the most important of those assets in the summer of 1942 was his ability to restore confidence in the 8th Army after its humiliating defeats at the hands of Rommel. Similar in some ways to Union General George McClellan during the American Civil War, Montgomery emphasized intense training and preparation, and took a deep interest in his soldiers' welfare. As with McClellan, he consequently revived the spirits of his men and won their deep affection. But also similar to McClellan, Montgomery was as cautious on the battlefield as he was arrogant. Known as the master of the 'set-piece' battle, he would attack only after meticulous preparation and the achievement of overwhelming superiority in numbers and equipment. Although as a result he lost few battles (a distinct difference from McClellan), he often failed to achieve the decisive victories that could have resulted from greater daring.

Montgomery had not been Churchill's first choice for this assignment. That distinction went to one of Auchinleck's subordinates, Lieutenant General William 'Strafer' Gott. But when Gott was killed, Churchill turned to Montgomery on Brooke's strong recommendation. The new 8th Army Commander's strengths and weaknesses both emerged in late August–early September when Rommel made a second attempt at a breakthrough along the El Alamein front, this time focused on the Alam el Halfa Ridge for which the battle would be named. Montgomery foiled this effort by making extensive use of ULTRA intercepts that revealed Rommel's plans and forces, as well as the fortifications that Auchinleck had previously strengthened here and his defensive plan. Typically, however, Montgomery claimed total credit for the plan and then refused to counter-attack against the exposed and vulnerable German forces. Instead he built up his own forces for nearly two months until he possessed numerical superiority of nearly three to one (230,000 to 80,000), and even greater aircraft and tank superiority (1,200 to 350 in aircraft and 1,500 to 500 in tanks, of which only 260 were German).[2]

Numerous factors enabled the British to achieve such superiority: better logistics; the previously cited US willingness to send major tank reinforcements in the aftermath of the fall of Tobruk;[3] knowledge from ULTRA of the timing and location of German convoys in the Mediterranean; and maintenance of the British air and naval base at Malta from which those convoys could be attacked. Supported by Hitler, Rommel and the German High Command had compounded these problems by selecting the invasion of Egypt over the conquest of Malta that the Italians preferred (Operation HERCULES), relying instead on air attacks that failed to totally subdue the island with its critical air and naval base. Furthermore, the Germans never suspected that their convoy or other messages sent on the ENIGMA machine were vulnerable to interception.[4]

ULTRA was also used extensively before and during the actual Second Battle of El Alamein (Operation LIGHTFOOT), which Montgomery finally launched on 23 October. As at Alam el Halfa, it provided the British commander with detailed information on Rommel's deployments, supply situation, tactical plans, and even the morale of his forces. These two battles constituted the first such massive and direct use of ULTRA, and it gave Montgomery an enormous advantage over his opponent. Adding to this and Montgomery's other advantages was the fact that Rommel was ill and in Germany for medical treatment on the date the battle began.

Nevertheless, the limited size of the battlefield (only 36 miles wide) given its closed flanks in the north and south made offensive manoeuvre as difficult and limited for Montgomery as it had previously been for Rommel. The result was a battle of attrition in which British tank losses were four times greater than German losses. But Rommel could not afford even this rate of attrition given his small number of tanks (by 3 November he had only 30 left). Consequently, he ordered a tactical retreat using Italian motorized transport, thereby saving 40,000 men from his Afrika Korps at the sacrifice of the Italian army in Egypt.

TORCH

On 8 November, a few days after Rommel began his retreat from Egypt back to Libya, combined Anglo-American forces under the overall command of US Lieutenant General Dwight D. Eisenhower invaded Casablanca, Oran and Algiers in Vichy-controlled French North Africa. A West Point graduate of the famous class of 1915, Eisenhower was virtually unknown to the public at this time. Yet he had during the inter-war years developed an excellent reputation within the army as a staff officer for MacArthur and others. He had first achieved notoriety as chief of staff for the Third Army in the 1941 Louisiana manoeuvres, the largest such manoeuvres to date for the US Army, and after Pearl Harbor he had been called to Washington by General Marshall to serve as head of the War Plans Division (which became the Operations Division in March 1942). Here Eisenhower had played a major role in the development of US cross-Channel plans until May–June, when Marshall had sent him to London to head the US European Theater of Operations (ETO). In London he had continued to fight for British acceptance of US cross-Channel plans. With the July rejection of those plans in favour of TORCH, Marshall had selected him to command the North African invasion.

Eisenhower thus came to this first combined Anglo-American operation newly and rapidly promoted (he had risen from lieutenant colonel in early 1941 to one-star general by year's end and three-star general six months later) and with no battlefield experience, a shortcoming his critics would consistently cite in their attacks on his generalship throughout and after the war. What Eisenhower did possess, however, and what enabled him to function superbly as a coalition commander, was exceptional managerial and diplomatic skills, skills clearly linked to his sharp intelligence as well as his pleasant, outgoing personality. Only such skills, many have argued, could have enabled him to deal with the difficult British and American personalities who would serve under him. Most notable in this regard would eventually be both Montgomery and the American commander of the Casablanca invasion force, Major General George S. Patton, a brilliant but mercurial and highly eccentric cavalry/armour officer who possessed an apparent inability, as will be shown, 'to control either his emotions or his mouth'.[5]

Eisenhower set out to achieve a truly unified Anglo-American command in this first major combined operation. His deputy commander, chief of staff and western air commander were American – Major General Mark Clark, Brigadier General Walter Bedell Smith and Brigadier General James Doolittle – as were two of his three task force commanders – Patton at Casablanca and Major General Lloyd Fredendall at Oran. But all his other major commanders were British, including naval commander Admiral Sir Andrew B. Cunningham, eastern air commander Marshal William Welsh, Algiers task force commander Major General Charles Ryder, and British First Army commander Lieutenant General Kenneth A.N. Anderson. Eisenhower's aim was nothing less than the creation of an unprecedented headquarters whose members acted as if they belonged to a single nation.

That would be easier said than done. 'I'll never take orders from a Britisher,' one American general bluntly stated upon his 1942 arrival in England.[6] British officers reciprocated the sentiment. Eisenhower, however, was an admitted fanatic regarding Allied unity and made clear that he considered any quarrels between British and American officers as a 'cardinal sin which would be mercilessly punished'. After the first such quarrel he relieved the American officer involved and ordered him to return to the United States. The British officer appealed that decision on the grounds that 'He only called me a son-of-a-bitch', a term the British had learned was 'a colloquial expression which is sometimes used almost as a term of endearment' and should not be taken seriously. 'I am informed that he called you a British son-of-a-bitch,' Eisenhower responded. 'That is quite different. My ruling stands.'[7]

The TORCH operation that Eisenhower commanded had been designed not only to secure French North Africa for the Allies, but also to trap Rommel in the Libyan desert between this Anglo-American force on his rear and Montgomery's 8th Army on his front. Although the invasion itself would succeed, this larger objective would elude the Allied forces for a host of reasons. While Montgomery's pursuit of Rommel after El Alamein was insufficiently aggressive, the TORCH invasion forces proceeded more slowly than anticipated because of a series of political problems with the French as well as military problems with the rapidly arriving Germans in this first large-scale combined Anglo-American operation.

Morocco and Algeria were part of the French Empire, and the substantial French forces in the area remained loyal to the officially neutral but unofficially collaborationist government of Marshal Henri Pétain in Vichy. Britain and the United States had no desire to fight these French forces. To the contrary, their hope was that the French would not resist the landings and that Eisenhower could move quickly and unopposed all the way to Tunisia, trapping Rommel in a massive pincer movement in the Libyan desert in conjunction with Montgomery's advancing British 8th Army. Obtaining French acquiescence in this plan became a major Anglo-American preoccupation, dilemma, and to a large extent an Anglo-American failure. Numerous political strategies were attempted, but all of them failed.

The essential problem was that the British and the Americans were invading French territory (albeit colonial territory), the rhetoric of 'liberation' notwithstanding. Moreover, in the aftermath of the French surrender of 1940, the British had on 3 July of that year attacked and sunk part of the French naval forces at Oran and the neighbouring base of Mers-el-Kebir, killing more than 1,000 French sailors and almost precipitating a French declaration of war. So bitter were French feelings that the British readily agreed in 1942 to an American commander for TORCH, an American assault force in front of their own troops at Algiers, and American patches on their uniforms in an effort to downplay their own role in the operation.

The British also hoped that French officers and soldiers might rally to General Charles de Gaulle, who headed the so-called Free French Forces from his London headquarters and who had, in conjunction with the British, successfully taken control of other portions of France's empire, most notably in French Equatorial Africa and the Middle East (Syria and Lebanon). Such efforts had failed wretchedly at Dakar on the western 'bulge' of Africa, however, and most French officers in North and West Africa considered de Gaulle a traitor.

While different, American perceptions of de Gaulle were no more favourable. Unlike the British, the Americans had retained diplomatic ties with Vichy and had rejected de Gaulle as an arrogant, manipulative and untrustworthy individual, if not a British puppet. His late 1941 takeover of the French islands of St Pierre and Miquelon off the coast of Newfoundland, despite promises not to do so, further alienated and angered US leaders, especially Secretary of State Cordell Hull. As an alternative, Washington chose to work with Henri Giraud, a French general who had recently escaped from a German prison and whom the Americans hoped French officers would obey when he ordered them not to fight Eisenhower's forces. The British concurred.

Eisenhower also sent his deputy General Clark secretly to Algiers to help organize a coup by anti-Vichy officers to coincide with the invasion.

Neither of these efforts succeeded. When informed at the last minute of the invasion, Giraud refused to cooperate unless he was placed in charge of all Anglo-American forces. Eisenhower, of course, refused this demand. And when Giraud finally relented and did issue orders to French forces, those orders were ignored. Simultaneously, the attempted coup in Algiers failed miserably.[8] Consequently the 65,000 Anglo-American forces that landed faced serious French resistance – and suffered serious casualties.

While all these prior plans and hopes thus came to naught, Eisenhower was able to halt the French resistance to TORCH via a totally unexpected avenue. Admiral Jean Darlan, commander of all Vichy armed forces, was unexpectedly in Algiers visiting his very ill son when the invasion began. With the failure of the other approaches, Eisenhower and Clark opened negotiations with him. An opportunist who saw which way the military wind was blowing, Darlan agreed to change sides and to order French forces to cease fighting and join the Allies. In return, Eisenhower agreed to place the admiral in administrative charge of French North Africa. Such cooperation with a known Nazi collaborator infuriated British and American public opinion as well as de Gaulle, Giraud and their followers – until the admiral was conveniently assassinated by one of his countrymen on Christmas Eve.

By that time, however, Hitler had responded to these events by invading the previously unoccupied portions of France (the French responded by scuttling their fleet at Toulon, rather than allowing it to fall into German hands or joining the Allies in North Africa) and by deciding to send major forces into Tunisia under General Hans-Jürgen von Arnim. The previous Allied decision to land no farther east than Algiers now came back to haunt them. Moreover, limited rail capacity, logistical foul-ups, poor weather, inexperienced troops, incompetent commanders, the numerous problems of a new and unprecedented Anglo-American command, and superior German airpower all combined to slow down and eventually halt Eisenhower's advance. 'I think the best way to describe our operations to date,' he sardonically wrote to OPD chief and old friend Major General Thomas T. Handy in early December, 'is that they have violated every recognized principle of war, are in conflict with all operational and logistic methods laid down in text-books, and will be condemned, in their entirety, by all Leavenworth and War College classes for the next twenty-five years.'[9]

To make matters worse, whereas Vichy French leaders and forces had been quite willing to resist Anglo-American forces in Morocco and Algeria, they and their commander in Tunisia, Admiral Jean Esteva, refused to follow Darlan's orders or offer any resistance to the German takeover. Hitler was thus able to win the race for Tunisia, seizing the ports of Tunis and Bizerte and quickly establishing a defensive perimeter through the Tunisian mountains southward to the Mareth defensive line that the French had previously constructed along the Libyan border. Eisenhower's forces did advance to within

12 miles of Tunis by late November, but they were halted there by fierce German resistance as well as bad weather and supply problems.[10] Two months later, Rommel's forces would cross the Mareth Line and enter the relative safety of the Tunisian bridgehead.

Bloody Buna and Guadalcanal

While Allied forces struggled to seize the strategic initiative from the Germans on two fronts in North Africa, other Allied forces struggled on two very different fronts in the South Pacific to seize the strategic initiative from the Japanese.

Despite their failures in the battles of Coral Sea and Midway, the Japanese were continuing their efforts to cut communications between the United States and Australia-New Zealand via a takeover of the southern Solomon Islands and an overland assault from the north on Port Moresby, on the southern coast of New Guinea. The Americans were simultaneously planning to take advantage of Coral Sea and Midway by launching a counter-offensive to capture the major Japanese base at Rabaul on the eastern end of New Britain Island in the Bismarck Archipelago (Operation CARTWHEEL). The ensuing collision would lead to extensive warfare in some of the most inhospitable climates in the world. Located near the equator, both New Guinea and the Solomon Islands were dominated by exceptionally high temperatures and humidity, incessant rainfall, high mountains, and dense jungles containing an incredible and often hideous assortment of bugs and diseases, including malaria, dysentery and typhus.

Confused command relationships compounded these problems of climate and terrain for the Allies. As previously noted, serious inter-service rivalry and personality conflicts precluded following the principle of unity of command in the Pacific.[11] Instead the theatre was divided into the Southwest Pacific Area (SWPA) under General MacArthur in Australia and the Pacific Ocean Areas (POA) under Admiral Nimitz in Hawaii. Nimitz in turn divided his huge command into three areas: the North Pacific and Central Pacific, which he commanded personally; and the South Pacific, which he placed under Vice Admiral Robert Ghormley. Eastern New Guinea and the southern Solomons lay within MacArthur's command, but the navy would not countenance his control of its capital ships while he would not countenance their control of his forces.

In Washington, Admiral King and General Marshall worked out a compromise whereby the planned offensive against Rabaul would be divided into three tasks. Task One would be an attack on Tulagi in the southern Solomons (Operation WATCHTOWER) and would be under Ghormley and Nimitz, with the boundaries between the SWPA and the POA shifted westward one degree of longitude so as to include the island in the POA. Task Two would be simultaneous advances along the northern coast of New Guinea and up the Solomon Islands chain, both of which would be under MacArthur. So would Task

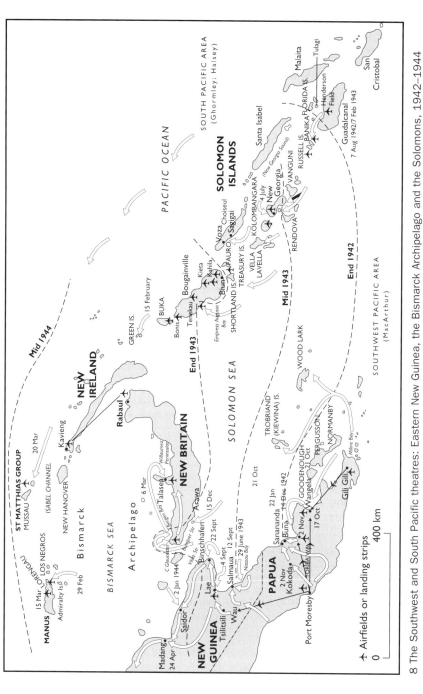

8 The Southwest and South Pacific theatres: Eastern New Guinea, the Bismarck Archipelago and the Solomons, 1942–1944

Three, the actual assault on Rabaul. On 2 July the Joint Chiefs issued the formal directive to launch Task One on 1 August, a date later postponed to 7 August. Simultaneously MacArthur's staff began to plan for Task Two, which would begin with the construction of an airfield near Buna Government Station on the northern coast of the Papuan Peninsula of eastern New Guinea.

Continued Japanese offensive moves quickly disrupted and necessitated changes in both sets of plans. Discovery in July of the Japanese construction of an airfield on Guadalcanal in the southern Solomons led to the addition of that island to Tulagi as a WATCHTOWER objective. Simultaneously, 16,000 Japanese troops under Major General Horii Tomitaro landed at Buna before MacArthur could occupy the area, and headed south in an effort to capture Port Moresby by land. By the end of the month they had crossed most of the Owen Stanley Mountains, a forbidding range of jungle-covered peaks rising to 13,000 feet and passable only via the Kokoda Trail, a route so steep, narrow and primitive as to challenge the most adventurous contemporary climbers, and were within 30 miles of Port Moresby. MacArthur's attention quickly shifted to halting this menace.

MacArthur would prove to be one of the most controversial American generals in World War II, and indeed in all of US history. Graduating first in his class at West Point in 1903, he had risen rapidly to high command and in 1930 became army chief of staff. After his term ended, he retired to accept an appointment as field marshal to train the Philippine Army prior to its scheduled independence, but he was recalled to active duty in July 1941 and placed in charge of all US forces in the Philippines. Here he had been badly defeated by the Japanese and ordered to evacuate to Australia in order to assume command of the SWPA. In this command, he would prove brilliant on many occasions but nearly incompetent on others. He would also continue to exhibit the extraordinary ego, vanity, imperiousness and paranoia for which he was already notorious, referring to himself in the third person and insisting that his theatre was more important than Europe and that dark forces were conspiring to thwart him. Roosevelt had labelled him one of the two most dangerous men in the United States during the 1930s and had been happy to see him depart for the Philippines. Nevertheless the president and Marshall had recognized his importance as a rallying point and his military abilities, and they had thus placed him in charge of the SWPA.

Although one would never know it from MacArthur's press releases, the Southwest Pacific Area was a combined Allied command in which non-US forces often predominated. That was certainly the case in New Guinea, where outnumbered Australian troops with Papuan and New Guinean volunteers had been involved in a desperate effort to halt, or at least to slow down, the Japanese advance across the Owen Stanley Mountains. By September these Australians and their allies had retreated to the southern foothills of those mountains, the last defensible barrier for Port Moresby. This led to a virtual panic in MacArthur's headquarters, along with numerous unfair slurs about Australian fighting ability and the competence of their commander, General

Sir Thomas Blamey. But at Milne Bay on the eastern tip of New Guinea, the reinforced Australian garrison, along with American combat engineers, stopped a second Japanese force of 2,600 moving against Port Moresby in late August–early September. Simultaneously, the Japanese High Command halted its main forces advancing on Port Moresby along the Kokoda Trail and ordered them to assume defensive positions, as scheduled reinforcements for Papua were diverted to the unexpected and fierce campaign taking place on Guadalcanal.

On 7 August, US marines had landed on the southern Solomon Islands of Guadalcanal and Tulagi (as well as the islets of Gavatu and Tanambogo), quickly taking them from their surprised and outnumbered Japanese defenders. But the Japanese High Command decided to retake Guadalcanal and dispatched major reinforcements to the island. The result would be a massive, six-month campaign of attrition on and around that island, including six major naval battles as well as numerous ground battles, which would divert Japanese forces from Port Moresby and eventually end their ability to conduct offensive operations in the South Pacific. Nobody had expected such a huge campaign for that island. Indeed, it had been added to US plans only at the last minute and only because of the discovery of a Japanese airfield being built there. But the struggle for Guadalcanal would become one of the fiercest and most decisive campaigns of the Pacific War.

The key to the campaign for each side was the ability to land troops and supplies on the island. Here the Americans had an enormous advantage in their possession of the airfield that the Japanese had begun and that the marines quickly seized and completed. Named Henderson Field after a marine air commander killed at Midway, it enabled US forces on the island both to receive supplies by air and to interdict Japanese supply efforts – provided the Americans could hold the airfield. They would be hampered in that effort and the entire campaign, however, by a paucity of available resources and serious naval problems. These problems stemmed partially from the fact that Admiral Ghormley's headquarters were 900 miles away in Noumea on New Caledonia, partially from the caution of naval task force commander Admiral Frank Jack Fletcher, who feared Japanese air attacks on his carriers, and partially from the naval superiority that the Japanese still possessed in surface ships and night fighting.

Much to the consternation of Rear Admiral Richmond Kelly Turner and marine Major General Alexander A. Vandegrift, the amphibious task force and ground commanders, Fletcher had insisted that his three aircraft carriers would stay in support of the landings for only two days. He had then withdrawn them on 8 August, 12 hours earlier than scheduled and before Turner had completed unloading supplies for the 11,000 marines on the island. Consequently, those marines would lack the materials they needed, including food and ammunition, to hold the airfield and island against the Japanese counter-attacks.

Those counter-attacks began on the evening of 8–9 August when, in the Battle of Savo Island, a Japanese surface naval force under Admiral Mikawa

Gunichi attacked and crippled the Allied surface fleet off Guadalcanal, sinking one Australian as well as three US cruisers and severely damaging another cruiser along with two destroyers. Luckily for the Americans, Mikawa did not know of Fletcher's withdrawal and, fearful of air attacks on his surface ships, himself withdrew at dawn instead of attacking the American transports. Nevertheless Savo Island was one of the worst defeats in US naval history, and it left the marines nearly isolated as the Japanese began to land major reinforcements on the island under General Kawaguchi Kiyotake. Their ensuing effort to land even more troops on 24 August led to the naval Battle of the Eastern Solomons, during which they would damage one of Fletcher's carriers (the *Enterprise*) but lose one of their small carriers to Fletcher's aircraft as well as two destroyers and a supply ship to land-based US aircraft.

For the next five months the Americans would use their control of Henderson Field to attempt to land supplies and reinforcements by day while the Japanese would use their naval surface force (dubbed the 'Tokyo Express' by the Americans) to land supplies and reinforcements by night and to bombard Henderson Field, running down the narrow body of water between the western and eastern Solomons known as 'the Slot'. So fierce was the fighting in Savo Sound between Guadalcanal and Tulagi, and so extensive the naval losses on both sides, that the body of water became known as 'Ironbottom Sound'.

On the evening of 13 September, Kawaguchi's troops launched a series of savage attacks against the marine position defending Henderson Field, later known as 'Bloody Ridge', in a failed effort to take the airstrip. The marines suffered 20 per cent casualties but killed more than 50 per cent of the attacking force. Far from halting the Japanese effort, however, this defeat led them to pour even more reinforcements into the island and to place their overall commander in the Solomons, General Hyakutaka Harukichi, in charge of the Guadalcanal campaign. The Americans in turn sent in army troops to reinforce the marines and on the evening of 11–12 October their naval forces surprised a Japanese convoy in the Battle of Cape d'Esperance, sinking a Japanese cruiser and destroyer but losing one cruiser and destroyer of their own.

Soon thereafter Nimitz replaced Ghormley with Vice Admiral William F. Halsey, an officer far more aggressive and, as a naval aviator, far more knowledgeable regarding the importance and use of airpower. Reversing Ghormley's prior policy, Halsey committed his carriers to the campaign in an effort to clearly gain the initiative. The results at first were far from encouraging. In the 26 October daylight naval air battle off the Santa Cruz Islands, east of Guadalcanal, the Japanese did lose numerous planes and pilots and suffered damage to two of their carriers, but in return they sank the US carrier *Hornet* and seriously damaged the *Enterprise*. On 13–15 November, however, Halsey scored a decisive victory in the so-called 'Naval Battle of Guadalcanal' – a series of daylight and night engagements involving battleships and smaller surface ships as well as carrier- and land-based aircraft. At the end of those engagements the Japanese had lost most of the ground reinforcements they had attempted to land and a substantial portion of their naval power. On the evening of 30 November they did achieve a tactical victory over American naval forces at the Battle of Tassafaronga Point, but it was too little and too late. With their ground forces heavily outnumbered and naval forces unable to continue to take the losses they had experienced, the Japanese High Command evacuated Guadalcanal in early February.

Meanwhile, reinforced and resupplied Australian ground forces succeeded in pushing the Japanese all the way back to the north coast of New Guinea by November, while American forces under Major General Edwin F. Harding were transported to the area for a combined assault on the remaining Japanese strongholds of Buna, Sanananda and Gona. Lacking the heavy weapons necessary to knock out the Japanese bunkers, the Americans suffered frightful casualties and failure in frontal assaults against what became known as 'Bloody Buna'. MacArthur unfairly blamed Harding and replaced him with Lieutenant General Robert L. Eichelberger, whom he ordered to 'take Buna or don't come back alive!'[12] At first Eichelberger fared no better. But increased air and naval strength brought him the reinforcements, supplies and tanks he needed to assault the Japanese bunkers, while seriously limiting Japanese reinforcements. Allied casualties continued to be quite heavy, but on 9 December the Australians took Gona and on 2 January the Americans took Buna. Sanananda fell to combined forces on 22 January.

The campaigns for Guadalcanal and the Papuan Peninsula on New Guinea were not the immediate, striking successes that Midway had been. Whereas, at Midway, US naval air forces achieved decisive victory in two days (and actually within 15 minutes), the Guadalcanal and Papuan campaigns lasted six months and included numerous American and Australian defeats. Nevertheless these campaigns were just as much decisive 'turning points' as Midway had been, if not more so. Despite their victories in some of the specific battles, the Japanese had failed to halt this first Allied counter-offensive against them. In the process their navy had taken additional heavy losses it could neither afford nor replace, and it had been forced to withdraw from the southern Solomons. Equally important, Japanese ground forces had been defeated for the first time in the war and had been shorn of their aura of invincibility. Although still very powerful, the Japanese Army and Navy were both now on the defensive in the Pacific, with the strategic initiative resting in Allied hands.

Stalingrad and the Eastern Front

El Alamein, TORCH, Guadalcanal and Papua were not the only, or even the most important turning point battles/campaigns taking place in the second half of 1942. Dwarfing all of them in terms of size and casualties was the Russo-German campaign of 1942. Shifting his sights after his failure to take Moscow in 1941, Hitler sent his *Panzers* southward toward the Caucasus oilfields and Stalingrad on the Volga River – more than 300 miles east of Moscow.

In a titanic six-month struggle, the Red Army first halted the Germans in both the Caucasus and at Stalingrad, and then surrounded the German 6th Army in the rubble of that now-destroyed city, forcing both its surrender on 31 January/2 February and the withdrawal of German forces in the Caucasus. The cost had been enormous: at least 300,000 and perhaps as many as 500,000 Soviet dead – more combat deaths than the British or the Americans suffered in the entire war. But, in turn, the Russians killed approximately 147,000 Axis troops, made prisoners of another 91,000, and destroyed any possibility that the Germans would be able to achieve total victory on the Eastern Front.[13]

In virtually all theatres, the Allies had thus by late 1942/early 1943 succeeded in halting major Axis offensives and launching successful counter-offensives of their own. Clearly, a major turning point in the war had been reached.

On no account, however, did these Allied successes mean that their Axis enemies were now doomed to total defeat. To the contrary, Germany and Japan still possessed enormous power and controlled extensive territories rich in human and material resources. What the Allies had succeeded in doing by early 1943 was halting the Axis bid for total victory. But that was a far cry from ensuring their own total victory. Military stalemate and a consequent negotiated peace that left the Axis governments and empires intact were quite possible, if not probable.

Such a scenario was even more likely when one looked at the sorry state of the Allied coalition. Of all the major Allied operations launched in 1942, only TORCH and the Papuan campaign had been combined ones. The former was hardly a striking success at year's end, and the latter's success had been partially dependent on what was occurring on and around Guadalcanal. That campaign, as well as El Alamein, Midway and Stalingrad, had been won by a single Allied power, not the coalition, and the individual victories bore no direct, supporting relationship to each other. To the contrary, they illustrated a continued *lack* of Allied coordination, as each power had in effect gone its own way in 1942. One result was that by year's end more US combat forces were deployed against Japan than against Germany, continued formal agreement to a Germany-first approach notwithstanding. This was by no means limited to naval forces, an imbalance one might expect given the nature of the Pacific war: 464,000 army troops were in the Pacific at the end of 1942 – 200,000 more than planned – while only 378,000 were in North Africa and the United Kingdom – 57,000 less than planned.[14]

Another result of this lack of coordination was increased and intense bitterness and distrust within the Grand Alliance, especially from the Soviets, who felt betrayed by the Anglo-Americans, and the Americans, who felt manipulated by the British. Such negative feelings were not modified by the combined Anglo-American victory in North Africa, an operation the American High Command had bitterly opposed and deeply resented, or the combined US-Australian victory in Papua, during which MacArthur had both insulted the Australians and downplayed their role in defeating the Japanese.

What was clearly needed, and lacking, was greater Allied confidence and trust in as well as respect for each other. What was equally needed, and also lacking, was a fully coordinated and accepted Allied plan for combined operations and victory.

The Casablanca Conference

Churchill and Roosevelt understood this latter need and made plans for a major Allied meeting during January of 1943 in the recently conquered Moroccan city of Casablanca. Stalin was invited but declined to attend, claiming he was too busy with ongoing operations while warning that he now expected his allies to make final arrangements for the 1943 second front that Churchill had promised him in August. But, barring a German collapse, no such front was likely to be established in that year. Anglo-American forces remained heavily engaged in Tunisia and would continue to be so engaged until May, while Australian and American forces remained heavily engaged in New Guinea and the Solomons as the year 1942 ended.

In effect, two diversionary fronts had been established in 1942, one in North Africa and the other in the Pacific. Neither could be halted in mid-campaign. Moreover, each ally wanted continuation and expansion of one of these campaigns during 1943. For the British, North Africa was supposed to be, in Churchill's words, 'a springboard and not a sofa' to further Mediterranean offensives designed to reopen that sea to shipping and knock Italy out of the war.[15] For the Americans, especially Admiral King and General MacArthur, a much greater percentage of US and Allied strength should be devoted to offensive action against the Japanese – even though more American forces were already deployed against Japan than against Germany. 'Germany-first', in the words of historian David Reynolds, had become 'a slogan not a strategy'.[16]

Compounding these problems was the fact that the U-boat menace was far from eliminated in early 1943, and that supply lines to both Britain and Russia remained threatened. Indeed, the Allies in 1942 lost 1,662 ships with a tonnage total of 7.8 million. Convoys to Russia via the northern route were totally halted for more than two months after the disastrous losses suffered by Convoy PQ-17 in June–July 1942 (only 11 of 37 ships in that convoy reached their destination) and again in September in preparation for TORCH, while British imports fell in 1942 to one-third of their pre-war level.[17]

At Casablanca the British and American military chiefs would quickly agree that defeat of this U-boat menace had to be the first Allied priority for 1943, and that Soviet forces 'must be sustained by the greatest volume of supplies that can be transported to Russia without prohibitive cost in shipping'.[18] Unfortunately, however, the CCS could agree to little else in terms of strategic priorities and operations for 1943.

Continued disorganization and lack of consensus over the proper approach for 1943 plagued the Americans as they prepared for the Casablanca Conference. While most US Army planners continued to favour a cross-Channel attack, some argued that continuation in the Mediterranean made more sense. This argument was indirectly reinforced by the insistence of the navy and MacArthur that greater emphasis needed to be placed on the Pacific, for Mediterranean operations would require fewer men and less material than cross-Channel operations. Consequently General Marshall was forced to inform Roosevelt on 7 January that 'there was not a united front' on 1943 cross-Channel operations, particularly among the planners, and that within the JCS itself 'the question was still an open one'.[19] Without such a united front among the planners and their chiefs, one between the president and his military advisers was out of the question.

This was certainly not the case with Churchill and his chiefs of staff, who were heirs to a long history of politico-military coordination. Roosevelt had warned his advisers in this regard that the British would 'have a plan and stick to it' at Casablanca, a warning that proved to be prophetic.[20] Their plethora of planners overwhelmed and out-argued the small American contingent, while Churchill and the COS noted and exploited the splits within the JCS and Roosevelt's continuing interest in the Mediterranean. As a result, the JCS were soon forced to acquiesce in British plans for Operation HUSKY, the invasion of Sicily in 1943, with operations for the European continent limited to a bombing offensive against German cities (Operation POINT-BLANK) and the continued build-up of forces in the United Kingdom for an eventual cross-Channel assault.

In return, however, the Americans demanded that more attention be given to the war against Japan. The irascible Admiral King pressed for a much greater percentage of the Allied war effort to be allocated to the Pacific (30 per cent), arguing that this was preferable to the build-up of a 'dormant' force in Britain 'awaiting an opportunity', while General Marshall pressed for a campaign in Burma (Operation ANAKIM) to reopen the supply route to China. The British countered that such an approach would violate the Germany-first strategy – a strategy the JCS openly threatened to abandon if their demands were not met. The CCS were able to compromise their differences by agreeing to the somewhat contradictory statement that 'adequate' forces would be allocated for Pacific and Burma offensives, but that those offensives were to be 'kept within such limits . . . as not to jeopardize the capacity of the United Nations to take advantage of any favorable opportunity that may present itself for the decisive defeat of Germany in 1943'.[21]

Ironically, the creation of any such opportunity continued to depend primarily on the Red Army, and Stalin would be anything but pleased to find out that no cross-Channel operations were likely in 1943 and that, indeed, no European ground operations were definitely planned for that year beyond the invasion of Sicily – an effort so limited that presidential adviser and confidant Harry Hopkins bluntly called it 'feeble' for two great powers.[22] Indeed, as the conference began, Stalin had complained to Roosevelt over the fact that even North African operations had come to a 'standstill' and had enquired as to why.[23] Consequently, Churchill and Roosevelt pressed their military chiefs at

3 Roosevelt and Churchill pose with their staffs after the Allied conference at Casablanca. Standing (left to right): Lt. Gen. H.H. Arnold, Adm. Ernest J. King, Gen. George C. Marshall, Sir Dudley Pound, Sir Charles Portal, Sir Alan Francis Brooke, Sir John Dill, Lord Louis Mountbatten and Brehon H. Somervell, January 1943 © Bettmann/CORBIS

4 Churchill and Roosevelt discuss details of Germany's surrender at Casablanca. © Hulton-Deutsch Collection/CORBIS

Casablanca for expansion of their plans so as to include a specific possible cross-Channel assault in August (Operation HADRIAN), creation of a combined staff to plan this and related operations, a British effort to bring Turkey into the war, and possible additional 1943 operations in the eastern Mediterranean and the Balkans. The CCS quickly complied with their superiors' wishes, but General Marshall made clear to both leaders that no matter what was put on paper, a 1943 cross-Channel assault would be 'extremely limited' in size and 'difficult if not impossible' to launch in conjunction with HUSKY unless German morale collapsed. Perhaps influenced by such warnings, Churchill and Roosevelt now avoided specifics by informing Stalin that the combined bomber offensive and planned build-up in Britain would enable them to cross the Channel 'as soon as practicable'.[24] Stalin would not be pleased or mollified by such vagueness about 1943. Nor would Chiang Kai-shek, whose China theatre remained a very low priority in Anglo-American planning.

Unconditional Surrender

Stalin and Chiang were far from the only individuals in the Allied camp displeased with Anglo-American plans and policies in early 1943. Eisenhower's November collaboration with Darlan in North Africa had deeply upset Anglo-American public opinion and led to sharp criticisms in both Britain and the United States, with Churchill forced to defend the policy in the House of Commons. Darlan's late December assassination had removed the immediate issue, but not the public outcry or the expressed fear of more 'deals' with Nazi collaborators. Indeed, some critics asked, what would prevent the Allies from using the same 'logic' to strike a deal with one of Hitler's high-ranking Nazi subordinates? Furthermore, Darlan's assassination had also created a politico-administrative power vacuum in French North Africa and an ensuing struggle for control between the British-backed de Gaulle and the American-backed Giraud, who refused to cooperate with each other.

During a press conference on 24 January, the last day of the Casablanca meeting, Roosevelt attempted to resolve these problems via two surprises. First, he invited de Gaulle and Giraud to the conference without telling either that the other would be present and forced them to agree both to a power-sharing accord and to shake hands before the cameras, thereby creating at least the appearance of cooperation. He then informed the press that 'peace can come to the world only by the total elimination of German and Japanese power', and that such elimination meant 'the unconditional surrender by Germany, Italy and Japan'.[25]

This enunciation of the Allied wartime policy of Unconditional Surrender has been the subject of numerous myths: that it came as a complete surprise and as a result merely of a momentary presidential whim; that it lengthened the war by encouraging the Axis powers to fight to the bitter end and by providing them with a propaganda statement to get their people to do so; that it was a purely military statement and a poor substitute for a statement of Allied political goals; and that as such it illustrated Roosevelt's political bank-ruptcy.[26] In actuality, none of the above is correct.

Unconditional Surrender had previously been discussed and agreed to by Roosevelt, Churchill and their advisers. Indeed, it had for quite some time been the de facto policy of Britain, Russia and the United States. As Roosevelt asserted on 24 January, 'we have all had it in our hearts and heads before . . .'.[27] The reasons were clear. The Allies considered Fascist militarism to be a major cause if not the major cause of the war, and this ideology could be uprooted only if they obtained an unconditional surrender that would enable them to thoroughly remake the governments and political systems of the Axis powers. Furthermore, conditional surrender was impossible with Adolf Hitler, a man who had broken just about every international agreement that he had signed. Another key factor was that Hitler had risen to power by using the 'stab in the back' myth – that Germany had not lost World War I militarily but instead had been betrayed by internal 'traitors' – a myth made popular by the conditional German surrender in 1918 that had led Allied armies to halt before they entered and occupied Germany. Repetition of that error had to be avoided this time.

Roosevelt also stated explicitly on 24 January that Unconditional Surrender did not mean the destruction of the German, Italian and Japanese people – only their governments and the Fascist ideologies of those governments. Nazi Propaganda Minister Josef Goebbels would of course distort the message to get the German people to fight to the bitter end, but he did not need a Roosevelt statement in order to manufacture his propaganda lies, and there is no evidence that this particular statement led the German people to fight longer (the Japanese are another, and a more complex story, as related later in this volume).[28] Nor was this statement a poor substitute for a political policy. Such a policy already existed in general terms within the Atlantic Charter.

But why enunciate this Unconditional Surrender as a policy in January of 1943? Roosevelt did so for some very clear and specific political reasons. First and foremost, he hoped it would reassure Stalin in the absence of more spe-cific pledges to launch a 1943 second front. As the president told his son Elliot, Unconditional Surrender was 'just the thing for the Russians'.[29] Similarly, it was 'just the thing' for the Chinese in light of the low priority Asia maintained in Anglo-American plans, and to reassure the British and American people that there would be no more 'Darlan deals' with other high-ranking collaborators or Nazi officials. It was also a wonderful way to post-pone the specific post-war territorial discussions that Stalin had pressed for in 1942 and that Roosevelt feared would seriously weaken both the alliance and domestic support for the war effort.[30]

But words were no substitute for actions in war, and Churchill and Roosevelt would soon discover that they had been far too optimistic at Casablanca regard-ing what their military forces could accomplish in 1943. Furthermore, the Americans left the conference intensely bitter over what they experienced as a major defeat at British hands. 'We lost our shirts and are now committed to a subterranean umbilicus operation in mid-summer,' US Army planner Brigadier General Albert C. Wedemeyer wrote to General Handy near the end of the conference. 'One might say we came, we listened and we were conquered.'[31] So bitter were American feelings that Eisenhower found it necessary to warn Handy immediately after the conference that 'one of the constant sources of danger in this war is the temptation to regard as our first enemy the partner that must work with us in defeating the real enemy'.[32]

Rather than reducing inter-Allied suspicions and tensions, the Casablanca Conference had thus in many ways exacerbated them. And rather than achieving a strategic plan on which all the Allies could agree, it had instead highlighted their continued strategic disagreements and set the stage for additional and heated arguments throughout the year 1943.

6

ASPECTS AND IMPACTS OF TOTAL WAR: THE IRREGULAR, INTELLIGENCE, NAVAL AND AIR WARS

World War II is often referred to as the first truly total war. The concept of non-combatant virtually disappeared during this conflict, as all aspects and components of society were mobilized for the war effort – and targeted by opposing forces. Already discussed in this regard were Anglo-American economic and human mobilization and coordination.[1] This chapter analyses several additional aspects of their total war effort, all of which were addressed directly or indirectly in the January 1943 Casablanca Conference accords: support for European resistance movements; issues of collaboration, resistance and decolonization in the Far East; the scientific and intelligence revolutions; the 'Battle of the Atlantic'; and the strategic bombing campaign.

The organization of European resistance

As previously noted, the Mediterranean focus in the Casablanca accords was a key component of Britain's peripheral strategy. But such Mediterranean activity to 'close the ring' around German-occupied Europe was not the only component of the British strategic approach. Equally important were actions to weaken Germany inside the 'ring' then being established so as to eventually force its collapse.

Support for European resistance movements was a key aspect of this effort. Such resistance movements, it was hoped, could aid the Allied war effort by providing vital intelligence and by engaging in sabotage and other forms of irregular warfare against Axis military forces. The early British decision to establish governments-in-exile for the European nations conquered by Germany was part of this approach. So was the July 1940 establishment of the British Special Operations Executive (SOE), whose key tasks were to organize military resistance and conduct covert operations within Nazi-occupied Europe. Once the United States entered the war Roosevelt established the Office of Strategic Services (OSS) under Major General William J. Donovan for similar purposes, as well as intelligence-gathering and analysis. The overall aim of such resistance organization and covert operations was, in Churchill's famous words, to 'set Europe ablaze'.

The resulting effort has been the subject of much mythology. Contrary to that mythology, the bulk of the European populations did not resist German occupation, and those who did resist were not always allied with their governments-in-exile. Indeed, in many countries, resistance that did take place was part of a pre-war and ongoing domestic conflict between Rightist and Leftist forces. Furthermore, the Allied governments did not always support these resistance movements, and their impact on the military outcome of the war was quite limited. So was the impact of the romantic but often ineffectual SOE and OSS activities.

Nazi occupation policies were so horrible that, from our contemporary perspective, they clearly should have led to wide-scale European resistance. The Germans plundered the material wealth of the nations they conquered, forced segments of the conquered populations into slave labour, and murdered millions. This behaviour resulted primarily from the Nazi ideology of racial superiority, which rated non-Germans as genetically inferior and therefore subject to expropriation, forced labour and/or death. Particularly noteworthy in this regard was the Nazi programme to exterminate all the Jews of Europe and the entire Slavic intelligentsia, and to severely diminish the Slavic population of Eastern Europe as a whole so as to provide *Lebensraum*, or 'living space', for German colonization. Such policies were first implemented by mobile killing squads known as *Einsatzgruppen* during and immediately after the 1939 conquest of Poland, and then again during the 1941 invasion of the Soviet Union. In 1942 extermination camps such as Auschwitz were established, some within or connected to pre-existing concentration camps already possessing very high death rates. Mass starvation also took the lives of millions.

Yet Nazi brutality did not lead to wide-scale resistance in many areas. In retrospect, the reasons were rather simple. First of all, resistance appeared futile to many in light of the stupendous German military victories of 1939–41 and the apparent invincibility of the *Wehrmacht*. It also appeared suicidal, as the Germans usually exacted a terrible toll for any resistance. Often they retaliated by killing civilians at the ratio of 50 or more to 1 for every German soldier killed. Even worse was the retaliation when SOE-trained Czech resistance fighters assassinated high-ranking SS official Reinhard Heydrich in the spring of 1942: Hitler ordered the total destruction of the village of Lidice, with all of its male inhabitants shot, its women sent to concentration camp or prison, and its children abducted.

Furthermore, the Nazis held no monopoly on racism. Anti-Semitism, for example, had a long history in Europe, and the Nazis found many collaborators more than willing to participate in their 'Final Solution' to what they called the 'Jewish Problem'. Moreover, many groups were willing to collaborate with the Germans as a means of gaining or retaining political power and destroying their domestic enemies; consequently, conservative forces in many

European countries made common cause with their Axis occupiers and eagerly participated in the carnage that followed.

Further complicating matters, many Europeans resented the fact that their leaders had fled to London to form governments-in-exile, and they consequently refused to fight for those governments. Moreover, not all European governments agreed to go into exile in London; the Belgian and Danish monarchs remained in their occupied countries, for example, and thus could not countenance armed resistance, while France and many East European nations had governments that openly collaborated with the Axis powers. Furthermore, while resistance movements tended to lean to the Left, many of the governments-in-exile did not.

Compounding this problem was the fact that after the Soviet Union was invaded in June of 1941, Moscow ordered all local Communist parties to work with native resistance movements. Many of these local Communist parties had been outlawed before the war, and their resulting clandestine tradition and secret cell structure made them perfect for organizing armed resistance. It also led to their members assuming leadership roles within the resistance movements. That in turn not only alienated conservatives in these countries, but also led to conflict with the governments-in-exile – and with the Allied governments. In Greece, for example, the major resistance movements refused to support the post-war return of the king, who had headed the Greek government-in-exile, even though the British Government did. London was in turn wary of supporting a heavily Communist movement that would probably align with the Soviet Union after the war, and indeed used force against it in late 1944. This problem was by no means limited to the British and the Greek resistance. The Soviet Government was similarly loath to support Polish resistance that was clearly anti-Communist and anti-Russian, and in August 1944 it refused to aid that movement's underground army when it rose up in Warsaw, thereby allowing the Germans to destroy it.[2]

The result of all this was a series of conflicts: between pro-British and pro-Soviet groups, Communist and non-Communist groups, indigenous rebels and governments-in-exile, the different Allied powers, and Rightists vs Leftists. In many countries the struggle to organize resistance was thus superimposed upon a virtual civil war as well as serious inter-Allied conflict, all of which seriously impeded organized resistance against the Germans.

The most successful resistance movements took place in the occupied portions of the Soviet Union, where partisan warfare was directed by the Soviet High Command as a key component of Soviet strategy,[3] and in Yugoslavia. In the latter country two very different resistance groups fought the German occupiers – and each other: the Chetniks under the leadership of Draza Mihailovic, a Serbian loyal to the Yugoslav royal government-in-exile; and the anti-royal government Partisans under the leadership of the Croat Communist Josip Broz (Tito). The British at first supported the Chetniks, but London shifted in 1943 after SOE operatives reported that Tito was more effective and willing to fight the Germans no matter how viciously they retaliated.

Mihailovic, on the other hand, was unwilling to risk such retaliation. He also appeared willing to collaborate passively with the Germans against the hated Partisans. Consequently Churchill once again subordinated his deep hostility to Communism, as he had in 1941 when he welcomed the Soviet Union as an ally, in favour of supporting those who could most effectively fight Hitler. With SOE support, Tito conducted the most widespread and effective guerrilla warfare against the Germans, tying down 15–20 Axis divisions that could otherwise have been used against Allied armies. In the process he also succeeded in liberating his own country without the help of any Allied army, Anglo-American or Soviet, and thus succeeded in controlling his nation's post-war government and destiny.

In Western Europe resistance tended to be of more limited effectiveness, and then only with the approach, or the promise of approach, of Allied armies; otherwise German retribution was simply too high a price to pay. In Norway, for example, the resistance movement, fearing reprisals and decimation at the hands of the large occupying German army, refused at first to conduct sabotage as desired by SOE and confined itself to intelligence-gathering and helping Jews and slave labourers to escape. Eventually it did agree to the important and successful sabotage of German atomic research and heavy water plants and to support for British military raids, but little beyond that. Resistance in Denmark, Belgium and the Netherlands was similarly limited by fears of retaliation, and by the continued presence of the royal family in the first two as well as terrain in all three that was not conducive to guerrilla warfare.

Resistance in France was limited not only by similar factors, but also by the fact that the German Army had occupied and administered northern and western France while the remainder of the country, as well as large segments of the French overseas empire, was governed by the collaborationist and conservative French Government in Vichy under the titular leadership of World War I hero Marshal Henri Pétain. At first, this government, not the British-supported Free French movement under General Charles de Gaulle, retained the allegiance of most French citizens as well as the French armed forces and most of the overseas French Empire. As previously noted, it also retained diplomatic relations with the United States from 1940–42. The invasion of French North Africa in November of 1942 ended these relations and resulted in a German military takeover of Vichy France. At that point the French scuttled their fleet in Toulon rather than either sail to North Africa to join the Allies or allow their ships to fall into German hands. Nevertheless, the German occupation of Vichy France left Pétain and Prime Minister Pierre Laval as total German puppets. But the United States still refused to have anything to do with de Gaulle, whom Roosevelt and Hull distrusted and detested. Instead, they supported General Henri Giraud. When neither de Gaulle nor Giraud proved able to get French forces in North Africa to stop fighting, however, Britain and the United States agreed to work with Vichy official Admiral Jean Darlan until his assassination in December of 1942. Roosevelt's arrangement of a public 'shotgun wedding' between de Gaulle and Giraud at the Casablanca Conference a month later was an effort to forge a unified French resistance movement that both powers could support.[4]

De Gaulle quickly outmanoeuvred the politically inept Giraud, however, and established a virtual government-in-exile at Algiers. He also managed, with SOE support, to bring together all resistance groups within France under his leadership (which in turn enabled him to preclude any Communist takeover of the resistance). Simultaneously, German military defeats in 1943–44 and the promise of forthcoming Anglo-American invasion turned the still-limited French and other West European resistance groups into mass movements that clearly aided Anglo-American military operations. So did the uniformed armed forces that de Gaulle and his supporters were able to organize and that fought alongside the Anglo-American armies in Tunisia, Italy and France. Not until August of 1944, however, would the distrustful Roosevelt agree to recognize de Gaulle's movement as a government, and even then he did not do so willingly. The resulting poisonous atmosphere would lead to very negative consequences for Franco-American relations in the post-war era.[5]

Resistance groups also emerged within Italy and Germany. In Italy, Mussolini's conservative opponents within the government succeeded in overthrowing and arresting him in July of 1943, after the invasion of Sicily, and then obtained a conditional surrender whereby Italy actually became an Allied power. It also became an occupied nation and a bloody battleground, however, as Anglo-American forces invaded from the south and German forces invaded from the north.[6] A daring German commando mission then freed Mussolini from prison and established him as head of a puppet government, the Salo Republic, in northern Italy. That government in turn became the target of a large partisan movement, one that captured and executed Mussolini when Germany collapsed in the spring of 1945.

Resistance in Germany was far less successful. It clearly existed, but given the nature of the Nazi police state, civilian resisters were powerless and usually wound up arrested and executed. Only the German Army possessed the capacity to overthrow Hitler. Some officers had been attempting to do just that since 1938, as there was no love lost between these Prussian aristocrats and the Austrian World War I corporal. But they were consistently thwarted by their own ineptitude and small numbers as well as Hitler's diplomatic and military successes, which undercut any appeal they might have within the officer corps in general. Furthermore, the anti-Hitler German officers received no support or encouragement from London or Washington, both of which considered them to be Prussian militarists little better than the Nazis. As revealed by the 'Unconditional Surrender' policy, Britain and the United States were also determined to occupy and thoroughly remake Germany, and to avoid any new 'stab in the back' myth via a conditional surrender. Nevertheless, a group of German officers led by Colonel Klaus von Stauffenberg attempted to assassinate Hitler in July of 1944 by planting a bomb in his East Prussian headquarters, and they almost succeeded. Hitler survived the bomb blast, however, and responded with a bloody purge that involved thousands of brutal executions and the virtual destruction of the old, aristocratic German General Staff that he detested.[7]

Although SOE, OSS and the European resistance movements did not play the major role in Allied victory that British strategists had hoped for, they did play a significant if auxiliary role by their sabotage of key German facilities, intelligence-gathering activities, and tying down of German troops. They did not precipitate a German collapse, however, or significantly weaken the German war effort. That task would be left primarily to the Allied armed forces.

Collaboration, resistance and decolonization in the Far East

In the Far East, OSS/SOE-supported indigenous resistance to the Japanese was also quite limited. The primary problem here was the pre-existing European/American colonialism, and Japanese efforts to portray the war as an anti-colonial, racial conflict to free Asians from white oppression. Consequently, numerous Asian nationalists agreed to collaborate with the Japanese, and even to form auxiliary military units to fight with them. Most notable in this regard were the Indian nationalist leader Subhas Chandra Bose and the Burmese nationalist leader Ba Maw. But the list of high-level nationalist collaborators also included Sukarno in the Dutch East Indies, Wang Ching-wei in China, former Chinese Emperor Pu Yi in Manchuria, and Filipino leaders such as Jose Laurel and Manuel Roxas. Moreover, Mohandas K. Gandhi's Congress Party in India practised a form of passive collaboration by refusing to aid the British war effort and by continuing to press for immediate independence, moves that led to a major crisis and to Gandhi being jailed from 1942 to 1944.

Verbally and on paper the Japanese promised national self-determination. Indeed, by the end of 1943 they had officially granted independence to Burma and the Philippines, allowed Subhas Chandra Bose to establish a provisional government for India, and hosted a Greater East Asia Conference in Tokyo for Asian nationalist leaders. Japanese anti-colonialism was largely rhetorical, however. In reality, the Japanese came as conquerors determined not to destroy colonialism, but to replace the Europeans and the Americans as the new colonial masters of the Far East. Furthermore, the combination of wartime demands and Japanese arrogance and brutality led to nationalist disenchantment with Tokyo, and eventually to some highly effective resistance against them.

As the major colonial power in Asia, Britain had mixed feelings at best about these nationalist resistance movements. The United States, on the other hand, was deeply interested in aiding them. It had no fear of, and indeed it supported their demands for post-war independence – which led to major policy clashes with Britain.

What the Americans did fear was the ability of Japanese anti-colonial propaganda to turn the Asian-Pacific conflict into a full-scale race war that would be unwinnable. And as one high-level US military estimate pointedly noted in 1943, Japanese success in such an endeavour and in the war, 'permitting a coalition under Japan's hegemony of the people of East Asia (about 55 per cent of the world's population), would appear likely to offer, indeed, a greater ultimate threat to the United States than would a similar outcome in Europe'.[8] Consequently, the Americans placed heavy emphasis on supporting nationalist resistance against the Japanese.

The Philippines contained one of the most notable such resistance movements, primarily because the United States had previously promised its inhabitants independence and had supported the development of an autonomous Philippine government and army. Trained by General MacArthur during the 1930s, that army fought with the Americans on Bataan. And although some Filipino leaders stayed and collaborated with the Japanese, others such as Manuel Quezon and Sergio Osmena were evacuated with MacArthur and formed a virtual government-in-exile. Furthermore, Philippine Army officers and men not captured by the Japanese joined with their American counterparts to form the core of a guerrilla resistance movement that eventually totalled over 200,000 and proved quite effective.

An American-supported resistance movement also developed in French Indochina, where the Japanese ruled through the existing Vichy French colonial government until March of 1945. At that time they overthrew the French and took over direct control. But the Japanese soon found themselves facing a nationalist guerrilla movement led by the Vietnamese Communist Ho Chi Minh, who worked closely with and received assistance from the OSS. Determined to free his people from colonial domination of any variety, Ho fought both the Japanese and the French and in late 1945 declared Vietnamese independence in words taken directly from the US Declaration of Independence. By this time World War II had ended, however, and the Soviet-American Cold War was beginning. Washington consequently refused to support Ho in his ensuing war against the French.[9] To the contrary, the United States worked actively against this Vietnamese Communist/nationalist, first by supporting the French and then, after their defeat in 1954, by establishing an alternative government in South Vietnam. The result would be one of the great tragedies of American, and Vietnamese history.

The largest and most important resistance movements from the American strategic perspective were in China. Should Chiang Kai-shek be defeated by the Japanese or agree to a negotiated peace, the results could be catastrophic, militarily and politically. Militarily, the bulk of the Japanese army, which was still bogged down fighting the Chinese, would then be free to concentrate against the Americans. Politically, Chiang's collapse would deeply reinforce Japanese propaganda that this was a race war against white imperialists. Consequently, the Americans launched a major effort to keep China in the war. This included extensive financial and military aid, and the sending in early 1942 of Joseph W. Stilwell, considered one of the best generals in the US Army, to serve as Chiang's Chief of Staff, train the Chinese armies and supervise Lend-Lease assistance. It also included consistent American calls at the Casablanca Conference and later for major military operations with the British to reopen the Burma Road supply route to Chiang's forces. Until that road could be opened, Lend-Lease supplies were flown in from India over the Himalayas, the highest mountain range in the world and one that those involved in the effort nicknamed 'the Hump'.

The Asian mainland remained a low priority in Anglo-American global strategy, however, and a major military offensive in Burma would be postponed as consistently as it appeared on the list of future Anglo-American operations. Furthermore, as General Stilwell quickly discovered, Chiang had no intention of using his American-trained and equipped forces against the Japanese. These were to be reserved for a post-war resumption of the civil war against the Communists under Mao Tse-tung, while the Americans and the British defeated the Japanese.

Mao's forces had escaped destruction by Chiang during the 1930s via their famous 'Long March' of 6,000 miles to the isolated province of Shensi. On paper they and Chiang's *Kuomintang* Party (KMT) then agreed to call a halt to their conflict and forge a united front against the Japanese invaders. In reality, however, each side prepared for a post-war resumption of their civil war. But whereas Chiang's preparations for this conflict precluded fighting the Japanese first, Mao's did not. To the contrary, extensive military conflict against the Japanese via guerrilla warfare was a key component of his overall military and political strategy.

Like Tito in Yugoslavia, Mao used guerrilla warfare as a means not only of hurting a hated conqueror, but also of gaining adherents and power for his post-war struggle to control his country. He was substantially aided by the extraordinary brutality of the Japanese Army, which gave him millions of potential recruits, and by his own development of a complex politico-military strategy based upon having the guerrilla army carry agrarian reform into the villages as a means of winning peasant support, using that support to attack outlying Japanese forces and take their weapons, and then disappearing into the countryside. Unable to find the guerrillas, the Japanese would retaliate against the villagers, thereby giving Mao even more recruits. By 1944 the comparison between his successes and Chiang's failures and corruption was so striking that Stilwell sought to make contact with the Communists – a decision that would play a major role in Chiang's late 1944 demand that he be recalled. Contact with the Chinese Communists was established in July of 1944 when a small group of Americans under Colonel David Barrett, the so-called 'Dixie Mission', visited Mao's headquarters in Yenan. Favourably impressed, they made plans for future collaboration. Those plans came to naught for a host of political reasons, however, and throughout the remainder of the war the Americans would thus do nothing to aid what in retrospect was the single most important and effective Asian resistance movement against the Japanese.[10]

The Americans did collaborate with Chiang's intelligence and guerrilla operations, primarily through SACO, the Sino-American Co-operative Organization headed by US Navy Rear Admiral Milton E. Miles and Chinese General Tai Li. Tai, however, was a notorious individual who also headed Chiang's secret police, and who used his extensive network of spies and assassins primarily to eliminate Chiang's domestic enemies, not the Japanese. Indeed, OSS reports called his organization the 'Chinese Gestapo' and Tai himself 'the Chinese Himmler' who, according to historian Michael Schaller, was 'notorious as an assassin, torturer, dope smuggler, and thief'. Nevertheless he was able to establish a strong friendship with Miles and receive US aid that was used to train additional secret police as well as guerrilla units. The latter fought not only the Japanese but also the Communists, which Tai Li saw as their primary purpose. Indeed, in Schaller's opinion, SACO's 'essential policy had been to help prepare the KMT for civil war', not attack the Japanese.[11]

Mao's guerrilla forces and operations did not defeat the Japanese Army in China, but they did hold that army in check and helped to keep China in the war. Ironically they also strengthened Mao's hand for the post-war conflict with Chiang by increasing enormously the territory and population he controlled, and by giving him both the experiences and the doctrine he would need to defeat Chiang between 1946 and 1949. Furthermore, they provided a model for the Vietnamese Communists under Ho Chi Minh in their struggles against the Japanese, French and Americans. As with resistance movements in Europe, those in Asia thus had consequences for the post-war world far more significant than their consequences for the military conduct of the war.

The scientific and intelligence revolutions

World War II witnessed a revolution in weapons technology. Related to this revolution was a redefinition and broadening of the relationship between scientists and the armed forces. Science and scientists had of course always played an important role in the development of new weapons. In World War II, however, that role was expanded enormously and institutionalized as a key component of the total war effort.

At the highest levels this resulted in the establishment within the United States of the important Office of Scientific Research and Development (OSRD) under Dr Vannevar Bush. In Britain, a Scientific Advisory Committee was attached to the War Cabinet. More importantly, Churchill maintained a personal and very powerful scientific adviser, his close friend Frederick Lindemann (Lord Cherwell).

At lower levels scientists actually studied operations so as to make their new weapons more effective in battle. Known as 'operational research', such analysis actually went far beyond weapons. It included food, clothing, medicine and even psychological studies. It also came to include turning the most advanced theoretical work, such as nuclear physics, into weapons. Churchill aptly summarized the overall result of this marriage of science to war by calling it 'the wizard war'.[12]

The list of both new and improved weapons developed during World War II is staggering. Armies, for example, obtained bigger and better tanks, anti-tank guns, hand-held anti-tank rockets (bazookas) and hand-carried automatic weapons as well as better clothing and scientifically determined food rations. Navies obtained radar and sonar. The new air forces were probably the biggest gainers, obtaining radar for offensive operations as well as defence, bigger and longer-range monoplane fighters and bombers, the Norden bombsight, jet engines, pilotless aircraft and rockets. The air forces were also some of the earliest users of scientists for military purposes, with Britain's Committee on Air Warfare under eminent physicist Sir Henry Tizard being established as far back as 1934.

Operational research constantly improved these inventions and came up with new ones. Particularly notable in this regard was the work of scientists within Britain's Combined Operations, under Admiral Lord Louis Mountbatten. Charged with developing methods for amphibious operations, these scientists came up with some of the most important, and some of the most bizarre, weapons of the war. In the former category were the landing craft, oil pipeline (PLUTO) and artificial harbours (MULBERRIES) that made possible the successful landing of the Allied armies and their equipment on the Normandy beaches in June of 1944. In the latter category was Pykrete, non-melting and shatterproof ice (made of sawdust and sea water) that Mountbatten wished to use in the creation of special aircraft carriers (code-named Project HABBAKUK).

As in other aspects of total war, the Axis powers originally held the lead in scientific research but squandered it as the war progressed. Nowhere was this more true than in the realm of intelligence, where a revolution was occurring.

Seeking to obtain and make effective use of vital military information about the enemy is as old as warfare itself, and it has traditionally involved the use of both spies and secret codes. Such traditional espionage activities continued throughout World War II, in Britain under MI5 and MI6 as well as the SOE, and in the United States under the OSS, the wartime predecessor to today's Central Intelligence Agency (CIA). During World War II, however, secret messages were for the first time sent in complex codes and ciphers created by machines rather than humans and transmitted via radio. Radio signals could of course be intercepted, but the key problem was how to break the new codes and ciphers. The revolutionary answer was a combination of the earliest and most primitive digital computers combined with human intelligence.

As previously noted, the British led the way with their code-breaking operations at Bletchley Park.[13] These focused on breaking the daily ciphers used by the Germans on their portable radio machines, ciphers the Germans considered unbreakable. Inside these machines, letter keys when pressed would electronically connect to three cylinders that were reset daily and send a coded message in which no key ever sent the same combination of coded letters twice in one message. The only way to read this message was to possess a copy of the machine and a copy of the codebook that revealed the daily cylinder settings.[14]

Unknown to the Germans, the British had obtained from the Poles and French a copy of the machine, which they named ENIGMA. They had then gathered at Bletchley Park, a Victorian mansion 50 miles northwest of London, some of the best minds in the country – most notably the brilliant mathematician Alan Turing, in an effort to crack the German codes (which they named ULTRA). As part of that effort they in effect created the first primitive computers. The entire effort was enormous, with the staff growing from 150 in 1939 to more than 10,000 by 1945, and the results were critical to Allied victory.

ULTRA had numerous limits, however. First of all, the codes had to be deciphered on a daily basis. Second, they covered only a small percentage of total German radio traffic. The entire effort also had to be kept top secret. That meant ULTRA information could not be acted upon unless the Germans could be convinced that the information came from another source. It also meant that distribution of this information was limited to senior commanders and placed outside normal intelligence channels. These procedures enabled the secret to be kept (it was not revealed until 1974), but at a cost of numerous missed opportunities. The early claim that Churchill allowed Coventry to be bombed in order to protect the secret is not true,[15] but in other situations action was not taken in order to maintain the secret, and senior commanders either missed or refused to believe what ULTRA revealed. On occasions, such as the September 1944 Battle of Arnhem, the intelligence 'pieces' were not put together. Two months later the massive build-up in the Ardennes revealed by ULTRA simply was not believed, and in the ensuing counter-offensive the Germans did not use radio messages.[16]

Throughout the war British and American cryptographers supplemented the intelligence supplied via ULTRA by breaking numerous other Axis codes and ciphers. The Americans had created a copy of the Japanese coding machine and cracked the Japanese diplomatic code even before Pearl Harbor (PURPLE/MAGIC). By 1942 they had also succeeded in cracking the key Japanese naval code, and would go on to break Japanese army and convoy codes as well, while the British broke the German U-boat code. In that year and in 1943, the British and Americans would agree to share these and future intelligence breakthroughs. Their successes and cooperation would play a major role in many of their military victories, including Midway and El Alamein.[17]

The Axis powers also broke numerous Allied codes and ciphers, however, and would often change their own, thereby necessitating a new round of code-breaking by the Allies. Furthermore, breaking a code or cipher by no means assured military victory. No British code-breaking success could overcome the massive Axis military superiority in 1941, for example. And even after that date, proper use of the information provided by code-breaking merely allowed for the possibility of victory. Moreover, such proper use was by no means guaranteed. Indeed, numerous senior Allied commanders misused or refused to believe the intelligence provided by ULTRA.

The intelligence revolution would nevertheless have a profound impact on the outcome of World War II. So would the scientific revolution. Nowhere was this impact more decisive than in the Anglo-American struggle throughout World War II against the German U-boats, a campaign known by Churchill's label as the 'Battle of the Atlantic'.[18]

The Battle of the Atlantic

As the historian Richard Overy has correctly noted, the United States and Great Britain were both primarily naval powers whose success in World War II depended first and foremost on their continued control of the seas.[19] Such control was necessary to implement the blockade and commando raid components of Britain's peripheral strategy. Furthermore, all of America's growing economic and military power would be worthless unless it could be projected overseas – both to support its British and Soviet allies via Lend-Lease supplies and to launch any offensive military operations. Indeed, without such control of the seas, no BOLERO concentration of American forces in England for Continental operations could take place, while Britain itself could be starved into submission (as Churchill later wrote, 'dominating all our power to carry on the war, or even keep ourselves alive, lay our mastery of the ocean routes and the free approach and entry to our ports')[20] and the Soviet Union could be forced to surrender, thereby ending any possibility of victory over Germany and leaving the United States totally isolated and forced to fight on its own soil. Consequently, the first two and the most important items in the Casablanca military accords concerned the related issues of the submarine menace on the high seas and assistance to Russia. 'The defeat of the U-boat', the Combined Chiefs of Staff insisted in their first major recommendation to Churchill and Roosevelt, 'must remain a first charge on the resources of the United Nations', while the Soviet Union, they maintained in their second point, 'must be sustained by the greatest volume of supplies that can be transported to Russia without prohibitive cost in shipping'.[21]

The problem, of course, was that German submarines were at that moment creating quite a 'prohibitive cost' in the shipping of supplies both to England and to Russia. Whereas the German surface navy may have been no match for the British fleet, Hitler's underwater vessels were more than a match for the combined Allied fleets. Indeed, despite Hitler's ground strength and relative naval weakness, the 'Battle of the Atlantic' may ironically have constituted his best chance of winning World War II by starving Britain into submission. Churchill later stated in this regard that 'The only thing that ever really frightened me during the war was the U-boat peril . . . I was even more anxious about this battle than I had ever been about the glorious air fight called the Battle of Britain.'[22]

A major U-boat campaign against Britain had not been part of the original German plan in World War II. Indeed, when the war began in 1939, Germany had a total of only 57 submarines, just 18 of which were operable

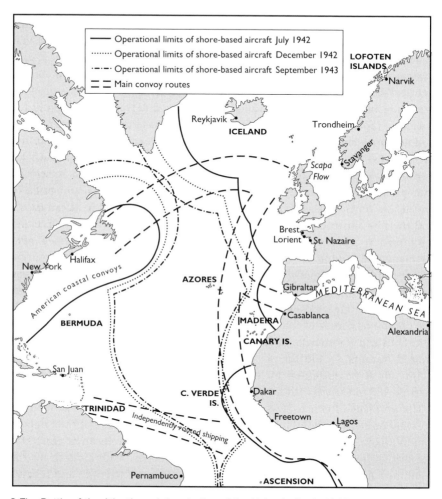

9 The Battle of the Atlantic and the closing of the 'Atlantic Gap', 1942–43

in the Atlantic. This was partially due to the fact that the Germans did not expect or plan for a long war of attrition, and because German naval commander-in-chief Admiral Erich Raeder's building programme was still far from complete in 1939. A veteran of the World War I Battle of Jutland, Raeder was also a proponent of surface warships and combat. U-boat commander Admiral Karl Dönitz, of course, thought differently, but he was unable to put his ideas fully into effect until he replaced Raeder as naval chief in early 1943.

An additional and related reason for the opposition Dönitz faced was the fact that his ideas ran counter to standard naval doctrines at the time. Those doctrines continued to be based on the writings of Alfred Thayer Mahan, a late nineteenth-century American naval captain and later admiral. In his classic and extraordinarily influential *The Influence of Seapower Upon History*[23] and other works, Mahan had maintained that naval supremacy was the key to national greatness and that it depended not upon commerce raiding, which he denigrated, but upon concentrated firepower in the form of the battleship fleet. These ideas found ready acceptance in all the world's major naval establishments – British, German and Japanese as well as American – where they quickly achieved the status of Holy Writ. US Secretary of War Henry L. Stimson would complain in this regard that the admirals 'frequently seemed to retire from the realm of logic into a dim religious world in which Neptune was God, Mahan his prophet, and the United States Navy the only true Church'.[24]

Against such a belief system, proponents of commerce raiding could at first make little headway, despite the successes German U-boats had achieved during World War I. Nevertheless, the very small German U-boat fleet did quite well against British naval and merchant vessels in the early years of World War II. So did the German surface fleet, in both its successful though costly amphibious invasion of Norway and its commerce raiding, and the *Luftwaffe* in its attacks against British shipping from new bases on the French and Norwegian coasts. Making use of broken British codes as well as those bases and new tactics (most notably 'wolf pack' submarine attacks at night), these combined German forces proceeded to sink over 1,000 British ships in 1940, totalling more than 4 million tons – 25 per cent of all British merchant shipping. Some 2 million more tons went down in just the first four months of 1941[25] and U-boats accounted for 70 per cent of these losses. To make matters even worse, Italy's entry into the war in June of 1940 added the large Italian surface and submarine forces in the Mediterranean to the naval enemies the British Navy and the merchant fleet had to face. Despite their defeats in the 1940–41 battles of Taranto and Cape Matapan, these Italian naval forces wreaked substantial damage on British Mediterranean shipping and naval forces – most notably in their successful submarine attack on the British fleet in Alexandria, Egypt, in December 1941.

As in World War I, the British responded to the submarine threat with naval convoys. Unlike World War I, however, they now possessed no naval bases in

France or Ireland from which to counter the threat to their shipping, while their enemies did possess naval and air bases on the Atlantic from which to attack them. Nor did the British possess after the fall of France any Allied naval support or sufficient naval escorts for effective convoy duty, even with the September 'destroyer–bases' deal with the United States. Nevertheless they were able to achieve temporary success by mid-1941 as a result of a series of new, favourable developments. These included ASDIC – better known as sonar – which could 'spot' submerged submarines; production of new small 'corvette' escort vessels; the addition of Canadian and US escorts; and the May capture of a U-boat with its ENIGMA machine and ciphers. ULTRA was indeed decisive at this time, but only for a brief period. Moreover, sonar was ineffective against night-time surface attacks by German wolf packs and was not capable of determining the depth of submerged U-boats. Consequently the British had to rely upon limited depth charge patterns (400 feet) that submarines could dive below.

The entry of the Soviet Union and the United States into the war in June and December of 1941 diverted German attention from the naval campaign but simultaneously added two new and highly vulnerable targets to their list: American coastal shipping and Arctic convoys proceeding to northern Russia. As a result of the lack of blackouts in American cities, German submarines had a field day sinking unprotected and silhouetted merchant ships in American coastal waters (over a million tons in May and June 1942 alone). And from their Norwegian bases, German surface, underwater and air forces devastated Allied convoys sailing from Britain to the north Russian ports of Murmansk and Archangel. In one of the worst shipping disasters of the war, the Germans in the summer of 1942 sank two-thirds of the ships in one such convoy, PQ-17, and thereby forced a total halt in northern convoys to Russia at a critical moment in the war.[26]

In early 1942 the Germans also changed their U-boat ciphers, thereby creating a virtual intelligence blackout that would last for nearly a year. Simultaneously, they succeeded in breaking the British naval cipher. The result was striking success in the first half of the year. Dönitz had estimated that he needed to sink 700,000 tons of Allied shipping a month to starve Britain into submission; by June he had reached that magic figure.

Anglo-American forces responded to this mortal threat in multiple ways. Expanded convoys with US warships were introduced, while blackouts were instituted in US coastal cities and American merchant ship production expanded in an effort to compensate for previous losses. Especially notable in this regard were the mass-production techniques that Henry Kaiser introduced to make 'Liberty Ships', techniques that cut the time needed to build one of these merchant vessels from 355 to 41 days.[27] The Allies also made use of non-ULTRA intelligence to avoid submarines as well as locate them for attack by their own forces, and began to commit ground and naval air forces in the form of long-range, ground-based aircraft and the new 'escort' carriers – former merchant ships converted via the addition of a flight deck for naval aircraft.

They also refined radar so that their aircraft could detect surface submarines at night, and improved their anti-submarine tactics.

Such methods were at first successful in reducing the quantity of Allied tonnage sunk, but the Germans in turn countered with a new device that could detect radar (METOX) and thereby enable their U-boats to dive before being attacked, plus additional and improved submarines. By November they were back up to Dönitz's magic figure of 700,000 tons per month. By year's end the total was 1,662 ships with a combined tonnage of 7,800,000 tons.[28] That was one million tons more than the Allies had been able to build in 1942. Some 80 per cent of this tonnage had been sunk by U-boats, with the largest percentage being sunk in the so-called 'Atlantic Gap' or 'Black Pit', an area beyond the reach of ground-based, long-range aircraft. In early 1943 Dönitz replaced Raeder as German naval commander and brought in even more submarines. By March he had reached the peak of his success, sinking over 600,000 tons of Allied shipping in three weeks and forcing another halt to all Arctic convoys. Allied merchant seamen had by this time developed what one scholar has aptly called 'a grim appreciation of their chances' for survival, measured in how one slept:

> If you carried iron ore, you slept on deck, for if hit by a torpedo, there were only seconds to get clear. If you carried general cargo, you could sleep below decks, but had to leave your door open, and sleep with your clothes on so you would have time to get out. If you were a tanker carrying aviation gas, you could undress, close your cabin door, and have a good night's sleep, because if you were hit, it wasn't going to make any difference at all; you'd never get out anyway.[29]

Given Dönitz's successes, the Allies during the January Casablanca Conference had to make defeat of the U-boat threat their top priority. They were able to achieve dramatic success within five months, primarily as a result of a major intelligence breakthrough and a massive, coordinated Anglo-American campaign.

In the intelligence realm, ULTRA came back on line, thereby enabling the British not only once again to 'read' German submarine traffic, but also to realize that their own naval cipher had been broken and to take appropriate counter-measures. Under British Admiral Max Horton, the new and highly co-ordinated anti-submarine campaign included support groups of fast frigates as well as destroyers to aid convoy escorts by hunting down submarines, the High Frequency Direction Finding (HF/DF, or 'Huff-Duff') technology that enabled the Allies to detect any U-boat using its radio, better anti-submarine ordnance and delivery systems ('hedgehog' mortars and contact fuses for depth charges), and major air support via expanded use of both long-range, shore-based aircraft to close the Atlantic Gap (including the B-24 'Liberator' bomber) and escort carriers to provide the convoys with close air support. Anti-submarine aircraft in turn possessed greatly improved technology, including new, undetectable air-to-surface radar and large searchlights for evening patrols, as well as better training for their pilots. Simultaneously, American ship production continued to accelerate and began to surpass losses.

The climax occurred during the months of March, April and May, when the rate of loss for Allied shipping was at first slowed and then reversed. Simultaneously, Dönitz began to lose more U-boats to Allied attacks. In May, the number of losses reached the prohibitive figure of 41, bringing the total for the first five months of 1943 to nearly 100.[30] This forced Dönitz to call off the offensive and withdraw his submarines from the North Atlantic. At the same time, the success of Allied ground forces in Tunisia provided new air bases from which to control Axis submarine attacks in the Mediterranean.

Dönitz regrouped his forces during the summer of 1943 and in September renewed his U-boat offensive in the Atlantic. By this time he possessed the new Walter high speed submarine, a homing torpedo, and a snorkel device that enabled his boats to remain submerged indefinitely. But the Walter was plagued by numerous technical problems that precluded its use in combat, and the Allies were able to foil the homing torpedo with a 'fixer' device that diverted it. Consequently, his renewed offensive accomplished little. Indeed, by early 1944, U-boat losses far exceeded Allied merchant ship losses, forcing Dönitz once again to halt operations. Simultaneously the British in late 1943–44 sank two of Hitler's few remaining capital ships along the Arctic convoy route: the battlecruiser *Scharnhorst* and the battleship *Tirpitz*. Dönitz continued to build submarines, however, and by March of 1945 his fleet had reached a high point of 462 ships. But technical difficulties continued to plague the Walter, and by this time fuel shortages precluded extensive use. In reality, the campaign had ended in failure by the end of 1943.

It had been an extremely costly campaign for both sides. The Allies lost 21.6 million tons of merchant shipping during the war. The U-boats were responsible for 14 million of these tons – a total of 2,828 ships. The British alone lost 60,000 men at sea, half of them merchant seamen and half of them navy personnel. Yet they and the Americans sank 784 of Germany's 1,170 submarines and killed 28,000 of the 39,000 total German submariners – one of the highest casualty rates for any branch of any national service during the war – and in the end won the campaign. The reasons for their success were numerous, with no one factor directly responsible. As Richard Overy has noted, those factors reached a critical combined mass in the late spring of 1943 with the simultaneous introduction of improved anti-submarine training, tactics and weaponry, expanded use of airpower, the revival of ULTRA, and the introduction of new Allied codes. The revival of ULTRA was certainly important, but by itself far from decisive. Indeed, Overy and others have concluded that expanded use of Allied airpower was probably the most important factor in closing the Atlantic Gap and ensuring victory – not only by sinking submarines, but more importantly by forcing the U-boats to stay under water to avoid detection and thereby precluding their ability even to keep up with the convoys.[31]

Only 37 long-range aircraft were needed to close that gap. Yet the British and American Air Forces strongly resisted any such use of their planes and crews for this mission. So did the US Navy, which consistently diverted needed aircraft to the Pacific and rejected any unity of command in the Atlantic until April. Two related reasons for this navy obstructionism were US inter-service rivalries and Admiral King's Anglophobia. Air Force resistance, on the other hand, was primarily the result of an insistence on concentrating all long-range aircraft for a task most British and American air officers considered more vital: the bombing of German cities. As historian John Buckley has aptly noted, 'The fact that defeat in the Atlantic would in fact have meant defeat in the war curiously evaded the minds of those who saw no value in the redeployment of a small fraction of the Allied air forces to keep the U-boat menace at bay.'[32] That evasion was primarily the result of their continued belief that strategic bombing could by itself force a quick and complete German surrender, all evidence to the contrary notwithstanding.

The strategic bombing campaign

As previously noted, airpower theorists had argued during the inter-war years that fleets of independent bombers could win a war quickly, decisively and with relatively low casualties by attacking enemy cities, thereby destroying the industrial capacity of the enemy and/or the civilian will to resist.[33] (Although they usually used the term 'vital centres' instead of cities per se, such centres were usually in urban areas.) British and American air officers firmly believed in this approach and attempted to implement it even before the Casablanca Accords made it a high Allied priority. Indeed, strategic bombing of Germany had long been a major component of British peripheral strategy, and it remained a major component of Anglo-American combined strategy throughout the war.

It was also one of the most controversial components of the Anglo-American war effort. Both during and after the war, three major controversies emerged regarding the theory and practice of Allied strategic bombing. The first concerned the validity of the theory and the effectiveness of the actual campaign, with critics arguing that it did not work and that it resulted in massive casualties as well as the diversion of Allied resources from more productive uses. The second controversy focused on the relative effectiveness of daytime 'precision' strategic bombing as espoused by the Americans vs night-time 'area' bombing as practised by the British. The third controversy concerned the morality of the entire campaign, with critics arguing that it constituted unjustified war against an entire civilian populace and consequent indiscriminate killing.

Although the German *Luftwaffe* had bombed civilians as far back as the Spanish Civil War (as immortalized in Pablo Picasso's painting 'Guernica'), they did so primarily as a terror tactic designed to help disrupt enemy communications and ground forces. Their air doctrine and campaigns thus remained essentially tactical in nature. Even in the Battle of Britain, their overall aim was to make possible a successful invasion of England – not replace it. Britain's Royal Air Force (RAF), on the other hand, embraced strategic bombing during the inter-war years and began to apply it in 1940, both out of belief and out of desperation: by the summer of 1940 London had virtually no other weapon with which to hurt the Germans.

The results, however, were quite disappointing. The bombers proved to be wildly inaccurate, while the inter-war belief that 'the bomber will always get through' proved to be totally false. In reality, British bombers could not defend themselves against the faster and more agile German fighters, which shot the former down with frightening frequency. Nor did the British possess any fighter with adequate range to protect their bombers from this German counter-assault. Consequently the British turned to night-time bombing, which in turn only increased their inaccuracy as well as German civilian deaths. An August 1941 British study revealed that only one in five sorties reached within five miles of the target, leaving Churchill deeply upset over the 'awful thought that perhaps three quarters of our bombs go astray'.[34]

By early 1942 the RAF's high casualties and inaccuracy had forced the British to agree to a fundamental shift and modification in their air strategy. Henceforth Bomber Command would focus its efforts on undermining German morale and destroying its productive capacity through massive night-time air attacks aimed at sections of German cities (supposedly where workers' housing was located but in reality a far larger area given the inaccuracies of night-time bombing). Although initiated before his appointment, new Bomber Command Chief Air Marshal Sir Arthur 'Bomber' Harris was one of the firmest adherents to this approach and soon came to be totally associated with it. As airpower historian Tami Davis Biddle has aptly stated, 'Harris's goal was destruction by the square yard; if he could destroy large stretches of Germany's largest cities, he would bring the war to a close'.[35]

The result of this shift in British air strategy was a series of thousand-plane night-time 'firebombing raids' against major German cities, beginning with Cologne in May and moving on to Lübeck, Rostock, Essen and Bremen. As with the Battle of Britain, these resulted in a large number of civilian deaths and much destruction, but with very little impact on German industry or port facilities and virtually no impact on civilian morale, save perhaps to strengthen it just as German bombing had strengthened British morale in 1940.

The US Army Air Forces (AAF) refused to accept the British approach and maintained their faith in daylight precision bombing of specific industries. Possessing excellent and heavily armed long-range bombers in the B-17 'Flying Fortress' and the B-24 'Liberator' as well as the new and accurate Norden bombsight, the Americans continued to maintain that such an approach could destroy Germany's industrial capacity to resist without prohibitive Allied losses. The newly established US 8th Air Force in England under Major Generals Carl Spaatz and Ira Eaker launched major daylight raids

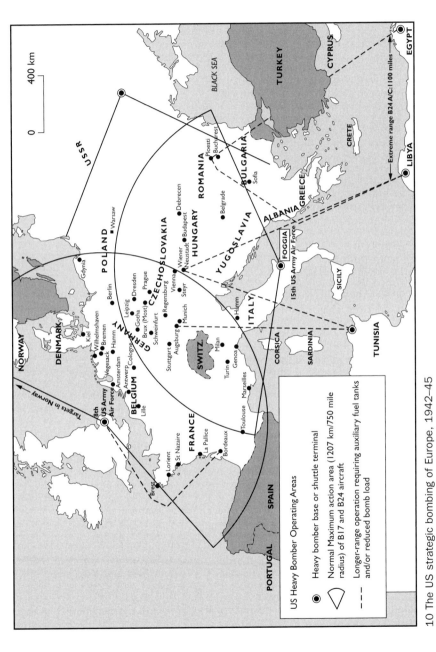

10 The US strategic bombing of Europe, 1942–45

US Heavy Bomber Operating Areas

⊙ Heavy bomber base or shuttle terminal

△ Normal Maximum action area (1207 km/750 mile radius) of B17 and B24 aircraft

--- Longer-range operation requiring auxiliary fuel tanks and/or reduced bomb load

0   400 km

Extreme range B24 A/C:1100 miles

Targets in Norway

8th US Army Air Force

15th US Army Air Force

FOGGIA

NORWAY
DENMARK
GERMANY
Kiel Wilhelmshaven Bremen Hamm
Wegesack
Amsterdam
Antwerp Cologne
BELGIUM
Lille
Brux (Most) Leipzig Dresden
Gotha
Schweinfurt Regensburg Prague
Stuttgart Augsburg Munich
Wiener
Neustadt Vienna Steyr
SWITZ.
Milan
Turin Genoa
Toulouse
Marseilles
FRANCE
La Pallice
Bordeaux
St Nazaire
Lorient
Brest
PORTUGAL
SPAIN
POLAND
Gdynia
Berlin
Warsaw
CZECHOSLOVAKIA
HUNGARY
Budapest Debrecen
YUGOSLAVIA
Belgrade
ROMANIA
Ploesti
Bucharest
BULGARIA
Sofia
ALBANIA GREECE
ITALY
Hamm
CORSICA
SARDINIA
SICILY
TUNISIA
CRETE
TURKEY
BLACK SEA
CYPRUS
LIBYA EGYPT
USSR

beginning in August of 1942. As with the 1940 British effort, however, the successes were few and the casualties very high.

Despite these failures, Churchill, Roosevelt and the Combined Chiefs of Staff agreed at the Casablanca Conference to expand the strategic bombing of Germany and make it a very high military priority; 1943 operations in the European theatre were to include 'the heaviest possible bomber offensive against the German war effort', with a special CCS directive defining the object of this offensive, code-named Operation POINTBLANK, as 'the progressive destruction and dislocation of the German military, industrial and economic system, and the undermining of the morale of the German people to a point where their capacity for armed resistance is fatally weakened'.[36]

In light of previous failures, this expanded commitment to strategic bombing at Casablanca does not appear very rational – at least not from the point of view of past military effectiveness. Of course, airpower advocates argued that past failures had been due to inadequate resources, and that an expanded campaign would be more successful. But when their superiors agreed, they did so primarily for political as opposed to military reasons: with the decision to focus on Italy in the Mediterranean and in all likelihood not cross the Channel in 1943, *some* major military activity against Germany was mandatory for public opinion – and for the Russians. Far from coincidentally in this regard, Churchill during his August 1942 visit to Moscow had attempted to soften the news of no second front that year with an emphasis on the destruction his bombers could wreak on the Germans. Stalin warmed to the news and, 'Between the two of them', according to American eyewitness W. Averell Harriman, 'they soon destroyed most of the important industrial cities of Germany.'[37] That such destruction could be wrought without the massive casualties of World War I trench warfare remained a key factor in the continued appeal of strategic bombing within Great Britain and the United States, as it had been since the inter-war years. And with so much already invested in this approach and a massive bomber force in the process of being created, abandoning or downgrading the campaign would have been extremely difficult, if indeed possible.

At Casablanca, Churchill, Roosevelt and the CCS resolved the Anglo-American dispute over daylight precision vs night-time area bombing with a simple compromise which was, in effect, 'an agreement to disagree':[38] both approaches would be used, with each air force proceeding in its own way. Targets were prioritized, with first priority going to German submarine construction yards. But the priority order could be 'varied from time to time according to developments in the strategical situation', while 'other objectives of great importance either from the political or military point of view must be attacked'. Examples of such objectives included submarine operating bases and Berlin, 'which should be attacked when conditions are suitable for the attainment of specially valuable results unfavorable to the morale of the enemy or favorable to that of Russia'.[39]

A series of major campaigns would be launched against Germany in 1943 as a result of this Casablanca directive: against German submarines and construction yards; against German aircraft production; and against German cities. From March to July, the bombers focused on the industrial Ruhr area; then against the large port city of Hamburg in July and August; and then against Berlin from November through to March of the following year. Using foil strips known as 'Window' to confuse German radar, the bombers dropped incendiary bombs to create an enormous conflagration. Known as a 'firestorm', it sucked in enormous quantities of air and spread with incredible rapidity, destroying everything in its path and killing tens of thousands by suffocation as well as immolation. Three-quarters of Hamburg was destroyed by British bombers in this manner, with at least 40,000 and perhaps as many as 100,000 civilians killed.

Despite the massive devastation and death toll, these raids were strategic failures by the definitions the strategic airpower advocates had previously established. German morale did not collapse, and war production actually increased under the brilliant leadership of the new armaments minister, Albert Speer. Furthermore, the Germans learned how to counter 'Window' and developed better radar and anti-aircraft tactics. They also expanded their fighter aircraft production. As a result, they inflicted very heavy losses on Allied planes and crews.

Given the conflicting British and US air doctrines and resulting activities, the 1943 campaign was for the most part not a combined offensive at all. In the words of the official British history, it was 'on the contrary, a bombing competition'.[40] British Bomber Command continued to focus on German cities in the continued incorrect belief that the German economy was already stretched to its limits and therefore could not stand any additional strain. In line with their own continued belief in precision daylight bombing, the US 8th Air Force responded by focusing on key components of the German aircraft industry so as to decrease, if not halt, the production of new German fighters. This was to an extent successful, but again at the cost of very heavy casualties. The October raid on the Schweinfurt ball-bearing plant, for example, resulted in the destruction of 60 and damaging of 138 of the 291 bombers involved.

Such losses were prohibitive and could not be maintained. Indeed, by the end of 1943, Operation POINTBLANK had to be considered a costly failure. If the bombing offensive was to continue and succeed, some protection had to be found for the Allied bombers. The obvious answer was Allied fighter aircraft to escort them and counter the German fighters. The problem was that no British or US fighters possessed the range to accompany the bombers over Germany. By late 1943, however, detachable extra fuel tanks, known as 'drop tanks', had been effectively added to the P-38 Lightning and P-47 Thunderbolt fighters, increasing their range dramatically. At the same time the Allies developed in the P-51 Mustang, an American aircraft with a powerful British engine, a long-range fighter superior in speed and manoeuvrability to German fighters. These new escorts helped the expanded and reorganized US Strategic Air Forces in Europe (USSTAF) now under Spaatz's overall command to achieve great success in their February 1944 attacks (later called 'Big Week') on German aircraft and air engine plants.[41]

By this time, however, the Allies had agreed to cross the Channel in the spring of 1944, and invasion commander General Dwight D. Eisenhower and his British deputy commander, Air Chief Marshal Sir Arthur Tedder, insisted that the US and British Air Forces must be diverted from their missions over Germany to missions in direct support of the invasion – most notably via the destruction of railroads and bridges in northern France so as to isolate the bridgehead and via support of the Allied armies after their 6 June landing. These missions were highly effective and played a major role in Allied success on the ground,[42] but they were tactical missions that, according to the strategic airpower proponents, hindered their ability to accomplish what they considered their more important and decisive strategic mission. Additional diversions occurred in the summer of 1944 when they attempted in Operation CROSSBOW (unsuccessfully as it turned out) to destroy the sites from which Hitler was launching against England his V-1 'Flying Bombs' and V-2 rocket bombs as revenge and terror weapons; these would kill another 9,000 British civilians before the sites were overrun by Allied armies.

Whether primarily the result of such diversions or doctrinal fallacies, the strategic bombing campaign clearly was not working – save in two very important and unexpected senses. By early 1944 it was obvious that bombing had not destroyed either German industrial capacity to resist or German civilian will to resist, as its proponents claimed it would. But it was diverting German war production from weapons that could be used against Allied armies, such as artillery pieces, to weapons such as anti-aircraft guns for use against the bombers. Equally, if not more important, with the establishment of long-range fighter escort and the American capacity to produce enormous quantities of these fighters, the air campaign was destroying the German *Luftwaffe* via simple attrition.

Recognizing this fact, and realizing that achievement of air superiority was critical to the success of OVERLORD, the Allies increasingly emphasized as a key goal of their bombing campaign in late 1943–early 1944 the destruction of the German Air Force through a 'counter-force' campaign of attrition. In effect, the bombers and their crews became the 'bait', attacking targets the Germans felt they had to defend and thereby luring their limited number of fighters and trained pilots into the sky where increasing numbers of superior Allied fighters with extended range could destroy them. The *Luftwaffe* would be literally blown out of existence by this campaign, with 98 per cent of all German fighter pilots either killed or maimed by war's end.[43] That in turn provided the Allied armies with total control of the air, which would be critical to their success on the ground in 1944. Indeed, the Germans would be able to mount only a handful of air sorties against the Anglo-American armies landing at Normandy in June of 1944. The successful attrition campaign also eased the strain on both the American 'precision' and British 'area' campaigns of 1944–45 and thus played a major role in their ensuing successes.

Even during the spring and summer of 1944, Eisenhower had agreed to allow those campaigns (most notably against German oil production) to proceed with excess bombers that were not needed for the OVERLORD campaign. Then in the autumn Allied bombers began an expanded campaign that focused, first, on the oil industry and then on transport within Germany, given the success of the transport campaign around Normandy, but with Harris and Bomber Command free to attack cities whenever poor weather precluded such precision attacks. With greatly expanded bomber forces now available and virtually no *Luftwaffe* resistance to face, these oil and transport campaigns appeared to be highly effective in crippling the German war effort and thereby proving the validity of strategic bombing doctrine. But the Red Army simultaneously seized the Ploesti oilfields and key resources in Upper Silesia while Anglo-American ground forces attacked the industrial Ruhr, thereby questioning just how pivotal the bombing campaign really was in the final collapse of the German war machine.

Allied bombing attacks continued and actually increased throughout the rest of 1944 and well into 1945. Approximately one and a half million tons of bombs would be dropped on Germany, more than 70 per cent of them after 1 July 1944. Officially, the Americans continued to maintain their doctrine of precision bombing. As Arnold's staff had argued in 1943, 'our own concept of the proper role of air power in war . . . works on the principle of the old adage to the effect that for the lack of a nail the house fell down. We take away the nail.' Such precision, the staff maintained, was 'the keynote of America . . . We hold no brief for terror bombing.'[44] Yet the distinction between the American precision approach and British area bombing tended to blur and often disappear in reality, especially in light of the heavy cloud cover and bad weather that covered much of Europe during the autumn and winter months. This tendency increased as obvious industrial targets disappeared. The classic case occurred on 13–15 February 1945, when continuous bombing of Dresden by both British and American air forces resulted in a firestorm that destroyed the entire city and killed 35,000 civilians – most of them women, children and the elderly. And in the war against Japan, the Americans were totally abandoning their precision doctrine in favour of the British area approach. By the time Germany surrendered, every one of its major cities had been destroyed with a human cost of 400,000 civilian dead and 400,000 more injured. In the process, the British and Americans lost 40,000 planes and 160,000 men. Most of the latter were bomber crews, with the death and total casualty rates for such crews in Bomber Command over 50 and 75 per cent, respectively.[45]

This constituted one of the highest casualty rates for any branch of Allied service, and it led critics to question whether what had been accomplished had been worth the enormous cost. As previously noted, strategic bombing did not accomplish what its proponents said it would. Indeed, German industrial production actually went up 300 per cent from 1941–44, and German civilian morale was not destroyed. Furthermore, critics charge, the indiscriminate killing of civilians inherent in strategic bombing, and to some extent planned by the air strategists, did not differ much from Nazi treatment of civilians. It thus reduced the Allies to the barbaric moral level of their enemies.

Supporters of the air campaign counter that there are no non-combatants in total war and that industrial workers, be they male or female, are just as valid targets as soldiers. They also maintain that the bombing prevented German production from going up even more than it did by preventing Speer from reaching his production goals. Moreover, it negatively affected German morale in that German workers became tired, highly strung and cautious. This in turn negatively affected their productivity. The bombing campaign also diverted German resources away from the fronts to fighter production and anti-aircraft defence, with very positive consequences for Allied ground forces. Similarly, the attrition campaign effectively destroyed the *Luftwaffe* and provided the Allies with critically important control of the air during the 1944–45 campaigns in Europe.

These were largely tactical air successes, however, in that they assisted rather than replaced ground forces. By the standards airpower theorists had themselves established before the war, the campaign was a failure. It did not result in a brief war, lower overall casualties, break enemy morale, destroy the enemy economy, or make irrelevant massive ground forces. It did help those ground forces enormously, however, and it played a major, perhaps a decisive role in their eventual victory. Whether that was worth the cost in lives lost and moral opprobrium incurred remains an open question.

7

SEIZING THE INITIATIVE AND REDEFINING THE COALITION, JANUARY–NOVEMBER 1943

The Allies would not be able in 1943 to complete all the military tasks they had set themselves at the Casablanca Conference. Nevertheless their accomplishments during the year were substantial, and in effect completed the seizing of the strategic initiative from the Axis that they had begun in late 1942. While the Soviets forced the surrender of the German 6th Army at Stalingrad, threw back a third German offensive at Kursk and then launched a major counter-offensive of their own,[1] Anglo-American forces completed the conquest of North Africa in May and successfully invaded Sicily in July and the Italian mainland in September. The Sicilian invasion also resulted in Mussolini's ousting and Italy's surrender. In the Pacific, the Americans in 1943 successfully completed the critical Guadalcanal campaign, continued to advance with their Australasian allies in the Solomon Islands and New Guinea, largely isolated the major Japanese base at Rabaul, and began a second line of advance through the Gilbert Islands in the Central Pacific.

1943 was also the year of numerous and critical Allied meetings, beginning with the previously discussed Casablanca Conference in January. At two ensuing strategic summit conferences, in Washington during May and Quebec during August, the British and Americans agreed to a major cross-Channel attack for the spring of 1944 and to multiple offensives against Japan on the Asian mainland as well as in the Pacific. Then during the autumn of 1943, a series of tripartite conferences with Soviet and Chinese leaders in Moscow, Cairo and Teheran firmly established a global Allied strategy for the duration of the war and basic plans for the post-war era.

In the process of making these plans and achieving these victories, however, the Allies redefined their relationship. On the basis of the growing American and declining British contribution to the war effort, the United States began to emerge as the senior partner in the 'special relationship'. It also emerged as a nation that appeared more interested in close relations with the other ascendant power, the Soviet Union, than the weakened United Kingdom. This would be fully illustrated at what was in many ways the most important of the 1943 conferences – the first Anglo-Soviet-American summit meeting at Teheran in late November.

Victory in Tunisia

As previously noted, the British 8th Army under General Montgomery had in late October defeated Rommel's Afrika Korps at El Alamein in the Egyptian desert, while Anglo-American forces under General Eisenhower had successfully invaded French North Africa in early November of 1942. Eisenhower's forces had failed to beat the Germans in the race to occupy Tunisia, however, an area Hitler quickly seized and heavily reinforced under the command of General von Arnim in late 1942. This provided Rommel with a defensible sanctuary behind the old French Mareth Line in southern Tunisia where the Afrika Korps could regroup and link up with von Arnim's forces. They did so in late January, thereby creating a large and formidable Axis force in a very defensible position.[2]

Facing that force, however, would be even larger Allied forces on two fronts: Eisenhower's Anglo-American army in the west, and Montgomery's British 8th Army advancing from the east. Once Montgomery reached the Mareth Line in southern Tunisia, Axis troops would be trapped in what resembled a huge automotive cylinder, with Eisenhower's troops and the Mediterranean Sea as the 'walls' and Montgomery's army as the potential 'piston'. Rommel considered the situation strategically hopeless and recommended complete withdrawal from Tunisia, leaving all of North Africa in Allied hands but saving hundreds of thousands of Axis soldiers. Hitler, however, refused to agree and instead continued to pour reinforcements into the area. Had he so reinforced Rommel a year earlier, he could have won all of North Africa and perhaps the Middle East. Now he merely multiplied his losses.

Forced to defend Tunisia, Rommel in February decided to turn westward and attack the still 'green' American troops at Kasserine Pass before Montgomery arrived in full force at the Mareth Line. Despite ULTRA, the American 2nd Corps under General Fredendall was caught by surprise and suffered a humiliating defeat. But Rommel fell short of his desired breakthrough, primarily because of non-cooperation from von Arnim, who was not under his control, and because of limits placed upon his operations by superiors who insisted that he pursue objectives more limited than he wished. Instead of his desired attack on the Tebessa supply base, they ordered him to attack northwestward through Kasserine Pass toward Thala and Sbiba — exactly where the Allies expected him. Consequently they were able to stop him and limit their losses to a tactical, as opposed to a major strategic defeat. Rommel then shifted his forces southward and on 6 March attacked the segments of the 8th Army that had arrived opposite the Mareth Line at Medenine, but ULTRA warnings enabled Montgomery to rush additional forces to the area and force the Germans to withdraw. When Rommel again urged evacuation, Hitler instead relieved him of command and placed all Axis forces in Tunisia under von Arnim.

By this time all Allied forces in North Africa had been combined and reorganized as the 18th Army Group, consisting of the British 8th Army in the south and the Anglo-French-American 1st Army in the west. Eisenhower was the overall commander. General Sir Harold Alexander, former commander of all British forces in the Middle East, became his deputy and the overall ground commander. Finding the Allied command situation abysmal, Alexander warned Eisenhower that British, French and US units were all mixed up, that there was no overall plan, and that the Germans had regained the initiative. As a result of these warnings and the Kasserine Pass débâcle, Allied forces were soon reorganized. Montgomery remained in command of the British 8th Army, but Fredendall was relieved of command of the US 2nd Corps and replaced by Patton, who quickly restored discipline and morale.

George S. 'Old Blood and Guts' Patton ('our blood; his guts' was the GI rejoinder to that nickname) would quickly emerge as one of the most brilliant US generals in World War II. He would also be one of the most controversial. Indeed, in all likelihood he was simultaneously the most brilliant and the most controversial. A former cavalry officer, World War I veteran and armoured warfare expert, he was already a major general when the United States officially entered the war. But he was also extremely outspoken and eccentric, to the point of being considered by many to be unbalanced and dangerous. Contemptuous of the British, extremely right-wing in his political views and consistently unable to keep his mouth shut, he was the proverbial 'loose cannon' and not exactly an individual capable of promoting Anglo-American cooperation. He was more than capable of whipping the 2nd Corps into shape, however, and of leading it to success against the Germans. Throughout the war he would provide his old friend Eisenhower with some of his greatest victories – and greatest headaches.

In the second half of March, Montgomery launched first an unsuccessful direct attack and then a successful flanking attack on the Mareth Line while Patton applied pressure from the west, forcing a series of German retreats by mid-April into a pocket around Tunis and Bizerte. Simultaneously Allied naval forces and a reorganized and unified air command under British Air Marshal Sir Arthur Tedder took full control of the sea and air and prevented major supplies or reinforcements from reaching von Arnim. On 22 April, Alexander launched a major offensive by all his ground forces that succeeded in taking Tunis and Bizerte by early May and forcing the remaining 170,000 Axis forces onto the Cape Bon peninsula. Surrounded, with virtually no fuel, ammunition or hope of rescue, they surrendered on 13 May, bringing the total of Axis prisoners of war in the campaign to a staggering 238,000.

The TRIDENT and Algiers Conferences

The final German surrender in Tunisia took place as Roosevelt, Churchill and the Combined Chiefs of Staff were beginning another major strategic conference in Washington, code-named TRIDENT. As at Casablanca, the British pressed for continuation of their Mediterranean strategy, with Churchill proposing that Italy be invaded and knocked out of the war after the conquest of

Sicily (Operation HUSKY), while cross-Channel operations were postponed until 1944. Such operations, he argued, could not be launched before that date anyway, and Anglo-American forces could not remain inactive after HUSKY – for diplomatic as well as military reasons: such inactivity, the prime minister noted, would have a 'serious effect on relations with Russia'. Italian collapse, on the other hand, was the 'great prize' now available to the Allies. It would lead not only to the surrender of the Italian fleet and armies, but also to the entrance of Turkey into the war and the opening of the Dardanelles, thereby providing a new and short supply route to Russia and forcing Hitler either to give up the Balkans or reinforce the area by withdrawing troops from the eastern front. Only in this way could large-scale relief be given to the Russians in 1943. Drawing parallels with the Bulgarian surrender of 1918, Churchill further argued that Italian collapse would 'cause a chill of loneliness over the German people, and might be the beginning of their doom'.[3]

The Americans disagreed vehemently – and this time with a unified voice. Infuriated by their defeat at Casablanca, the Joint Chiefs had totally revamped their committee structure during the spring of 1943 and now presented a strong united front against British Mediterranean proposals, which they considered a politically inspired effort to advance British post-war political interests in the area as well as militarily counter-productive. General Marshall argued that the Mediterranean would prove to be a 'vacuum' that would suck in resources and men, thereby delaying cross-Channel operations even beyond 1944 and with them the defeat of Japan as well as Germany. Joined by the rest of the JCS, the US Army Chief threatened in return to focus on the Pacific as the favoured American 'sideshow' if the British insisted on continued focus on their Mediterranean 'sideshow'.[4]

British General Ismay had noted an 'unmistakable atmosphere of tension' at the beginning of the conference that promised a 'battle royal'.[5] His assessment was accurate. As deadlock ensued, the CCS at Marshall's suggestion went 'off the record', with all planners and assistants as well as minute-takers dismissed. The British and American Chiefs then had a series of 'off-the-record', 'heart-to-heart' talks – and heated arguments.

Out of these sessions eventually emerged a compromise strategic plan for 1943–44. In the European theatre, the British agreed to a definite cross-Channel assault with a target date of 1 May 1944, while the Americans agreed to additional Mediterranean operations in 1943 after HUSKY 'to eliminate Italy from the war and to contain the maximum number of German forces'. But these were to be undertaken with a specifically limited force, and with provisions for seven veteran divisions to be held in readiness by 1 November for withdrawal from the Mediterranean in order to take part in the 1944 cross-Channel assault. In the Far East, the British agreed to an extension of the war against Japan on multiple fronts. In the South and Southwest Pacific, Allied forces were to continue their campaigns so as to capture the rest of the Solomon Islands and New Guinea as well as the Bismarck Archipelago. Simultaneously the US Navy would begin its Central Pacific drive with the seizure of the Marshall and Caroline Islands, while the Japanese were to be ejected from the Aleutian Islands in the North Pacific that they had seized in 1942. On the Asian mainland, the air supplies to China over the 'Hump' were to be expanded while land and amphibious operations were launched into Burma, though here the Americans agreed to a smaller scale than the operation that had been planned at Casablanca (ANAKIM).[6]

Churchill objected strongly to this compromise. He had come to Washington this third time 'only' for the purpose, he told his physician, of obtaining agreement to invade Italy proper – a commitment the Americans refused to give. Correctly fearing that they might insist instead on a minor attack against Sardinia, he vehemently attacked the CCS compromise accord on 24 May and pleaded instead for an agreement to invade Italy – and perhaps the Balkans as well. This time, however, Roosevelt did not support him. Humiliated by the fact that their president had throughout 1942 and early 1943 supported Churchill's strategic arguments against their own, the American Joint Chiefs had since the Casablanca Conference devoted much effort to achieving a united front with Roosevelt as well as among themselves. That effort now paid off. Feeling that the prime minister was acting like a 'spoiled boy', the president at one point told him point-blank to 'shut up' and, with Hopkins' assistance, forced him to accept the CCS compromise.[7]

In return, however, Roosevelt acceded to Churchill's request that General Marshall accompany the prime minister to Algiers for a strategy conference with Eisenhower and his associates. Here Churchill once again tried to convince the American Army chief to commit to an invasion of the Italian mainland, including the capture of Rome. Such an invasion, he argued from 29 May to 3 June, was the only 1943 operation capable of diverting German forces not only from the eastern front, but also from northern France – which would be necessary for success in any 1944 cross-Channel assault.

By now Marshall had learned the futility of engaging in prolonged strategic debate with the eloquent prime minister. Instead he continued to insist that the final decision on exactly how to eliminate Italy from the war await the results of HUSKY, Eisenhower's recommendations and the looming battles on the Eastern Front. Eisenhower in turn made it clear that he would indeed recommend invasion of the mainland if HUSKY proved to be an easy operation, a statement that mollified Churchill and convinced him that the Americans would 'almost certainly' pick the mainland over Sardinia.[8] They eventually did, albeit with far more limited objectives in mind than the prime minister.

The invasion of Sicily and the fall of Mussolini

The Anglo-American invasion of Sicily, Operation HUSKY, was led once again by Eisenhower, with British Air Marshal Tedder, Admiral Cunningham and General Alexander remaining as his British deputies in charge of air, naval and ground forces, respectively, and Bedell Smith once again his chief of staff. Organized as the 15th Army Group, the ground forces were composed of the

British/Commonwealth 8th Army under Montgomery and the US 7th Army under Patton. The revised invasion plan called for Montgomery to land in the southeast near Syracuse and drive north along the east coast to Messina, while Patton landed to the west along the southern beaches and played a subsidiary role protecting Montgomery's left flank. As with most military plans, however, this one was dramatically modified by events on the battlefield.

Eisenhower began the campaign in June with a six-day and night naval and air attack on Pantelleria, an island in the strait between Tunisia and Sicily. That attack so demoralized the Italian defenders as to force their surrender without an invasion, thereby fulfilling one of the prophecies of inter-war airpower advocates – the ability to obtain a surrender without any ground invasion. Unfortunately it was the only such example in the war save for Hiroshima/Nagasaki.

The actual landings in Sicily on 10 July were also successful. Hitler, unsure of exactly where the Allies would next attack, had sent forces to Sardinia, Greece and the Italian mainland as well as Sicily. Partially this had resulted from the success of an extraordinary British deception, made famous after the war in book and movie form. Code-named Operation MINCEMEAT, it involved the dumping off the Spanish coast of a dead body dressed as a British officer with phony papers implying that Greece was about to be invaded while Sicily was merely a cover.[9] As a result of this deception and ensuing German dispersion, as well as Hitler's massive losses in Tunisia, only two German *Panzer* divisions under the operational command of General Hans Hube and the overall command of Field Marshal Albert Kesselring on the Italian mainland, were in Sicily to buttress the demoralized Italians. To make matters worse, Axis leaders had incorrectly anticipated that any Anglo-American invasion of Sicily would come in the southwest, the coast closest to Tunisia, and at a later date because of bad weather and surf conditions. They were thus caught by surprise on 10 July.

After landing, however, Montgomery paused to regroup before pushing northward to Messina. He thereby squandered any opportunity he might have had to take the city quickly and cut off the Axis escape route across the narrow straits of Messina to the Italian mainland. Instead, the Germans were able to strengthen their defences south of Mount Etna, thereby delaying the British advance. Patton, on the other hand, requested and received permission from Alexander to expand his objectives and move through weak Italian resistance to capture Palermo on Sicily's north coast. He successfully did so in four days, took the city on 22 July, and then turned eastward along the north coast in an effort to beat Montgomery in a 'race' for Messina. Now, however, he faced the same fierce German resistance as Montgomery rather than the weak Italians, and his advance subsequently stalled. But the Germans were heavily outnumbered and the Italians by this point nearly useless. Consequently, Hitler in early August agreed to a withdrawal of his forces across the straits of Messina. Patton did reach Messina just before Montgomery, on 16–17 August. In reality, however, it was Kesselring who won the race, for by that time his forces, totalling approximately 40,000 German and 62,000 Italian troops, had escaped across the straits to the mainland.

The Sicilian campaign was thus a military success, albeit a limited one, for the Allies. It was also a political success, in that it led to the overthrow of Mussolini on 23 July and his replacement by Marshal Pietro Badoglio, whose government began secret negotiations with Eisenhower for Italy's surrender. Simultaneously, Marshall and Eisenhower agreed that the next Allied object-ive should indeed be the Italian mainland as Churchill desired. But whereas the US Army chief saw such an invasion in limited terms and as a way to close down the Mediterranean in preparation for cross-Channel operations, the British saw Mussolini's fall and Italy's defection as opening major new oppor-tunities in that theatre. Consequently, they requested a delay in the TRIDENT Conference agreement to transfer seven divisions from the Mediterranean to England. Seeing this as yet another effort to delay crossing the Channel, the Americans refused. The stage was thus set for yet another Anglo-American strategic confrontation, this time in Quebec.

The QUADRANT Conference

When Churchill, Roosevelt and their chiefs of staff met in Quebec from 12–24 August for the strategic summit conference code-named QUADRANT, the long-running Anglo-American strategic dispute reached a climax. On the one hand, Mussolini's fall and Italian surrender negotiations had opened up the possibility of major gains in the Mediterranean; indeed, the Italians made it clear that they would renounce their alliance with Hitler if the Allies agreed to invade Italy so as to preclude a German military takeover of the country. On the other hand, the Allies now had before them an actual plan for a 1944 cross-Channel invasion, which the Americans argued could succeed only if Mediterranean operations were severely limited.

At the Casablanca Conference in January, the Allies had agreed to the for-mation of a combined staff to plan future cross-Channel operations. In late July that staff and its chief, British Lieutenant General Sir Frederick Morgan (formally titled COSSAC for Chief of Staff, Supreme Allied Commander [Designate]), completed plans for Operation OVERLORD, a May 1944 invasion of the Normandy coast. Success in this operation, they made clear, would depend upon successful fulfilment of numerous preconditions – including a massive Anglo-American build-up in the United Kingdom and a severe limi-tation on available German strength in the Normandy area.[10]

The British Chiefs of Staff were willing to agree at Quebec that future Mediterranean operations be subordinated to OVERLORD, but they argued that COSSAC's insistence on limiting available German strength across the Channel required major operations in Italy to further disperse enemy forces. The American chiefs countered that such operations would disperse the Allies more than the Germans and preclude the necessary massive build-up of forces in the United Kingdom. OVERLORD, they insisted, would have to have 'overriding priority' in the allocation of personnel and resources, including the immediate transfer of seven divisions from the Mediterranean to England as called for in the TRIDENT accords. This the British rejected, arguing instead that 'overriding priority' would be 'too binding' and that transfer of the seven divisions should be postponed until fresh American forces could replace them, thereby allowing the Italian campaign to continue along with the OVERLORD build-up. That, however, would hinder planned Pacific operations, further delay the already-behind-schedule build-up in the United Kingdom, and create a continuous drain on OVERLORD resources, according to the JCS, who refused to agree.

To the Americans, the British were once again being duplicitous and remained more concerned with political gains in the Mediterranean than crossing the Channel and winning the war quickly and decisively. To the British, such charges were not only incorrect but also hypocritical in light of American insistence on maintaining scarce landing craft in the Pacific, rather than transferring them to the European theatre for further Mediterranean action and/or an increase in the size of the OVERLORD assault.

Compounding these suspicions were continued serious differences on how to proceed in the war against Japan that had previously erupted at the Casablanca and Washington Conferences, and that now erupted once again at Quebec. The fundamental disagreement involved the priority to be given to the war against Japan as a whole, with the Americans insisting on a much higher priority than the British. But beneath that were a series of additional disagreements over which operations in Asia and the Pacific should be undertaken and given priority. The JCS pressed for greater allocations of resources to the Pacific so as to pursue a Central Pacific drive under Admiral Nimitz and MacArthur's Southwest Pacific drives simultaneously, additional operations to liberate Burma and reopen the supply route to China, and agreement to plan to defeat Japan within a year of German defeat. The British objected to this timetable, the larger Pacific allocation, the dual advance and the extensive plans to liberate Burma. Instead they proposed far more limited operations in north Burma so as to leave resources available to retake Singapore, as well as the creation of a new British-led Southeast Asia Command to pursue this and related objectives.

As at the previous TRIDENT Conference, the CCS were forced into 'off the record' conversations, during which all planners left the room and extremely harsh words were exchanged. Among other things this resulted in an amusing episode. Immediately after one of those 'off the record' conversations, Admiral Mountbatten wheeled in a new invention of his Combined Operations Staff, a block of the previously discussed shatterproof ice known as Pykrete for Project HABBAKUK.[11] To illustrate the fact that the Pykrete was indeed shatterproof, Mountbatten fired a pistol into it as well as into a block of regular ice. This was a serious mistake, as the bullets richocheted and one almost hit Admiral King. When the Pykrete was then covered and wheeled out of the meeting room on a litter, one of the officers still waiting outside exclaimed in regard to the bitterly arguing chiefs, 'My God! They're shooting one another!'[12]

Things had not quite reached that stage, and by 19 August the CCS were able to report a compromise to Churchill and Roosevelt. That compromise was highly favourable to the American position. OVERLORD and an Italian campaign would both be launched, but the former would be the 'primary' operation with a target date of 1 May 1944, while the latter would take place within the TRIDENT limits established the previous May regarding the seven division transfer, and with the goal limited to Rome rather than the Po River in northern Italy as originally proposed by the COS. Also mentioned was the possibility of then using the forces in Italy for an invasion of southern France (Operation ANVIL) to further divert German forces from the Normandy area. In the Pacific the British acquiesced both in the dual advance and the 12-month timetable. They did obtain their desired Southeast Asia Command under Lord Mountbatten, but with the American General Stilwell in China as his deputy and a major focus remaining on Burma.

The American victory was due to two factors. First, the British were reaching the limits of their war mobilization and productivity, whereas the American mobilization was still growing and beginning to dwarf London's contribution. Second, and for the first time in the war, US preparations for an Anglo-American conference and united front tactics were superior to those of the British. That united front extended to Roosevelt. Visiting FDR at his Hyde Park home from 12–14 August, prior to departure for Quebec, Churchill found the president solidly supporting the positions of his military chiefs.

Unusually, the same could not be said at this time for Churchill, who had split with the COS over his insistence, despite their opposition, on operations to capture Aegean islands in the eastern Mediterranean and the northern tip of Sumatra in the East Indies rather than Singapore. To keep these pet military projects alive in light of British as well as American military opposition, he proved willing to acquiesce in JCS proposals as enunciated in the CCS compromise. Indeed, at Hyde Park he went even further. Recognizing that American forces would outnumber the British in any 1944 cross-Channel operations, he approved an American commander for OVERLORD in return for a British commander in the Mediterranean and Admiral Mountbatten as the British commander for the new Southeast Asia Command (SEAC), despite previous promises to Brooke that he would command the cross-Channel operation.[13] And in Quebec a few days later, Churchill approved the CCS proposals with only minor and fairly meaningless modifications: further examination and study of the Sumatra project that no one else favoured; the unstated but implied possibility of using landing craft in the eastern Mediterranean after the capture of Rome should this not interfere with OVERLORD; and mention of an alternative invasion of Norway (Operation JUPITER) if OVERLORD could not be mounted. JUPITER had long been one of Churchill's pet projects, but no one else favoured it and it was added to the QUADRANT accords merely to humour the prime minister. Brooke referred to Churchill's 'mad plans to go back to Norway', and acidly commented as follows: 'Why he wanted to go back and what he was going to do there . . . we never found out. The only reason he ever gave was that Hitler had unrolled the map of Europe starting with Norway, and he would start rolling it up again from Norway.'[14]

More important in retrospect than any of these fairly meaningless concessions – and perhaps part of their agreement that an American would command OVERLORD – was a document that Churchill and Roosevelt signed at Hyde Park re-establishing combined research in the atomic bomb project and virtually pledging to maintain an Anglo-American monopoly on any weapon that would result from that research.[15] This agreement, as well as the QUADRANT accords on cross-Channel operations, in turn reflected a crisis that had developed in Anglo-American relations with the Soviet Union.

Stalin had not been informed after the Casablanca Conference of the likely postponement of cross-Channel operations until 1944. Indeed, when Churchill had in the previous August flown to Moscow to inform the Soviet leader that the Channel would not be crossed in 1942, the prime minister had promised 'a very great operation in 1943'.[16] That promise had never been officially rescinded; indeed, it had been vaguely reaffirmed in early 1943. Thus, when Churchill and Roosevelt informed Stalin in June of the TRIDENT Conference decisions regarding 1944 cross-Channel operations, he angrily responded with a litany of broken Anglo-American promises regarding those operations and a warning that his government 'cannot become reconciled to this disregard of vital Soviet interests in the war against the common enemy'. Calling Anglo-American military sacrifices 'insignificant' compared to those of the Soviet armies, he further warned that 'the point here is not just the disappointment of the Soviet Government, but the preservation of its confidence in its Allies, a confidence which is being subjected to severe stress'.[17] Subsequently Stalin recalled his ambassadors from London and Washington, cancelled a proposed summit meeting with Roosevelt, and complained bitterly over his lack of inclusion in Italian surrender negotiations. Rumours of a possible Russo-German separate peace filled the air. Simultaneously, the Red Army in July demolished Hitler's third and final offensive at the Battle of Kursk and launched a massive counter-offensive that would liberate much of the Soviet Union by the year's end and much of Eastern Europe in the following year. And in Moscow, a 'Free Germany' Committee composed of German Communists and captured *Wehrmacht* officers called upon the German people to overthrow Hitler. Anglo-American intelligence now began to fear not simply a separate Russo-German peace, but a Soviet attempt to create a Communist government in Berlin and to dominate all of post-war Europe.[18]

American insistence on cross-Channel operations had previously been motivated in large part by the desire to keep Russia in the war. In 1942 that desire had been primarily military – i.e. to relieve the pressure on the Red Army and thus avoid Soviet military defeat. Now in 1943 it became largely political – to preclude the possibility of Russia voluntarily leaving the war by providing Stalin with the operation he had consistently demanded. But by this time fear of Communist expansion into Eastern and Central Europe led to an additional reason to support cross-Channel operations: preclude Soviet post-war domination of Europe by placing a large body of Anglo-American troops on the continent. To cover this contingency, COSSAC had also developed a series of plans, code-named RANKIN, to land major Anglo-American forces on the Continent should Germany weaken or collapse before the May 1944 OVERLORD target date.[19]

The JCS and CCS discussed and approved these plans in principle at QUADRANT and directed that they be kept under continuous review regarding the forces required. Roosevelt also showed great interest in the plans and by conference's end had joined Churchill in expressing anger over Stalin's behaviour.[20] Their secret agreement on full cooperation in the development of an atomic bomb and never to help a third party develop such a weapon without mutual consent (as well as never to use it against each other or against a third party without the other's consent) reflected their growing fear of the USSR, a fear that counter-balanced their growing differences and helped keep them closely aligned. For in signing this agreement Roosevelt rejected the policy that his scientific advisers had proposed in late 1942 with an eye on post-war as well as wartime issues, and that he had originally accepted, to avoid additional 'joint enterprise' with the British on this project and maintain at most 'restricted interchange'. The Hyde Park agreement re-established and formalized full interchange, albeit, as historian Martin Sherwin has noted, with the British now 'as junior rather than equal partners'.[21]

In September and October, however, relations with the Soviets would warm considerably under the impact of renewed Anglo-American pledges to cross the Channel in 1944 and the invasion of Italy. During that time Stalin agreed to both a tripartite summit conference with Churchill and Roosevelt in November and a preliminary meeting of their three foreign ministers in Moscow during October. At the same time, the Anglo-American strategic dispute erupted once again in the Mediterranean.

The invasion and surrender of Italy

While Churchill, Roosevelt and their advisers met in Quebec during August, Eisenhower prepared to invade Italy and simultaneously negotiated for an Italian surrender in the aftermath of Mussolini's 23 July ousting from power. As if these tasks were not difficult enough, he simultaneously had to deal with a flood of telegrams from individuals in London and Washington who could not be ignored. Harold Macmillan, his British political adviser and a future prime minister, noted in his diary on 29 July that 'poor Eisenhower is getting pretty harassed' as a result of these missives from:

(i)   Combined Chiefs of Staff (Washington) – his official masters
(ii)   General Marshall. Chief of U.S. Army – his immediate superior

(iii)   The President
(iv)   The Secretary of State
(v)   Our Prime Minister (direct)
(vi)   Our Prime Minister (through me)
(vii)   The Foreign Secretary (through me)

All their instructions, Macmillan noted, 'are naturally contradictory and conflicting'. So he and Bedell Smith developed 'a sort of parlour game in sorting them out and sending back replies saying what *we* think ought to happen. As this rarely, if ever, coincides with any of the courses proposed by (i), (ii), (iii), (iv), (v), (vi), or (vii),' Macmillan concluded in classic British understated and dry humour, 'lots of fun ensues'.[22]

On 3 September, portions of Montgomery's 8th Army crossed the straits of Messina and landed successfully on the toe of the Italian 'boot' (Operation BAYTOWN). Five days later news of Italy's surrender was officially announced, and early the following morning Montgomery's forces landed on the inside heel (Operation SLAPSTICK). Simultaneously the US 5th Army landed at Salerno below Naples (Operation AVALANCHE) under General Mark Clark rather than Patton, who had created a furore in Sicily by verbally abusing and slapping the faces of two soldiers suffering from combat exhaustion.

In the period between Mussolini's 23 July overthrow and the 8–9 September announcement and Allied landings, however, Hitler had poured 16 additional German divisions into Italy, bringing his total there to 20. Under the overall command of Kesselring and the operational command of General Heinrich von Vietinghoff, those forces now counter-attacked Clark's forces at Salerno and almost succeeded in throwing the Americans back into the sea. Simultaneously, German commandos led by Otto Skorzeny rescued Mussolini from his prison and re-established him at Lake Garda in northern Italy as head of a puppet state known as the Salo Republic. Officially Italy under the Badoglio government now changed sides and became an Allied co-belligerent. In reality, however, it became a battleground occupied by Allied forces south of Naples and German forces north of that city.

That battleground proved to be particularly bloody due to the rugged terrain of Italy, whose mountain spine and numerous rivers negated the effective use of armour for breakthroughs, and the impressive defensive capabilities of Kesselring and von Vietinghoff, who now constructed the formidable Gustav Line defences south of Rome. Heavy autumn rains only compounded these problems for the Allies, and by October a bloody stalemate and campaign of attrition was evident in the mud of the Italian theatre.

At the optimistic beginning of the Italian campaign, however, Churchill had moved to get British forces into the eastern Mediterranean so as to take over key areas from demoralized Italian occupation troops before the Germans could. On 9 September, the same date Eisenhower announced Italian surrender and landed at Salerno as well as the heel of Italy, the prime minister proposed to Roosevelt a movement of troops from Italy into the Balkans. Simultaneously

Middle East Commander General Sir Henry Maitland Wilson, pressed by Churchill, sent troops the Dodecanese Islands of Cos, Leros and Samos before the Germans could. The *Wehrmacht* beat him to the main prize, however – the island of Rhodes – from which the Germans soon launched counter-attacks that succeeded by October in retaking Cos, the only one of the three Dodecanese Islands with an airfield. Churchill and Wilson both pressed Eisenhower to spare forces and landing craft for an invasion of Rhodes (Operation ACCOLADE) in order to avoid a humiliating defeat on Leros and Samos, as well as to bring Turkey into the war and force a German withdrawal from the entire eastern Mediterranean and the Balkans. This the Americans refused to sanction on the grounds that any campaign against Rhodes would be lengthy and would have to use resources needed for OVERLORD, Italy – and Burma. The October stalemate in Italy only reinforced that opposition by making it clear that a choice between Rome and Rhodes was necessary, with Rome obviously more important.

Churchill, however, had by this time 'worked himself into a frenzy of excitement about the Rhodes attack', according to Brooke, and had 'magnified its importance so that he can no longer see anything else and has set his heart on capturing this one island even at the expense of endangering his relations with the President and the Americans, and also the whole future of the Italian campaign'.[23] When Eisenhower thus requested a minor delay in transferring the seven divisions and landing craft to OVERLORD so as to avoid stalemate or defeat in Italy, Churchill expanded the requested delay so as to enable him to attack Rhodes and bring Turkey into the war as well. He also requested a summit meeting with Roosevelt before any meeting with Stalin. This brought the Allies to their final set of arguments over strategy in the European theatre.

The Moscow Foreign Ministers Conference

From 18 October to 1 November, British Foreign Secretary Anthony Eden and US Secretary of State Cordell Hull met in Moscow with their Soviet counterpart, Foreign Minister Vyacheslav Molotov, to discuss post-war issues and set the stage for their superiors' summit conference. For the Soviets, however, establishment of the second front remained the prerequisite for any future understandings. This they made clear even before, as well as during the Moscow meeting. Consequently British General Ismay, Churchill's personal representative on the COS, and Major General John Deane, former secretary of the JCS and head of the new US Military Mission to Moscow, made detailed presentations of the OVERLORD plan at the beginning of the conference. Reassured on this point, the Soviets then agreed to discuss numerous post-war political issues.[24]

Anglo-American differences of opinion now emerged on those issues as well as strategic ones. For Hull, the important thing was to obtain Soviet agreement to broad principles – most notably the unconditional surrender and tripartite occupation of Germany and the establishment of a post-war collective security organization to replace the League of Nations – as well as a tripartite summit conference. The British, however, were far more concerned with explicit agreements regarding the future of Europe and therefore pressed for the establishment of a tripartite European Advisory Commission in London to plan occupation policies and specific accords regarding the nations of Eastern and Central Europe, particularly Poland.

The Soviets were amenable to all of Hull's points. In signing the State Department's Declaration on Germany and Four Power Pact, they agreed to the unconditional surrender and tripartite occupation of Germany as well as post-war cooperation within the framework of a new League of Nations. Moreover, Stalin continued to show interest in a summit meeting and, without being asked, promised to enter the war against Japan once Germany was defeated. The Soviets were far less amenable to British proposals, however. While willing to agree to the establishment of a European Advisory Commission in London to plan occupation policies, they would not agree to any specific accords regarding Poland or the other nations of Eastern Europe. The same was true of Hull, who refused to support Eden over East European accords he called 'piddling little things'.[25] On post-war political as well as wartime strategic issues, the United States thus appeared to be making common cause with the Soviet Union against Great Britain.

As the Moscow Conference neared its end Churchill pressed for a delay in OVERLORD so as to invade Rhodes and bring Turkey into the war as well as break the stalemate in Italy, and for an Anglo-American summit conference with Roosevelt before any tripartite meeting with Stalin. Roosevelt agreed to meet Churchill in Cairo before moving on to meet Stalin in Teheran, but he was unwilling to discuss changes in European strategy without Stalin present. Consequently, he invited Chinese leader Chiang Kai-shek to Cairo, thereby guaranteeing that Far Eastern affairs would dominate the conference.

The war against Japan and the first Cairo Conference

By late 1943 the Allies were sorely in need of a conference that focused on the Far East and the war against Japan. The TRIDENT and QUADRANT agreements regarding that war had essentially listed all the different avenues of approach to victory, rather than prioritizing them and focusing on one or two. By late 1943 such focusing appeared more necessary than ever.

In the Pacific, strategic disputes during 1943 had continued to divide the US Army from the US Navy, as well as the United States from the British. In the aftermath of the Guadalcanal campaign, Admirals King and Nimitz had in early 1943 renewed their calls for a shift to their preferred naval drive across the Central Pacific through the Marshall, Caroline and Mariana Island chains and then to Formosa, while MacArthur pressed instead for continuation in his theatre, the Southwest Pacific, both up the Solomon Islands chain and along the northern coast of New Guinea to take the major Japanese base at Rabaul (Operation CARTWHEEL) and then to liberate the Philippines.

Rather than select one line of advance or the other, the Joint Chiefs in April of 1943 decided to pursue both avenues of approach simultaneously, a decision based on political and economic as well as military factors. The Central Pacific was the most direct approach and the one the navy had planned to use since the old pre-war ORANGE war plans, but closing down the South and Southwest Pacific would be difficult to justify given the effort already made and the lives lost on Guadalcanal and Papua. Of perhaps equal importance was the fact that the Central Pacific was under a naval commander while the Southwest Pacific was under an army commander – and a living legend by this time. Most important of all, growing war production along with the postponement of cross-Channel operations to 1944 and new, efficient strategies in the Pacific now gave American strategists the luxury of pursuing both approaches simultaneously – and the power to force British acquiescence at the TRIDENT and QUADRANT Conferences.

Consequently, MacArthur's forces in the Southwest Pacific continued throughout 1943 to advance westward from Buna, albeit slowly and in the face of fierce Japanese resistance. Indeed, after their defeat at Guadalcanal the Japanese were determined to hold New Guinea and therefore sent major air and ground reinforcements, including an entire air army as well as a ground army under General Adachi Hatazo, who set up his headquarters at Lae on the north side of the Huon Gulf, 175 miles west of Buna. Still determined to take Port Moresby, his forces in January attempted to destroy the recently reinforced Australian guerrilla Kanga force and take its airstrip at Wau, 25 miles south of the Japanese stronghold at Salamaua on the south side of the gulf (see the map on p. 80).

MacArthur was able to defeat these expanded Japanese forces via the development of a technique, for which he incorrectly claimed credit, known as 'leapfrogging'. This involved the use of land-based airpower as well as amphibious forces to attack the Japanese in unexpected and therefore weakly held areas behind their main fortifications and troop concentrations (thus the 'leapfrogging'), thereby bypassing and isolating the latter while achieving local superiority against smaller forces, then 'rolling up' equipment and reusing it for the next offensive 'jump'. Despite his claim to having seen the advantages of this approach from the moment he landed in Australia in 1942, in point of fact MacArthur was a late convert to this strategy, which the Joint and Combined Chiefs of Staff forced on him with their 1943 decision to isolate and bypass rather than conquer Rabaul.[26] But when ULTRA intelligence revealed to MacArthur the strength of Japanese garrisons in his theatre, he proved capable of using the technique very effectively.

MacArthur did admit after the war that leapfrogging was 'as old as war itself' and 'merely a new name, dictated by new conditions, given to the ancient principle of envelopment. It was the first time that the area of combat embraced land and water in such relative proportions.'[27] But the key to the technique and the ensuing advance of his forces was neither ground nor naval forces. Rather, it was air superiority, something his air commander, Lieutenant General George

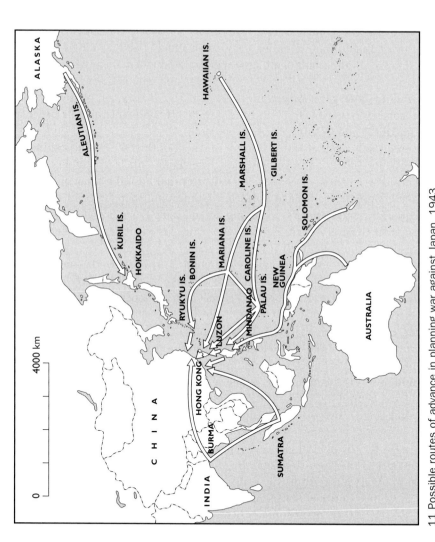

11 Possible routes of advance in planning war against Japan, 1943

C. Kenney, brilliantly achieved during the spring and summer of 1943. In the early March Battle of the Bismarck Sea, Kenney used ULTRA intelligence and low-level attacks by B-25 Mitchell medium bombers to destroy a Japanese convoy of transports containing 7,000 troops with accompanying destroyers that had been headed from Rabaul to reinforce the garrisons at Lae and Salamaua. This was the first time land-based bombers had accomplished such a feat. Fearing the growing American air superiority, Admiral Yamamoto responded with a series of air raids against Guadalcanal, Tulagi and Allied bases in New Guinea, but he suffered aircraft losses at least as great as those his pilots inflicted. Equally if not more damaging to the Japanese cause, Yamamoto himself was killed on 18 April en route to Bougainville in the northern Solomons when the Americans, having intercepted cryptographic messages with the details of his trip, shot down his plane. When ULTRA revealed a major Japanese air concentration at Wewak, far beyond the range of Kenney's fighters, he secretly constructed a new airstrip 60 miles west of Lae and on 17–18 August launched bomber raids that destroyed three of the four Wewak airstrips and all but 38 of the Japanese aircraft stationed there.

While Kenney was achieving air superiority, MacArthur reorganized his troops into the US Alamo Force and the Australian New Guinea Force and began a campaign to take both Salamaua and Lae. In January he had transported part of an Australian brigade by aircraft to Wau in the midst of the battle for that village and airstrip, thereby enabling the Australians to repulse the Japanese attack and go on the offensive. Then in late June US forces landed at Nassau Bay, opening a supply route to Wau and focusing Japanese attention on defending Salamaua, which was only 15 miles away from the American landings. MacArthur, however, was focused not on Salamaua but on Lae, 25 miles further north. While his feint at Nassau Bay led the Japanese to send reinforcements to Salamaua, Australian troops made a successful amphibious landing along the Huon Gulf coast 20 miles east of Lae on 4 September. One day later, US airborne troops seized the airstrip at Nadzab northwest of Lae, enabling an Australian division to land there and advance on Lae from that direction. This pincer movement forced the Japanese to abandon both Lae and Salamaua by mid-September, with the Australians pursuing them by land and sea through the Huon Peninsula.

While MacArthur advanced on Lae and Salamaua, naval, marine and army forces in the South Pacific under his general command but Admiral Halsey's operational control began after Guadalcanal an advance northwest up the Solomon Island chain in the naval version of leapfrogging known as 'island hopping'. In June they invaded New Georgia (and neighbouring Rendova) and, after suffering heavy casualties, took the critical Munda garrison and airfield, and the rest of the island, in early August. Halsey then bypassed the heavily garrisoned Kolombangara Island and instead successfully attacked the lightly defended island of Vella Lavella, thereby forcing the Kolombangara garrison to evacuate in September–October so as to avoid being cut off. In the process his naval forces engaged in a series of battles with the Japanese fleet, the last of which on 6–7 August resulted in the first American night victory. Halsey then attacked the northernmost Solomon Island of Bougainville, with the 3rd marine division invading Empress Augusta Bay on the west coast on 1 November. Japanese Admiral Omori Sentaro tried to sink the transports that evening but was thwarted and forced back to Rabaul by Rear Admiral A. Stanton Merrill in the Battle of Empress Augusta Bay.

By the time of the QUADRANT Conference in August, the CCS had concluded that these twin axes of advance were isolating Rabaul, and that the huge base could therefore be bypassed rather than conquered as MacArthur had planned to do in Operation CARTWHEEL. By that time the Americans had also retaken the Aleutian Islands of Attu and Kiska, which the Japanese had seized as part of their Midway plan in 1942.[28] Japanese defenders forced a brutal struggle for the former but evacuated the latter before the Americans landed. Then in October–November Nimitz began his Central Pacific drive with an attack on the Tarawa and Makin atolls in the Gilbert Islands, on the edge of the Japanese defensive perimeter, so as to provide bases for the attack on the Marshall Islands.

By this time the US fleet under Admiral Spruance had been massively expanded and improved via the introduction 12 new carriers, six of them the new 'Essex' class, as well as numerous battleships, cruisers and destroyers – a feat of productivity the Japanese could not come close to matching quantitatively. Nor could they qualitatively match the new naval aircraft, the F6 Hellcat, which had been specifically designed to outperform the Japanese Zero. Nevertheless the 20 November American attack on Tarawa, led by Rear Admiral Richmond Kelly Turner in charge of the amphibious forces and marine Major General Holland M. 'Howlin' Mad' Smith in charge of the ground forces, turned into a bloodbath as the marines faced 5,000 entrenched defenders who withstood a massive naval and air bombardment and fought virtually to the last man (only 17 Japanese survived). A limited number of new amphibious tractor landing craft (AMTRACS) brought the first waves of marines from the 2nd Division successfully to Betio, the most heavily defended island in the atoll, but regular landing craft proved unable to surmount the coral reef surrounding the island, forcing the remaining marines to wade hundreds of yards through high water just to reach the beach. Some 1,500 of them were killed or wounded on the first day alone, 3,000 by the time the battle ended on 23 November. Such heavy casualties shocked the American people but unfortunately would be repeated many times during the navy's bitterly contested advance across the Central Pacific.

Problems also plagued Allied operations on the Asian mainland during 1943 in what the Americans called the China-Burma-India Theater (CBI). By March, a shortage of resources and of progress had led to further postponement of the Casablanca-approved Operation ANAKIM to reconquer Burma. Disagreements throughout 1943 over this and related operations on the Asian mainland split not only the British from the Americans, but also the Chinese from the Americans and the Americans from each other in a complex web that made up part of what one historian appropriately called the 'China Tangle.'[29] With good reason many Americans during the war referred to CBI as standing for 'Confused Beyond Imagination'.

The Anglo-American disagreement focused specifically on operations to retake Burma so as to reopen the Burma Road land supply route to China, but more basically on the importance of China to the Allied war effort and the post-war world. Roosevelt and his advisers saw China as critical to both. Militarily its continued survival was necessary to keep the bulk of the Japanese Army tied down on the Asian mainland, prevent Japan from turning the conflict into an unwinnable race war for the Allies, and provide future bases for attacks on the Japanese home islands. Politically Roosevelt saw China as a future great power, one of his 'Four Policemen', which would replace Japan as the stabilizing force in post-war Asia. Churchill and his advisers disagreed on virtually all of these points, seeing Chiang's China as incapable of fulfilling any important role either during or after the war and thus unworthy of a major effort to retake Burma. Instead they desired operations against the Dutch East Indies and to retake Singapore. Yet, in a parallel irony, any Burma operation would have to rely on British troops from India, as well as Chinese forces that Stilwell was training, while amphibious operations in Southeast Asia would have to depend on scarce American landing craft. Each side thus possessed an effective veto over the other's proposed operations.

The British had no objections to some limited operations in Burma, specifically against Arakan in western Burma so as to protect India, and under Field Marshal Wavell they launched such an operation with British and Indian troops in December of 1942 to take the port of Akyab. That effort failed, however, as did two additional attempts in early 1943. The Japanese successfully counter-attacked and by the time of the TRIDENT Conference in May, they had pushed Wavell back to his starting point.

The Sino-American and intra-American disputes focused on the type of aid to be sent to Chiang, and the type of warfare to be emphasized in China against the Japanese. Stilwell was training Chinese ground forces to fight the Japanese and thus wanted supplies to support this effort, but he was opposed on both grounds by Major General Claire Chennault, formerly head of the group of pilots known as the 'Flying Tigers' who had volunteered to fly and fight for Chiang before Pearl Harbor, and now the commander of the 14th US Army Air Force in China. A firm believer in strategic airpower, Chennault argued that a small number of bombers alone, operating from Chinese bases, could defeat the Japanese, and that US supplies should focus on the creation of such a force for use in 1943. Supported by both Marshall and King, Stilwell countered that trained and supplied ground forces were necessary to protect the air bases from Japanese counter-attacks; but Chiang supported Chennault so as to preserve his troops for the anticipated post-war conflict against Mao. So did the British, who saw the air campaign as a way out of Burma operations, and Roosevelt, who personally favoured air over ground operations and who saw no reason to argue with his British and Chinese allies over this issue.

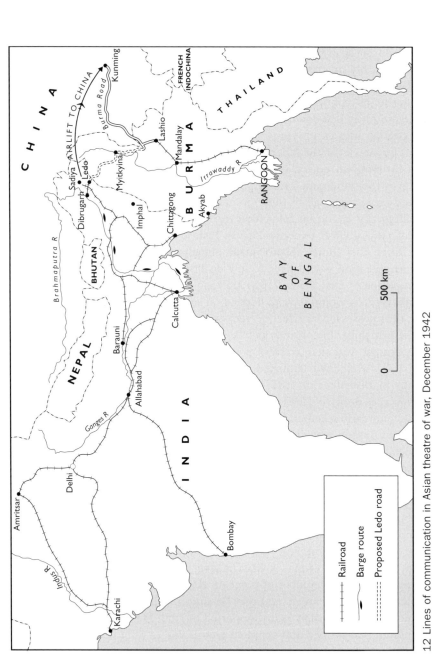

12 Lines of communication in Asian theatre of war, December 1942

After listening to Wavell, Stilwell and Chennault at the TRIDENT meeting, the conferees decided to increase tonnage delivered over the 'Hump', with the majority going to Chennault but enough going to Stilwell to continue his training. They also in effect dropped ANAKIM and with it any effort to reopen the Burma Road in 1943. Instead they agreed to more limited operations in northern Burma that could lead to the creation of a new land route, the so-called Ledo Road, from India to China. But supply problems and continued foot-dragging and defeatism by Wavell in India and by the Chinese further delayed even those limited operations.

At the QUADRANT Conference, Burma operations received two boosts. The first came from the presence of the charismatic and eccentric British Brigadier General Orde Wingate, who had organized a special commando force known as the Chindits and had led them in a series of daring raids behind Japanese lines in Burma earlier in 1943. Although he lost a third of his 3,000-man force and annoyed the Japanese more than he truly hurt them, his exploits and personality raised Allied morale, convinced many that the Allies could indeed best the Japanese in jungle warfare, and psychologically galvanized the QUADRANT conferees to more action in the area – including the creation of a similar American unit, which was code-named GALAHAD and would be nicknamed 'Merrill's Marauders', after its commander, Brigadier General Frank Merrill. The second boost came from the establishment of the new Southeast Asia Command (SEAC) under Admiral Mountbatten, with Burma operations given top priority within this new command. To ensure such operations and proper coordination, Stilwell was appointed as Mountbatten's deputy.

The establishment of SEAC and appointment of Mountbatten and Stilwell created additional problems, however. First of all, it placed within the same theatre and under British command not only Burma, but also such former European colonies as Singapore, Malaya, Indochina and the East Indies – areas in which the British also had greater interests. Indeed, before long, Americans were referring to SEAC as standing for 'Save England's Asian Colonies'. Second, Stilwell's appointment added yet another title and responsibility to the many he already shouldered: chief of staff to Chiang; commander of Chinese forces in India responsible both to Wavell in India and Chiang in Chungking; commander of US Army forces in the CBI responsible to Marshall and the JCS in Washington; and Lend-Lease administrator responsible to Roosevelt and his Lend-Lease administration. As one wartime reporter quipped, 'The only one, it seems, that the general was not responsible to was God.'[30] The result was administratively incomprehensible even to Churchill. To make matters worse, Stilwell loathed both Chiang and the British. Nicknamed 'Vinegar Joe', the acerbic general lambasted the Chinese leader in his diary for *Kuomintang* corruption and his refusal to fight the Japanese, derisively calling him 'Peanut' and his party 'a gang of fascists' similar to the Nazis save for their inefficiency. British officials fared no better, receiving such epithets as 'monocled ass', 'pisspot' and 'pig-fucker'.[31]

5 Chiang Kai-shek, Franklin Roosevelt and Winston Churchill during the Cairo Conference ©
Bettman/CORBIS

6 Lord Louis Mountbatten pictured during a visit to Chiang Kai-shek, Head of the Chinese
Government. Left to right: Gen. Ho Yin-Chen, China's War Minister, Lt. Gen. Brehon Somervell,
U.S. Chief of Supply, Chiang Kai-shek, Lord Louis Mountbatten, Madame Chiang Kai-shek and
Lt. Gen. Joseph Stilwell © Bettmann/CORBIS

Matters came to a head at the November Cairo Conference, code-named SEXTANT. By that time Chiang had made it clear that he would not commit his forces to planned operations in North Burma (Operation CHAMPION) unless the British and Americans committed to an additional, amphibious operation in the Bay of Bengal against southern Burma so as to relieve Japanese pressure on his troops. One such operation against the Andaman Islands in the Bay of Bengal, BUCCANEER, was indeed under discussion within the CCS. Churchill, however, still intent instead on his pet amphibious operations against northern Sumatra in Southeast Asia and the island of Rhodes in the eastern Mediterranean, refused to agree. But the Americans would not agree to either of these operations, with Marshall making clear that the landing craft assigned to BUCCANEER would be transferred to the Pacific, not to Sumatra or the eastern Mediterranean ('not one American soldier is going to die on [that] God Damned beach', an angered Marshall replied when Churchill pressed him on Rhodes),[32] should the Bay of Bengal operation not be approved. Furthermore, Roosevelt, seeking to reassure and build up Chiang both during and after the war, now made the Chinese leader a series of critical promises.

The most famous of these were contained in the Cairo Declaration, a public document in which Churchill, Roosevelt and Chiang stated that Japan would at war's end lose all the territories it had conquered since World War I, that those taken from China would be returned, that Korea would become an independent state, and that all three leaders had reached accord at Cairo on future military operations against Japan. To obtain Chiang's agreement to that latter statement, however, Roosevelt privately promised him the BUCCANEER amphibious operation. With landing craft so scarce, that meant the Allies would have to give up on Rome, or Rhodes, or OVERLORD on schedule. They simply did not have enough landing craft to do all three operations as scheduled *and* BUCCANEER.

Such American placement of Asia and the Pacific before Europe infuriated the British, much as their insistence on the Mediterranean over cross-Channel operations had infuriated the Americans. According to Stilwell, one CCS session over Burma almost ended in a brawl when 'Brooke got nasty and King got good and sore. King almost climbed over the table at Brooke. God, he was mad. I wish he had socked him.'[33]

The Anglo-American strategic conflicts over the war against Germany and the war against Japan had thus been fully joined. And, ironically, final decisions would now depend on Josef Stalin.

The Teheran Conference

Despite their multiple and global military campaigns in 1942 and 1943, Anglo-American military activity paled in significance when compared to the massive Soviet effort on the Eastern Front. The statistics in this regard are staggering. In the single battle of Stalingrad, the Soviets suffered more combat deaths than the Americans or the British suffered in the entire war. While Anglo-American forces faced two German divisions in Sicily during July and August, the Red Army faced 180. More than 90 per cent of all German Army casualties by late 1943 had occurred on the Eastern Front.

These facts led Anglo-American military and political leaders properly to conclude that victory necessitated continued and active Soviet participation in the war. That in turn necessitated Anglo-American assistance in the form of both supplies and military operations, most notably the second front that Stalin consistently demanded, in order to divert the Germans, relieve the pressure on the Eastern Front, and reassure the highly suspicious Soviet leader of Anglo-American commitment to victory so that he would not sign a separate peace with Germany – as he had in effect done in 1939. By 1943 it was also apparent that continued Soviet participation in the war and a total Allied victory would result in an enormous expansion of Soviet post-war power, along with a serious decline in British power.

Long known for his antipathy to Communism, Churchill was not sanguine regarding this expansion of Soviet power. Roosevelt, however, believed it required befriending Stalin and reducing his suspicions of the West so as both to win the war and to create a workable post-war peace. He was also convinced that with his personal charm he could accomplish this task, whereas the British could not. As he informed Churchill in 1942, 'Stalin hates the guts of all your top people. He thinks he likes me better, and I hope he will continue to do so.'[34]

Roosevelt has come in for sharp criticism for what appears to be his extraordinary naïveté regarding both his personal powers of persuasion and the true nature of Stalin and his regime. But his approach to Stalin was more fundamentally based on his recognition of growing Soviet power combined with British decline, and continued Anglo-American strategic disagreement. In point of fact, Russia was in 1943 fast becoming more important than Britain, both to the war effort and to the post-war order. Moreover, Allied strategic disagreements found Russia and the United States aligned against the British regarding cross-Channel operations.

All of these factors led Roosevelt into a secret effort in the spring of 1943 to arrange a private meeting with Stalin, an effort he duplicitously denied when queried by Churchill.[35] That effort foundered on the continued postponement of the second front, replaced in the autumn of 1943 by renegotiation of the original plans for a tripartite conference. By October agreement had been reached to hold that conference, code-named EUREKA, in the Iranian capital of Teheran.

All three leaders appear to have planned originally on a conference that would focus on post-war issues. But Churchill's desire to postpone OVERLORD so as to pursue objectives in the Mediterranean reopened the old strategic debate in September–October and made it the dominant issue at Teheran in November; three out of the conference's four days would be dominated by this issue.

Despite Stalin's repeated demands since 1941 for cross-Channel operations, the Soviets had been attracted to Churchill's most recent proposals because they promised immediate assistance, in the form of both Anglo-American action in the Mediterranean and the strongly desired entrance of Turkey into the war, at the expense of delay in a cross-Channel operation not possible for another six months under any circumstances. Consequently no one was sure what Stalin would say when formally presented with the strategic options now available.

Roosevelt presented those options during the first plenary session of the conference on 28 November, but only after giving a lengthy discourse on the war against Japan. He then made clear that numerous immediate campaigns were possible in the Mediterranean but only if OVERLORD was delayed. Stalin responded by stating that Russia would enter the war against Japan once Germany was defeated and then came down squarely for OVERLORD on schedule on the grounds that no Mediterranean operations could be decisive. In effect, he was promising Roosevelt a Soviet 'second front' in the Far East on condition that the Americans provided him with a second front in Europe. Churchill of course objected and pressed for delay in OVERLORD so as to launch multiple and immediate offensives in the Mediterranean. But in response Stalin noted that the proposed Mediterranean operations were not related to each other and would result in an unwise dispersion of forces. OVERLORD should be launched on schedule, and Allied forces in Italy should be used for a diversionary operation in southern France before OVERLORD, a possibility previously raised at the August QUADRANT Conference as Operation ANVIL, rather than sent to the eastern Mediterranean. Roosevelt concurred.

In effect, a forceful Soviet-American front had been formed at this meeting in opposition to British strategy. Given that fact and the growing strength of the two powers vis-à-vis the declining British, Churchill stood no chance of winning this strategic debate, all his eloquence notwithstanding. Indeed, Stalin, on the second day, cut off that eloquence with 'an indiscreet question, namely, do the British really believe in OVERLORD or are they only saying so to reassure the Russians?' And at dinner that evening, he taunted the prime minister mercilessly on his attitude toward OVERLORD.[36]

Roosevelt joined in that taunting (and on other occasions initiated it) as part of his preconceived effort to win Stalin's trust and convince the Soviet leader that no Anglo-American front existed in opposition to the Soviets. When Stalin suggested shooting 50,000 German officers at war's end and Churchill vehemently objected, FDR humorously responded with a 'compromise' proposal of 49,000 and his son Elliot with a toast in favour of the executions that led Churchill to stalk out of the room in anger. Stalin and Molotov brought him back, but the hopelessness of his position was by that point clear.[37] On 30 November, the third day of the conference and his 69th birthday, he formally surrendered. By the CCS accord as approved by all three men, OVERLORD would be launched in May of 1944. Operations would continue in Italy within limits imposed by OVERLORD, and the ANVIL invasion of southern France would be launched from Italy in conjunction with OVER-LORD. At lunch that day, Stalin expressed 'great satisfaction' and promised an offensive on the Eastern Front to coincide with and divert German forces from the OVERLORD landings. That evening, Churchill hosted a dinner party to mark his birthday. In sharp contrast to the previous evening, all three now joined in a series of effusive toasts. As the American minutes noted, 'It was clear that those present had a sense of realization that historic understanding had been reached and this conception was brought out in the statements and speeches.'[38]

Although the debate over future military operations dominated this first tri-partite Allied summit conference, the 'Big Three' did find time to discuss numerous post-war political issues. And although those discussions were inconclusive, they set the stage for definite agreements at later occasions, most notably the February 1945 Yalta Conference. Particularly noteworthy in this regard were the discussions regarding the occupation and division of Germany, a possible movement of Poland's boundaries westward, and post-war international organization.[39]

Churchill later stated that he was forced to realize at Teheran what a small nation Britain was: 'There I sat with the great Russian bear on one side of me, with paws outstretched, and on the other side the great American buffalo, and between the two sat the poor little English donkey who was the only one . . . who knew the right way home.'[40] That comment aptly summarized the declin-ing position in which the British now found themselves vis-à-vis their American as well as their Soviet allies. Illustrative of that declining position was not only their defeat on strategic issues, but also the fact that Roosevelt chose to stay at the Soviet rather than the British embassy throughout the conference (the US embassy was distant from both, and the Soviets claimed to have discovered an assassination plot); the fact that Roosevelt met privately with Stalin but not with Churchill during the conference; and the needling that Churchill experienced at the hands of Roosevelt as well as Stalin in the former's efforts to befriend the latter. On one occasion, the president teased the prime minister mercilessly 'about his Britishness, about John Bull, about his cigars, about his habits', until Churchill got red in the face and Stalin 'broke into a deep, hearty guffaw . . . I kept it up', Roosevelt later told one of his cabinet members, 'until Stalin was laughing with me' – at Churchill's expense.[41]

Equally illustrative of Britain's declining position within the alliance was Churchill's declining health. He had come to Cairo and Teheran with a cold, and it grew progressively worse as the conferences progressed. By December it had turned into pneumonia.

8

MILITARY SUCCESSES AND EARLY POST-WAR PLANNING, DECEMBER 1943–SEPTEMBER 1944

The Cairo–Teheran Conferences firmly established Allied global strategy for the duration of the war. What followed was a series of extraordinary military successes that brought the Allies to the verge of total victory over their Axis opponents. Given the approach of that victory, the Allies also began detailed planning for the post-war world. As in 1943, Anglo-American conflicts would occur in both the strategic and the political realms. And as in 1943 these conflicts would be successfully resolved. Once again, however, such resolution would be largely on American terms, as US preponderance within the alliance continued to grow.

The second Cairo Conference

Churchill, Roosevelt and their staffs returned to Cairo from 3 to 7 December for yet another conference to clean up loose ends from the Teheran and first Cairo Conferences. They reaffirmed that OVERLORD and ANVIL would be 'the supreme operations for 1944' that 'must be carried out during May',[1] but on that basis they needed to make a host of additional decisions. Two of the most important of these concerned appointment of the OVERLORD commander and what to do about the continued landing craft shortage.

During the second plenary session at Teheran, Stalin had asked who would command OVERLORD. When Roosevelt replied that no final decision had yet been reached, Stalin shot back, 'Then nothing will come of these operations.'[2] Given that comment, as well as the importance of the Teheran agreement on OVERLORD both militarily and diplomatically, immediate appointment of a commander was now mandatory.

Churchill had in August ceded that appointment to the Americans, and it was widely expected that Roosevelt would select Marshall and replace him in Washington by appointing Eisenhower as army chief of staff. The president had delayed, however, primarily because Marshall had become so vital to the effective functioning of the JCS and CCS, where he had clearly emerged as the 'first amongst equals'.[3] Consequently, many individuals – including his JCS colleagues and his mentor, World War I American commander and former chief of staff General John J. Pershing – questioned the wisdom of removing him from Washington for a field command. Moreover, that field command would be geographically limited to northwest Europe, as the British insisted the Mediterranean remain a separate theatre and be under British command. Nevertheless OVERLORD would be the most important Anglo-American operation of the war, and one of the most prestigious commands in military history. And it was an honour Roosevelt clearly wished to bestow upon Marshall, whom Churchill would call 'the noblest Roman of them all' as well as the 'organizer of victory',[4] for his selfless service in Washington.

That selflessness, however, had previously led Marshall to refuse to reply when Roosevelt had pointedly asked him, on numerous occasions, whether he wanted the command. Of course he did, but by his professional and ethical standards he could not and would not say so. His personal desires, he replied, were irrelevant; the president needed to act in the best interests of the country, not the best interests of George Marshall.

At Cairo, Roosevelt attempted one last time to elicit a reply from Marshall. When the army chief once again refused, the president informed him that Eisenhower would command OVERLORD because 'I could not sleep at night with you out of the country.'[5] British General Sir Henry Maitland 'Jumbo' Wilson was then selected as overall Mediterranean commander, combining his own pre-existing Middle East Command with Eisenhower's North African and Italian theatres.

The landing craft shortage, particularly the shortage of landing ship tanks (LSTs), proved to be a far more difficult problem to resolve. Indeed, it was the key limiting factor in all Anglo-American amphibious operations, and thus the fulcrum of many strategic disputes. 'How it is that the plans of two great empires like Britain and the United States should be so hamstrung and limited by a hundred or two of these particular vessels', a frustrated Churchill wrote to Marshall in April, 'will never be understood by history.' The fact is that what he called 'the absurd shortage' of these landing craft truly did so hamstring and limit Anglo-American operations. At Teheran, Marshall stated that 'prior to the present war he had never heard of any landing craft except a rubber boat. Now he thinks about little else.'[6] As previously noted, at the first Cairo and the Teheran Conferences, their lack had forced choices that cost Churchill his much-desired operation against Rhodes, Operation ACCOLADE. Now at the second Cairo Conference, the prime minister attempted to revive his Mediterranean plans by obtaining cancellation of Operation BUCCANEER, the amphibious operation in the Bay of Bengal that Roosevelt had recently promised Chiang Kai-shek.

Churchill argued after the return to Cairo that launching BUCCANEER would delay both OVERLORD and ANVIL, and that Stalin's promise to enter the Pacific war negated the military importance of Chinese bases and thus the Bay of Bengal operation. When Admiral Mountbatten simultaneously insisted that he needed additional landing craft and men for BUCCANEER, Roosevelt agreed to cancel the operation and transfer its landing craft to the Mediterranean, where they would be used first for Italian operations and then for ANVIL. Churchill also hoped to use them to take Rhodes before they would be needed for the southern France invasion.

This cancellation of BUCCANEER followed logically from the Anglo-American reassertion at Cairo that OVERLORD and ANVIL were the 'supreme operations for 1944' and that 'Nothing must be undertaken in any other part of the world which hazards the success of these two operations.'[7] But the cancellation also released Chiang from his commitment to operations in northern Burma and illustrated once again that the Asian mainland remained near the bottom of the Anglo-American priority list. In the war against Japan, greater emphasis would clearly be placed on the dual campaigns in the Pacific, which the British were now to join but which would remain under JCS direction.[8]

With the cancellation of BUCCANEER, success for Churchill's Mediterranean plans with their tight timetable now hinged on two additional factors: prior Turkish entry into the war, and the conquest of Rome in January so as to free up the landing craft for use against Rhodes before they were needed for ANVIL. Unfortunately for the prime minister, neither occurred. At Cairo Churchill 'pleaded, cajoled, and almost threatened' Turkish President Ismet Inonu, according to Admiral Leahy,[9] but to no avail: Turkey would not enter the war at this time – or indeed at any time until it was nearly over (February of 1945). Furthermore, Allied attempts to break Kesselring's Gustav Line and take Rome continued to fail wretchedly in early 1944.

Anzio and the Italian campaign

In May and June of 1944, Allied forces in Italy finally did break that line and take Rome. They had expected to do so months earlier, however, and with far fewer casualties than they experienced. Furthermore, the victory was incomplete and once again involved serious coalition controversy.

When Eisenhower departed in early 1944 for the OVERLORD command in England, he took Montgomery with him as his ground commander. Alexander remained in charge of the Italian theatre, with British General Sir Oliver Leese taking over command of the 8th Army while US General Clark continued to command the 5th Army.

In the midst of these command shifts, Churchill proposed a bold stroke to break the bloody stalemate in Italy: an amphibious assault on the west coast of Italy behind the Gustav Line (Operation SHINGLE). To launch this operation, he further proposed that the transfer of Mediterranean landing craft to OVERLORD be postponed by three weeks, arguing that this would not affect the date of the invasion itself and offering to drop the Rhodes operation completely in return. On the basis of those conditions the Americans agreed both to the transfer delay and the SHINGLE operation. So did the Mediterranean commanders, who under more stable circumstances might have pointed out numerous problems with the plan and/or clarified its objectives in greater detail. But with one group of commanders leaving, another coming in and a third remaining, a degree of confusion occurred and no one did so.

On 22 January forces from Clark's 5th Army under US Major General John Lucas totally surprised the Germans with an amphibious landing near the town of Anzio, behind the German lines and only 33 miles from Rome. Alexander expected Lucas to move quickly inland to the Alban Hills so as to cut German communications between Rome and the Gustav Line's anchor at Monte Cassino, a formidable mountain, thereby forcing a withdrawal of General Vietinghoff's 10th German Army. But in light of the quick German reaction and near-disaster at Salerno the previous September, Clark had ordered Lucas to build up his strength on the beachhead before any inland movement, a decision he refused to alter despite the surprise achieved and supporting ULTRA intelligence. Nor was the overly cautious Lucas willing to request a change in his orders. Consequently he remained on the beach, a blunder that enabled Kesselring to shift forces, attack him and come very close to throwing the entire beachhead back into the sea. Saving it required a major reinforcement effort that temporarily made Anzio the fourth largest port in the world and delayed numerous operations elsewhere. In the process, it also turned what was supposed to have been an offensive operation to dislodge the Germans and break a military stalemate into a desperate defensive operation that only reinforced the stalemate. 'I had hoped that we were hurling a wildcat onto the shore,' Churchill complained, 'but all we had got was a stranded whale.'[10]

Clark fared no better in his simultaneous effort to outflank Monte Cassino and link up with the Anzio beachhead by moving along the Rapido and Liri rivers. His failure resulted not only in heavy US casualties, but also in the destruction of the famous medieval abbey on Monte Cassino's summit prior to the next attempt to break the Gustav Line, officially for military but at least partially for coalition political reasons.

In February, Alexander sent Lieutenant General Bernard Freyberg's New Zealand corps, including an Indian division famous for its mountain fighting abilities, from the 8th Army to reinforce and relieve the depleted 5th Army forces around Monte Cassino. Believing that the Germans were using the abbey as an observation outpost, Freyberg insisted that it be bombed before he would launch any ground assault. Clark, who was Freyberg's immediate superior, did not believe the abbey was being so used and refused to agree. But Alexander feared that Freyberg would respond to rejection by withdrawing his New Zealand and Indian troops from the line. To avoid a coalition crisis, he therefore supported Freyberg. Clark thereupon agreed, and on 15 February Allied heavy bombers destroyed the historic abbey. The destruction did no good, however, and an ensuing frontal assault by the Indian division failed. In fact, Clark had been correct in his belief that the Germans were not using the abbey as an observation post. Now, however, they did so within its ruins, which provided them with effective cover.

In March, the Allies launched yet another attack, preceded this time by an air assault on the town of Cassino itself at the base of the mountain. Again the ground attack was repulsed with heavy casualties. Only in May, on their fourth try, were the Allies able to break the German lines by shifting much of the 8th Army westward to join the 5th, thereby giving them the necessary numerical superiority. By this time Alexander's forces included units not only from the United States, Britain and the Commonwealth and Empire, but also from numerous other Allies, most notably France, Poland and Brazil. French and Polish troops were particularly important in outflanking Monte Cassino and then taking it, thereby forcing a German withdrawal from the Gustav Line. Simultaneously the reinforced Americans at Anzio under Major General Lucian Truscott, who had replaced Lucas in February, broke out of the beachhead.

Rather than use this breakout to trap the German 10th Army with a movement into the town of Valmontone as Alexander desired and ordered, Clark directed Truscott northward so as to take the prestigious prize of Rome. Truscott did so on 4 June. But Clark's glory was short-lived, as the event was all but forgotten in the aftermath of the Normandy invasion two days later. Furthermore, ordering Truscott to Rome instead of Valmontone enabled the Germans to escape, slow the Allied advance and establish a new defensive position, the Gothic Line, 150 miles north of Rome in the northern Appenine Mountains. Alexander's forces did not even reach that line until August. They broke through it in September, but by that time Alexander had been forced to give up seven divisions for the invasion of southern France, Operation ANVIL, and his depleted forces made little progress against the Germans. ANVIL, however, had by that time led to yet another round of intense Anglo-American strategic controversy.

ANVIL: the Mediterranean controversy continued

Throughout the first half of 1944 the British had argued for cancellation of the southern France operation on numerous grounds: that insufficient landing craft were available to launch it in conjunction with OVERLORD; that it was unnecessary in support of the cross-Channel operation; that the troops and landing craft were needed in Italy; and that from Italy those troops could and should move not westward, but eastward into Yugoslavia, down the Dalmatian coast and through the Ljubljana gap to Vienna and the Hungarian plain. The Americans countered that ANVIL remained crucial to the success of OVER-LORD and that it had been promised to the Soviets at Teheran. It was therefore as sacrosanct as OVERLORD, and if the landing craft shortage precluded launching it in conjunction with OVERLORD, it should be launched after the cross-Channel assault rather than cancelled.

Unstated save in their internal correspondence was the American belief that ANVIL was necessary to prevent the very descent into southeastern Europe that the British desired by denying London the forces capable of making that descent. According to JCS planners, the Balkans had always been the hidden

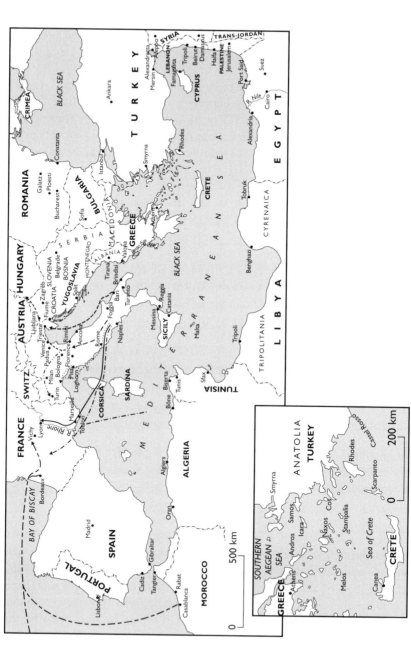

13 Possible strategies in the Mediterranean, April–August 1944

goal of British Mediterranean strategy and had to be avoided at all costs for both military and political reasons. Militarily, the mountainous terrain would preclude effective operations against the Germans, much as Italy had done. Politically, entering the Balkans would place Anglo-American forces in an area of intense and historic Anglo-Russian rivalry — which was exactly, the Americans believed, why the British wanted to invade the area. But resurrection of this historic clash invited a dangerous split in the alliance. It also involved manipulation of US forces for British political goals in an area of no particular interest or value to Washington, what Stimson bluntly called 'another diversion in the interest of the British Empire and contrary to our American interests'.[11]

Consequently Roosevelt and the JCS refused to agree to ANVIL's cancellation and used their growing power to bludgeon the British into acquiescence by threatening to withhold the Far Eastern landing craft they had previously agreed to send to the Mediterranean. Brooke at one point bluntly called American behaviour 'blackmail' for which 'History will never forgive them.'[12] Churchill did not accept defeat until July, and when he did so it was without the good grace he had shown in defeat at the end of the Teheran Conference. Indeed, when ANVIL was re-code-named DRAGOON for security reasons, he found the new name quite appropriate and spoke of being 'dragooned' into accepting the operation.[13]

Throughout 1942 and 1943 the Mediterranean theatre had been an arena of intense Anglo-American controversy that had boldly illustrated the problems inherent in coalition warfare. Such controversy and problems clearly continued into 1944. The decisions to land at Anzio in January, to bomb the abbey on Monte Cassino in February and March, to take Rome in June instead of trapping the retreating Germans, and to invade southern France instead of the Balkans, were all the result of coalition politics. Interestingly, each of these decisions save the last one in favour of ANVIL also resulted in costly military failure and loss of life, a pattern the Americans clearly feared would be reproduced in northern Italy and Yugoslavia.

Indeed, so lengthy, bloody and indecisive was the entire Italian campaign as to call into question whether it ever should have been undertaken. Its defenders argue that it led Hitler to send 20 divisions to Italy, a dispersion of his forces that clearly helped OVERLORD to succeed. But critics argue that this same goal could have been accomplished merely by the threat of invasion, without the actual, bloody and unnecessary operations on the Italian mainland — and definitely without the movement beyond Rome that British military theorist Major General J.F.C. Fuller bluntly labelled 'daft'.[14]

Controversy also continues to swirl around the decision to invade southern France rather than the Balkans, with critics arguing that ANVIL-DRAGOON was unnecessary for OVERLORD and that the British Balkan strategy could have precluded post-war Soviet control of much of Eastern Europe. Defenders of the American position counter that the invasion of southern France was indeed necessary for OVERLORD's success — especially in light of the

Anglo-American inability to obtain a usable port in northern France,[15] and that events in the mountains of Italy clearly illustrated that military operations in the mountainous Balkans would have failed. Italy and the Balkans, these individuals argue, did not constitute a 'soft underbelly' as Churchill had earlier claimed. Rather, as General Marshall later told his biographer, 'the soft underbelly had chrome steel baseboards'.[16]

OVERLORD and the liberation of France

Much greater and more important Allied military success occurred in France during the late spring and summer of 1944. Prior to that time, the last successful cross-Channel invasion had occurred nearly 900 years earlier, in 1066, when the Normans had successfully invaded England. This fact weighed heavily on Allied planners, especially British planners. But the Americans were by late 1943 aware of the dangers as well. During the Teheran Conference, Roosevelt had called the English Channel 'a disagreeable body of water' (Churchill shot back that 'the British had every reason to be thankful that the English Channel was such a disagreeable body of water'). And when Soviet Marshal Kliment E. Voroshilov compared crossing the Channel to crossing a large river, General Marshall politely yet forcefully corrected him by noting that

> The difference between a river crossing, however wide, and a landing from the ocean is that the failure of a river crossing is a reverse while the failure of a landing operation from the sea is a catastrophe, because failure in the latter means the almost utter destruction of the landing craft and personnel involved.[17]

An amphibious landing is by its very nature one of the most complex and dangerous types of military operation to undertake. It requires extraordinary logistical preparation and inter-service cooperation, and even under the best of circumstances it places the attackers at a severe disadvantage vis-à-vis entrenched defenders. The Allies did by 1944 have a history of successful amphibious operations stretching back to 1942, but many of those operations had been near-disasters, most recently and notably Salerno and Anzio. Moreover, and unlike all the previous amphibious landings, the Germans fully expected a cross-Channel assault and had prepared extensive fortifications along the entire northern French coast.

General Morgan and his COSSAC planning staff had emphasized in this regard the need to make sure that no more than 12 'full-strength first-quality' German divisions would be available in reserve for use against the invasion, a prerequisite that the British continually emphasized in their calls for greater Mediterranean activity to divert and disperse the *Wehrmacht*. COSSAC had also emphasized the need for surprise and had therefore rejected landing near Calais, a French port at the narrowest point of the English Channel but for that very reason the most likely invasion site and the one the Germans would most heavily defend. Furthermore, the raid against Dieppe in August of 1942, one in a series launched by Mountbatten's Combined Operations but a disaster during which the 5,000 Canadians suffered a staggering 68 per cent casualties, provided additional evidence, if any was needed, against attacking fortified ports.[18] Consequently COSSAC suggested an assault on the open beaches of Normandy, far to the west of Calais but near the ports of LeHavre to the east and Cherbourg on the Cotentin Peninsula to the west.[19]

Churchill, Roosevelt and the CCS had approved COSSAC's plans during the August 1943 QUADRANT Conference. So did Eisenhower and Montgomery in early 1944. Each general concluded, however, as had Churchill earlier, that COSSAC's proposal for a three-division assault over a 25-mile front at Normandy was inadequate even against limited German strength. Consequently they expanded the assault plan (Operation NEPTUNE) to more than five regular as well as three airborne divisions over five beaches covering 55 miles, with the airborne divisions to be sent in behind enemy lines on the flanks a few hours before the actual assault. They also postponed ANVIL until August, and the OVERLORD invasion itself for one month, so as to obtain additional landing craft from the Mediterranean and from American production for the additional troops.

The assault on Normandy would be the largest amphibious operation in history, comprising over 2 million men, 4,000 ships and 12,000 aircraft. Preparing for such an undertaking would require an enormous effort. To ensure Anglo-American cooperation and coordination, Eisenhower arranged for an integrated command structure at his Supreme Headquarters, Allied Expeditionary Forces (SHAEF), similar to the one he had created in the Mediterranean. Directly beneath him would be four British commanders. Air Marshal Sir Arthur Tedder, who had previously served as his air chief in the Mediterranean, would be the deputy commander. Replacing him as chief of the air forces would be Air Marshal Sir Trafford Leigh-Mallory. Admiral Sir Bertram Ramsay would command all naval forces, and General Montgomery all ground forces. US Lieutenant General Walter Bedell Smith would again be Eisenhower's chief of staff, but Morgan and two other British officers would serve as deputy chiefs of staff. Actual combat forces would remain nationally distinct on the division and corps levels, but SHAEF itself would be a fully integrated Allied command structure.

Differences in such matters as word usage, pronunciation and national as well as military cultures would of course continue to exist and create problems in such an integrated staff. In North Africa, for example, Eisenhower had been puzzled by a British requisition for 10,000 'sleepers' until informed that this referred to railroad ties, not Pullman cars! Similarly a British officer had asked his American counterpart 'Where the devil' Americans had learned to mispronounce the word 'schedule' as 'skedule' instead of 'shedule' ('I learned in school,' the US officer quickly shot back). Such difficulties, General Bedell Smith humorously noted soon after the war, could usually be 'overcome with a little gin'.[20] But national chauvinism and animosity were another matter.

7 Allied Supreme Command at their British headquarters. Left to right: Lt. Gen. Omar N. Bradley, Senr Cmdr of US Ground Forces; Adm. Sir Bertram Ramsay, Naval Cmdr; Air Chief Marshal Sir Arthur Tedder, Deputy Supreme Cmdr; Gen. Dwight Eisenhower, Supreme Cmdr; Gen. Sir Bernard L. Montgomery, Cmdr-in-Chief of the British forces; Air Chief Marshal Sir Trafford Leigh Mallory, Air Cmdr-in-Chief; and Lt. Gen. Walter Bedell Smith, Chief of Staff, 11 February 1944 © Bettmann/CORBIS

8 Lt. Gen. George S. Patton, Lt. Gen. Omar N. Bradley and General Sir Bernard Montgomery meet to discuss the progress of the French campaign © CORBIS

Exhibitions of such chauvinism and animosity would of course occur on an individual level, but one of Eisenhower's greatest strengths remained his refusal to tolerate such behaviour and his insistence on cooperation as mandatory among his subordinates. Already cited is the famous 1942 story about his insistence on sending home an American officer for using 'British' as an adjective in front of the otherwise-acceptable epithet 'son-of-a-bitch'.[21] Such a stance became even more important in 1943–44, with the arrival and continued presence of so many American soldiers in England for OVERLORD and POINTBLANK (over one and a half million by June 1944) as to constitute a virtual 'American Occupation of Britain', in the words of British historian David Reynolds.[22]

Ensuing clashes were unavoidable, with the British stereotyping the arriving Americans as 'oversexed, overpaid, overfed, and over here' and the Americans responding that the British were 'undersexed, underpaid, underfed, and under Eisenhower'. Authorities on both sides launched major efforts to minimize these clashes. As General Spaatz noted and warned, there were three crimes a member of the AAF in England could commit: 'murder, rape and interference with Anglo-American relations. The first two might conceivably be pardoned, but the third one, never.'[23]

Eisenhower himself must have been sorely tempted by 1944 to apply the adjective and epithet he had found so objectionable in 1942 to some of his British associates – most notably the arrogant Montgomery, who appeared not to know or care how offensive his behaviour was. But another one of Eisenhower's great strengths was his ability to deal with such individuals without losing his temper – most of the time, anyway. Such self-control and cooperation by example would both be crucial to OVERLORD's success.

A successful invasion would also require major deception plans regarding the exact location of the landings, for unlike Mediterranean operations in 1943, the Germans were fully aware that the Channel coast would be invaded in 1944. Indeed, Hitler had ordered creation of an 'Atlantic Wall' of defences and placed two of his best commanders in charge of German forces in the area. Field Marshal Gerd von Rundstedt, who had led the German forces that broke through the Ardennes in 1940, was brought out of retirement and appointed Commander-in-Chief West, while Rommel was appointed commander of Army Group B defending the Channel coast. To deceive these men and their intelligence as to exactly where and when the invasion would take place, the Allies developed a massive and highly effective deception plan code-named BODYGUARD after Churchill's comment at Teheran that 'In wartime . . . Truth is so precious that she should always be attended by a bodyguard of lies.'[24]

BODYGUARD was designed to convince the Germans that the Allies intended to invade at Calais rather than Normandy, in the summer rather than the spring, and with a diversionary attack against Norway (interestingly, where Hitler had long expected an attack and where Churchill had long wanted to attack with Operation JUPITER). To convince the Germans that Calais was the primary target, Allied intelligence created in southeastern

England what one historian has aptly called 'a work of artistic mendacity' – the phony US First Army (FUSAG) of a million men under Patton, including phony camps, supply depots, airfields, landing craft and tanks (Operation FORTITUDE SOUTH).[25]

COSSAC had insisted that a successful invasion also had to be preceded by control of the air, isolation of the beachhead, creation of artificial harbours for supply across the open beaches until a port had been taken, and the ability to limit German forces in the area to 12 first quality divisions with no more than 15 available for transfer from the east. Even then, it warned, there was only a 'reasonable prospect of success'.[26] While two huge artificial harbours (MULBERRIES) were being created and prepared for towing to Normandy in 200-foot-long concrete sections, the new Anglo-American long-range fighter aircraft that accompanied the bombers on Operation POINTBLANK against the German aircraft and oil industries were decimating the *Luftwaffe* in what had become a campaign of attrition the Germans could not win.[27] In that sense they were gradually achieving overall command of the air – a vital prerequisite for success at Normandy. SHAEF, however, needed and demanded a more immediate and direct air campaign to achieve local air superiority and preclude potential German reinforcement of the invasion area. Tedder's plan to achieve this called for use of the heavy bombers engaged in POINTBLANK as well as SHAEF's own air forces to destroy the French railway system, attacking the marshalling and repair yards first and then focusing on isolation of the coast and destruction of German air defences. Furthermore, Eisenhower hoped to create in England a fully integrated bomber command similar to the one he had created in the Mediterranean. But POINTBLANK commanders Spaatz and Harris objected to the transfer of their heavy bombers to Leigh-Mallory and to what they considered a tactical diversion of those bombers from their more important strategic missions against German industry, particularly the oil and aircraft industries. They were supported by Churchill, who further objected both to SHAEF's proposed railway campaign because it would kill thousands of French citizens and to an integrated bomber command because it would deprive Britain of one of its last independent commands. That he raised such objections at the same time as the ANVIL debate illustrates his multiple efforts in early 1944 to retain some equality in the alliance amidst the ever-growing American preponderance of power.[28]

So fierce was the ensuing struggle over the air campaign that in the midst of it Eisenhower threatened to resign. A compromise was worked out on the command and priorities issues in late March whereby Eisenhower and Tedder (but not Leigh-Mallory) were given temporary control of the heavy bombers for operations in support of OVERLORD, including the attack on the French railway system, but Spaatz and Harris were in effect allowed to continue their attacks against oil installations and the aircraft industry as well as their independent commands with residual bombers not needed for SHAEF's targets. It took until May to get Churchill to concede formally on the issue of French casualties. The ensuing campaign was massive, with more than 11,000 aircraft flying more than 200,000 sorties and dropping 195,000 tons of bombs. It was also highly successful, though most notably and ironically in its final phase when Leigh-Mallory's small bombers, not POINTBLANK's large ones, destroyed more than 70 bridges and tunnels, thereby isolating northwestern France and precluding major German reinforcement of the invasion area. By early June, SHAEF also possessed total control of the air above Normandy.[29]

Eisenhower received additional assistance prior to the invasion in the form of divided German command relationships and conflicting defence proposals. Neither von Rundstedt nor Rommel had control of German air or naval forces, and the two generals disagreed as to whether they should focus on stopping the invasion on the beaches as Rommel maintained, or inland via a large mobile reserve as von Rundstedt held to be the only viable option. Neither option was properly pursued, though Rommel did heavily reinforce the Atlantic Wall. But the Allied air campaign severely hampered his efforts, as did sabotage by the SOE and OSS-supported French resistance. Furthermore, Hitler divided his armoured reserves between Rommel and his own High Command, leaving Rundstedt with none. And in early June the weather along the French coast was so bad that Rommel went home for his wife's birthday.

The invasion itself was originally scheduled for the morning of 5 June along five beaches. Under Montgomery's overall command, two American divisions and elements of a third comprising the nucleus of the US First Army under Lieutenant General Omar N. Bradley were to land on 'Utah' and 'Omaha' beaches on the western end of the invasion area near the base of the Cotentin Peninsula; farther east, two British and one Canadian division from the British Second Army under Lieutenant General Miles Dempsey were to land on 'Gold', 'Juno' and 'Sword' beaches and capture the town of Caen, an important road junction. Preceding these landings, two US airborne divisions were to land to the west of Utah beach while one British airborne division landed to the east of Sword, the easternmost British beach.

Despite all the preparations and advantages, the invasion proved to be a very near thing (realizing this fact, Eisenhower prepared and carried with him on 6 June a message taking total personal responsibility for the failure).[30] First, bad weather postponed the operation from 5 June to 6 June, when Eisenhower's meteorologist predicted a temporary break in the storms pounding the Channel coast. Then many of the American parachute and British glider-based airborne forces landed far from their targets. And while the air campaign had previously succeeded in isolating the beachhead, it had not knocked out the German defences. Naval guns had to be turned on those defences in support of the Allied troops.

The worst problems occurred at Omaha beach, where German defences both on the beach itself (including a seawall and an anti-tank ditch) and above the cliffs at the beach's end decimated the Americans. Failure on Omaha beach could have wrecked the entire invasion, for without it Utah beach would be isolated from the three British beaches, which in turn could have been isolated and overwhelmed by German reserves. The Americans lost 2,500 men

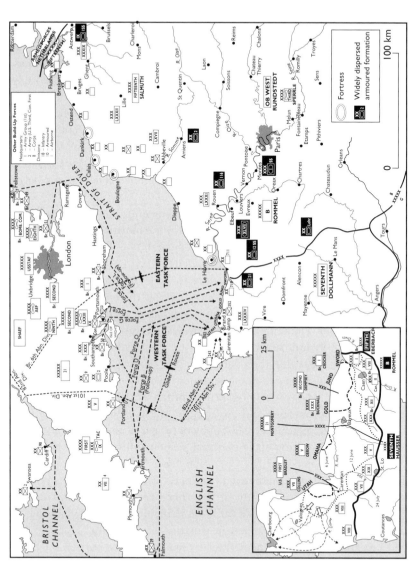

14 Allied invasion force and German dispositions in northwestern France, 6 June 1944. The inset shows the operations since 6 June and the situation on 24 July 1944.

on Omaha beach on 6 June, but by day's end they had succeeded in taking the cliffs.

Those landing at Utah, Gold, June and Sword beaches had an easier time, partially because Hitler originally saw the landings as a diversion from the main assault at Calais and therefore refused to commit his armoured reserves until it was too late to destroy the beachhead, which by 8 June contained 100,000 troops. But on all five beaches Anglo-American forces moved inland far slower than expected. Indeed, the British could not take their main objective of Caen on the first day, or indeed for the next six weeks as the Germans counter-attacked and rushed major reinforcements into the area. The Americans fared little better due to the terrain around their beaches – high banks of earth planted with thick hedges (hedgerows) by Normandy farmers to delineate their separate fields – which precluded effective use of their armour and provided the Germans with excellent defensive shields. The Americans did manage to cut off the Cotentin Peninsula to the west and capture Cherbourg on 27 June, but German destruction precluded any use of the port until mid-July and full use until September – a major loss given the destruction of one of the two MULBERRIES in a major Channel storm on 19 June.

Despite this loss, Eisenhower was able to build up his forces within the constrained beachhead and by the end of June had almost a million men within it. These were organized by late July into two army groups: the British-Canadian 21st under Montgomery, consisting of the British 2nd Army under Dempsey and the new Canadian 1st Army under Lieutenant General Henry Crerar; and the American 12th Army Group under Bradley, consisting of the US 1st Army under Lieutenant General Courtney Hodges and the new US 3rd Army under Patton, who was now moved from his phony deception army in England to a real one in France.

Patton had been available for the successful FORTITUDE SOUTH deception because his behaviour in Sicily during 1943 had led Eisenhower to suspend him temporarily from active command, replacing him with Clark in Italy and promoting Bradley, Patton's subordinate corps commander, to command US troops in northern France. A classmate and friend of Eisenhower from the famous West Point class of 1915, Bradley had exhibited a solid and quiet competence in 1942–43 operations in both North Africa and Sicily that stood in sharp contrast to Patton's flamboyance and tendency to get into trouble – especially with his mouth. That tendency was illustrated once again in the spring of 1944, leading Eisenhower to warn Patton bluntly that he was 'thoroughly weary of your failure to control your tongue' and to threaten to send him home. But with Marshall giving him free rein in the matter, Eisenhower decided to keep Patton and gave him command of the US 3rd Army once it was activated in France.[31] Patton would henceforth serve under Bradley, however, who would command the entire 12th Army Group. Bradley's supporters argue that this was the correct and most effective command relationship, with the brilliant but erratic Patton under the more stable Bradley. But others argue that Bradley has been vastly overrated and was far from the super-competent 'soldier's general of media legend'.[32]

Throughout June and early July, Rommel focused his armoured forces not against Bradley, but against what he perceived to be the more dangerous threat of Montgomery's army group at Caen, thereby precluding any breakthrough on that front despite a major effort (Operation GOODWOOD). Only on 20 July was Montgomery able to take the town. By that time, however, Eisenhower had turned to Bradley's forces, which had taken the pivotal town of Saint Lo two days earlier, for the desired breakthrough (Operation COBRA). After, an intense 'carpet bombing' of the area that killed not only the German defenders but also many Americans (including US Lieutenant General Lesley McNair, who had been responsible for the training of all American army ground forces), the 1st Army's VII Corps under Lieutenant General J. Lawton Collins broke through at Saint Lo, opening a gap in the German lines through which Patton sent most of his 3rd Army sweeping eastward while two armoured divisions were detached westward in an unsuccessful effort to quickly capture ports on the Brittany coast. The sweep eastward was highly successful, however, partially because Hitler chose to counter-attack against the American flank at Mortain near Avranches rather than withdraw. With the failure of that counter-attack, Bradley saw the possibility of sweeping around the German rear and linking up with the Canadian 1st Army attacking south, thereby trapping an entire German army. But the trap did not close completely, as the Americans halted to avoid collision with the Canadians, who were slowed by strong resistance and Montgomery's failure to reinforce them. Some 35,000 German soldiers thus escaped from the so-called Falaise pocket before it closed on 19 August. Within the pocket, however, 10,000 Germans died and 45–50,000 surrendered. The remaining German forces proved unable to stop the rapid Anglo-American advance that now took place.

Compounding this military disaster (and indeed, partially a cause and partially an effect of it), a major crisis erupted within the German High Command. Unhappy with von Rundstedt's performance, Hitler on 2 July replaced him with Field Marshal Gunther von Kluge as Commander-in-Chief West. Two weeks later, on 17 July, Rommel was badly injured by an Allied air attack. Three days after that, on 20 July, high-ranking army conspirators led by Colonel Klaus von Stauffenberg attempted to assassinate Hitler with a bomb at his East Prussian headquarters.[33] But Hitler survived the attempt and quickly began a purge of all those involved – a group that included Rommel, who committed suicide. So did von Kluge, who had flirted with the conspirators, after Hitler replaced him on 16 August with Field Marshal Walther Model. Such disarray within their High Command only compounded the disaster now facing the Germans.

Once again, however, Allied coalition arguments erupted. With his forces racing eastward against the demoralized Germans, Eisenhower ordered Bradley and Hodges to bypass Paris. That proved intolerable to the French. Inside the

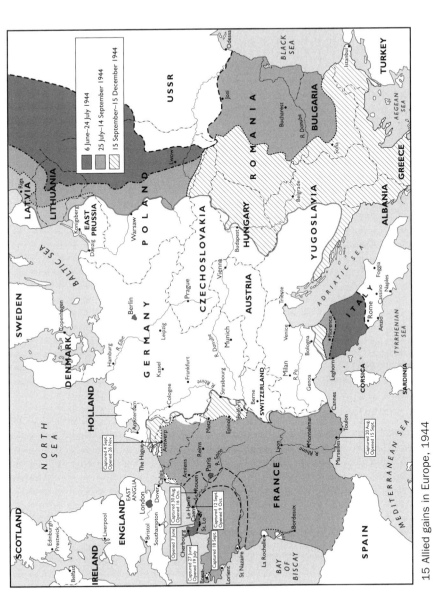

15 Allied gains in Europe, 1944

Legend:
- 6 June–24 July 1944
- 25 July–14 September 1944
- 15 September–15 December 1944

SCOTLAND
IRELAND
Belfast
Edinburgh
Prestwick
Liverpool
Bristol
ENGLAND
EAST ANGLIA
London
Dover
Southampton
Calais
NORTH SEA

Captured 4 Sept.
Opened 26 Nov.
HOLLAND
The Hague
Amsterdam
Antwerp

Cherbourg
Opened 7 June
Captured 27 June
Opened 9 July
Brest
Captured 18 Sept.
St Nazaire
Lorient
La Rochelle
Bordeaux
BAY OF BISCAY

Captured 30 Aug
Opened 16 Oct.
Le Havre
Caen
St Lo
Captured 12 Sept.
Opened 9 Oct.
Amiens
Rouen
Reims
Paris
R. Seine
FRANCE
Lyon
R. Rhône
Montélimar
Marseilles
Toulon
Captured 20 Aug
Opened 15 Sept.
Cannes

SPAIN
MEDITERRANEAN SEA

SWEDEN
DENMARK
Copenhagen
BALTIC SEA
Hamburg
R. Elbe
Berlin
Leipzig
GERMANY
Kassel
Frankfurt
Cologne
Metz
Epinal
Belfort
Berne
SWITZERLAND
R. Rhine
Strasbourg
R. Danube
Munich
Milan
Venice
R. Po
Genoa
Bologna
Leghorn
Florence
ITALY
Rome
Anzio
Cassino
Naples
Foggia
TYRRHENIAN SEA
SARDINIA
CORSICA

Königsberg
Danzig
EAST PRUSSIA
LATVIA
Riga
LITHUANIA
Warsaw
POLAND
Lwow
CZECHOSLOVAKIA
Prague
Vienna
AUSTRIA
Budapest
HUNGARY
Trieste
ADRIATIC SEA
YUGOSLAVIA
Belgrade
ALBANIA
GREECE

USSR
Odessa
BLACK SEA
Jassi
ROMANIA
Bucharest
R. Danube
BULGARIA
Sofia
Istanbul
TURKEY
AEGEAN SEA

city resistance forces rose in revolt against the German garrison. Outside, de Gaulle protested Eisenhower's decision while Major General Jacques Leclerc defied Ike's orders and sent Free French forces to take the city. Bowing to the demands of coalition warfare, Eisenhower approved and Bradley sent American units to aid the French. Paris fell on 25 August.

The effort hardly slowed the Allied advance, as both army groups moved rapidly into Belgium and Lorraine. That advance was aided by the belated invasion of southern France, Operation ANVIL-DRAGOON, by Lieutenant General Alexander Patch's US 7th Army on 15 August, followed by Free French forces under General Jean de Lattre de Tassigny. They quickly captured the French naval base at Toulon and the port of Marseilles, which would prove vital to supply the Allies in light of the destruction at Cherbourg and the failure to take the Brittany ports. Organized as the 6th Army Group under the overall command of US Lieutenant General Jacob Devers, they then made very quick progress up the Rhône River valley as Hitler ordered his forces to withdraw, and by 12 September had made contact with Patton's US 3rd Army.

By mid-September Anglo-American forces had thus liberated most of France and much of Belgium and Luxembourg as well as southern and central Italy, were approaching the German border, and had so badly mauled the German Army as to call into question its ability to defend Germany itself in the West. An equally if not more threatening situation had developed for Hitler on the Eastern Front. 1944 was in Soviet history the year of the 'Ten Great Victories' by which the Red Army totally expelled the Germans from Soviet soil, knocked Finland out of the war, and conquered much of eastern Europe. Indeed, by August the Red Army had reached the Vistula River outside Warsaw.[34] Germany was reeling under combined assaults from west, east, south and in the air, and total Allied victory before year's end now appeared possible.

The dual offensive in the Pacific and the destruction of Japanese naval airpower

Allied offensives in the Pacific during 1944 achieved equally spectacular results. While MacArthur and Halsey completed the encirclement of Rabaul and invaded the Philippines, Nimitz's forces advanced successfully through the Marshall Islands, neutralized the major Japanese base at Truk in the Carolines, and then took Saipan, Guam and Tinian in the Marianas. Both advances mortally threatened the Japanese and led to decisive naval battles that effectively destroyed Japan's naval power and rendered the Japanese position hopeless.

While Australian troops fought the Japanese on the Huon Peninsula,[35] US Army and Marine forces in December 1943 invaded first the southern tip of New Britain and then Cape Gloucester near the northwestern tip, thereby continuing the encirclement of Rabaul that the JCS had ordered during the August QUADRANT Conference as an alternative to invasion. They completed that encirclement on 29 February 1944, with a landing on Los Negros Island in the Admiralty chain to the northwest. Simultaneously they subjected Rabaul itself to a continuous and furious pounding from the air, forcing the withdrawal of major surviving air and naval forces to Truk by March. This successful isolation and neutralization of Rabaul avoided what could have been frightful casualties had the base been invaded, for at its eventual surrender it still contained 90,000 personnel.

While Rabaul was being isolated, MacArthur simultaneously continued to 'leapfrog' along the northern New Guinea coast with amphibious landings at Saidor on 2 January and then, with carrier cover for Nimitz, all the way to Aitape and to Hollandia in Dutch New Guinea, more than 500 miles to the west. On 22 April, he thereby bypassed Hansa Bay and Wewak while cutting off General Adachi's escape route. MacArthur then jumped 130 miles farther west to the island of Wakde on 17 May (along with the mainland village of Sarmi), and ten days later to the island of Biak, another 190 miles to the west. In July his forces took the island of Noemfoor and the village of Sansapoor on the Vogelkop Peninsula, the westernmost section of New Guinea. But the Japanese garrison at Biak Island was both much larger than anticipated and deeply entrenched in a series of fortified, interconnecting caves. The result was a series of bloody contests that lasted until mid-August and brought back memories of 'Bloody Buna'.

Between Buna and Biak, however, MacArthur's campaign was exceptional in terms of the ability to avoid and cut off heavy concentrations of Japanese troops via use of ULTRA intelligence and the leapfrogging technique. Nevertheless MacArthur was a late convert to the idea for which he later became famous, and the New Guinea campaign as a whole exacted a fearful casualty toll on the troops involved. Since the total number of Allied troops on New Guinea remained small, those casualties were not huge by World War II standards. Relatively speaking, however, they were actually far worse than the bloodletting on Guadalcanal: 1 in 37 Allied servicemen died taking that island, whereas 1 in 11 died on New Guinea.[36]

While MacArthur's and Halsey's forces were winning these major victories in the South and Southwest Pacific, Nimitz's forces in the Central Pacific successfully moved westward and bypassed Japanese concentrations at an even more rapid pace. As in New Guinea, ULTRA played a key role, revealing to Nimitz that the Japanese expected the next attack in the eastern Marshall Islands and had heavily reinforced the area. Consequently Nimitz ordered Spruance, Turner and Smith to attack instead Kwajalein Atoll in the middle of the Marshall chain, preceded by air raids from the Gilberts and from the new and fast US carriers under the command of Vice Admiral Marc Mitscher against Japanese airfields throughout the Marshalls. Outnumbering the Kwajalein defenders five to one, army and marine forces took the atoll between 1 and 4 February with far fewer casualties (373 dead and 1,500 wounded) than they had experienced at Tarawa (1,000 dead and 2,000 wounded). Given the relative ease and success of this operation, Nimitz then jumped to Eniwetok in the western Marshalls on 17 February. To protect his forces from Japanese air

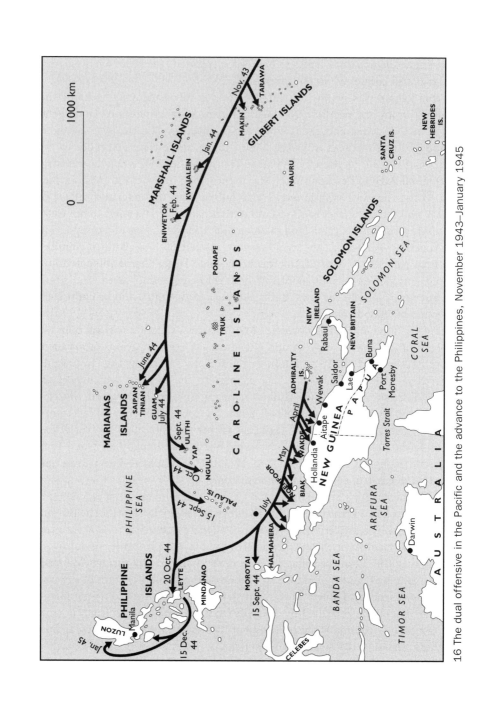

16 The dual offensive in the Pacific and the advance to the Philippines, November 1943–January 1945

attacks, Mitscher's carrier task force launched simultaneous and devastating raids on the base at Truk, destroying 265 planes and sinking eight warships as well as 24 merchant ships totalling 140,000 tons. Eniwetok fell four days later, thereby giving Nimitz total control of the Marshalls and cutting off numerous Japanese garrisons and other islands in the chain.

Given these victories and the vulnerability of Truk as proven by Mitscher's successful raids, Nimitz now decided to bypass the base and the Carolines entirely and instead take a huge jump 1,000 miles westward to the Marianas, a chain within striking distance of both the Philippines and the Japanese home islands. The island of Saipan within this chain was the first objective, with Spruance once again in command of the fleet, Turner the amphibious landing, and Smith the ground forces. The invasion began on 15 June but encountered fierce resistance from the island's 32,000 defenders that lasted for three weeks rather than the three days US planners had anticipated. As in previous Pacific battles, Japanese soldiers fought virtually to the last man, inflicted heavy casualties on the Americans, and chose suicide to surrender. So did 8,000 of Saipan's civilian population, who at the end of the campaign committed suicide rather than face American occupation.

More important than the ground campaign on Saipan was the naval battle that ensued just a few days after the amphibious landings. Correctly viewing the struggle for the island as critical and searching for a decisive, Mahanian naval battle and victory to halt the Americans, Admiral Toyoda Soemu, Yamamoto's successor as Combined Fleet Commander, ordered an attack on Spruance's Fifth Fleet by the First Mobile Fleet in the Philippines under Vice Admiral Ozawa Jisaburo. The resulting Battle of the Philippine Sea on 19–20 June was the largest naval air battle of the war and, as the Japanese had planned, a decisive one. Unfortunately for them, however, it was decisive in favour of the Americans and resulted in the destruction of the Japanese naval air arm.

Ozawa's fleet contained the newest Japanese warships, but they were far inferior to Spruance's and Mitscher's forces numerically, with the Americans outnumbering the Japanese in carriers and aircraft by a factor of two to one. The qualitative difference in pilots was even greater, for the Americans had been rotating their veteran pilots so as to train new ones, whereas the Japanese had not. Consequently, the new Japanese pilots were not as well trained as the Americans, while most of the old Japanese veteran pilots had by this time died in previous campaigns. Furthermore, Spruance knew the Japanese plan and refused to be drawn toward Ozawa's fleet as called for in that plan. He and Mitscher did allow Ozawa to attack first, but the Japanese admiral's four air attacks accomplished nothing save the destruction of his naval air arm. The Japanese lost an incredible 275 out of 373 planes in these attacks without sinking a single US ship, while the Americans lost only 29 aircraft. With good reason the latter nicknamed this battle 'the Great Marianas Turkey Shoot'. To make matters worse, Ozawa also lost 17 of 25 submarines in futile attacks on Mitscher's fleet. US submarines, on the other hand, sank two of his carriers, one of them the largest in Japan's navy. Then on the afternoon of 20 June Mitscher's aircraft attacked Ozawa, shot down 65 more of his planes, sank a third Japanese carrier and seriously damaged three more.

Nevertheless, numerous critics were and have remained deeply upset with Spruance's handling of the battle, particularly his refusal to allow Mitscher to steam westward in order to engage and thoroughly destroy Ozawa's fleet on 19 June. Spruance rejected this Mahanian vision on the grounds that his primary responsibility was protection of the Saipan invasion force, and that Ozawa might be attempting to lure him westward with part of his fleet as the bait so that the other part could destroy the troop transports (which, interestingly, was exactly what the Japanese attempted to do in the next major naval battle at Leyte Gulf). Spruance also knew of the near-disaster and severe criticism that had followed Admiral Fletcher's early withdrawal from the waters around Guadalcanal in 1942.[37] Consequently, he ordered Mitscher to fall back towards Saipan, and by the time his forces located Ozawa's fleet on the afternoon of 20 June it was 340 miles away – perilously close to the range limit of his own aircraft. Nevertheless Mitscher launched over 200 aircraft, with the devastating results enumerated above, and ordered his ships to risk night submarine attack by turning their lights on so as to guide the returning pilots. Some 80 planes were lost when they ran out of fuel and either crash-landed or ditched in the sea, but most of the crews were recovered the following day. That in turn ruled out further pursuit of what remained of Ozawa's fleet. Nevertheless, many if not most historians agree that Spruance was correct to consider protection of the invasion force his primary objective. And even with his caution, he had still dealt the Japanese naval air arm a mortal blow from which it would never recover.

These defeats were devastating to Japan. Its naval air arm was now destroyed, its surface fleet weakened and vulnerable without adequate air cover, its veteran pilots dead, its empire about to be cut in half, and the Americans with their new long-range B-29 'superfortress' bombers within bombing distance of the home islands. Less than two weeks after the fall of Saipan on 9 July, the Tojo government in Tokyo resigned in failure and was replaced by a new military government under General Koiso Kuniaki.

Nor was this the end of the bad news for the Japanese war effort. By month's end the Americans had also seized Tinian and retaken Guam in the Marianas. To make matters worse, US submarines, armed since late 1943 with new and now highly accurate torpedoes as well as ULTRA intelligence, were quickly destroying the already undersized Japanese merchant fleet on which the home islands relied, much as Great Britain relied on its own and the US merchant fleet. Indeed, during 1944 alone the Japanese lost 600 merchant ships totalling more than 2.7 million tons. And in Burma, despite heavy casualties (including Wingate's own death in a plane crash) and numerous setbacks, Chinese, American and British forces had by mid-1944 finally achieved major success.

In late 1943 and early 1944, Stilwell's Chinese forces as well as Wingate's Chindits and Merrill's Marauders, their American counterparts, launched a series of operations that succeeded in taking Myitkyina in the northern part of the country by the summer, thereby opening the way for the extension of the new Ledo Road from India as an alternative to the old Burma Road supply route to China. Then, in January, Lieutenant General Sir William Slim and his 14th Army in India launched another offensive against Arakan. Again, however, he was stopped by Japanese counter-attacks. In March the Japanese 15th Army under General Mutaguchi Renya invaded India to foil additional Chindit raids or another offensive by destroying Slim's supply bases, establish Subhas Chandra Bose and his Indian National Army within India, and perhaps thereby start a revolt against the British. Mutaguchi's forces quickly surrounded and laid siege to the key British positions at Imphal and Kohima. Slim was able to reinforce the defenders, however, who held on in fierce fighting until Slim's army, supplied by air, broke the sieges in April and May. The ensuing retreat of Mutaguchi's ill-supplied and by now diseased and exhausted troops turned into a rout. Out of 85,000 men, an extraordinary 53,000 were casualties (the majority dead), at the cost of 17,000 British casualties, thereby opening the way for additional operations against the now seriously weakened Japanese forces in Burma.

As in Europe, total victory now loomed on the horizon in the war against Japan. But Allied successes in the Southwest and Central Pacific opened a strategic argument regarding the next goal of the dual offensive. MacArthur, of course, favoured a combined focus on the Philippines, including the main island of Luzon, but some planners argued that the entire archipelago could perhaps be bypassed and a major attack launched directly against Formosa, or even under certain circumstances against the Japanese home island of Kyushu. King of course concurred, but, somewhat surprisingly, so did Marshall. MacArthur, however, protested vehemently that American interests and honour, not to mention his personal 1942 promise to return, required liberation of, rather than island-hopping over, the Philippines.

In July, Nimitz agreed that the southern Philippine islands should be taken, but maintained that Luzon should be bypassed in favour of Formosa. Later that month, Roosevelt met Nimitz and MacArthur in Hawaii. Although no final decision was reached at this time, Roosevelt as a politician sympathized with MacArthur's arguments. Furthermore, all parties by this time did agree to tentative plans to attack the southern Philippine island of Mindinao in October.

Post-war planning begins

The apparent approach of victory, combined with the success of the Moscow–Cairo–Teheran Conferences in late 1943, led to the initiation of serious Allied post-war planning in 1944. As agreed during the Moscow Foreign Ministers Conference in October, Britain's proposed European Advisory Commission was established in London in late 1943 to plan surrender terms and occupation policies for Germany and its satellites. Then during the summer, the Allies moved on the economic and political fronts to implement the post-war

9 General MacArthur, President Roosevelt and Adm. Nimitz discuss the progress of the war, July 1944 © Bettmann/CORBIS

international cooperation envisioned in the American-sponsored Four Power Pact that had also been approved at the Moscow Conference. In July, representatives of 44 nations met at Bretton Woods, New Hampshire, to plan post-war monetary policy. And from late August through to early October representatives from 39 nations met at the Dumbarton Oaks estate in Washington, DC, to discuss the framework for a new international organization to replace the League of Nations.

Each of these meetings would result in major post-war agreements. Expanding upon a preliminary division first proposed by COSSAC in 1943, the European Advisory Commission would eventually agree to occupation zones in, as well as basic occupation policies for, Germany. The Bretton Woods Conference would result in agreement to establish two major post-war financial organizations: an International Monetary Fund to make liquid reserves available in order to maintain stable national currencies without resort to restrictive trade practices; and an International Bank for Reconstruction and Development (the World Bank) to provide funds for reconstruction projects and, in the process, promote world trade. Both would be largely funded by the United States, with the US dollar becoming the key world currency. The Dumbarton Oaks Conference would lead to Allied agreement on the basic principles and organizational structure of what would become the post-war United Nations, including a General Assembly of all participants, a Security Council with each of the major Allies as permanent members possessing a veto power, and a Secretariat. Major Allied conflicts occurred over all of these agreements, however, with many of the disagreements still unresolved in September.

Allied representatives on the European Advisory Commission had no trouble agreeing as to what the boundaries should be between their respective occupation zones in Germany. Their inability to agree in early 1944 focused primarily on which nation would occupy which zone. Even though the British would enter Germany from the northwest and the Americans from the southwest, Roosevelt refused to accept a southwestern occupation zone for the United States because it would force him to rely for his logistics upon post-war France, which it appeared the detested de Gaulle would indeed control, and leave Washington with post-war responsibilities for that nation as well as southern Europe, which FDR wished to avoid. Instead FDR demanded from late 1943 onwards that the United States occupy northwestern Germany, with the Anglo-American armies somehow swapping geographic positions once Germany surrendered. 'I do not want the United States to have the post-war burden of reconstituting France, Italy and the Balkans,' he informed Acting Secretary of State Edward Stettinius in February. 'Do please don't ask me to keep any American forces in France,' he told Churchill at the end of the month. 'As I suggested before, I denounce in protest the paternity of Belgium, France and Italy. You really ought to bring up your own children. In view of the fact that they may be your bulwark in future days, you should at least pay for their schooling now!'[38]

Equally if not more serious disagreements simmered beneath the surface of the July Bretton Woods Accords on the post-war financial order. By this time the pre-existing State Department and general American belief that trade restrictions led to war, while their absence led to peace and prosperity, had been heavily reinforced by the fact that the Axis enemies practised closed, autarchic economic systems in an effort to achieve economic self-sufficiency – and indeed had gone to war partially to create such systems and self-sufficiency. Consequently, the Americans continued to ignore or deny the fact that free trade tended to reward the economically strong and penalize the economically weak, as well as their own trade barriers. The British did not. They continued to view the American position as dangerous to themselves as well as hypocritical.[39]

By 1944 it was obvious that the war effort had exhausted Britain economically, that its post-war situation would be even worse than it had been during the 1930s, and that its need for protected markets in the post-war world would be both desperate and even greater than it had been during the Great Depression. Consequently the British continued to argue for both bilateral trade pacts and retention of their Imperial Preference System as necessary to avoid economic ruin. The Americans refused to agree and continued to press the British to acquiesce in their non-preferential and multilateral position. That acquiescence occurred at Bretton Woods, as it had previously in the 1942 Master Lend-Lease agreement and would again later in the war. It was similar to Churchill's acquiescence on the invasion of southern France, however, in that it was forced by American economic pressure and it led to irritation, acrimony and additional strains on the alliance.[40]

Allied conflict over post-war issues in 1944 was by no means limited to the United States and Britain. Although it sent representatives to Bretton Woods, the Communist Soviet Union did not sign the ensuing plans for a post-war capitalist world order. Moreover, as will be discussed in the next chapter, it disagreed sharply with its Anglo-American allies at Dumbarton Oaks regarding some of the specifics of the post-war international organization.[41]

Although dwarfed in hindsight by these conflicts between Russia, on the one hand, and its two western allies, on the other, the British and Americans also collided at Dumbarton Oaks over American proposals for an expansive trusteeship system with the post-war United Nations. Whereas the British saw such a system as limited to former Axis territories, the American saw it as including at least portions of the European colonial empires – including the British Empire.

The OCTAGON Conference

Many of these issues were joined at the next Anglo-American summit conference in Quebec (OCTAGON), from 12–16 September 1944. Churchill aptly summarized the extraordinary military victories of 1944 by noting that since the last Anglo-American conference in Cairo the past December, Allied affairs 'had taken a revolutionary turn for the good. Everything we had touched had turned to gold.'[42] Indeed, a CCS intelligence estimate predicted German surrender by 1 December, and the good military news from the Pacific continued to pour in while the conference was in progress.

Admiral Halsey's carrier air strikes against the Philippines in early September had revealed unexpected Japanese weakness in the area. Consequently Halsey, MacArthur and Nimitz all recommended that the original plan for a movement onto the southern Philippine island of Mindinao be scrapped and that the island be bypassed in favour of an attack in October, two months before it had been scheduled, on the more northern island of Leyte. The Joint and Combined Chiefs meeting in Quebec quickly agreed.

These events lent additional urgency at OCTAGON to the unresolved question as to what Britain's future contribution would be in the war against Japan. With victory in Europe on the horizon, the British were pressing for a larger role in that conflict. But where to focus that role led to major controversies in both London and Quebec. Churchill favoured Southeast Asia. His chiefs of staff favoured instead the dispatch of a fleet to join the Americans in the decisive Pacific theatre. And the US Joint Chiefs favoured neither.

At Cairo the Allies had agreed to tentative plans for the dispatch of a British fleet to the Pacific in June. In March, however, Churchill had informed Roosevelt of his renewed preference for a major effort to retake Singapore and other Southeast Asian colonies. The JCS opposed what they considered such politically inspired diversions, but neither they nor Roosevelt saw any pressing need for a British fleet in the Pacific before mid-1945. The British chiefs thought otherwise, however, and in effect threatened in March to resign if Churchill demanded this strategic shift.[43] The prime minister backed off at this time, then raised his proposal once again just before the OCTAGON meeting began. At the conference itself, however, he backed down a second time in the face of COS opposition and, on 13 September, offered 'the British Main Fleet' for the Central Pacific under US command. Simultaneously, however, he continued to emphasize his desire for both the reconquest of Singapore and an amphibious operation along the Adriatic Coast so as to give Germany 'a stab in the armpit', counter the 'dangerous spread of Russian influence' in the Balkans, and beat the Russians to Vienna. A startled General Brooke, already furious over Churchill's recent behaviour, recorded in his diary that according to Churchill, Britain's 'two main objectives' had suddenly become 'an advance on Vienna and the capture of Singapore!' – despite the fact that the COS had no plans for either.[44]

The Singapore proposal was obviously designed to rebuild British prestige in the Far East after the humiliating defeats of 1941–42. Indeed, Churchill said so at the 13 September meeting. He stated that the loss of Singapore 'had been a grievous and shameful blow to British prestige which must be avenged. It would not be good enough for Singapore to be returned to us at the peace table. We should recover it in battle.'[45] But that motivation was also important in the fleet proposal given the decisive nature of the Central Pacific campaign, along with London's desire to strengthen the British position and Anglo-American ties within the alliance – especially in light of the Bretton Woods disagreements over economic matters and Britain's desperate need for American financial assistance in the post-war world.

Neither motivation made much of an impression on Admiral King, however. Anglophobic to begin with and still smarting over the British refusal to offer naval assistance when he had desperately needed it in early 1942, the US naval chief rationalized his opposition to the fleet proposal on efficiency grounds, maintaining that it would necessitate the needless removal of American ships in the Central Pacific that were doing quite well on their own. Better to leave the British Navy in the Indian Ocean and Southeast Asia, he argued – areas in fact doomed by the rapid American advance in the Pacific to remain backwaters despite the recent progress in Burma.

More concerned with the future of Anglo-American relations than his naval chief, Roosevelt overruled King and immediately accepted the British offer on 13 September. King continued to object at the 14 September CCS meeting, however, and in effect denied that the president had accepted the offer that he clearly had accepted. Representing FDR, Admiral Leahy shot back, according to the official minutes, that 'if Admiral King saw any objections to this proposal he should take the matter up himself with the President'. According to a British witness, Leahy warned King, 'I don't think we should wash our linen in public.'[46] Nevertheless the final OCTAGON agreement left open exactly how the British fleet would be used in the Pacific.

In the political realm, Roosevelt reversed himself at Quebec and acceded to an American occupation of southwestern rather than northwestern Germany that he had been demanding for months, albeit with the caveat that the Americans would have the ports of Bremen and Bremerhaven in the British northwestern zone so as to minimize reliance on the French. Interestingly, he also agreed at Hyde Park a few days later to a new atomic sharing agreement with the British and at Quebec to a desperately needed post-war continuation of Lend-Lease aid to the British during 'Phase II', the time period after German but before Japanese surrender. Most likely in return, however, Churchill agreed to the plan proposed by US Treasury Secretary Morgenthau to preclude the reindustrialization of Germany (the notorious 'pastoralization' plan), even though this went against previous British proposals and had been condemned by the prime minister early in the conference as 'unnatural, unchristian and unnecessary'. Furthermore, Roosevelt toyed with and, consciously or inadvertently, humiliated Churchill by delaying his signature on the Phase II Lend-Lease accord, to the point that the prime minister angrily asked, 'What do you want me to do? Get on my hind legs and beg like [your dog] Fala?'[47]

At OCTAGON Churchill was proud to state that the British Empire was deploying as many divisions in Europe as the Americans. But many of these were deployed in what was now considered a peripheral area: the Mediterranean. Those in northwestern Europe constituted in November only 12 divisions of 820,000 men — a quarter of Eisenhower's total forces.[48] Furthermore, many of these divisions, as well as the British Isles themselves, were now being supplied by the Americans. From the ANVIL decision through Bretton Woods and OCTAGON, the Americans had used their now-massive productive and financial power to get their way with their British ally. Moreover, the American troop contribution continued to grow. US forces would henceforth totally outnumber the British, who had reached their mobilization limit. OCTAGON was the last time Churchill could even claim any sort of equality with the Americans, who more and more would consider his opposition to their plans nearly irrelevant.

OCTAGON also marked the high point of Anglo-American optimism regarding when and how the war would end. Unfortunately it turned out to be gross over-optimism. The remaining months of 1944 would be marked by military setbacks and heavy casualties. They would also be marked by some very serious and related conflicts within the Grand Alliance.

9

ALLIANCE PROBLEMS
AND THE DEFERRAL OF VICTORY,
SEPTEMBER 1944–JANUARY 1945

Hopes for quick victory evaporated during the autumn of 1944 under the impact of stiffening Axis resistance. Along with that resistance came not only Allied military setbacks and mounting casualties, but also serious coalition conflicts. Resolution of those conflicts, as well as military victory, would be deferred until 1945.

Arnhem and the slowing of the Anglo-American advance

By early September Eisenhower had taken over from Montgomery as overall ground commander and had three army groups racing for the German border: Montgomery's 21st Army Group composed of Crerar's Canadian 1st Army and Dempsey's British 2nd Army in the north; Bradley's 12th Army Group consisting of Hodges' US 1st Army and Patton's US 3rd Army in the centre; and Dever's 6th Army Group containing Patch's US 7th Army and de Lattre de Tassigny's French 1st Army in the south. All of these armies were fast outrunning their supplies, however, most notably but far from exclusively the petrol required for rapid armoured warfare.

The problem was a result partially of the previous Allied air campaign that had so successfully disrupted the French transportation system in northern France, and partially the continued Allied failure to capture intact Channel ports. German strategy had been to hold those ports as long as possible and/or to destroy their facilities so as to deny them to the Allies, and overall they had been highly successful. The much maligned mid-August invasion of southern France had prevented a crisis by opening up the port of Marseilles, which carried nearly 40 per cent of Allied supplies for the remainder of the year.[1] And on 4 September Montgomery had been able to capture intact the critical Belgian port of Antwerp, whose use would be essential in the invasion of Germany itself. But with his eyes on crossing the Rhine as soon as possible and ending the war in 1944, Montgomery failed to give adequate attention or resources to cutting off and trapping the German 15th Army on the southwest side of the 60-mile Scheldt estuary that connected Antwerp to the North Sea at a time when he could have easily done so. Nor did he or Eisenhower pay attention to ULTRA intelligence warnings that Hitler intended to hold the estuary. Consequently, the 15th Army escaped and was able both to reinforce German defences to the east and to hold the estuary. The result would be a bloody campaign that would not end until late November, during which time the port remained totally unusable.

With petrol and others supplies dwindling, individual commanders began to argue that they could continue their rapid advance if given the supplies of other commanders, who would have to be halted. Given the different nationalities and personalities of these commanders, the ensuing conflicts were as political as they were military and posed serious problems for Eisenhower's coalition forces.

In the north, Montgomery argued that he could invade the Ruhr, Germany's critical industrial region, move on Berlin, and end the war in 1944 if all supplies went to Dempsey's British 2nd Army in his 21st Army Group and Hodges' US 1st Army, which would be placed under his direction for this campaign; all the other armies – Crerar's Canadian 1st Army, Patton's US 3rd Army and Devers' 6th Army Group – would go on the defensive. Patton, on the other hand, argued that his 3rd Army could advance rapidly to Berlin and end the war in 1944 if provided with Montgomery's supplies.

Eisenhower rejected such appeals on both military and political grounds, opting instead for a slower and more gradual approach, the so-called 'broad front' strategy, by all of his armies simultaneously. Militarily, the 'single thrust' being proposed by Montgomery and Patton ran the risk of being cut off by a German counter-attack – a risk that would not be faced should the numerically superior Allied armies all advance simultaneously. Politically, giving either the British Montgomery or the American Patton all the supplies at the expense of the other would create a crisis in the alliance. So would removing Hodges' US 1st Army from Bradley's 12th Army Group and placing it under Montgomery.

Neither Montgomery nor Patton was known for humility or tact, and neither accepted Eisenhower's decision gracefully. Montgomery was particularly upset and offensive in his reaction, for he did not respect Eisenhower's strategic abilities. Partially for this reason and partially out of personal pride and ego, he had vigorously protested against Eisenhower's decision to take his place as overall commander of Allied ground forces. Indeed, his 'single thrust' proposal would partially reverse that decision by putting the US 1st Army back under his overall command.

Churchill and Brooke supported Montgomery not only out of national pride, but also in recognition of the fact that his approach offered possible victory in 1944 and that continuation of the war into 1945 would not be in Britain's interest. Although Churchill had boasted at the OCTAGON Conference that there were as many British Empire divisions as there were US divisions in the European theatre, that was rapidly ceasing to be the case. In truth, the British had already passed the peak of their war mobilization, whereas the Americans had not. Indeed, a brand new US army, the 9th under Lieutenant General William H. Simpson, would by month's end be activated and added to Bradley's army group, giving the Americans four armies to one for the British (plus one Canadian army). The British contribution to the war effort, and with it British power and influence within the coalition, could only decline precipitously if the war did not end soon.

Brooke had additional reasons to support Montgomery, for he fully shared the latter's sentiments and conclusions about Eisenhower as well as appropriate strategy and command relationships. Brooke's previous support for Ike had been based primarily on alliance politics and had been coupled with the belief that the American did not possess 'the tactical or strategical experience required' for supreme command. During the Mediterranean campaigns, Alexander had served as ground commander under Eisenhower, an arrangement Brooke had supported and called 'flattering and pleasing' to the Americans,

> who did not fully appreciate the underlying intentions. We were pushing Eisenhower up into the stratosphere and rarified atmosphere of a Supreme Commander, where he would be free to devote his time to the political and inter-allied problems, whilst we inserted under him one of our own commanders to deal with the military situations and to restore the necessary drive and co-ordination which had been so seriously lacking of late![2]

The low opinion of Eisenhower's military abilities paralleled a low British opinion of American military abilities in general. Alexander in April of 1943 had bluntly informed Brooke that Americans as a whole 'simply do not know their job as soldiers, and that this is the case from the highest to the lowest, from the General to the private soldier . . . they are soft, green and quite untrained'.[3] Despite American battlefield successes in the summer of 1944, Brooke and Montgomery continued to believe that they needed British direction.

Eisenhower refused to give up command of the ground forces, but he did relent on strategy to the extent of giving Montgomery priority in September so that he could attempt a dramatic outflanking of German defences in the north. If the British commander succeeded in this manoeuvre, he would be able to overrun the sites from which the Germans were launching their unmanned V-1 aircraft and V-2 rockets against England, capture the critical Ruhr industrial area of Germany, and be on both the flattest terrain and shortest route to Berlin – all solid justifications in Eisenhower's mind for providing Montgomery with the extra means at this time.

Montgomery's daring plan, Operation MARKET GARDEN, focused on the use of three airborne divisions, two American as well as one British, to seize bridges over the Rhine and a series of preceding rivers and canals in the

Netherlands in advance of a British armoured corps. The US 101st Airborne Division was to focus on a bridge over the Maas River near Eindoven, the US 82nd on another bridge over the Waal near Nijmegen, and the British 1st on the northernmost bridge across the Lower Rhine at Arnhem. Simultaneously the British 30th Armoured Corps under Lieutenant General Brian Horrocks was to advance 64 miles along the ground to relieve these divisions, which being airborne did not possess heavy equipment. But both airborne and ground forces ran into fierce resistance when the operation began on 17 September, most notably from two German *Panzer* divisions refitting near Arnhem. The Americans did capture their bridges at Eindoven and Nijmegen, and were rescued from further German counter-attacks by Horrocks' corps, but the British at Arnhem were unable to take their bridge over the lower Rhine, the now-famous 'bridge too far',[4] and Horrocks was not able to reach and rescue them. Less than a third of the British airborne force eventually broke through the German lines and escaped.

Simultaneously German resistance also stiffened along the rest of the Allied line. Crerar's Canadians faced fierce resistance in the Scheldt estuary. Hodges' US 1st Army suffered massive casualties in what turned into a lengthy and bloody campaign in the Hürtgen forest along the German-Belgian border. Patton faced strong German defences around Metz in Lorraine. In all three areas Allied forces also faced the rainy, cold weather of late autumn and terrain that favoured the defenders. So did Devers in the Vosges mountains of Alsace. As winter set in, it became obvious that the war would not end in 1944 after all.

The Battle of the Bulge

With his empire and his options rapidly dwindling, Hitler now decided to throw his last reserves into a major counter-offensive against Eisenhower in the Ardennes, the same heavily forested area where his forces had achieved their dramatic breakthrough in 1940. Code-named Operation AUTUMN FOG and under the overall command of von Rundstedt, whom Hitler had reinstated as Commander-in-Chief West, it once again involved a very large force – 200,000 soldiers and 600 tanks organized into three separate armies totalling 30 divisions, including ten armoured divisions – but with more limited objectives than in 1940. As in that previous operation, the military aim was to split Allied forces, this time by capturing the now usable and critical port of Antwerp. But the political goal in 1944 was far more limited than it had been in 1940 – to obtain not Allied surrender but a negotiated peace in the west that would break the Allied coalition and allow Hitler to concentrate all his forces against the Soviets in the east.

Facing this huge German force would be only four American divisions from Hodges' 1st Army (with a fifth in reserve), approximately 80,000 men thinly spread over a 70-mile front. The area had been lightly defended in 1940 because of a belief that tanks could never get through its steep and heavily

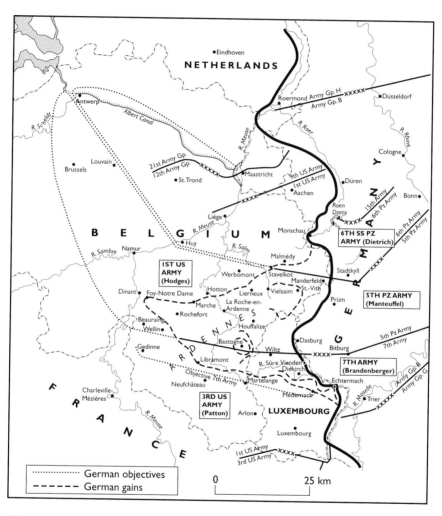

17 The Battle of the Bulge, December 1944–January 1945

wooded terrain. Despite the German success in doing just that in 1940, it remained lightly defended again in 1944, primarily as a result of Allied over-confidence and belief that Hitler was neither capable nor mad enough to attempt such a gamble, given his limited resources and desperate situation on the Eastern Front. German radio silence and poor weather precluded know-ledge of the offensive through ULTRA or air reconnaissance, while over-confidence led to the dismissal of ULTRA warnings that did come in regarding a German build-up in the area.

The Germans began their attack on 16 December in weather so poor as to ground Allied aircraft, and they made quick progress against the surprised and overwhelmed American forces. Further aiding German efforts was their use of English-speaking commandos in American uniforms, whose presence and activities behind US lines created confusion and fear. That fear was only reinforced by massacres of American prisoners by an SS *Panzer* division, most notably at Malmédy. Within a matter of days the Germans had created a dan-gerous 'bulge' in the Allied lines more than 40 miles wide and more than 60 miles deep.

Allied lines did not break, however, as Eisenhower moved quickly to contain the damage by sending in reinforcements and by ordering attacks against the sides of the German salient. Given its size, however, he concluded that Bradley would not be able to maintain effective contact with all of his forces on both of its sides and therefore, in a controversial move, temporarily transferred control of the US 1st and 9th Armies to Montgomery, who was directed to counter-attack from the north while Patton counter-attacked from the south.

The German offensive failed even to cross the Meuse River, let alone reach Antwerp 100 miles to the northwest. It was halted by a combination of factors. Stiffening and fierce American resistance by individual units, most notably at the key road juncture at Bastogne, slowed their advance. Here the surrounded but reinforced Americans under Brigadier General Anthony McAuliffe replied to a German surrender demand with the famous 'Nuts!' – translated for the non-comprehending German officer who received the reply as equivalent to 'Go to Hell!'[5] Fuel shortages also slowed the Germans, while clearing weather enabled Allied air forces to launch devastating attacks on the *Panzers* from the air. Furthermore, in what many consider to have been his most brilliant manoeuvre of the war, Patton successfully completed an excep-tionally rapid, 90-degree shift of his forces and counter-attacked from the south, relieving Bastogne by 26 December. Montgomery followed with an attack from the north on 3 January, while Stalin, in response to a personal plea from Churchill on 6 January, initiated an offensive in Poland ahead of sched-ule as a way of diverting German forces from the west.[6] Hitler was forced to call off the offensive, and by the end of January Allied forces had eliminated the bulge that had originally been created.

By that time Hitler also had to call off the counter-offensive he had launched at the end of December against Devers in Alsace from the so-called 'Colmar Pocket', in a failed effort to divert Patton from the bulge. All the

German dictator had accomplished by both offensives was a temporary respite at the cost of his last reserves and the further weakening of his forces against the Russians in the east, who had now opened a 200-mile wide gap in the German lines and advanced to within 45 miles of Berlin. Hitler thereby and ironically guaranteed that Russian rather than British or American troops would take the German capital.

The German winter offensive had been quite threatening, however, and it had precipitated two separate Allied crises. One occurred in Alsace, where the German attack had threatened the provincial capital of Strasbourg and led Eisenhower to authorize its evacuation. But the 1st French Army refused to retreat from a French city and Eisenhower, encouraged by Churchill, decided to bow to what was in effect de Gaulle's demand for a change in orders in order to maintain the coalition.

The second political crisis would not be as easily resolved. The Battle of the Bulge had been almost entirely an American battle, and indeed the largest battle in the history of the US Army. Montgomery, however, who had been given temporary command of the US 9th and 1st Armies, had publicly and arrogantly taken credit for halting the German advance and had stated that the American soldiers made great fighters when properly led. He thereby infuriated, as Eisenhower biographer Stephen Ambrose has noted, 'Bradley, Patton, and nearly every American officer in Europe'.[7] Equally if not more troublesome, he resumed his attacks on Eisenhower's broad-front strategy and his calls for a single thrust from the north. For this purpose he also recommended retention of the US forces that Eisenhower had temporarily placed under his command, thereby precipitating another Allied strategic conflict in early 1945.

New Japanese tactics in the Pacific

Japanese resistance also stiffened during the autumn of 1944. As previously noted, the weakness of Japanese defences in the Southwest Pacific had led Halsey to recommend, and MacArthur and Nimitz as well as the Joint and Combined Chiefs of Staff meeting in Quebec to approve, a major shift and speed-up in their timetable.[8] The large southern Philippine island of Mindinao would now be bypassed in favour of an October landing on the island of Leyte farther north, with a preparatory invasion of Peleliu in the Palau Islands during September. Both invasions would succeed, but only at heavy cost in American lives due to new Japanese tactics.

In all previous Pacific campaigns the Japanese had fought ferociously and virtually to the last man. Indeed, once their eventual defeat had become apparent, they had usually launched one final and suicidal *banzai* charge against the Americans that had resulted in their virtual obliteration, while their commanders committed ritual suicide. Such charges and ritual suicides had been primarily a means of retaining honour by their *Bushido* warrior code, which considered surrender or capture to be dishonourable. Given the growing desperateness of their situation, the Japanese in late 1944 shifted to different suicide tactics designed to maximize American casualties and thereby convince Washington to agree to a negotiated peace.

The most famous of these tactics was the *kamikaze* ('divine wind'), suicide pilots who crashed their aircraft into Allied ships. While individual Japanese pilots had occasionally done so throughout the war, their deliberate and mass use began only in October of 1944, when a special force was formed to attack American aircraft carriers supporting the Philippine invasion. They would make their first appearance on 25 October during the battle of Leyte Gulf.[9]

Much more damaging than the *kamikazes* in terms of total casualties were new Japanese ground tactics that were first used during the mid-September invasion of Peleliu in the Palaus. Here the Japanese had created a concrete-reinforced and interconnecting series of caves and tunnels into which their garrison of more than 10,000 men retreated after inflicting heavy casualties on the assaulting US 1st Marine Division. These defences could not be destroyed by naval shelling or aerial bombardment, and would instead have to be taken, one by one, by ground assault and flamethrowers. That effort took more than two months and resulted in one of the bloodiest if lesser-known campaigns of the Pacific War. The Americans would suffer over 6,500 total casualties, including more than 1,250 dead. That was not a high number by European standards, but given the size of the invasion force, it translated into a casualty rate of 40 per cent, the highest casualty rate for any American campaign in the war. Peleliu was a clear precursor of what the Americans would face throughout the remainder of the war – especially on the islands of Iwo Jima and Okinawa in 1945.

The Battle of Leyte Gulf

On 20 October, a massive American force began the reconquest of the Philippines by invading Leyte, with General MacArthur himself landing in one of the most famous photographs of the war and announcing that he had returned. Completing that return would take a long time and be quite bloody, however, for the Japanese had decided to defend the islands at all costs. Unbeknownst to the Americans, they had also decided to shift major forces from Luzon to Leyte and, despite their disastrous defeat in the June Battle of the Philippine Sea, to use what remained of their fleet to destroy the American invasion force. The resulting Battle of Leyte Gulf on 24 and 25 October would be the first major surface engagement since early 1942 and the largest naval battle of the war, and indeed of all naval history. The Japanese almost succeeded, but in the end lost most of what remained of their fleet.

The Japanese realized they could not hope to defeat the enormous US covering fleet, which now included 16 aircraft carriers and which had been placed under Halsey's command for this operation (Halsey and Spruance were now alternating in their control of the fleet, which was the 3rd Fleet under the former and the 5th Fleet when commanded by the latter). Instead Japan's naval leaders hoped to use their four remaining and new carriers (which contained only 110 aircraft) under Admiral Ozawa Jisaburo to lure Halsey northward, while nearly all of Japan's remaining surface ships converged in a massive pincer movement on the American transports and the relatively small US 7th Fleet under Vice Admiral Thomas Kinkaid guarding those transports in Leyte Gulf.

The first part of the plan worked perfectly. Convinced by a 23 October encounter with and ensuing withdrawal of the northern arm of the pincer under Kurita Takeo in the Sibuyan Sea that the Japanese vice admiral had given up, and far less cautious than Spruance had been at the Philippine Sea battle, Halsey took the bait and steamed northward with his entire fleet to attack Ozawa's carriers. But Kurita turned back around toward the now unprotected San Bernadino Strait to the north of Leyte, while the southern arm of the pincer under Vice Admiral Nishimura Shoji, followed by a second supporting fleet under Vice Admiral Shima Kiyohide, steamed into Surigao Strait in the south to close the trap. Halsey had thus left the invading force exposed to the entire Japanese surface fleet.

Kinkaid's 7th Fleet battleships and cruisers, under the command of Rear Admiral Jesse Oldendorf, all but annihilated Nishimura's fleet in the Surigao Strait, leading Shima to retreat before he met the same fate. But Kurita's still powerful northern force suddenly emerged from San Bernadino Strait on the morning of 25 October. The only US naval force between him and the transport and supply ships at Leyte Gulf was Rear Admiral Clifton Sprague's small and weak fleet composed of five escort carriers and three destroyers (plus four destroyer escorts), which Kurita overwhelmingly outgunned and could easily destroy (see map on p. 180). He began to do just that but in the midst of the battle suddenly withdrew, apparently unnerved by air attacks from the escort carriers as well as virtually suicidal torpedo attacks by the destroyers, and fearful of another attack from Halsey and Mitscher, whom he thought might have returned. That was not the case, as they were still far to the north destroying the four remaining Japanese carriers. Under pressure from Nimitz, Halsey finally did send a task force south to intercept Kurita, but it was too late and the remaining Japanese ships were able to escape.

Nevertheless the Japanese gamble had failed, and their losses were staggering: 4 aircraft carriers, 3 battleships, 6 heavy cruisers, 4 light cruisers and 11 destroyers totalling 300,000 tons (to American losses of 37,000 tons), as well as 500 aircraft. Although they still possessed individual warships, including the enormous *Yamato*, the largest battleship in the world, they no longer possessed any naval air forces or indeed any surface fleet to speak of. But they were far from ready to surrender, and would now turn more and more to the *kamikazes*, which they introduced at this battle, and suicidal ground defences to combat the overwhelming American power arrayed against them. On Leyte they would consequently suffer 25 Japanese deaths for every American death and lose 80,000 men. Even at that ratio, however, the struggle for Leyte would cost the Americans 3,000 dead and 12,000 wounded.

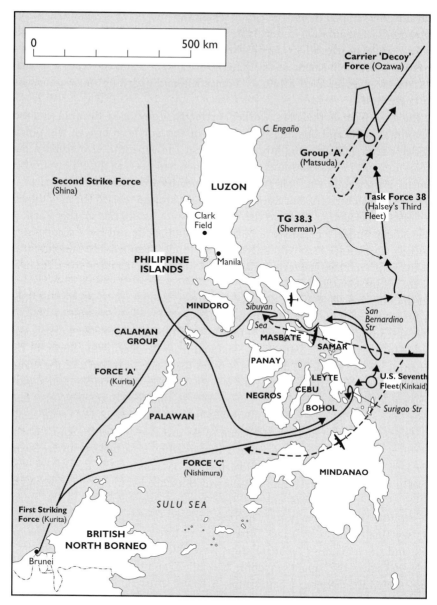

18 The Battle of Leyte Gulf, October 1944.
Note, in particular, Ozawa's 'decoy' of Halsey's fleet; Kinkaid's destruction of
Nishimura's fleet in the Surigao Strait; Kurita's withdrawal from the Sibuyam Sea; and
his return to San Bernardino Strait.

Before Leyte, the American dual offensive in the Pacific had never had to face such large numbers of Japanese troops – partially because of the nature and size of the islands involved and the bypassing of such strongholds as Rabaul, but also because the bulk of the Japanese Army had remained tied down in China. By the autumn of 1944, however, China was on the verge of military collapse, a collapse that could free much of the Japanese Army for future bloody combat against the Americans.

Military and political crises in China

Throughout 1944, the one exception to the string of Allied military victories had been the China theatre. By October a major diplomatic as well as military crisis had erupted in this troubled area.

The military crisis resulted from a major Japanese offensive during the spring and summer of 1944, Operation ICHIGO. As Stilwell had warned,[10] the Japanese had responded to Chennault's air offensive with a ground campaign to overrun his air bases, and Chiang's forces had failed miserably in defending them. Indeed, Chinese troops had abandoned Changsa, a key communications centre, without a fight. Consequently, the Japanese not only captured most of Chennault's air bases, but also expanded substantially the territory they controlled and completed their conquest of the Chinese coastline. They thereby created a land link to Southeast Asia, threatened what remained of the Chinese war effort, and led Chiang to consider the withdrawal of Stilwell's trained forces from the North Burma front – at the very moment those forces were about to clear remaining Japanese forces from the Ledo Road area.

Throughout 1942 and 1943 Roosevelt had supported Chiang and rejected calls by Marshall as well as Stilwell for a showdown with the Chinese leader. But FDR could not ignore the military catastrophe now unfolding. Furthermore, he had begun to sour on Chiang and his Wellesley-educated wife, whose vanity and arrogance were revealed during a lengthy 1942–43 visit and stay at the White House.[11] Consequently FDR strongly recommended to Chiang in July of 1944 that he place Stilwell in charge of all Chinese as well as US forces, including Mao's Communist forces. Chiang at first appeared to accede, but actually was stalling for time. The result was a second and even stiffer note in September threatening Chiang with a cut-off of all aid unless Stilwell was both reinforced in Burma and placed in charge of all Chinese forces. Stilwell personally delivered this second ultimatum and gleefully noted in his diary that 'The harpoon hit the little bugger right in the solar plexus and went right through him.' The American general's full fury and contempt for Chiang after years of frustration emerged in a vicious poem he wrote and sent to his wife at this time:

I've waited long for vengeance
At last I've had my chance,
I've looked the Peanut in the eye
And kicked him in the pants

The old harpoon was ready
With aim and timing true,
I sank it to the handle
And stung him through and through.

The little bastard shivered,
And lost the power of speech.
His face turned green and quivered
And he struggled not to screech.

For all my weary battles,
For all my hours of woe,
At last I've had my innings
And laid the Peanut low.

I know I've still to suffer,
And run a weary race,
But oh! The blessed pleasure!
I've wrecked the Peanut's face.[12]

Stilwell's victory was short-lived, however, for Chiang quickly made clear his belief that the real problem was the American general, whose recall he now demanded. In effect, the Chinese leader was calling a presidential bluff. While FDR did control Lend-Lease aid, China was simply too important to his post-war plans to risk Chiang's defeat and/or alienation. Moreover, Chiang's vocal supporters within the United States had throughout the war built up the Chinese leader's image among the American people. Known as the 'China Lobby', those supporters included such influential individuals as *Time-Life* publisher Henry Luce, a son of Chinese missionaries, who portrayed Chiang (a convert to Christianity) as the George Washington of China and a vital US ally. Roosevelt, intent on making China one of his 'Four Policemen' in the post-war world, had joined in this effort. He had thereby helped to create a Frankenstein monster that now came back to haunt him, for any break with Chiang could seriously affect public support for the war and his post-war plans. Consequently, FDR agreed to recall Stilwell, replacing him with Major General Albert C. Wedemeyer, a former member of Marshall's staff who since mid-1943 had been serving as Mountbatten's Chief of Staff in SEAC. Promoted to Lieutenant General in early 1945, Wedemeyer would prove to be much more diplomatic than Stilwell and thus much more successful in his relations with Chiang. But both the president and the JCS now began to minimize what they could expect from the Chinese war effort.

That minimization had dramatic consequences for both US military strategy in Asia and the Pacific, and for relations with the Soviet Union. Throughout the first half of 1944, the American armed forces had continued to argue over future objectives of the dual offensive in the Pacific. All had agreed by September to the accelerated drive to take the island of Leyte in the Philippines, but beyond that the navy still wanted to bypass the northern and main island of Luzon in favour of an assault on Formosa so as to connect with the China theatre, particularly the Chinese air bases. MacArthur had already objected furiously and perhaps already won Roosevelt's support during a July presidential conference with his Pacific commanders; but the general's hand was tremendously strengthened in the ensuing months by the fact that the Formosa operation would require far more troops than originally anticipated and by the Japanese successes in China, which eliminated the air bases as a factor at the very moment alternative bases were becoming available in the Marianas as a result of Nimitz's Central Pacific drive. Consequently the navy finally agreed to drop Formosa and focus on Luzon after the conquest of Leyte, followed by a movement northward to obtain air bases in the Pacific even closer than the Marianas to the Japanese home islands. On 9 January MacArthur's forces under Lieutenant General Walter Krueger landed at Lingayen Gulf on Luzon.

But what was to prevent the Japanese, in the absence of effective Chinese resistance, from transferring the bulk of their army from the China theatre to defence of those islands as well as the home islands, or perhaps even from moving their government to the Asian mainland? Only the Red Army could replace the Chinese in keeping the Japanese Army in China tied down. Obtaining Soviet entry into the war against Japan had always been a major JCS desire, but it now achieved an even higher priority than previously. Unfortunately, that higher priority took place at the same time that serious conflict erupted with the Soviets, conflict which in turn exacerbated numerous Anglo-American conflicts.

Anglo-Soviet-American conflicts

As previously noted, the Allies had been able during 1944 to reach major post-war agreements within the European Advisory Commission and at the Bretton Woods and Dumbarton Oaks Conferences regarding the occupation of Germany, post-war economic policies and post-war international organization. But serious disagreements had also emerged at these conferences. Anglo-American conflicts had centred on Roosevelt's demand for a northwestern rather than a southwestern occupation zone in Germany, the American insistence on British abandonment of the Imperial Preference System and bilateral trade agreements in favour of multilateralism and a global 'Open Door', and the future of colonialism. Many of these conflicts had been settled during the July Dumbarton Oaks meeting and the September OCTAGON conference in Quebec, though not without bitter feelings.[13]

Other conflicts had not been settled, however, and to them were added additional ones in the autumn as many of the OCTAGON agreements collapsed.[14] Regarding colonialism, despite their apparent backing away at Dumbarton Oaks from expansive trusteeship plans for the post-war United Nations to replace the old League of Nations Mandate system, the Americans continued to attack European colonial empires and support anti-colonial post-war policies that the British continued to resist. Illustrative of this continuing conflict were Churchill's angry comments at the Quebec Conference about US 'lack of understanding' regarding British policies in India, Roosevelt's continued rejection of British and French proposals to incorporate a French military contingent into Mountbatten's Southeast Asia Command, and Churchill's October decision to approve a French mission to SEAC anyway but not to inform FDR.[15] Simultaneously, Roosevelt retreated under bureaucratic and political pressure from his OCTAGON pledges regarding the use of Phase II Lend-Lease aid to assist in British post-war economic reconstruction, while State Department negotiators demanded in return for any such aid further reduction in British trade barriers. Those negotiators clashed with their British counterparts not only over this issue, but also over policies regarding Argentina and the Italian government as well as post-war international civil aviation. At a November conference in Chicago to establish rules for such aviation, the Americans demanded an 'Open Door' policy that the British argued would virtually eliminate them. In late November, Roosevelt made blatant use of US economic power by warning Churchill that British obstinacy on this issue would endanger future Lend-Lease aid. Churchill's pained reply noted the enormous preponderance of American economic as well as military power, while politely yet forcefully informing Roosevelt that American proposals would take unfair advantage of previous war-time air agreements so as to 'virtually monopolise' post-war air traffic and 'run out of the air altogether' everyone else.[16]

By that time, however, equally if not more serious disagreements had erupted between the British and Americans, on the one hand, and the Soviets, on the other. As a Communist country, the Soviet Union had no interest in the Bretton Woods Conference beyond the reconstruction loans it might receive and therefore refused to sign on and become part of this planned post-war capitalist world economic order. Equally if not more disturbing was its behaviour at Dumbarton Oaks. Fearing that they might be outvoted by the British Commonwealth and/or American-controlled Latin American nations, the Soviets demanded 16 seats in the UN General Assembly, one for each supposedly 'independent' republic within the Soviet Union. They also demanded an absolute veto in the Security Council, even on matters to which they were a party. The United States and Britain were deeply upset by these demands and united in their opposition to both. Stalin, however, refused to back down on either one. Consequently, the Dumbarton Oaks Conference broke up in October with no agreement on these two critical points. Equally if not more threatening by then was a dispute that had broken out in August and September over Soviet behaviour in Poland.

Polish boundaries, governments, Katyn, and the Warsaw Affair

Poland had been a contentious issue in Allied relations throughout the war. Under the Nazi-Soviet Pact, the Soviets had in 1939 taken over eastern

Poland. They had also refused to recognize the Polish Government-in-Exile that had been established in London and became known as the 'London Poles'. Diplomatic relations between that government and Moscow were reestablished after the German invasion of the Soviet Union in June of 1941, but had remained cool. The Poles refused to accede to the 1939 loss of eastern Poland, and Stalin refused to give back what he had gotten from his pact with Hitler – and what in effect had been part of the Russian Empire from the late eighteenth-century partition of Poland to its seizure during and after World War I, first by the Germans and then by the recreated Polish state.

Stalin also failed to account for approximately 15,000 Polish officers who had been taken prisoner in 1939 along with their troops. He would not do so for a simple reason: his secret police had shot most of those officers in 1940. In the spring of 1943, the Germans had announced discovery of the graves of some of them in the Katyn Forest and asserted that the Soviets had murdered them. Moscow had denied the charge and blamed the Germans. When the Polish Government-in-Exile accepted a German offer of a Red Cross investigation, Stalin had broken off diplomatic relations with the Poles and begun to build up an alternative Communist puppet government, known as the Union of Polish Patriots, or 'Lublin Poles'.

By the time the Big Three met at Teheran in late 1943 there were thus two separate and contentious Polish issues to deal with: the boundary of post-war Poland and its post-war government. At Churchill's suggestion, the Big Three discussed and informally agreed to a resolution of the boundary issue whereby eastern Poland, which even the British Lord Curzon had proposed after World War I remain in the Soviet Union via his famous 'Curzon Line', would stay in Soviet hands but Poland would be compensated with German territory in the west. The London Poles refused to agree, however, and relations remained frozen as Soviet forces in 1944 entered pre-war Polish territory. As they approached Warsaw in August of 1944, the Polish Underground or 'Home' Army rose up in an effort to seize the city from the Germans before the Russians arrived. The Red Army thereupon halted on the east bank of the Vistula River and allowed the Germans to utterly destroy both the Home Army and the city of Warsaw.

Stalin claimed, accurately, that his forces faced fierce German resistance and needed to regroup. But he also had no interest in helping these Poles who remained loyal to London. Consequently, he rejected pleas by Churchill and Roosevelt that he come to their aid, or that at the very least he allow his allies to drop supplies to them by air and land behind Soviet lines. He eventually did accede to one such drop and landing, but by that time it was too little and too late.

This so-called 'Warsaw Affair' led many American as well as British officials to question the future of Allied relations. US ambassador W. Averell Harriman, for example, warned that Moscow's refusal to aid the Poles had been based on 'ruthless political considerations' and left him 'gravely concerned'. Relations with the Russians, who he claimed were 'bloated with power', had taken a 'startling turn' for the worse.[17]

Churchill had been concerned about Russia long before the Americans but had previously been unable to convince Roosevelt or his advisers to take a tough, united stand against the Soviets, or to support military actions in the Balkans that held out the possibility of placing limits on the westward advance of the Red Army. Indeed, Roosevelt consistently rejected such a united stand in favour of a role as mediator between Churchill and Stalin. Similarly, the US Joint Chiefs and their planners had consistently and forcefully rejected the Balkan strategy throughout the war and any support for the British in a Balkan conflict with the Russians. By the summer of 1944 they were explicitly warning that any such conflict must be avoided, and that the post-war world would see a shift in the global balance of power unparalleled since the fall of Rome. Britain would be in serious decline, the Soviet Union and the United States would emerge as the new superpowers, and neither would be capable of militarily defeating the other, even if aligned with Britain. For these reasons as well as the continued need for Soviet military action to defeat the Axis powers, conflict with Russia had to be avoided.[18]

Such attitudes only added to the British belief that American power was, in the words of one 1944 British Foreign Office document, a 'great unwieldy barge . . . likely to continue to wallow in the ocean, an isolated menace to navigation' unless properly 'steer[ed]' by British pilots. Harold Macmillan was even blunter in this diplomatic parallel to the beliefs of Brooke and Montgomery regarding American military leadership, informing a subordinate in 1943 that 'we are Greeks in this American empire' who 'must run' Allied headquarters in Algiers, and by implication Allied headquarters elsewhere, 'as the Greek slaves ran the operations of the Emperor Claudius'.[19] The Warsaw episode gave the British their first opportunity to play Macmillan's Greeks and successfully 'steer' the Americans by calling into question previous US attitudes toward the Soviets. During the Quebec Conference, Churchill openly listed as an 'added reason' for an amphibious operation in the Adriatic towards Vienna, 'the rapid encroachment of the Russians into the Balkans and the consequent dangerous spread of Russian influence in this area. He preferred to get into Vienna before the Russians did as he did not know what Russia's policy would be after she took it.'[20] The JCS for the first time offered no objections to such a possible amphibious assault along the Yugoslav coast toward the Ljubljana Gap, should operations in Italy go well. As for Roosevelt, it may be far from coincidental that a few days later in Hyde Park he joined Churchill in rejecting Danish physicist Niels Bohr's call for atomic sharing with the Soviets and agreed instead to a post-war Anglo-American monopoly on any atomic weapon that might be developed.[21]

Operations in Italy did not go well, however, and by mid-October the proposed amphibious assault in the Adriatic was all but dead. Nor did US policy shift in its opposition to specific political and territorial agreements while the war was in progress. Given these facts, as well as Stalin's behaviour in Poland

and the Red Army's rapid advance through eastern Europe and the Balkans, Churchill now decided to bypass the Americans and strike a spheres-of-influence deal directly with Stalin.

The TOLSTOY Conference in Moscow and crisis in Greece

As early as May, Churchill had initiated a tentative arrangement whereby the Soviets would accede to his wartime control of Greece in return for their control of Romania. By October the combination of Soviet military advances and their behaviour in Poland, along with the failure of his Ljubljana Gap strategy, led him to fly to Moscow to formalize and expand this arrangement as well as attempt to deal with Poland. Code-named TOLSTOY, the ensuing second Moscow Conference between Churchill and Stalin would result in one of the most famous, or infamous, Allied agreements of the war. As reported in his memoirs, Churchill proposed on the evening of 9 October that the two of them

'settle about our affairs in the Balkans. Your armies are in Rumania and Bulgaria. We have interests, missions, and agents there. Don't let us get at cross-purposes in small ways. So far as Britain and Russia are concerned, how would it do for you to have ninety percent predominance in Rumania, for us to have ninety percent of the say in Greece, and go fifty-fifty about Yugoslavia?' While this was being translated I wrote out on a half-sheet of paper:

Rumania		
	Russia	90%
	The others	10%
Greece		
	Great Britain (in accord with U.S.A.)	90%
	Russia	10%
Yugoslavia		50–50%
Hungary		50–50%
Bulgaria		
	Russia	75%
	The others	25%

I pushed this across to Stalin, who by then had heard the translation. There was a slight pause. Then he took his blue pencil and made a large tick upon it, and passed it back to us. It was all settled in no more time than it takes to set down.

Of course we had long and anxiously considered our point, and were only dealing with immediate war-time arrangements. All larger questions were reserved on both sides for what we then hoped would be a peace table when the war was won.

After this there was a long silence. The pencilled paper lay in the centre of the table. At length I said. 'Might it not be thought rather cynical if it seemed we had disposed of these issues, so fateful to millions of people, in such an offhand manner? Let us burn the paper.' 'No, you keep it,' said Stalin.[22]

Eden and Molotov later altered the percentages to 80–20 in favour of the Soviets for Bulgaria and Hungary, but Churchill's eyes were set on Greece. Indeed, almost immediately he made use of this agreement to send in a British force to replace the retreating Germans in that country and to install a royalist government under the premiership of Georges Papandreou. In the following month when the Italian Government collapsed, Churchill refused to allow a new government to be formed with Count Carlo Sforza as prime minister or foreign minister, a move widely interpreted in the United States as resulting from Sforza's opposition to the Italian monarchy. And when negotiations with the EAM-ELAS Communist resistance forces in Greece broke down and resulted in open Communist revolt against the Greek Royal Government in December, Churchill ordered its forceful suppression by the British Army. Abiding by his October agreement, Stalin said nothing and did nothing to aid the Greek Communists. But in negotiations with Polish Prime Minister Stanislaw Mikolajczyk, the Soviet leader in turn refused to compromise on the post-war boundary and demanded Polish agreement to that boundary for any return to normal relations. Bowing to the inevitable, Mikolajczyk favoured agreement. But he was unable to convince his London colleagues to agree and consequently he resigned in late November. In early January Stalin responded by recognizing the Lublin Poles as a provisional government, despite entreaties by Churchill and Roosevelt that he not do so.

The Moscow territorial agreements and ensuing British as well as Soviet behaviour directly violated Roosevelt's policy of postponing all territorial settlements until the war's end. That behaviour also fulfilled his worst fears by upsetting the American people and led to a frightening resurgence of isolationist sentiments in late 1944. Although 'a plague on both your houses' appeared to summarize public anger against their British and Russian allies, the British bore the brunt of American press and public wrath. *The New York Times* accused Churchill of being a 'product of nineteenth century thought fighting a twentieth century war for eighteenth century aims', while a majority of those polled in one survey blamed the British (54 per cent) rather than the Russians (only 18 per cent) for the events and problems taking place.[23]

So did the administration. In early December Edward R. Stettinius, Jr, who had recently replaced the physically ailing Hull as secretary of state, publicly criticized British behaviour in the Mediterranean. While Churchill in a long message to Roosevelt objected strongly to what he called the 'acerbity' of this 'public rebuke to His Majesty's Government', a rebuke far stronger than anything previously said about Russia or any other Allied government, Admiral King ordered his naval commander in the area to halt British use of US landing craft to ferry their troops and supplies from Italy to Greece. Simultaneously the JCS rejected a British request for formal CCS approval of their Greek operations. As historian Terry Anderson has aptly concluded, Anglo-American relations had by year's end 'deteriorated to their war-time nadir'.[24]

As the 1944 Moscow Conference had illustrated, Britain and the Soviet Union were now intent on making post-war territorial arrangements and Roosevelt could not stop them. Yet the consequences of such arrangements were, as he had feared, placing great strains on the alliance and on the domestic consensus he had built up. Clearly, it was time for another Big Three conference to try to patch up Allied disagreements as well as make additional strategic decisions. This time, however, any such meeting would have to deal extensively with the host of post-war issues that had arisen in 1944. The result would be the most famous, or infamous, Allied meeting of the war – at Yalta in the Crimea.

10

FINAL VICTORY AND THE CHANGING OF THE GUARD, FEBRUARY–SEPTEMBER 1945

1945, appropriately labelled 'Year Zero' by John Lukacs,[1] was one of the most eventful years of the twentieth century. During its winter and spring months the Allies achieved final and total victory over Germany, a victory made possible by the successful compromising of their differences at the February Yalta Conference as well as the successful and coordinated military campaigns that followed in Europe. But this was also the period of the bloodiest battles to date in the Pacific War, the breakdown of both the Yalta Accords and the alliance as a whole, and the near-simultaneous death of Roosevelt. The summer months were equally eventful. In July, Churchill was defeated for re-election in the midst of the final Allied Summit Conference in Potsdam, a conference marked by much acrimony and disagreement; that left only Stalin from the wartime 'Big Three'. July was also the month in which the United States successfully tested the first atomic bomb. In August, it used that weapon twice against the Japanese, while the Soviet Union declared war on Tokyo and invaded Manchuria. Formal Japanese surrender followed in early September, officially ending the war. With Churchill and Roosevelt both gone and relations with Stalin rapidly deteriorating, however, the world quickly moved from the World War II era to the Cold War era.

The Yalta Conference

Code-named ARGONAUT, the Yalta Conference of 4–11 February 1945, remains the most famous, or infamous, of the many wartime Allied summit conferences. It was the second Big Three meeting of the war, and it had numerous aims. First and foremost was, as with previous Allied summit meetings, to plan future military operations against Germany and Japan. But Yalta was also a political conference designed to ratify post-war agreements tentatively discussed at Teheran and/or reached by subordinates in 1944, to attempt to compromise differences that had arisen and that those subordinates had been unable to resolve, and to deal with other post-war issues the three leaders had previously postponed or avoided. If successful in all these endeavours, the Allies would be able to achieve both total military victory in the war and post-war cooperation that would ensure a lasting peace. If they failed, the war could end short of total victory and/or simply set the stage for Axis revival and another war in the future.

It was because the stakes were so high, and because Stalin refused to leave the Soviet Union, that an obviously ill Roosevelt agreed after his re-election to a fourth term in November to a conference at such a lengthy distance from the United States. Situated on the Black Sea, Yalta had been a resort of the Russian czars and aristocracy, and it possessed a very temperate climate as well as numerous beautiful palaces. It was in that sense a very suitable spot for a winter Big Three meeting. But it had only recently and forcefully been liberated from the German Army and was thus hardly ready for their arrival, despite massive Soviet efforts to clean it up. Furthermore, Yalta was situated on the southern end of the Crimean peninsula, an extremely distant and difficult location to reach even today. 'We could not have found a worse place for a meeting if we had spent ten years on research,' Churchill told Hopkins just before the conference.[2]

The Yalta discussions and agreements were quite lengthy and complex. Most important were those concerning future military operations against Germany, the ensuing military occupation of the country, the post-war United Nations organization, the boundaries and government of Poland, future governments in the rest of Europe, and Soviet entry into the war against Japan. Each of these subjects had a long history before Yalta, and on each the three leaders compromised in order to maintain unity.

On Germany they agreed both to combined military operations for the spring and to post-war division of the country into occupation zones. Both matters had been subjects of controversy throughout 1943–44 and had been partially resolved in the past. They were further resolved at this time.

Preliminary discussion of future military operations against Germany actually took place at the little-known Anglo-American conference in Malta that directly preceded the Yalta meeting. Here the 'broad' vs 'narrow' front debate of 1944 continued, with Eisenhower presenting plans for continuation of the former approach and the British once again pressing instead for a single thrust by Montgomery's 21st Army Group in the north. The JCS would, of course, not agree, and given their preponderance at this stage, the COS had little choice but to concur with Eisenhower's plans, albeit with continued misgivings. By those plans a series of Allied offensives would first destroy all German forces west of the Rhine, after which Montgomery would cross the river from the north, followed by a crossing by Bradley to the south and a link-up to surround the critical Ruhr industrial area. For these purposes some additional forces would be transferred from the Mediterranean to western Europe. At Yalta the Soviets were informed of these plans and in turn presented their own military plans for the spring, albeit in very general terms. The Combined Chiefs proposed closer and more flexible collaboration and coordination regarding future land and air operations, but the Soviet military chiefs preferred to rely upon existing institutional arrangements that had been established during and soon after the Moscow–Teheran Conferences of late 1943 and to await the results of the planned spring military campaigns. They thereby in effect left the matter for Eisenhower to attempt to resolve in March and April, which would in turn lead to additional Allied conflict at that time.[3]

In regard to German occupation zones, as previously noted, Roosevelt in September had finally agreed to COSSAC's 1943 proposal for an American zone of occupation in southwestern rather than northwestern Germany, on condition that he have control of Bremen and Bremerhaven in the north-western British zone.[4] Once this problem had thus been resolved, the European Advisory Commission had been able to proceed with its work, which the Big Three then ratified with modifications at Yalta. The Soviets would control the eastern section of Germany, the British the northwestern and the Americans the southwestern sections, with the capital of Berlin within the Soviet zone similarly divided. As Churchill wished, however, Roosevelt and Stalin also agreed that a fourth zone in Germany be created for France out of the British and American zones. Within these zones the victorious powers were to possess supreme authority, including the power to disarm, demilitarize and dismember Germany 'as they deem requisite'. Furthermore, reparations were to be made in kind via equipment, tools and labour, with the amount to be determined by an Allied Reparations Committee in Moscow. The Soviets and Americans but not the British agreed to the figure of 20 billion dollars 'as a basis for discussion' in Moscow, with 50 per cent going to the Soviet Union. War crimes trials were to take place, with the foreign secretaries directed to arrange and report on this matter, and an Allied Control Commission composed of the occupation army commanders (including the French) would be established to coordinate administrative matters.[5]

On the post-war United Nations organization, the Big Three succeeded in compromising their differences over structural issues that had been left unresolved at Dumbarton Oaks. Stalin now agreed to three rather than the 16 seats in the General Assembly that he had previously demanded, and to the same number of seats for the United States if Roosevelt needed them to obtain congressional approval of the organization. The Soviet leader also gave up his insistence on an absolute veto in the Security Council and accepted the more limited American proposal that the veto not include procedural matters and that abstention be used instead on matters in which one was a party. Moreover, he and Roosevelt agreed to veto power for France as Churchill wanted, while he and Churchill agreed to veto power for China as Roosevelt wanted. All three further agreed that a conference would take place in San Francisco in late April to actually write the charter for the new international organization, and on an invitation to the conference that included guidelines for the charter. Simultaneously, Roosevelt backed down on his earlier proposal for UN trusteeships that would include European colonies as a means of decolonizing Asia and Africa, agreeing instead to

Churchill's proposal that trusteeships be limited to old League of Nations mandates, conquered enemy territory, and colonies voluntarily placed in the system.

As informally agreed at the previous Teheran Conference, Poland was to lose territory in the east to the Soviet Union but be compensated with German territory in the west, though exactly how far west was not fully determined at this time. The Lublin Polish Government that the Soviets had recently recognized was to be reorganized so as to include individuals from within Poland and abroad, meaning the London Poles, and recognized by all the Allies, with free elections to follow. In the Declaration on Liberated Europe, the three Allies also promised democratic elections and institutions throughout the continent as promised in the Atlantic Charter.

In the Far East, Stalin once again agreed to enter the war against Japan, as he had previously at the 1943 Moscow and Teheran Conferences. This time the date of that entry was set at two to three months after the defeat of Germany and the territorial price made explicit: retention of the pro-Soviet status quo in Outer Mongolia; the Japanese Kurile Islands; and return of all special rights in China as well as territory that Russia had lost in its 1904–05 war with Japan. These included possession of the southern half of Sakhalin Island, a lease on Port Arthur, internationalization of the Chinese port of Dairen with preeminent Soviet interests, and joint operation of the Chinese railroads to that port. The United States was to obtain Chiang's agreement to these terms, and the Soviet Union in return would conclude a treaty of alliance with Chiang.[6]

For nearly six decades now western critics have attacked Yalta as craven appeasement of Stalin, primarily by Roosevelt but also on occasion by Churchill, that gave away half of the world to the Soviet dictator and thereby guaranteed the Cold War that would follow. That FDR remained physically disabled from polio and confined to a wheelchair is correct. That he was dying from serious heart disease is also correct, and within two months of the Yalta Conference he would indeed be dead. But whether his illness impaired his mental abilities at Yalta remains very questionable, for his behaviour at the conference was similar to the behaviour he had exhibited throughout his presidency. And in reality, neither he nor Churchill gave away anything at the conference that they actually possessed. To argue that they did misreads the situation in February of 1945 and incorrectly projects later issues and values onto this time period.

As previously noted, each Yalta agreement had a long history prior to the conference. Indeed, some historians have concluded that many of those agreements were actually determined at the preceding Teheran Conference and simply ratified at Yalta. Furthermore, as noted above, each of the Big Three compromised in order to obtain agreement, and each one of them as well as their advisers left Yalta convinced that these compromises had ensured continuation of the alliance and thus both total military victory and post-war peace. General Marshall told the press a few weeks later that the Yalta Accords constituted a major German defeat in that they precluded the Allied split on which Berlin had always planned.[7] Hopkins later stated:

> We really believed in our hearts that this was the dawn of the new day we had all been praying for and talking about for so many years. We were absolutely certain that we had won the first great victory of the peace – and by 'we' I mean *all* of us, the whole civilized human race. The Russians had proved that they could be reasonable and farseeing and there wasn't any doubt in the minds of the President or any of us that we could live with them and get along with them peacefully for as far into the future as any of us could imagine.[8]

One must also recognize that some of these agreements were designed to be temporary in nature, with permanent accords reserved for the expected formal peace conference at war's end. A few also reflected uncertainty within individual allied countries as to the appropriate policies to pursue. This was especially true in regard to future policies in Germany. Permanent dismemberment was listed only as a possibility because the powers had not yet made up their minds internally, let alone with each other, as to whether or not this was a good idea. The basic problem in this regard, at least from the British and American perspectives, was that a unified and economically strong Germany appeared necessary for the post-war economic health and thus the peace of Europe, but a potential menace to the rest of Europe militarily. At the 1944 OCTAGON Conference in Quebec, Churchill and Roosevelt had appeared to conclude that the military menace was paramount when they agreed to the Morgenthau Plan for the 'pastoralization' of Germany,[9] but objections from the US State and War Departments as well as the British Foreign Office that this would create economic and political chaos throughout Europe soon led to second thoughts. No final decisions had been reached by February of 1945, and none was stated as absolute in the Yalta Protocols.

Poland was the most controversial issue, and it would end up being a major factor in the break-up of the Grand Alliance and the advent of the Cold War. Discussions regarding Poland took up more time at Yalta than any other topic, occurring during seven of the eight plenary sessions and encompassing nearly 18,000 words between the Big Three.[10] But Poland's boundary shift had been discussed and virtually determined at Teheran, and the Warsaw Affair of 1944 as well as the ensuing advances of the Red Army had left Stalin and his puppet government in total control of the country by the time the conference opened. Churchill argued at Yalta that Britain had gone to war for Poland in 1939 and that the issue of Polish independence was thus a matter of honour for his country; but Stalin bluntly responded that in light of past history it was to Russia a matter of security as well as honour, for the Polish plains had twice in the twentieth century served as a German invasion route.[11] The most that Stalin would concede given this fact, and his physical occupation of the country, was agreement to allow London Poles into the government and

10 Stalin, Roosevelt and Churchill seated together during the Yalta Conference. Behind them stand their respective foreign ministers: Molotov, Stettinius and Eden, 4–11 February 1945 © Hulton-Deutsch Collection/CORBIS

eventually to hold free elections. (Those elections, Roosevelt asserted, 'should be like Caesar's wife. I did not know her but they said she was pure.' 'They said that about her,' Stalin replied, 'but in fact she had her sins.'[12]) Roosevelt clearly realized how limited these concessions were. When Admiral Leahy objected that the Polish accord was 'so elastic that the Russians can stretch it all the way from Yalta to Washington without technically breaking it', Roosevelt responded, 'I know Bill – I know it. But it's the best I can do for Poland at this time.'[13]

Although Churchill felt similarly, he would have preferred greater support from Roosevelt in an effort to obtain additional concessions from Stalin. But the president was more concerned with other and more readily obtainable Russian concessions, most notably in regard to the United Nations, German occupation, and the war against Japan. Without Soviet concessions on the UN disagreements, he feared a revival of isolationism within the United States that would in turn guarantee an Axis revival and World War III. Lack of Allied agreement on post-war Germany similarly promised only German revival and a third world war. On both issues Stalin offered concessions to Roosevelt and Churchill. In light of the virtual collapse of Chinese resistance in the summer and autumn of 1944, lack of specific agreement on the terms of Soviet entry into the war against Japan meant that the bulk of the Japanese Army would be freed to fight US forces. But such terms for Soviet entry were reached. Similarly, a post-war Soviet refusal to work with Chiang instead of

Mao could have doomed what remained of Roosevelt's post-war plans in China. And, similarly, Roosevelt obtained Stalin's agreement to recognize and work with Chiang.

As for the Cold War that would soon replace cooperation, it was neither desired nor expected by any of the three leaders. All of them wanted cooperation – even Stalin, albeit on his own terms. Belief that such cooperation would occur may have been a mirage, but if so it was a mirage shared by all three and by no means the monopoly of Roosevelt and Hopkins. Despite his famous and long-held distrust of the Russians and hatred of Communism, even Churchill was optimistic. 'Poor Nevile [sic] Chamberlain believed he could trust Hitler', the prime minister stated on his return. 'He was wrong, But I don't think I'm wrong about Stalin.'[14]

Finally, the Anglo-American military position vis-à-vis the Soviets was anything but strong enough to have obtained a better deal than the one obtained at Yalta. In this regard, the western Allies 'gave away' absolutely nothing that they actually possessed in February of 1945. The Red Army occupied all of Poland and was less than 45 miles from Berlin, whereas Eisenhower's forces were just recovering from the Battle of the Bulge and remained on the west side of the Rhine River, more than 250 miles from the German capital. Indeed, at that time it appeared possible that the Red Army might reach the Rhine before Eisenhower crossed it. Furthermore, in light of the Chinese collapse, the continued fanatical and suicidal Japanese resistance that US forces were facing, and the ensuing hideous casualties those forces were taking, Roosevelt's military advisers desperately desired Soviet entry into the Far Eastern War at a specified time and considered the price paid to be well worth it. Indeed, a very pleased General Marshall stated that 'for what we gained' on this matter alone, 'I would have gladly stayed [in Yalta] a whole month'.[15] As for the atomic bomb that critics argue precluded the need for Soviet entry, it did not even exist in February of 1945.

It might exist before the war ended, however, and it was clearly something that interested Roosevelt and Churchill as a method of balancing Soviet power should Stalin prove unwilling to cooperate. Indeed, immediately after the OCTAGON Conference the president and prime minister had agreed at Hyde Park to maintain an Anglo-American monopoly over any weapon that might be developed and not to share the secret with Stalin as the Danish nuclear physicist Niels Bohr had proposed.[16] Consequently, neither western leader even mentioned their nuclear project at Yalta. Simultaneously, the additional bait Roosevelt held out to Stalin for cooperation was the possibility of a massive post-war loan from the United States.

Admittedly, appeasement of Stalin did take place at Yalta as critics have charged, especially on the issue of Poland. But so did Soviet appeasement of the British and Americans, as well as Churchill's and Roosevelt's appeasement of each other, on issues ranging from occupation zones in Germany and Berlin (interestingly, Stalin during the conference halted an immediate assault by his forces on Berlin that could have advanced his armies even farther westward),[17] through an occupation zone and UN veto for France, to the territories that would be placed under UN trusteeship – where Roosevelt agreed to limits that clearly compromised his previous anti-colonialism. He continued to compromise that anti-colonialism over the next few months, even going so far as to sanction military assistance for a French return to Indochina that he had previously vowed never to allow.[18] It is important to note in this regard that while appeasement became a dirty word as a result of the events of the 1930s and remains so to this day, it had long been an accepted diplomatic practice among allies and nations with an otherwise close relationship, and that all three leaders practised it at Yalta.

Allied discord and final victory in Europe

Unfortunately, however, the Yalta Accords began to break down even before the ink was dry, as Stalin brutally established his dominance in Poland, Romania and everywhere else his armies moved, thereby making a mockery of the Yalta agreements to a coalition government in Poland and free elections throughout Europe that he probably dismissed as mere window dressing. Indeed, in all likelihood he viewed his behaviour as parallel to Churchill's December behaviour in Greece, and Anglo-American protests as tantamount to their breaking of the Yalta Accords – an interpretation not totally lacking in merit.[19] By April, he had forcefully imposed Communist governments on Romania and Poland, even going so far as to arrest leaders of the Polish Underground Army who had survived the Warsaw uprising of 1944. He also refused to send Molotov to the UN Conference in San Francisco, making the Soviet Union the only sponsoring country not to send its foreign minister.

Far from coincidentally, German resistance simultaneously weakened considerably and then collapsed in both the west and the south, which in turn fuelled Stalin's suspicions and led him, when he heard of secret surrender negotiations in Switzerland regarding German forces in northern Italy, to accuse his allies of attempting to secure a separate peace with Germany. That was too much for Roosevelt, who was 'furious' and 'outraged' over the charges, according to Charles Bohlen, and who uncharacteristically responded with a very sharply worded message on 4 April expressing to Stalin both 'astonishment' and 'bitter resentment' over what he bluntly labelled 'such vile misrepresentations of my actions or those of my subordinates'.[20]

The German weakening and the breakdown of the Yalta Accords also reignited the Anglo-American debate over the broad vs narrow front strategies. Throughout early 1945, Eisenhower had continued to reject Montgomery's proposals for the latter and instead pursued his approach to have all Allied armies 'close on the Rhine' before anyone crossed that large river. With Hitler determined to defend every inch of territory rather than withdraw to the east side of the Rhine, the result was a series of bloody battles in early 1945, much of it over purposefully flooded terrain in the Netherlands and the Roer River area.

Eisenhower's plan once all forces had reached the Rhine was once again to give Montgomery in the north priority in crossing the river, the last major German defensive barrier, and in moving on to the Ruhr and Berlin. For that reason Montgomery retained Simpson's 9th US Army from the December Ardennes crisis, though Hodges' 1st Army was returned to Bradley over Montgomery's protests. On 7 March, however, units from that 1st Army unexpectedly found and took the Ludendorff railroad bridge over the Rhine at Remagen that the Germans had attempted but failed to blow up. Hodges quickly established a bridgehead on the east side of the river, while Patton's 3rd Army and Patch's 7th Army swept northward and quickly cleared all remaining resistance on the west bank of the Rhine. Eisenhower decided to take advantage of this situation by shifting his main thrust from Montgomery in the north to Bradley farther south, a decision reinforced by Patton's successful crossing of the Rhine and establishment of a second bridgehead on 22 March at Oppenheim, southwest of Frankfurt. He thereby won a second 'race' with Montgomery and left the British field marshal to cross the Rhine last rather than first, on 24 March at Wesel. By 27 March, all seven Allied armies, a full 80 of the 91 divisions under Eisenhower's command, were across the Rhine while 290,000 Germans had been taken prisoner on the west side.

Eisenhower now had elements of Simpson's US 9th Army and Hodges' US 1st Army encircle the key Ruhr industrial area, a task they successfully completed by 1 April. At that time the 9th Army reverted to Bradley's command, which also added the new US 15th Army. Simultaneously the rest of the 12th Army Group drove rapidly eastward toward Dresden, with Montgomery's forces protecting Bradley's northern flank and racing northeastward to seal off German forces in Denmark and Norway. Hitler refused to retreat from the Ruhr and ordered it defended down to the last man. Instead 325,000 trapped troops surrendered by 19 April, less than three weeks after the encirclement had been completed (German Army Group B commander Field Marshal Walther Model committed suicide), making the Ruhr pocket the largest such surrender of the war.

A similar scenario simultaneously occurred in northern Italy in April, as Allied forces finally broke through the German defences now under Vietingoff's overall command (Hitler had moved Kesselring back to Germany to replace Rundstedt in the west after the Remagen Bridge disaster). Those defences now collapsed. On 28 April Italian partisans captured and executed Mussolini and his mistress before they could reach Switzerland, and on 29 April German commanders in Italy agreed to an unconditional surrender effective 2 May.

In Germany, Simpson's 9th Army spearhead reached and crossed the Elbe River on 11–13 April, leaving him only 50 miles from Berlin. As a result, he as an American commander now joined Montgomery, Churchill and the COS in pressing Eisenhower to advance on the German capital. Again Ike's reply was negative. Instead he insisted that the Ruhr Pocket campaign be completed and that Montgomery advance on Lübeck so as to seal off Denmark in the

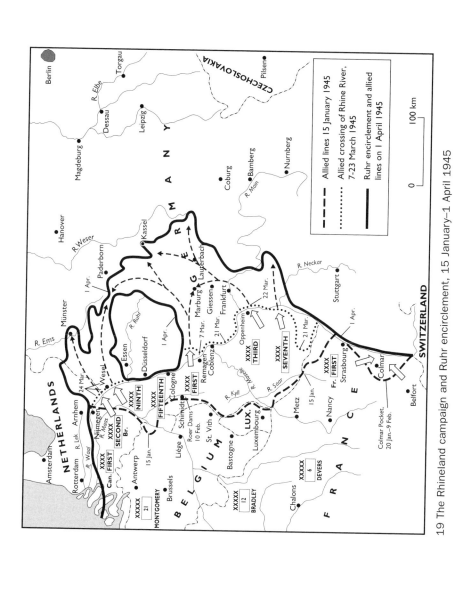

19 The Rhineland campaign and Ruhr encirclement, 15 January–1 April 1945

north, while Allied armies advanced in the south into Bavaria and Berlin be left to the Russians. A few weeks earlier he had informed Stalin of these tentative plans. Now he decided definitely to halt his armies and meet the advancing Red Army on the Elbe River, far west and south of Berlin.[21]

Eisenhower had numerous reasons for making these highly controversial decisions. Militarily his intelligence reported that Hitler was preparing to leave Berlin for a 'national redoubt' in the Bavarian mountains from which he would continue the war via guerrilla operations. While these intelligence reports turned out to be totally false, Eisenhower could not and did not know that. In April, he believed he had to move to get to the redoubt before Hitler did or face an extension of the war by months if not years. He also needed to prevent a head-on collision with the advancing Red Army that would result in needless casualties and could create a diplomatic crisis. Already his forces in Germany had moved beyond the occupation zones allotted to the western powers at Yalta. A clear demarcation line had to be established immediately.

Furthermore, only Simpson's spearhead had crossed the Elbe, and this relatively small force could easily have been cut off and decimated had it attempted a rapid advance on Berlin. The Russians, after all, would suffer at least 100,000 and perhaps more than 300,000 casualties taking the German capital. Moreover, Berlin as well as Germany had already been divided into occupation zones at the Yalta Conference, and over one and a quarter million Red Army troops were massed for a final assault on the city. Why lose lives for a political prize you had already obtained at Yalta? And why assume that the Soviets would not speed up their offensive in response to any Anglo-American effort to 'race' for the city and not respond with their own 'race' — not only for the German capital, but also for still-unoccupied territories such as Denmark?[22]

Churchill and the British Chiefs of Staff disagreed strongly. Consequently, they pressed the US Joint Chiefs and Roosevelt to stop Eisenhower's message to Stalin and reject his strategy. Instead they called for Anglo-American forces to focus on meeting the Red Armies 'as far to the east as possible', as Churchill suggested to Roosevelt on 5 April, 'and if circumstances allow, enter Berlin' before the Russians did.[23]

Previously Roosevelt had fully supported Eisenhower, and had he lived longer he would in all likelihood have joined the JCS by once again doing so now, despite his conflicts with Stalin. But on 12 April the president suffered a massive stroke and died. Six days earlier he had admittedly informed Churchill that 'Our armies will in a few days be in a position that will permit us to become "tougher" than has heretofore appeared advantageous to the war effort', but he did so right after he had rejected a Churchill plea for an advance on Berlin. And in his last message to Churchill on 11 April he downplayed recent problems with Stalin on the grounds that such problems 'in one form or another, seem to arise every day and most of them straighten out', as in the case of the recent blow-up over negotiations in Switzerland for the surrender of German forces in Italy. 'We must be firm, however,' FDR continued, 'and our course thus far is correct.'[24] On the following day he complained of a 'terrific headache' while sitting for a portrait in Warm Springs, Georgia, and suddenly collapsed from a massive stroke. Within a few hours he was dead, taking with him whatever specific plans and ideas for Soviet-American relations he may have had.

'Our friendship is the rock on which I build for the future of the world, so long as I am one of the builders,' Churchill had written to Roosevelt less than a month earlier. Now the man he would publicly eulogize as 'the greatest American friend we have ever known' had died, leaving him feeling 'as if I had been struck a physical blow'.[25]

Hitler's reaction was of course quite different. Sitting in his underground Berlin bunker with the Red Army rapidly closing in on him, the German dictator interpreted Roosevelt's death as a harbinger of an Allied split, much as the death of the Russian Empress Elizabeth in 1763 had broken the coalition against Prussia and saved Frederick the Great at the last minute from a total defeat in the Seven Years' War. He was almost correct, as Anglo-American relations with the Soviets continued to deteriorate throughout April. The alliance held, however, and on 24 April US 1st Army forces made contact with the Red Army at Torgau on the Elbe River, thereby splitting Germany in half. Simultaneously new US President Harry S. Truman joined his military advisers in supporting Eisenhower's decision to bypass Berlin. While Crerar's Canadian 1st Army took the rest of the Netherlands and together with Dempsey's British 2nd Army conquered northwestern Germany and its major ports, in the south de Lattre de Tassigny's French 1st Army and Patch's US 7th Army crossed the Rhine and, joined by Patton's 3rd Army, moved rapidly through southern Germany and toward the Austrian border. Crossing the Czech border on 25 April, Patton requested permission to take Prague. But Eisenhower refused on grounds similar to his Berlin refusal and ordered Patton instead to advance through southern Germany and into Austria.

On 29 April, five days after the Allied link-up at Torgau and with Soviet troops closing in on his Berlin bunker, Hitler appointed Admiral Dönitz as his successor, married his mistress Eva Braun, and then shot both her and himself. Dönitz thereupon attempted to split the Allies by announcing on 1 May not only Hitler's death but also that the 'struggle against Bolshevism' would continue – a clear invitation to the British and Americans to negotiate a separate peace. He made that offer explicit on the following day, only to have it flatly rejected. His emissaries then surrendered unconditionally to Eisenhower at Rheims on 7 May and to all three Allies in Berlin on the following day.[26]

While Allied forces were completing the conquest of Germany in early 1945, they were simultaneously making major progress against the Japanese. In Asia, they succeeded in retaking much of Burma. In the Philippines MacArthur's forces liberated the island of Luzon and the capital of Manila, while combined Anglo-American naval forces moved northward and took the islands of Iwo Jima and Okinawa. They suffered frightful casualties in these campaigns, however, as Japanese suicide tactics took their toll.

The reconquest of Burma

In South Asia, Slim successfully counter-attacked against the remnants of Mutaguchi's 15th Army that had been shattered at Imphal and Kohima, and crossed the India–Burma border in December 1944.[27] The decimation of that 15th Army had seriously weakened but far from destroyed Japanese forces defending Burma. Indeed, those forces under Japanese General Kimura Hoyotaro remained numerically superior to those Slim now led into Burma and across the Chindwin River. His aim was nothing less than a crossing of the Irrawaddy River in order to take first Mandalay and then Rangoon, in the process retaking the main road and railroad running from Rangoon up to Mytkyina. (See map on p. 136.)

Slim's numerical problems in late 1944 and early 1945 were compounded by the endorsement of General Wedemeyer, Stilwell's replacement as CBI chief, of Chiang's continuing demands for return of his troops from northern Burma in order to halt the Japanese ICHIGO offensive, and by Wedemeyer's additional request for the transfer of two groups of SEAC transport aircraft that had been supporting Burma operations. Such aircraft had been and remained critical to the supply and ensuing mobility of Slim's forces given the inadequate roads and inhospitable terrain and climate in Burma. Historian Ronald Spector has aptly compared the value of a squadron of transport planes in this theatre to an aircraft carrier or amphibious task force in the Pacific. That the Americans, who had long demanded and were finally getting a major British offensive in Burma, would now propose 'to let the air out of its tires' was not lost on the British, who protested vigorously. Returning the American suspicion of their motives, some Britishers concluded that the real aim of the United States was not to halt the Japanese in China but to make sure SEAC remained a backwater in the war.[28]

Slim succeeded in early 1945 via a deception that convinced Kimura the main British crossing of the Irrawaddy would take place north and west of Mandalay, and therefore to rush reinforcements to this area. But Slim's main crossing actually occurred south of Mandalay in mid-February and succeeded in taking Kimura's major supply and communication centre at Meiktila. While Japanese counter-attacks failed, Slim's deception corps in the north then broke out and took Mandalay in March. Simultaneously Wedemeyer's Chinese forces advanced in northern Burma and captured Lashio at the western end of the Burma Road, but he then requested withdrawal of these forces, as well as transport planes to move them, in order to attack the Japanese in China and retake a portion of the coastline. Churchill's direct protest to Marshall led the JCS to agree to a temporary retention of the aircraft by the British in order to take Rangoon – provided they could do so before the monsoon rains hit. They did, despite the fact that those rains arrived early. At the beginning of May, the Japanese abandoned Rangoon under pressure from both Slim moving from the north and an amphibious assault by Mountbatten's SEAC forces in the south (Operation DRACULA).

In these 1945 and preceding 1944 operations, British Imperial forces had inflicted on the Japanese Army some of the worst defeats it had ever suffered. But the area was clearly of secondary if not tertiary importance by 1945, for the American successes in the Marianas and the Philippines had virtually cut the Japanese home islands off from the resource-rich parts of their empire in Southeast Asia. Reconquest of those areas thereby lost much of their military significance. They still possessed political significance for the British and other European colonial powers, but for that very reason the Americans had no desire to focus on the area. Instead they continued to focus on the decisive Pacific theatre, where far more important and very bloody battles were taking place and would continue to take place.

Bloodbaths on Luzon, Iwo Jima and Okinawa

In the Philippines, the battle for Luzon began in January with US landings at Lingayen Gulf in the north. The previous Japanese decision to send major forces to Leyte seriously depleted their strength on Luzon and virtually guaranteed their eventual defeat. Nevertheless, the ensuing campaign would be one of the largest and bloodiest of the entire Pacific War. More than ten American divisions organized into two armies would participate – more than the total number of US troops in North Africa, Sicily or southern France.[29] They would meet fierce and suicidal Japanese resistance that would not be overcome in some areas even by the time Japan surrendered in August/September.

The *kamikaze* suicide attacks began as the invasion armada approached Lingayen Gulf, resulting in 25 US ships sunk or damaged. The landings themselves were relatively easy, however, primarily because Japanese commander General Yamashita Tomoyuki, the conqueror of Malaya and Singapore in 1941–42, realized his weakness and decided on a strategy of delay. Instead of challenging the American landings or trying to hold Manila, he ordered the withdrawal of most of his troops into three military strongholds in the mountains north and east of Manila.

Nevertheless a very bloody battle for Manila ensued, primarily because Japanese Rear Admiral Iwabachi Sanji refused to agree to Yamashita's evacuation order, and General Yokoyama Shizuo in the city, unable to stop the admiral, agreed to stay and fight. What followed was a month of urban street fighting, often block by block and building by building, that virtually destroyed the city and rivalled the carnage at Stalingrad in 1942 and at Warsaw in 1944. Nor were the casualties limited to soldiers and sailors. Some 100,000 Filipino civilians would also die, many of them victims of yet another round of atrocities by the Japanese Army.

By late February–early March the Japanese had clearly been defeated in Manila, as well as Bataan and Corregidor. But Yamashita's main forces remained in a strong, mountainous defensive triangle. To make matters worse, MacArthur seriously weakened his own forces on the island by ordering Eichelberger with five of his divisions to take the rest of the Philippine

Islands while the Australians attacked Borneo. This resulted in 14 major and 24 minor amphibious landings in 44 days. Although successful, they were devoid of strategic significance and left a weakened American force on Luzon to face the wily Yamashita, who proceeded to conduct 'one of the shrewdest delaying campaigns of the war'.[30]

While this bloodbath took place in Manila and throughout Luzon, Nimitz moved his fleets northward in an effort to eliminate Japanese fighter bases and obtain US bases closer than the Marianas for the bombing and blockade of the Japanese home islands. His first target was Iwo Jima, an island in the Bonin chain only 660 miles from Tokyo.

Iwo Jima was a small island, only 5 miles long by $2\frac{1}{2}$ miles at its widest point. But the Japanese had placed 21,000 troops under General Kuribayashi Tadamishi in a series of concrete-reinforced pillboxes, blockhouses, bunkers, caves and tunnels, many of them 35 feet underground. Some 72 days of US aerial bombardment followed by three days of naval shelling proved totally ineffective against such defences. The landings themselves were successful on 19 February, and the high point of Mount Surabachi was taken a few days later in what became one of the most famous photographs of the war. But it took US marines more than a month to take the rest of the island, far longer than had been anticipated. The Japanese fought virtually to the last man, with only a few hundred of their 21,000 taken prisoner. In turn, they inflicted 26,000 casualties on the Americans, a casualty rate of 30 per cent that included more than 6,000 dead and nearly 20,000 wounded. For the first and only time in the Pacific War, US casualties exceeded those of the Japanese.

Nimitz's next target was Okinawa, a long and narrow island in the Ryukyus, only 350 miles from the southernmost Japanese home island of Kyushu. At 485 square miles, it was much larger than Iwo Jima and contained a much bigger garrison: 77,000 Japanese soldiers plus 20,000 Okinawan militia. Hundreds of *kamikazes* were also available from the home islands and Formosa. Consequently Nimitz gathered an enormous invasion force of 180,000 under Admiral Turner and Lieutenant General Simon Bolivar Buckner, as well as a huge fleet under Spruance that included more than 40 carriers, 18 battleships, and nearly 200 destroyers. Within this naval force was the British Pacific fleet that Roosevelt and Leahy had forced Admiral King to accept at the OCTAGON Conference.[31] With 4 aircraft carriers, 2 battleships, 5 cruisers and 15 destroyers, it was clearly the largest British fleet of the entire war. But it was dwarfed by the American fleet, a telling illustration of the enormous power the United States was now mobilizing compared to the British.[32]

On 1 April US army and marine forces organized as the 10th Army under Buckner successfully landed on the island and within a week had succeeded in cutting it in two at its narrowest point. But the entrenched Japanese under General Ushijima Mitsuru now inflicted hideous casualties on the invading forces, especially in the south, and dragged out the campaign for nearly three months. By the time it ended on 21 June, they had wounded nearly 32,000 American soldiers and marines, and killed more than 7,000, including Buckner himself, while all but 7,000 of their own 77,000 men were killed. Over 100,000 Okinawans also died in the fighting. Simultaneously, the largest *kamikaze* attacks of the war sank 36 ships and damaged over 360, including 4 carriers and 10 battleships, with nearly 5,000 sailors killed and another 5,000 wounded.

Nevertheless the Japanese lost both battles. In the process they also lost most of what remained of their surface fleet, including *Yamato*, the world's largest battleship. Simultaneously, US submarines continued their destruction of the Japanese merchant fleet while B-29 bombers under Major General Curtis LeMay, adopting the area bombing and targeting of civilians that the Americans had doctrinally rejected in Germany, launched massive firebombing raids from the Marianas against the highly flammable Japanese cities. The largest of these raids in March killed over 100,000 people in Tokyo while destroying 16 square miles and leaving 5 million people homeless.

By June of 1945 Japan was thus utterly defeated. It had no navy or merchant marine left to speak of, its major ally in Europe was totally conquered and occupied, and its home islands were under both total naval blockade and constant air bombardment. Okinawa had been lost, and the Americans were preparing to invade the southernmost home island of Kyushu in November. With its government still controlled by the fanatical armed forces, however, Japan refused to surrender.

Allied conflict and the Potsdam Conference

A few hours after Roosevelt's death on 12 April, Harry S. Truman was sworn in as president of the United States. Truman was a relatively unknown former senator from Missouri who had been selected as a compromise vice presidential candidate in late 1944. On 12 April he had been vice president for only three months and had in no way been admitted into Roosevelt's inner circle. Indeed, FDR had kept his new vice president totally uninformed regarding most of the major wartime and post-war issues that now needed to be addressed immediately. 'Is there anything I can do for you?' Truman asked the grieving Eleanor Roosevelt on that momentous day. 'Is there anything *we* can do for *you*?' she replied, 'For you are the one in trouble now.' Truman concurred. 'I felt like the moon, the stars, and all the planets had fallen on me,' he told his former Senate colleagues on the following day. 'I've got the most terribly responsible job a man ever had.'[33]

Truman publicly stated that he intended to pursue Roosevelt's policies. The problem was that neither Truman nor anyone else really knew what those policies were, or how the secretive FDR would have behaved had he lived past 12 April. On no issue was this more apparent than relations with the Soviets, which continued to deteriorate.

On one level, Truman did not change Roosevelt's cooperative approach. Despite Churchill's entreaties, the new president refused to overrule Eisenhower or his own military advisers by sanctioning a 'race' for Berlin or

Prague. On the other hand, Truman did exhibit a new toughness in tone toward the Soviets, a toughness that Harriman and other Americans as well as Churchill had been recommending for many months on the grounds that Stalin respected only force. The San Francisco Conference to draft the UN charter would open as scheduled on 25 April, the new president told his advisers on 23 April, 'and if the Russians did not wish to join us they could go to hell'. Eschewing diplomatic niceties, he bluntly lectured the visiting Molotov later that day on fulfilment of the Yalta Accords regarding free elections in Poland and warned him that future relations could not be based on the 'one way street' of the past. 'I have never been talked to like that in my life,' Molotov replied (a lie for anyone who worked for Stalin). 'Carry out your agreements,' Truman continued to lecture, 'and you won't get talked to like that again.'[34] Two weeks later, on the day Germany officially surrendered, Lend-Lease to the Soviet Union was abruptly halted, even to the extent of unloading ships bound for Russia.

Such tough talk and behaviour did not change Stalin's brutal policies in Eastern Europe, though it did lead him to conclude that US policies had indeed changed with the death of Roosevelt. Furthermore, additional disagreements now erupted at the San Francisco Conference regarding the UN, and in occupied Germany. Truman had already revoked the Lend-Lease cut-off, which had been initiated by the Washington bureaucracy without his knowledge, and in late May he sent Roosevelt's ailing confidante Harry Hopkins to Moscow in an effort to clear the air. Hopkins managed to do so via a series of meetings and agreements with Stalin between 26 May and 6 June that covered many of the issues that had been aggravating Allied relations. Agreement was also reached to conduct a third 'Big Three' meeting in July in the recently conquered Berlin suburb of Potsdam.

Code-named TERMINAL, that meeting would differ in numerous ways from its Teheran and Yalta predecessors. Whereas those had lasted only four and eight days, respectively, the Potsdam Conference would continue for two and a half weeks, from 16 July to 2 August. The cast of major characters would also be different. Truman had of course already replaced Roosevelt. Midway through the conference Churchill unexpectedly lost the British elections and was replaced by his wartime deputy prime minister, Clement Attlee of the Labour Party. That left only Stalin of the original 'Big Three'.

The conference was also more rancorous than previous meetings. And despite its length, very little was actually accomplished. The Big Three did agree to establish a Council of Foreign Ministers to determine boundaries, peace terms and other policies for post-war Europe, but the very creation of this body was illustrative of the inability of the three leaders to agree on such matters at the conference itself. The foreign ministers would subsequently do no better, despite numerous meetings over the next few years.

Potsdam also witnessed a continuation of Britain's declining position vis-à-vis its allies, a decline that had been apparent since Teheran but one that had dramatically accelerated during 1944–45 and was only reinforced during the conference by the replacement of the overwhelming Churchill with the much blander Attlee. One British official concluded that the plenary sessions at the conference were now between 'the Big Two and a Half'. The decline was visible on a host of Anglo-American as well as Anglo-Soviet-American issues. While disagreements continued over the Phase II Lend-Lease aid that Britain desperately needed, the US Joint Chiefs bluntly rejected COS efforts to remove the Pacific War from solely American jurisdiction and place it instead under CCS direction. They also refused to allow British participation in Soviet-American exchange of information regarding future operations against Japan, tabled discussion of continuation of the CCS into the post-war era as premature, and even asked Truman to abolish the Combined Munitions Assignment Board as 'no longer necessary or desirable'.[35]

In retrospect, the most important issue at the Potsdam Conference was one that does not even appear in the official minutes: the atomic bomb. On 16 July the first successful test of this weapon took place at Alamagordo, New Mexico. As reported by the project commander, US Major General Leslie Groves, the explosion released energy equivalent to more than 15–20,000 tons of TNT, with its light seen 180 miles away, its sound heard 100 miles away, and its mushroom-shaped cloud rising 36,000 feet.[36] These and related facts were relayed to Potsdam over the next five days and had a profound impact on the president and his advisers – and of course on the war and the post-war world.

As previously noted, Britain and the United States had for years been working on the development of such a weapon – at first separately and then together. The ensuing project (code-named MANHATTAN, TUBE ALLOYS and S-1) had been top secret, however, so secret that US Secretary of War Henry Stimson had earlier in the war refused to reveal its contents to the then-Senator Truman ('I can't tell you what it is,' he told Truman at that time, 'but it is the greatest project in the history of the world'[37]) and had only done so after he became president in April. Stimson also informed Truman at that time of the expectation of forthcoming success. A high-ranking Interim Committee had consequently been formed and concluded in June that any weapon developed from the project should be used against Japan without warning, despite the stated objections of some of the scientists involved in the project within their so-called Franck Committee Petition. The Interim Committee did alter its recommendations somewhat in response to the petition by recommending that America's major allies, including the Russians, be informed beforehand.[38]

The successful test of this new weapon in mid-July coincided with an ongoing policy debate over the best way to obtain Japanese surrender. As previously noted, Japan's military situation by this time was utterly hopeless. Its navy and merchant marine were largely sunk, its trained pilots dead, its major allies defeated, and most of its army still mired in China. Furthermore, it had already lost much of its empire, it was separated from what remained by an Allied naval blockade, and its home islands were under constant devastating air attacks that were reducing all of its cities to rubble. Yet as illustrated by

Luzon, Iwo Jima and Okinawa, the Japanese continued to fight fanatically, using *kamikaze* and other suicide tactics to inflict upon largely American but also British forces their worst casualties of the Pacific War. The home islands contained 5,000 of these *kamikazes* as well as 2,000,000 armed men, 250,000 on the island of Kyushu and ready to inflict similar casualties on any invading force. How to convince them not to do so, and instead to recognize and accept their defeat before the OLYMPIC invasion of Kyushu scheduled for November, was thus a key Allied goal by mid-1945.

Some argued that the key to achieving this goal was Allied modification of Roosevelt's Unconditional Surrender policy. Japanese moderates had been sending out peace feelers to the Russians, which Stalin shared with his allies at Potsdam but which they already knew about via their signals intelligence. No Japanese leaders would ever accept Unconditional Surrender as a basis for peace, however, for it threatened the continued existence of the emperor, whom the Japanese considered a god and the indispensable element for the continuation of their people and nation. In that sense Unconditional Surrender was not merely unacceptable to the Japanese; it was incomprehensible to them.

Modification of Unconditional Surrender might embolden the militants to fight on, however, by convincing them that Anglo-American will was weakening and that more bloodletting would weaken that will even further and thereby secure better peace terms. It might also lead to a domestic uproar against Truman in the United States, where the public and Congress strongly supported the policy – a factor that weighed heavily on Truman's new and very powerful Secretary of State, James Byrnes. What was needed instead of modification of Unconditional Surrender, he and others believed, was something to shock the Japanese into surrender. The atomic bomb fitted the bill perfectly. Some, such as Byrnes, also saw the weapon as an alternative to Soviet entry into the war and thus a way to avoid increased Soviet power in the Far East. Others, however, saw the two as complementary shocks.

At Potsdam the hardliners on Unconditional Surrender won out. An Anglo-American-Chinese public document issued on 26 July and known as the Potsdam Declaration demanded Unconditional Surrender of the Japanese armed forces and ensuing Allied occupation of the country to eliminate its militaristic government. It also called for war crimes trials, reaffirmed the terms of the 1943 Cairo Declaration, whereby Japan was to be stripped of all its imperial conquests, and warned that failure to surrender unconditionally would lead to 'prompt and utter destruction'. But in line with the recommendations of the Interim Committee, the Potsdam Declaration made no specific mention of any atomic weapon.[39]

Upon receipt of Groves' full report on 21 July, Truman, according to Churchill, was a 'changed man' who 'stood up to the Russians in a most emphatic and decisive manner'. Three days later the president fulfilled the letter if not the spirit of the Interim Committee recommendation regarding the Soviets by casually informing Stalin after the afternoon plenary session had

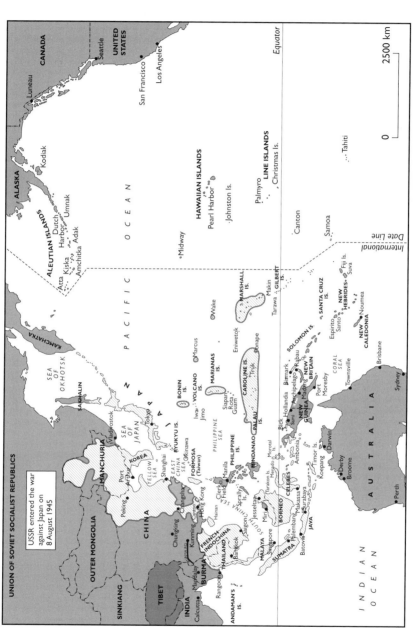

20 Areas under Allied and Japanese control, 15 August 1945

UNION OF SOVIET SOCIALIST REPUBLICS

USSR entered the war against Japan on 8 August 1945

SINKIANG

OUTER MONGOLIA

MANCHURIA

TIBET

INDIA

CHINA

Chungking

Kunming

BURMA

Rangoon

Mandalay

Calcutta

ANDAMAN'S IS.

THAILAND

FRENCH INDOCHINA

Bangkok

Saigon

MALAYA

Singapore

SUMATRA

Palembang

Batavia

JAVA

BORNEO

CELEBES

Makassar

Surabaya

Peking

Port Arthur

KOREA

Shanghai

Hong Kong

Hainan

YELLOW SEA

EAST CHINA SEA

FORMOSA (Taiwan)

Manila

Clark Field

PHILIPPINE IS.

Spratly Is.

Jesselton

Miri

Tarakan Is.

Menado

Morotai

Ambonia

Timor Is.

Koepang

SEA OF JAPAN

Vladivostok

Tokyo

RYUKYU IS.

Okinawa

PHILIPPINE SEA

MINDANAO

SOUTH CHINA SEA

SAKHALIN

KAMCHATKA

SEA OF OKHOTSK

BONIN IS.

VOLCANO IS.

Iwa Jimo

MARIANAS IS.

Siapan

Rota

Guam

PALAU IS.

Sami

Biak

Hollandia

NEW GUINEA

Port Moresby

Marcus

CAROLINE IS.

Truk

Ponape

Eniwetok

Wake

MARSHALL IS.

Makin

Tarawa

GILBERT IS.

Bismark Archipelago

Rabaul

NEW BRITAIN

Madang

SOLOMON IS.

CORAL SEA

Townsville

Brisbane

Sydney

ESPIRITO Santo

NEW HEBRIDES

SANTA CRUZ IS.

Fiji Is.

Suva

Noumea

NEW CALEDONIA

Samoa

Canton

PACIFIC OCEAN

Midway

ALEUTIAN ISLANDS

Attu

Kiska

Amchitka

Adak

Dutch Harbor

Umnak

Kodiak

ALASKA

Juneau

CANADA

UNITED STATES

Seattle

San Francisco

Los Angeles

HAWAIIAN ISLANDS

Pearl Harbor

Johnston Is.

Palmyro

LINE ISLANDS

Christmas Is.

Tahiti

International Date Line

Equator

INDIAN OCEAN

AUSTRALIA

Darwin

Derby

Broome

Perth

0   2500 km

ended that 'we had a new weapon of unusual destructive force'. Stalin nonchalantly replied that he was pleased to hear it and hoped his allies would make 'good use of it against the Japanese'.[40] While Truman may have walked away from this encounter convinced that he had 'put one over' on his erstwhile ally, Stalin knew exactly what he was talking about as a result of reports from his spies within the Anglo-American project and, either at this time or immediately after the 6 August atomic destruction of Hiroshima, he accelerated the Soviet atomic bomb project.[41] With the most dangerous common Axis enemy now totally defeated and occupied, the Grand Alliance was rapidly degenerating into the total mistrust that would mark the ensuing Cold War.

The atomic bomb and the Japanese surrender

Japanese Prime Minister Suzuki Sasaki responded to the Potsdam Declaration by asserting that the document contained nothing new and that therefore his government would 'ignore it entirely' – a translation of the Japanese word *mokusatsu* that the Allies interpreted as total rejection.[42] On 6 August a United States B-29 bomber obliterated more than 80 per cent of the city of Hiroshima with a single atomic bomb, killing approximately 130,000 people. Two days later the Soviet Union declared war on Japan, exactly three months after German surrender as Stalin had promised at Yalta but also one week earlier than he had told Truman at Potsdam that he would enter the war. On 9 August the United States dropped a second atomic bomb on the city of Nagasaki. Japanese army and navy leaders still refused to surrender, but these events threw them off-balance sufficiently to allow the moderates, supported by the emperor, to seize the initiative and offer surrender with the one proviso that the emperor be retained. That in turn led to a renewed debate among Truman's advisers, and a counter-offer to allow the Japanese to retain the emperor but leave him subject to the authority of the Supreme Allied Commander in charge of the occupation, who would be General MacArthur. (If the emperor was a god and now subject to MacArthur, some have quipped, what did that make the haughty American general?) On 14–15 August Japan accepted these terms, but only after another intervention and public statement by the emperor and the failure of an attempted military coup. On 2 September the Japanese signed the formal documents of surrender on board the US battleship *Missouri* in Tokyo Bay.

These final events of World War II have led to heated debate and an enormous literature over the last four decades regarding why the atomic bombs were dropped on Japan and whether they were indeed necessary to obtain Japanese surrender. Truman and his advisers argued immediately after the war that they were dropped to end the war as quickly as possible and thus to save hundreds of thousands of lives that would have been lost during any invasion of the home islands (Truman, Churchill and others cited the staggering figure of half a million American deaths in any invasion of the home islands), and that the bombs were necessary to accomplish these goals. Critics have labelled this a 'myth' if not an outright lie, and have argued that Japan would have surrendered without the bombs and before the planned invasion of Kyushu in November. Rather than ending the war quickly in order to save lives, the real motives for dropping the atomic bombs were to impress the Soviets with American power so they would change their behaviour in Eastern Europe and to end the war against Japan before the Soviets could enter and extend their power in Asia. Defenders of Truman have in turn attacked this interpretation as a 'cult' based upon a mythical re-reading of the past in light of present concerns.[43]

This debate has not and, in all likelihood, will not be resolved in the foreseeable future, for in many ways it reflects contemporary issues and cultural conflicts over memories and values more than it does what happened and why in 1945. It also involves 'counter-factual' history (i.e., what would have happened if the bomb had not been used), and counter-factuals cannot be proven or disproven because they did not actually occur. What can and should be noted, however, is a series of key facts that link the decision to use the bomb to previous events in the war itself.

First and foremost, the bombing of civilians did not begin at Hiroshima. As noted earlier in this volume, such bombing had been a key Allied policy throughout the war and had been consistently defended on numerous moral as well as practical grounds. In that sense the destruction of Hiroshima with an atomic bomb was to many of those involved in the decision no different than previous operations to destroy Tokyo, Dresden, Berlin, Hamburg or dozens of other cities, save that now a single bomb could accomplish such destruction.[44]

Second, Truman did not initiate the anti-Soviet components of US policy. Roosevelt did, in conjunction with Churchill, via their 1942–44 agreements to work together on the project, to keep it an Anglo-American monopoly and not even to inform the Soviets of its existence. The historians who first discovered this during the 1970s, Barton Bernstein and Martin Sherwin, also concluded that the conflicting interpretations could be synthesized. Impressing the Soviets with American power was, in Bernstein's words, a 'diplomatic bonus' that complemented rather than contradicted the primary desire to end the war as quickly as possible with minimum American casualties.[45]

Third, there was no decision in mid-1945 to 'use' the bomb against Japan as opposed to not using it. The Anglo-American project had begun as a 'race' to beat the Germans to develop any potential weapon, and its use if successfully developed had always been assumed, given the total war that was being fought and the belief that in such a war there was no such thing as a non-combatant. Had an atomic bomb been developed earlier, it certainly would have been used against Germany. Racism and a desire for revenge for Pearl Harbor may have been added factors in the decision to use it against Japan (more than 22 per cent in a December US public opinion poll agreed with the statement that more atomic bombs should have been quickly dropped before Japan had a chance to surrender).[46] But such additional factors were hardly necessary given the preceding years of strategic bombing and the mentality of total war. Furthermore, the question in 1945 was not *whether* to use the bomb, but *how* to use it, with critics arguing in the Franck Committee Petition for a demonstration on a deserted island before any use on the Japanese public for political as well as humanitarian reasons – i.e. the desire to avoid a 'wave of horror and repulsion' that would make post-war international control of atomic energy impossible and instead result in a nuclear arms race. The Interim Committee concluded that such a test was not technically work-able and would not produce the desired shock value. With the advantage of hindsight, one can see that numerous other options were available. But they were either rejected or not recognized at the time.[47]

Finally, the bombs by themselves did not cause the Japanese agreement to surrender. Equally important was the Soviet declaration of war and the American agreement to retain the emperor. The former turned the only great power left to mediate a negotiated peace into an enemy that quickly ripped through Japan's last major military asset – its army in northern China – and thereby left Japan diplomatically as well as militarily isolated. Retention of the emperor, and his strong and public support for the agreement, made sur-render tolerable.

As usual, Churchill had the best if not the last words on the significance of the bomb. 'Stimson,' he asked after the US Secretary of War informed him of the Alamagordo test results, 'what was gunpowder? Trivial. What was elec-tricity? Meaningless. This atomic bomb is the Second Coming in wrath.'[48] Hyperbolic or not, that quote, and this awesome weapon, were a fitting con-clusion to this most destructive war in human history.

11

AFTERMATH, CONSEQUENCES AND CONCLUSIONS

World War II was the largest and most costly war in history. The total number of human beings who died during and as a result of this enormous global conflict can only be estimated, and those estimates have consistently risen as previously classified documents have been opened and our knowledge of the war has increased. Recent estimates give the death toll at 60 million, a figure that is so large as to defy comprehension.[1] In addition to the human cost, the war also resulted in unprecedented dislocation and physical destruction, with most of Europe and Asia reduced to rubble. One writer has concluded:

> The years from 1939–1945 may well have seen the most profound and concentrated upheaval of humanity since the Black Death. Not since the 14th century had so many people been killed or displaced, disturbed, uprooted, or had their lives completely transformed in such a short period of time.[2]

Such an awesome conflict with such enormous destruction had to have enormous, multiple consequences over a long period of time. Indeed, those consequences are far from complete today, 60 years after the war ended. In many ways we still live with the results of World War II. What follows is a brief summary of those results to the extent that we are now able to see them, for the world as a whole, and for Britain, the United States and their relationship in particular.

Immediate consequences

The most immediate and obvious politico-military result of the war was the total destruction of German and Japanese power. Both nations were militarily occupied, demilitarized and temporarily removed from the list of great powers. The wartime leaders of both nations were also subjected, as the Allies had pledged, to war crimes trials. The highest-level Germans were tried by the major Allies as a whole at Nuremberg from 1945–47, others by individual allies within their zones of occupation or by the post-war governments of nations occupied during the war, with Nazi collaborators joining the Germans as defendants within these countries. Japanese war crimes trials were held in Tokyo from 1946–48 under an international tribunal, with regional trials by individual nations continuing until 1951.

Sentences for the major German officials found guilty at Nuremberg ranged from death by hanging for such individuals as Generals Albert Jodl and Wilhelm Keitel of Hitler's staff, to imprisonment for anywhere from ten years to life. The last prisoner for life, Rudolf Hess, died in Spandau Prison in 1987. No statute of limitations was ever set on the war crimes of Nazis and their collaborators, resulting in the Israeli capture, trial and execution of Holocaust architect Adolf Eichmann in 1960–61 and the trial and conviction by the French of Klaus Barbie and collaborator Paul Touvier as late as 1987 and 1994, respectively.

Key legal precedents were established at the Nuremberg and Tokyo trials. For the first time, violation of treaties and planning aggressive war, as well as 'crimes against humanity', were judged as punishable violations of international law. 'Following orders' was ruled an inadequate defence, in effect an assertion that orders could be illegal and that following an illegal order was a crime. Critics of the trials argued that much of this was in reality a series of *ex post facto* judgments on actions that had not been considered crimes when they were committed, and thus both illegal and merely a cover and rationalization for 'victor's justice'. Defenders argued that Axis aggression and barbarism had been unique, and that judging Germany and Japan by legal standards both preserved and expanded civilized behaviour in wartime while acting as a deterrent against future aggressive wars by punishing those who planned them.

Those who defended the trials were and have remained a clear majority regarding the Nuremberg judgments against the Nazis, with the standards set there being used today in international trials against such individuals as Serbian leader Slobodan Milošević. But criticism of the Tokyo trials was and remains much more widespread. Three of the 11 judges on the tribunal dissented from the verdicts at the time, with the Indian judge arguing that all the defendants were innocent of all the charges. Similar dissent emerged in some of the regional trials. Most notably, many felt that General Yamashita was unfairly blamed, found guilty, and executed for the atrocities committed by Japanese soldiers and sailors in the Philippines during the 1945 campaign. Yamashita's defence, that due to chaotic battlefield conditions he did not control and could not have controlled the troops even had he known of their actions, was rejected on the grounds that as overall commander he was directly responsible for their behaviour, with his death sentence upheld by the US Supreme Court. Yet the Americans themselves refused to apply this principle to the 1969 My Lai massacre in Vietnam, limiting those officers considered responsible to a lowly lieutenant.[3] Yamashita's true 'crime' for which he was tried and executed, critics have argued, was his brilliant delaying strategy on Luzon that tarnished General MacArthur's reputation.

Another major and immediate result of the Allied victory in the war was the formation of a new international body at the San Francisco Conference to replace the League of Nations. Between April and July of 1945, Allied delegates in San Francisco were able to reconcile their differences and agree to the actual charter of the new United Nations organization. That charter and organization still exist, with headquarters in New York and structure essentially the same as that which had first been proposed at Dumbarton Oaks in 1944 and then compromised and ratified at Yalta and San Francisco in 1945. Membership has quadrupled since the end of World War II, however, and the organization has seldom been able to act as its originators planned — primarily because disagreements between the great powers on the Security Council have precluded collective security based on Roosevelt's 'Four Policemen'.

The war destroyed much more than the power of Germany and Japan. It also destroyed or severely weakened the power of numerous other countries, most notably Great Britain, France and the other nations of Europe that had previously ruled much of the world. The result was a massive, global power vacuum that would be filled by the only two remaining powers: the Soviet Union and the United States. Indeed, both ended the war as rising 'superpowers', with their wartime ally Britain in serious decline. This situation had been foreseen during the war by numerous Americans — most notably the Joint Chiefs of Staff and their senior military advisers, who in 1944 had warned of a post-war shift in the world balance of power unparalleled since the fall of Rome.[4]

The phenomenal expansion of Soviet power was a direct result of the victories of the Red Army. Contrary to the popular mythology in Britain and the United States, the western democracies were not primarily responsible for the defeat of Nazi Germany. That bloody honour belonged to the Communist Soviet Union under the brutal dictatorship of Josef Stalin. From late June of 1941 until the formal German surrender in early May of 1945, the Soviets faced the overwhelming bulk of the *Wehrmacht* — anywhere from 67 to 98 per cent of all German combat divisions — and inflicted upon the Germans most of their combat casualties. Before the Normandy invasion the percentage had been more than 90. But even after June of 1944, the differences between the Anglo-American and Russian fronts remained enormous. Indeed, the total number of German combat casualties on the Eastern Front between June and September of 1944 — nearly 900,000 — exceeded by far not merely the total number of German casualties in the west, but also by 200,000 the total number of German troops engaged against Eisenhower's armies.[5] In May of 1945, a Red Army of more than 11 million consequently stood triumphant and in control of most of Eastern and much of Central Europe. Stalin did not intend to give that up. 'This war is not as in the past,' he told Yugoslav Communist Milovan Djilas, 'whoever occupies a territory also imposes on it his own social system. Everyone imposes his own system as far as his army can reach. It cannot be otherwise.'[6]

The Soviets had paid dearly for this victory. British and American casualties had been far from insignificant during World War II. Indeed, each nation suffered more than 400,000 deaths, a figure surpassed in British history only by World War I and in American history only by the Civil War of 1861–65. But even combined, these deaths do not reach the total number of Russians who died in the single siege of Leningrad, let alone the staggering total Soviet death toll of at least 25 million, approximately one-third of whom were military and two-thirds civilian.[7]

This is not to say that the Anglo-American contribution to victory had been insignificant. Far from it. The British had prevented a total German victory by fighting on alone after the 1940 fall of France and had provided the base from which Anglo-American naval, air and ground operations against Germany were launched. They had also provided millions of servicemen, from the Commonwealth countries and the rest of the empire as well as the United Kingdom itself, who had played major roles in the defeat of the Axis in North Africa, Italy and the rest of the Mediterranean (where they outnumbered American troops three to one in June of 1944),[8] as well as Western Europe, New Guinea and Burma – not to mention the strategic bombing campaign that diverted German resources from the Russian front and eventually crippled German industry as well as destroying the *Luftwaffe*. Through Lend-Lease, the Americans had provided both the British and the Russians with critical war material even before they officially entered the war, and by 1945 they were responsible for over 50 per cent of the total Allied war material produced during the war, 60 per cent of Allied combat munitions and 40 per cent of the world's armaments.[9] The United States also had in uniform in mid-1945 over 12 million soldiers, sailors and airmen, deployed around the globe, who had won major military victories against the Germans in conjunction with the British in North Africa, Italy and Western Europe, and who were primarily responsible for the military defeat of Japan. Truly, the Allied victory was a combined effort. But the military defeat of Germany was primarily the result of Soviet military victories on the ground, victories based not merely on Russian numbers, as German and western commentators originally maintained, but on Soviet military skill that grew throughout the conflict.[10]

The Cold War

Ambassador Harriman in Moscow had warned as early as the summer of 1944 that the Russians were becoming 'drunk with power' as a result of their military victories and needed to be firmly checked before they became a menace to Britain and the United States. Churchill made similar statements throughout 1944 and 1945, and attempted to enlist the Americans in a combined stance against Stalin that included military operations in the Balkans and to take Berlin, Prague and Vienna, as well as a forceful united diplomatic front against Russian behaviour in Poland and the rest of Eastern Europe. Roosevelt and his military as well as civilian advisers had refused, however, concluding that British proposals were militarily defective, capable of wrecking the alliance and designed to manipulate the Americans into a defence of British interests in areas of no real concern to the United States. By the time of Roosevelt's death, however, a major reassessment of American policy was under way. That reassessment continued throughout the spring and summer months and was greatly reinforced by Soviet behaviour, the atomic bomb and Japanese surrender. Roosevelt and his advisers had believed as late as the February 1945 Yalta Conference that post-war collaboration was both possible and highly desirable, that the Soviets were primarily interested in security in Eastern Europe, and that they were still needed to achieve total victory over Germany and to defeat Japan without horrendous American casualties. By August/September, however, both Germany and Japan had surrendered, the United States was in sole possession of the ultimate weapon, Soviet demands had extended far beyond security requirements in Eastern Europe, and Soviet behaviour was being perceived as more and more truculent and dangerous.[11]

The consequent inability of the increasingly suspicious wartime allies to agree to peace terms for the defeated Axis nations soon became apparent. In London, the first meeting of the Council of Foreign Ministers established at Yalta ended in total discord in October 1945, with the conferees unable to agree even on the public communiqué announcing their failure. A second meeting in Moscow during December was more successful, resulting in peace treaties for Germany's wartime satellites. But all the ensuing foreign ministers meetings in 1946 and 1947 failed to reach accord on terms for Germany. Consequently, no equivalent of the post-World War I Paris Peace Conference ever took place and no equivalent of the Treaty of Versailles was ever even written, let alone signed and ratified.

Instead of such a treaty and the peaceful world the Allies had hoped to create, what emerged very quickly from the ashes of World War II was the Cold War, a conflict that historian David Kennedy has aptly labelled 'the unwanted war baby conceived in the fragile marriage of convenience that was the Grand Alliance'.[12] The result would be the division of Germany, and the rest of Europe, for the next 45 years.

As early as February of 1946 Stalin publicly reasserted the primacy and correctness of Communist ideology, with its anti-capitalist emphasis, in a speech US Supreme Court Justice William O. Douglas labelled a 'declaration of World War III'. One month later former Prime Minister Winston Churchill warned during a speech in Fulton, Missouri, with President Truman on the stage, that an 'Iron Curtain' was descending across Central and Eastern Europe, 'From Stettin on the Baltic to Trieste on the Adriatic', and that this menace should be met by a strong Anglo-American front.[13] In effect, he was once again asking for American agreement to what he had called for during the latter stages of the war, a united Anglo-American front against the Soviets, and in effect a continuation of the Anglo-American wartime alliance but now redirected against Moscow. By 1947 the United States would agree via enunciation of the Truman Doctrine, the Marshall Plan, and its policy of 'Containment' of the Soviet Union, as publicly explained by State Department official George F. Kennan.[14]

The Cold War completed the demise of American political and military isolation from Europe. Admittedly, that demise had begun in World War I and continued through World War II. Isolationism had re-emerged after World War I, however, and throughout World War II Roosevelt consistently feared another appearance. Indeed, he did not believe the American people would tolerate their troops remaining in Europe for more than two years after German defeat. The rise of Soviet-American antagonism ended such fears once and for all and led to a full American commitment to the defence of Western Europe and the containment of Communist Russia.

In effect, the United States concluded that a hegemonic Soviet Union posed as much of a threat after the war as a hegemonic Germany had posed during the war, and that America in its own interest needed to continue to act so as to prevent any single power from controlling Europe. In that sense, Washington in effect adopted the same balance-of-power policy that had dominated British diplomacy for centuries. Indeed, American grand strategy during the war was similar in many ways to British grand strategy during the Napoleonic Wars: material and financial support of European allies combined with powerful expeditionary forces to support those allies. Furthermore, Americans such as Walter Lippmann had begun to assert during the war that Britain's previous enforcement of the European balance of power had guaranteed their own security during much of their history, and that if a weakened Britain could no longer enforce it, the United States would have to do so.[15] Far from accidentally the United States thus took over British policy in many parts of the world as British power retreated after the war.

Nowhere was this more apparent, or ironic, than in the eastern Mediterranean. Throughout World War II the Americans had objected vehemently to British proposals for military operations in this area, denigrating such proposals as politically inspired efforts to suck the United States into a revival of the historic Anglo-Russian clash in the area as an ally of Britain. But when London in early 1947 informed Washington that it could no longer afford to support the Greek Government against Communist rebels or the Turkish Government against Soviet territorial demands, the United States quickly accepted the not-so-subtle British offer to take London's place. The result would be the famous Truman Doctrine of early 1947, in which the president requested and received congressional funds to support the Greek Government against Communist guerrillas and the Turkish Government against Soviet pressure on the grounds that US policy 'must be . . . to support free peoples who are resisting attempted subjugation by armed minorities or by outside pressures'.[16]

A few months later General Marshall, now Truman's secretary of state, proposed that the United States use its awesome economic power to contain the

Soviets by funding the economic recovery and integration of Europe, thereby eliminating the poverty, devastation and despair upon which Americans believed Communism and all other forms of political tyranny thrived.[17] The result was what officially became the European Recovery Program and is unofficially known as the Marshall Plan, whereby the United States gave the participating nations of Europe 16 billion dollars to integrate and rebuild their economies, thereby squashing the popularity of local Communist parties as well as restoring European confidence and prosperity. The Marshall Plan was also designed revive the entire US-led global capitalist economy, and to minimize the possibility of future intra-European war by making the European nations dependent on each other economically. Such ideas dated back in US history to the 1920s.[18] In the context of 1947, however, the Marshall Plan was also a post-war continuation of wartime Lend-Lease, using the same tool of American economic power for the similar goal of preventing others from being forced to surrender to the enemy. It worked equally well, and it is generally considered one of the most successful international pro-grammes in US history. But it also played a major role in creating a half-century division of Europe into two armed camps, for Stalin interpreted it as a diplomatic offensive designed to take away his empire in Eastern Europe. Consequently he refused to allow his satellites or his own nation to partici-pate, tightened his control over the nations of Eastern Europe, and launched a coup that in early 1948 put Czechoslovakia behind the Iron Curtain.

That brought back memories of Munich a decade earlier and led to a war scare in the West, a war scare tremendously reinforced by what occurred a few months later in Germany. The European economic recovery that the Marshall Plan was designed to produce required a rebuilt and fully integrated German economy. With Allied negotiations over the future of that occupied wartime enemy stalemated, the United States, Britain and France agreed in 1948 to merge their three occupation zones and create a German state without the Soviet zone or Soviet concurrence. In a desperate effort to stop what he con-sidered this dangerous revival of his mortal German enemy, Stalin responded with a Soviet blockade of the land routes into the western zones of Berlin, which lay totally within the Soviet zone of Germany as a whole. But the effort boomeranged in that it only accelerated both the creation of West Germany (the Federal Republic) and a formal American military commitment to the defence of Britain and Western Europe via the sending of atomic-capable B-29 bombers to England and the 1949 North Atlantic Treaty Organization (NATO). One British policy in 1944–45 to defend against post-war Soviet domination of the continent had been creation of a West European bloc. Now the United States not only supported such a bloc, but actually joined it in the first peace-time military alliance in its history.

Despite the war scare, World War III did not take place in 1948 or 1949. The western powers responded to the Berlin blockade not via a humiliating with-drawal or a provocative armed convoy that could have led to hostilities, but instead with a successful airlift of supplies to their sectors of Berlin that the

Soviets did not militarily challenge. And when the Federal Republic of Germany was indeed formed out of the three western occupation zones, Stalin responded with the Communist Democratic Republic of Germany in his zone. Two German states would thus exist until the end of the Cold War.

On a broader level, no third world war ever developed from the Cold War. Indeed, the years of the Cold War coincided with the longest period of peace in the history of Europe – longer than the Metternichian period that followed the Napoleonic Wars in 1815 and longer than the Bismarckian period that followed the wars of German unification in 1871.[19] This was far from accidental or coincidental. In effect, the Soviet-American superpower confrontation in Europe kept suppressed the intra-European conflicts that had led to two world wars. It also kept Germany divided and thus incapable of beginning a third world war, with the American commitment to NATO and permanent stationing of troops in Germany further suppressing any revanchist tendencies that might develop in the Federal Republic. As a popular saying at the time (often credited to General Ismay) put it, NATO actually had three purposes: to keep the Russians out, the Americans in, and the Germans down.[20]

Some have argued that the absence of any third world war despite the intense hostility of the Cold War was primarily due to the advent of nuclear weapons. As Niels Bohr and the signers of the Franck Committee petition had warned, using these weapons without warning and without really informing the Soviets did indeed lead to a nuclear arms race and the inability to achieve international control over atomic energy. Stalin rejected the Anglo-American proposals for such control in 1946, and by 1949 he had successfully tested his own atomic bomb. But the nuclear arms race in turn resulted in a 'balance of terror' that ironically helped to preserve the peace in Europe. With each side possessing nuclear weapons and threatening to use them if the other side infringed upon its sphere in Europe, both sides developed an abiding interest in a peaceful preservation of the status quo.

That was not the case in Asia, however, specifically in China where US efforts to avoid a continuation of the civil war between Chiang's Nationalist government and Mao's Communists failed – despite a major mediation effort by General Marshall as presidential emissary in 1946. Whether that effort could have succeeded under any circumstances is questionable, given the pre-existing hatred between the two sides. But the emerging Cold War ended any possibility of successful US mediation by precluding the possibility of the United States dropping its support of Chiang in favour of the Communist Mao. Consequently, hardliners within the *Kuomintang* triumphed, for given the expected American support in any continuation of the civil war, there appeared to be no need to compromise.

Actually there was, for as previously noted, the war had seriously weakened the *Kuomintang* while strengthening the Communists.[21] In 1945 and 1946 they were further strengthened by a Soviet occupation and handover of Manchuria after the Japanese surrender and by Chiang's insistence on attempting to occupy all Chinese cities as the Japanese withdrew, despite American warnings that this would grossly overextend his forces and precipitate clashes with the Communists that he would lose. That is exactly what occurred over the next few years, as Mao's armies isolated and defeated Chiang's forces, using both guerrilla tactics they had perfected against the Japanese and American weapons they captured from Chiang's forces. By 1949 Chiang had fled to the island of Formosa and Mao had proclaimed the Communist People's Republic of China.

In that same year the Soviets exploded their first atomic device. The American response was a refusal to recognize Mao's government, which allied with the Soviet Union by early 1950, and a new national security policy – as enunciated in National Security Council (NSC) Paper #68 – that called for a full rebuilding of the military power of the United States and its allies around the globe as well as the creation of new allies. Most notable in this regard was the decision to sign a peace treaty with and rebuild Japan as a replacement for China in the Far East. Within five years the United States had thus decided not only to maintain and expand its wartime alliance with Britain and other West European powers, on the one hand, but also to rebuild its two major World War II enemies, on the other, in an effort to check and defeat its former ally and new enemy in Moscow. Its success in doing so ironically helped to create two of its major economic competitors in the late twentieth century.

Decolonization and revival of limited war

The Cold War, however, was but one of two major international events to dominate the post-war era. The other, which may well have been the most profound and long-lasting result of World War II for international relations, was decolonization of the European empires in Asia, Africa and the Middle East. As previously mentioned in this chapter, the membership of the UN has quadrupled since its inception in 1945. Most of this increase in size has been the result of decolonization.

World War II seriously weakened the European colonial powers, mostly via German occupation and exploitation as well as wartime destruction, and thus the ability of those powers to maintain physical control of their overseas empires. Britain had not been occupied by the Germans, but its enormous wartime effort shattered its economy, which had been in relative decline for decades, and left it almost totally economically and financially dependent on a United States deeply opposed to a continuation of colonialism. Churchill may have boasted in late 1942 that he had not become prime minister to preside over the liquidation of the British Empire, but in effect he had. Compounding the problem of European weakness were Japanese wartime conquests in Asia and the Pacific, which had provided dramatic illustration of both that weakness and the ability of non-Europeans to defeat them in battle, while raising the hopes of nationalist leaders and their supporters around the world. The Europeans would nevertheless attempt to resurrect their empires immediately after the war, but would fail wretchedly. In the ensuing decolonization the United States and Russia would superimpose their Cold War conflict on these areas in an effort to extend their own influence and check their opponent's influence. The results were often complex, bloody and tragic. This was most notably and immediately the case in Asia, where the confluence of decolonization and the Cold War led to lengthy and bloody wars in Korea and Vietnam.

As part of the Japanese Empire, Korea had been promised independence by the Allies in the 1943 Cairo Declaration. When Japan surrendered in August of 1945, the peninsula was occupied by American troops in the south and Russian troops in the north. As the Cold War then developed, the temporary dividing line of the 38th Parallel of latitude hardened into a permanent border. Each superpower established a friendly Korean Government in its zone and withdrew its own troops, thereby creating by 1950 two Koreas similar in some ways to the two Germanies that had recently been created in Europe. That seemed to suit the two superpowers as an acceptable compromise. It did not suit either Korean Government, however, both of which threatened to unify the peninsula by force. With Stalin's permission the North Korean Government of Kim Il-Sung struck first on 25 June 1950, quickly capturing the South Korean capital of Seoul. Perceiving this assault as Soviet-sponsored, and using comparisons to Axis aggression and Allied appeasement in the 1930s, the Truman Administration decided to oppose the North Koreans with force. While American occupation troops in Japan were rushed into South Korea around the port of Pusan, Washington took the matter to the United Nations. With the Soviets boycotting the Security Council over its refusal to replace the defeated Chiang with Mao's representative in China's chair, the Americans were able to obtain UN sanction and support for collective military action against North Korean aggression under the overall command of General MacArthur in Tokyo.

MacArthur quickly routed the North Koreans via a brilliant amphibious landing behind their lines at the port of Inchon, at which point Truman and his advisers decided to cross the 38th Parallel and unify the peninsula by force. Viewing the ensuing American advance to his Yalu River border as part of an American strategy to undo the results of his victory over Chiang, Mao responded with a massive Chinese counter-offensive that sent the Americans as well as the South Koreans retreating back down the peninsula. What followed was a major crisis in both the NATO alliance and US civil-military relations, as the Truman Administration and its European allies reverted to their original aim of preserving South Korea via a limited campaign to return to the 38th Parallel while MacArthur, refusing to accept such limits, publicly attacked administration policy and called for expansion of the war into China. Truman thereupon relieved MacArthur, replacing him with General Matthew Ridgway and unleashing a firestorm of protest within the United States that included calls for his impeachment.

While the opposition Republican Party supported MacArthur in the ensuing congressional hearings, the Joint Chiefs of Staff and now Secretary of Defense

George Marshall, supported Truman on the grounds that expanding the Korean conflict at this time would involve the United States in an open-ended commitment on the Asian mainland, would not have the support of Britain or the other NATO allies, and would leave both the United States diplomatically isolated and Western Europe open to a Soviet attack. In JCS chairman General Omar Bradley's famous words, expanding the war to China would be 'the wrong war, at the wrong place, at the wrong time, and with the wrong enemy'.[22] Although nearly six years had passed since the end of World War II, the Americans were in effect replaying their wartime debate over appropriate global strategy: once again the administration and the Joint Chiefs were insisting on the appropriateness of a 'Europe-first' approach in alignment with Great Britain and other European allies, and consequently on limits in the Far East. And once again the charismatic Far Eastern commander MacArthur, suffering from 'localitis', was refusing to agree. This time, however, he was fired.

Truman survived the firestorm of protest, and Ridgway fought his way back up to the 38th Parallel. An armistice was finally reached in 1953 by Truman's Republican successor as president, wartime Supreme Allied Commander General Dwight Eisenhower. But neither Eisenhower nor any other US president was able to turn that armistice into a peace treaty – even after the Cold War ended. Two Koreas still exist, the North now armed with nuclear weapons, and more than 30,000 US troops still defend the border established by the 1953 armistice near the 38th Parallel.

While events in Europe, China and Korea dominated the headlines from 1945–53, events in Indochina were leading to an equally if not bloodier and tragic war. With the Japanese surrender, Ho Chi Minh proclaimed the independence of Vietnam, using words taken directly from the US Declaration of Independence. France, however, refused to give up its Indochina colony and war ensued. Despite Roosevelt's wartime statements and OSS wartime support for Ho, the United States remained officially neutral and unofficially pro-French from 1945–50 due to the emerging Cold War and the subsequent desire to rebuild France as a major ally in Europe as well as antipathy towards Ho's indigenous Communist movement, which US policymakers viewed as a tool of Moscow. By 1950 US support of France had become official and extensive as Ho aligned with Mao and Stalin. He also used Maoist guerrilla tactics against the French and, despite massive American aid, had thoroughly defeated them by 1954. Eisenhower seriously considered American military intervention to rescue the French fortress of Dien Bien Phu in that year, but eventually decided not to do so – perhaps as a result of opposition from now army chief of staff Ridgway as well as others. Instead he decided to provide massive support for the former French puppet government that had been left temporarily in charge of the southern half of Vietnam via the Geneva Accords of 1954 that ended this 'first' Indochina War, in an effort to create the equivalent of the two Koreas in Southeast Asia. The failure of this effort would lead to the Americanization of the Vietnam War in the mid-1960s, and to a humiliating American defeat by 1975.[23]

Decolonization in the rest of Asia did not result in the United States going to war a third time, but it often did result in substantial bloodshed and Cold War competition for influence. Facing continued nationalist pressure as well as its own weakness, Britain in 1947 withdrew from India, its 'crown jewel' of empire, with two independent and warring states emerging based primarily on the religion of the inhabitants: Hindu India and Muslim Pakistan. Their mutual animosity and conflict, particularly over the province of Kashmir, continues to this very day and consistently threatens to lead to a regional nuclear war.

Over the next few years the Dutch would withdraw from their East Indies colonies, leading to the creation of Indonesia, while the British withdrew from virtually all their remaining colonies in South and Southeast Asia, leading to independence for Burma, Malaya and Singapore. In 1946 the Philippines also became independent from the United States. While some of these nations allied with their formal colonial masters and received aid in suppressing indigenous Communist rebellions, many declared their neutrality in the Cold War, leading to the use of the term 'Third World' to describe their status as opposed to the 'First World' and 'Second World' allies of the United States and the Soviet Union.

Also choosing neutrality in the Cold War were many of the newly independent nations emerging in Africa – a continent totally controlled by Europeans when World War II ended. Mussolini had in 1935–36 extinguished the independence of the only country in Africa that had previously been able to resist European conquest: Ethiopia. In the decades after World War II, however, the British, French, Belgians, Italians and Portuguese all gave up their colonial holdings on the entire continent. But the boundaries of the new nations were the boundaries that had been set by these European colonizers in their late nineteenth- and early twentieth-century competition, and made little if any sense given African tribal history. The result would be major conflicts both within and between the new African nations as well as the pre-existing tribes, many of them exceptionally violent. Violent conflicts also erupted between black Africans and their white colonizers, particularly in the former British colonies of South Africa and Rhodesia (present-day Zimbabwe), where those colonizers established white minority governments. Although most of the new African states chose non-alignment in the Cold War, the Americans and the Soviets often added to the bloodshed via efforts to extend their influence and/or check each other. One of the most tragic cases of this confluence of factors was the former Belgian Congo, which was plunged into an orgy of violence following Belgium's 1960 granting of independence.

In the Middle East the end of World War II brought full independence for a host of states, many of which had been part of the Ottoman Empire before World War I and had achieved during the inter-war years a degree of autonomy via the League of Nations mandate system. Most notable in this regard were the former French mandates of Lebanon and Syria and the British mandates of Iraq, Palestine and Transjordan. Full independence was also achieved for areas in North Africa over which the Europeans had obtained formal or informal control in the nineteenth century: Morocco, Algeria and Tunisia for France; Libya for Italy; and Egypt for Great Britain. Once again, however, the boundaries for these new states were artificial creations of the colonial powers who had replaced the Ottomans, and many of those boundaries made little sense given the history of the area.

The resulting conflicts in the Middle East were compounded by three additional factors. The first was the presence of huge oil deposits upon which the industrialized nations of the world were dependent for both their economic health and the viability of their armed forces. The second was an intense Cold War rivalry for influence in the area, both because of the importance of oil and because the Middle East is geopolitically and strategically critical as the meeting point of three continents: Africa, Asia and Europe. These two factors would lead to some of the earliest Cold War conflicts immediately after World War II. In Iran, which had been occupied by the British and the Soviets in 1941 to remove a pro-Axis government and establish a supply route to Russia, the British and Americans in 1946 pressured the Soviets to fulfil their wartime commitment to withdraw their troops in the first public display of a split in the alliance. In the following year, first British and then American support for Turkey in the face of Soviet pressure resulted in the Truman Doctrine. Iran came back to centre stage in 1953, when the US CIA organized a coup against the nationalistic Prime Minister Mohammed Mossadeq who threatened British oil interests and was therefore (incorrectly) considered a Soviet stalking horse. His overthrow led to the return to power of the young Shah that the British had first installed in 1941, Mohammad Reza Pahlevi, as a British-American friend until his overthrow in 1979 by Islamic fundamentalists. Those fundamentalists then seized the US Embassy in Teheran, precipitating the Iranian hostage crisis of 1979–80. To this day they consider the United States the 'Great Satan' for the 1953 coup and ensuing support of the detested Shah.

The third factor to compound the decolonization-related conflicts in the Middle East was the creation of Israel as a result of the UN's 1947 agreement to partition the British mandate of Palestine into Jewish and Arab states. That decision split the Truman Administration from the British, as well as from its own State and Defense Departments. It also led to the first Arab-Israeli War of 1947–49, and with it the Palestinian refugee problem that continues to this very day. For the nations that voted for partition of Palestine, the creation of Israel was the fulfilment of a pledge originally made by the British and supported by the League of Nations to recreate a homeland for Jews after nearly 2,000 years of wandering and persecution, a pledge that took on new urgency and morality in the aftermath of Hitler's attempt to exterminate all the Jews of Europe and the post-war need to find a home for the survivors of the Holocaust. To the Islamic states that opposed partition, however, the creation of Israel was simply another form of European imperialism in that it established a de facto colony for despised European Jews, by European Christians who did not want them, within the heartland of the Islamic world. That struggle too continues to the present day.

World War II also resulted in dramatic changes in warfare itself. As noted numerous times throughout this volume, war became 'total' and the concept of civilians virtually disappeared. Civilian populations were mobilized and militarized for total war efforts run by their governments, and they were killed in unprecedented numbers. The overwhelming majority of British and American casualties were admittedly military, but both powers inflicted heavy civilian casualties on their enemies, primarily via the bombing of German and Japanese cities. Furthermore, the overwhelming majority of deaths and casualties in other nations, most notably Poland, Russia and China, were civilian in nature.

The combination of total war on civilians and the advent of atomic weapons led many to conclude war could never take place again without destroying human civilization – and indeed the human race. That conclusion was quickly proven incorrect, as the world returned after 1945 to the concept of limited war that had dominated European history during the eighteenth century and again in the century between Napoleon's 1815 defeat and the outbreak of World War I. Indeed, one might argue that the world has been in a state of perpetual limited war since 1945.

Anglo-American relations

World War II had numerous specific consequences for Britain and the United States beyond those already enumerated, and for their relationship with each other. Although one of the victors, Britain emerged from the conflict severely weakened – and in some ways in no better condition than France and the defeated Axis enemies. Although not as physically devastated as those nations, it had suffered extensive destruction from German bombs and rockets. Even more damaging was its precarious economic and financial condition. The war had cost London a quarter of its national wealth and left it virtually bankrupt – and thus thoroughly dependent on the United States. It also emerged with a new Labour Government of democratic socialists and trade unionists who would nationalize its economy and seriously 'flatten' its pre-war social pyramid while overseeing the first and most important steps in the dismantling of the British Empire.

A flattening of the social pyramid also occurred in the United States, though in different ways and for far different, indeed, diametrically opposed, reasons. Whereas the British flattening occurred as a result of economic decline as well as shared wartime hardship and a post-war sharp leftward shift in British politics, the American one resulted from enormous economic growth with a shift to the right during and after the war.

The United States was the only major belligerent not to be bombed or invaded during the war. Consequently, it was able to fully mobilize and indeed expand what even before the war had been the largest economy in the world in order to supply its allies as well as its own forces with war material, thereby increasing its gross national product by 50 per cent. By war's end the United States possessed half of the manufacturing capacity of the entire world, more than half of its electricity, two-thirds of its gold supply and half its monetary reserves. The result was the end of the Great Depression and the beginning of the longest economic boom in US history. As a result of that boom, and the post-war GI Bill of Rights that provided loans and educational benefits to millions of veterans, the American middle class exploded. By 1960 it encompassed two-thirds of the entire US population.[24]

Furthermore, to organize the wartime economy Roosevelt made peace with big business, much of which had warred with him over the New Deal in the 1930s. The result was a sharp shift in American Liberalism, away from previous class-orientated attacks on big business and the idea that the economy was now 'mature' and incapable of further growth. Instead American Liberals restored to centre stage the concept of economic growth that American Conservatives had never abandoned, albeit an economic growth overseen and directed by a Federal government making use of the Keynsian deficit spending that had proven itself during the war. Given their experiences with Fascism, post-war Liberals also tended to be less trustful of the people and the state than they had been during the 1930s, and in effect more willing to accept conservative warnings about the dangers inherent in mass politics and government power.[25]

The explosion of the American economy also had world-wide economic consequences. During World War I the United States had shifted from a debtor to a creditor nation, with New York beginning to replace London as the financial capital of the world. During and after World War II that process was enormously accelerated. The International Monetary Fund and World Bank established at the 1944 Bretton Woods Conference were in effect the first steps in creating an American-focused, multilateral, free trade global economy, one that led not only to the post-war European Recovery Program, but also to the General Agreements on Tariff and Trade (GATT), and the contemporary World Trade Organization (WTO), the European Union, and the North American Free Trade Agreement (NAFTA).

The United States also now possessed the military power to match this economic power. In 1945 it had the largest and most powerful air force in the world, the largest and most powerful navy the world had ever seen, the second largest army in the world and a monopoly over the ultimate weapon, the atomic bomb. Much, but far from all, of this power was demobilized over the next few years, but by the end of the decade the United States had reinstituted the draft and was rebuilding its entire arsenal and rearming its allies.

Where a weakened Great Britain would fit into these American-centred economic and military systems, as well as the emerging Cold War geopolitical system, remained open questions at war's end. Clearly, the British desired continuation of the wartime relationship – out of desperate financial and strategic need, and out of a desire to 'steer' the 'unwieldy barge' of American foreign policy and thereby play the role of Greeks tutoring the new American Romans that Harold Macmillan had called for in 1943.[26] Under no circumstances would Washington accept such tutoring. Nevertheless, a 'special relationship' clearly did continue after the war. Whether it would have done so without the Cold War, however, is doubtful. As this volume has made clear, the wartime alliance was primarily the result of common fear of the Axis menace. Indeed, the alliance did not really begin to form until German victories and France's surrender in June of 1940 made clear how serious that menace was, and how much the two nations needed each other. In David Reynolds' words, 'The wartime alliance was neither natural nor inevitable, but the consequences of the unexpected global emergency of 1940–1.' And even after the fall of France, it would take 18 more months, Japanese attacks on both nation's Pacific possessions, and a German declaration of war on the United States, to make London and Washington formal allies. Furthermore, that Anglo-American alliance would be plagued by numerous conflicts over wartime strategy and post-war policies. Particularly noteworthy were the conflicts over military operations in the Mediterranean and the Balkans, decolonization, and post-war trade policies. The alliance was thus, in Reynolds' words, 'a marriage of necessity, uniting two major states whose recent history had been one of peaceful rivalry,' a rivalry reflecting different 'national interests and ideals' that continued throughout the war.[27]

From 1940 through early 1943 these differences were either swept under the rug or compromised, often to Britain's advantage. By late 1943, however, growing American power had shifted the balance. By 1944–45 that American power was so great, and British power so depleted, that the United States could and often did force its will upon its erstwhile ally. Indeed, so desperate was the British need for US post-war financial support as to leave London a supplicant.

US behaviour in 1944 and 1945 provides little evidence that the United States would have provided that financial support, or even desired post-war continuation of the alliance, if it had not been for the rise in Soviet-American tensions and the advent of the ensuing Cold War. Throughout 1945 there was a continued and notable cooling in Anglo-American relations, with a refusal by the United States not only to provide the financial support Britain needed, but also to continue military and strategic coordination via the CCS organization as London desired, or even to fulfil the terms of the Lend-Lease and atomic sharing agreements that Churchill and Roosevelt had initialled during the war. Indeed, with the Japanese surrender London quickly found the fiscal, military and nuclear collaboration doors slammed in its face while the Truman Administration refused to consider itself bound by previous Churchill–Roosevelt agreements and arrangements. Lend-Lease was abruptly terminated in August, for example, thereby cancelling the OCTAGON Phase II aid agreement, which the British desperately needed, while leaving an enormous quantity of goods recently delivered or in transit to be returned or paid for in cash that the bankrupt British treasury did not possess. Ensuing presidential and congressional actions also spelled the virtual end of any Anglo-American exchange of atomic information, the Churchill–Roosevelt agreements of 1943 and 1944 notwithstanding. Only as Soviet-American tensions grew did the Americans agree to post-war financial support of Britain – first through a multi-billion-dollar loan in late 1945/early 1946 whose tough terms, according to historian Randall Woods (agreement to make sterling freely convertible, finally ratify the Bretton Woods agreements and not discriminate against American goods), were counter-productive and actually contributed to 'a disintegration of Britain's international financial position';[28] and then through the European Recovery Program of 1947–48. Only at that point did the Americans cease their strategic opposition to involvement in the eastern Mediterranean and, via the 1947 Truman Doctrine and other measures, accept Churchill's wartime and post-war calls for a united Anglo-American front against the Soviets. In effect, the United States also replaced Britain in the eastern Mediterranean at this time, and in the rest of the world, as the guarantor of the balance of power. By 1949 Washington had joined the West European bloc that London had long desired in the form of the NATO. It had also replaced Britain as the chief military defender of such Commonwealth countries as Australia and New Zealand, and as the key financial investor in many parts of the world.

Admittedly, as US General Walter Bedell Smith noted soon after the war, common language had played a critical role in creating and maintaining an exceptionally successful alliance during World War II.[29] So had the similar (or, more accurately, the not-too-dissimilar) cultures and values of the two nations; the friendship that developed between Churchill and Roosevelt as well as their military and civilian subordinates; and the numerous agreements and combined boards that were established during the war. Equally important were the personal contacts and relations that developed between the officials, soldiers and common citizens of both nations, and the presence in positions of authority of individuals like Eisenhower, who recognized the importance of the Anglo-American special relationship and understood what it took to make that relationship work. (In Marshal Tedder's words, making a combined military command work 'comes back to having the right people and being ruthless'.[30]) But the necessary key to the creation and success of the wartime Anglo-American alliance, and indeed of most if not all alliances, had been the perceived need for each other in the face of a very threatening common enemy. That remained the key to the 'special relationship' in the Cold War era.

It also limited that relationship, for during both World War II and the Cold War years, national differences over policies and strategies led to serious disagreements that not only precluded closer collaboration, such as the common citizenship that Churchill desired, but that actually threatened to disrupt the existing coalition relationship. At each critical point in these conflicts, however, the commonalities and personalities managed to overcome or compromise the differences in a manner at least tolerable if not totally acceptable to both parties. The numerous and sharp World War II disagreements analysed throughout this volume threatened but never shattered the wartime alliance. Similarly, the numerous and sharp disagreements during the Cold War years, most notably but far from exclusively over the Middle East during the Palestine and Suez Crises of 1947–48 and 1956 and over Southeast Asia during the Vietnam War in the 1960s and 1970s, threatened but never shattered the anti-Soviet alliance. Indeed, the United States even chose Britain over a hemispheric ally (and thus over the Monroe Doctrine), in the 1982 Anglo-Argentina War over the Falkland/Malvinas Islands. Similarly, the British Government was and remains the strongest supporter of the United States in Iraq today, despite the opposition of other NATO allies and, indeed, its own people.

Whatever the relative importance today of those commonalities and personalities as opposed to the need for each other in the face of a common enemy, the 'special relationship' continues. As this volume has attempted to show, however, it was never as 'special' as Winston Churchill claimed or desired. But during the war it was indeed a 'special relationship' in many ways. Never before had two nations fused their military high commands and forces to such an extent and so successfully, or so collaborated in economic mobilization, the sharing of intelligence secrets, and the establishment of so many combined boards and committees to coordinate multiple aspects of their combined war effort. Nor had two heads of government ever before created such an extensive correspondence and strong personal friendship, a friendship duplicated by many of their subordinates and citizens. In those and numerous other ways the Anglo-American wartime relationship was 'special' compared to any other alliance in history.[31] And while that relationship has changed over the ensuing 60 years, it has remained 'special' to this very day.

NOTES

Preface

1 As quoted in Warren F. Kimball, 'Wheel Within a Wheel: Churchill, Roosevelt and the Special Relationship', in Robert Blake and William Roger Louis (eds) *Churchill* (New York, 1993), 294.

2 Winston S. Churchill, *The Second World War*, 6 vols: vol. 1: *The Gathering Storm* (1948); vol. 2: *Their Finest Hour* (1949); vol. 3: *The Grand Alliance* (1950); vol. 4: *The Hinge of Fate* (1950); vol. 5: *Closing the Ring* (1951); vol. 6: *Triumph and Tragedy* (1953) (Boston, 1948–1953; published 1954 in the UK).

3 Ibid.

4 See John Colville, *The Fringes of Power: Downing Street Diaries, 1939–1945* (New York, 1985), 658; and 'Roosevelt, Churchill, and the Wartime Anglo-American Alliance: Towards a New Synthesis', in William Roger Louis and Hedley Bull (eds) *The 'Special Relationship': Anglo-American Relations since 1945* (Oxford, 1986), 17–18. For an excellent, detailed analysis of the writing and publishing of Churchill's memoirs, see David Reynolds' new *In Command of History: Churchill* (London: Allen Lane, 2004), which was published in the UK as this volume went to press and is scheduled for publication in the USA in late 2005.

5 Arthur Bryant, *The Turn of the Tide* and *Triumph in the West: A History of the War Years Based on the Diaries of Field Marshal Lord Alanbrooke, Chief of the Imperial General Staff* (Garden City, NY, 1957, 1959). See also the more recent and complete *War Diaries 1939–1945: Field Marshal Lord Alanbrooke*, ed. Alex Danchev and Daniel Todman (Berkeley and Los Angeles, CA, 2001). See also Sir John Kennedy, *The Business of War* (New York, 1958), and Lionel Hastings Ismay, *The Memoirs of General Lord Ismay* (New York, 1960).

6 See below, Chapter 3, p. 50.

7 Christopher Thorne, *Allies of a Kind: The United States, Britain and the War against Japan, 1941–1945* (New York, 1978).

8 David Reynolds, *The Creation of the Anglo-American Alliance 1937–1941: A Study in Competitive Co-operation* (Chapel Hill, NC, 1982) and David Reynolds, 'Roosevelt, Churchill and the Wartime Anglo-American Alliance'; Warren F. Kimball, *The Juggler: Franklin Roosevelt as Wartime Statesman* (Princeton, NJ, 1991) and *Forged in War: Roosevelt, Churchill, and the Second World War* (New York, 1997); William Roger Louis, *Imperialism at Bay, 1941–1945: The United States and the Decolonization of the British Empire* (New York, 1978); Robert M. Hathaway, *Ambiguous Partnership: Britain and*

America, 1944–1947 (New York, 1981); Terry H. Anderson, *The United States, Great Britain, and the Cold War, 1944–1947* (Columbia, MO, 1981); Alan P. Dobson, *U.S. Wartime Aid to Britain, 1940–1946* (London, 1986); Fraser J. Harbutt, *The Iron Curtain: Churchill, America and the Origins of the Cold War* (New York, 1986); John J. Sbrega, *Anglo-American Relations and Colonialism in East Asia, 1941–1945* (New York, 1983); Randall Bennett Woods, *A Changing of the Guard: Anglo-American Relations, 1941–1946* (Chapel Hill, NC, 1990).

9 See, for example, my *Allies and Adversaries: The Joint Chiefs of Staff, the Grand Alliance, and U.S. Strategy in World War II* (Chapel Hill, NC, 2000).

10 Evan Mawdsley, *Thunder in the East: The Nazi-Soviet War, 1941–1945* (London, 2005).

11 See, for example, John Erickson, *Stalin's War with Germany*, 2 vols (London, 1975, 1983, 1999 reprint); and David M. Glantz and Jonathan M. House, *When Titans Clashed: How the Red Army Stopped Hitler* (Lawrence, KS, 1995).

12 Letter, Hew Strachan to author, 25 August 1994, in author's possession.

13 See Warren F. Kimball (ed.), *Churchill & Roosevelt: The Complete Correspondence*, 3 vols (Princeton, NJ, 1984), and Kimball works cited above in n. 8.

14 Waldo H. Heinrichs, *Threshold of War: Franklin D. Roosevelt and American Entry into World War II* (New York, 1988).

15 Rick Atkinson, *An Army at Dawn: The War in North Africa, 1942–1943* (New York, 2002), 656.

1 Axis threat and alliance forming

1 James D. Richardson (ed.), *A Compilation of the Messages and Papers of the Presidents, 1789–1897* (Washington, DC: U.S. Government Printing Office, 1907), vol. 1, 321–4.

2 See David Reynolds, *Rich Relations: The American Occupation of Britain, 1942-1945* (New York, 1995), 17–30.

3 John E. Moser, *Twisting the Lion's Tail: American Anglophobia between the World Wars* (New York, 1999); Steven T. Ross (ed.), *American War Plans, 1919–1941* (New York, 1992), vol. 2.

4 Reynolds, *Rich Relations*, 7.

5 Ibid., 6; Lloyd C. Gardner, *Safe for Democracy: The Anglo-American Response to Revolution, 1913–1923* (New York, 1984).

6 David Reynolds, *From Munich to Pearl Harbor: Roosevelt's America and the Origins of the Second World War* (Chicago, 2001), 38.

7 Ibid., 72–3.

8 See David MacIsaac, 'Voices from the Central Blue: The Air Power Theorists', in Peter Paret (ed.), *Makers of Modern Strategy: From Machiavelli to the Nuclear Age* (Princeton, NJ. 1986), 624–35.

9 See Brian Bond and Martin Alexander, 'Liddell Hart and de Gaulle: The Doctrines of Limited Liability and Mobile Defense', in *Makers of Modern Strategy*, 616–17.

10 See John Lukacs, *Five Days in London* (New Haven, CT, 1999), 4–5 and ff.

11 Winston S. Churchill, *The Second World War,* vol. 2: *Their Finest Hour* (Boston, 1949), 25–6.

12 Older works cite a superiority of approximately 4 to 1 in aircraft and 7 to 1 in trained pilots; newer works such as Stephen Bungay's *The Most Dangerous Enemy: A History of the Battle of Britain* (London, 2000), 107–8 and 379, see the actual ratio in relevant aircraft as closer to 1½ to 1 or 3 to 2 and note that British pilots were supported by hundreds of thousands of auxiliaries. Richard J. Overy, *The Battle of Britain: The Myth and the Reality* (New York, 2001), 34–41, cites virtual parity in fighters and fighter pilots in August and British superiority by September.

13 See below, Chapter 3, p. 50 and Chapter 6, pp. 101–2.
14 Churchill, *Their Finest Hour*, 340.
15 Ibid., 118.
16 Warren F. Kimball (ed.), *Churchill & Roosevelt: The Complete Correspondence*, vol. 1 (Princeton, NJ, 1984), 37.
17 Mark S. Watson, *Chief of Staff: Prewar Plans and Preparations*, a volume in *United States Army in World War II* (Washington, DC, 1950), 312; Reynolds, *From Munich to Pearl Harbor*, 81.
18 Kimball, *Churchill & Roosevelt*, vol. 1, 37.
19 Warren F. Kimball, *Forged in War: Roosevelt, Churchill, and the Second World War* (New York, 1997), 58.
20 See directly below.
21 See below, Chapter 2, pp. 20–1.

2 The alliance formed and the globalization of the war, 1940–1941

1 Winston S. Churchill, *The Second World War*, vol. 2: *Their Finest Hour* (Boston, 1949), 558–67; Warren F. Kimball (ed.) *Churchill & Roosevelt: The Complete Correspondence*, (Princeton, NJ, 1984), vol. 1, 87–109.
2 *Complete Presidential Press Conferences of Franklin D. Roosevelt*, vols 15–16, 1940 (New York, 1972); and State Department *Bulletin*, 4 (Washington, DC, 1941), 3–8.
3 *Public Papers and Addresses of Franklin D. Roosevelt*, 9, 1940 (New York, 1941), 663–78.
4 See Warren F. Kimball, *The Most Unsordid Act: Lend-Lease, 1939–1941* (Baltimore, MD, 1969).
5 Churchill, *The Second World War*, vol. 4: *The Hinge of Fate* (Boston: 1950), 569.
6 David Reynolds, *The Creation of the Anglo-American Alliance 1937–1941: A Study in Competitive Co-operation*, (Chapel Hill, NC, 1982), 166–7.
7 See below, pp. 27–8 and Chapter 3, pp. 38–41.
8 On US productive capacity, see Paul Kennedy, *The Rise and Fall of the Great Powers* (New York, 1987), 330–3, 353–61.
9 Steven T. Ross (ed.), *American War Plans, 1919–1941* (New York, 1992), vol. 3, 225–74.
10 Ibid., 305–22 (quote on p. 309).
11 David Reynolds, *From Munich to Pearl Harbor: Roosevelt's America and the Origins of the Second World War* (Chicago, 2001), 116–18; James Leutze, *Bargaining for Supremacy: Anglo-American Naval Collaboration, 1937–1941* (Chapel Hill, NC, 1977), 216–52.
12 Ross, *American War Plans*, vols 4, 1–109 and 5, 1–60; Maurice Matloff and Edwin Snell, *Strategic Planning for Coalition Warfare, 1941–1942*, in *United States Army in World War II* (Washington, DC, 1953), 32–48.
13 As quoted in Michael J. Lyons, *World War II: A Short History*, 4th edn (Upper Saddle River, NJ, 2004), 107.
14 John Colville, *The Fringes of Power: 10 Downing Street Diaries, 1939–1955* (New York, 1985), 404.
15 W. Averell Harriman and Elie Abel, *Special Envoy to Churchill and Stalin, 1941–1946* (New York, 1975), 75.
16 The Atlantic Charter is in State Department *Bulletin* 5 (Washington, DC, 1942), 125–6. For the conference itself, see Theodore A. Wilson, *The First Summit: Roosevelt and Churchill at Placentia Bay, 1941*, 2nd edn (Lawrence, KS, 1991). For the religious service, see ibid., 97–100.
17 Hadley Cantril and Research Associates in the Office of Public Opinion Research, *Gauging Public Opinion* (Princeton, NJ, 1944; Port Washington, NY, 1972), 222.

18   Warren F. Kimball, *The Juggler: Franklin Roosevelt as Wartime Statesman* (Princeton, NJ, 1991), 50–4.

19   See above, pp. 21–2.

20   See below, Chapter 3 for more detail on this disagreement.

21   See Ross, *American War Plans*, vol. 5, 145–298 (quote on p. 169); and Charles Edward Kirkpatrick, *An Unknown Future and a Doubtful Present: Writing the Victory Plan of 1941* (Washington, DC, 1990).

22   Henry L. Stimson Diary, Sept. 25, 1941, Yale University, New Haven, CT, quoted in Mark A. Stoler, *Allies and Adversaries: The Joint Chiefs of Staff, the Grand Alliance, and U.S. Strategy in World War II* (Chapel Hill, NC, 2000), 57.

23   Robert Murphy, *Diplomat Among Warriors* (Garden City, NY, 1964), 69.

24   Robert Dallek, *Franklin D. Roosevelt and American Foreign Policy, 1932–1945* (New York, 1979, 1995), 285.

25   Patrick Abbazia, *Mr. Roosevelt's Navy: The Private War of the U.S. Atlantic Fleet* (Annapolis, MD, 1975), 223–31; Waldo H. Heinrichs, *Threshold of War: Franklin D. Roosevelt and American Entry into World War II* (New York, 1988), 166–8.

26   There is scholarly disagreement as to whether Roosevelt truly desired such a total embargo, or whether it resulted from the way his subordinates implemented his order. See Jonathan Utley, *Going to War with Japan, 1937–1941* (Knoxville, TN, 1985) and Irvine H. Anderson, *The Standard-Vacuum Oil Company and United States East Asian Policy, 1933–1941* (Princeton, NJ, 1975) for the former argument vs Heinrichs, *Threshold of War*, for the latter.

27   *Hearings Before the Joint Committee on the Investigation of the Pearl Harbor Attack*, 79th Congress, 1st Session (Washington, DC, 1946), Part 12: 165; (as quoted in Dallek, *Franklin D. Roosevelt*, 307).

28   See Evan Mawdsley, *Thunder in the East: The Nazi-Soviet War, 1941–1945*, (London, 2005).

29   Elliot Roosevelt (ed.), *F.D.R: His Personal Letters* (New York, 1950, 1970), vol. 4, 1177.

30   Quotes from US Joint Board, 'General Strategy Review by the British Chiefs of Staff', 30 Sept., 1941, in Ross, *American War Plans*, vol. 3, 343. See also similar comments in Victory Program in ibid., 5: 173; and Stoler, *Allies and Adversaries*, 51–4.

31   Heinrichs, *Threshold of War*, 159, 179.

32   Ibid., 189–95, 213–14.

33   Stimson Diary, Nov. 26–27, 1941.

34   Winston S. Churchill, *The Second World War,* vol. 3: *The Grand Alliance* (Boston, 1950), 605.

35   Ibid., 606–8.

36   See, for example, Charles Tansill, *Back Door to War: The Roosevelt Foreign Policy, 1933–1941* (Chicago, 1952).

37   See Roberta Wohlstetter, *Pearl Harbor: Warning and Decision* (Stanford, CA, 1962).

38   For an excellent analysis of the numerous Japanese errors in attacking Pearl Harbor, see Gerhard Weinberg, *A World at Arms: A Global History of World War II*, 2nd edn (Cambridge, 2005), 258–63.

3 The Anglo-American muster against the Axis

1   See Chapter 2, pp. 21–2.

2   U.S. Department of State, *Foreign Relations of the United States: The Conferences at Washington, 1941–1942, and Casablanca, 1943* (Washington, DC, 1968), 375; Winston S. Churchill, *The Second World War*, vol. 3: *The Grand Alliance* (Boston, 1950).

Notes

3   See below, Chapter 4, and Evan Mawdsley, *Thunder in the East: The Nazi-Soviet War, 1941–1945*, (London, 2005) for details on these campaigns.

4   Warren F. Kimball (ed.), *Churchill & Roosevelt: The Complete Correspondence*, vol. 1 (Princeton, NJ, 1984), 294–309.

5   Alex Danchev and Daniel Todman (eds), *War Diaries, 1939–1945: Field Marshal Lord Alanbrooke* (Berkeley, CA, 2001), 209; Arthur Bryant, *The Turn of the Tide: A History of the War Years Based on the Diaries of Field-Marshal Lord Alanbrooke, Chief of the Imperial General Staff* (Garden City, NY, 1957), 225–6.

6   Anthony Eden, *The Memoirs of Anthony Eden, Earl of Avon: The Reckoning* (Boston, 1965), 334–8. See also Oleg A. Rzheshevsky, *War and Diplomacy: The Making of the Grand Alliance; Documents from Stalin's Archives* (Amsterdam, 1996), 1–62.

7   Churchill, *The Grand Alliance*, 630.

8   See Michael Howard, *The Causes of Wars* (London, 1983), 180, who labels the peripheral approach 'a strategy of necessity rather than choice, of survival rather than of victory'. See also his *The Mediterranean Strategy in the Second World War* (New York, 1968), especially pp. 1–18.

9   See David Reynolds, 'Churchill and the British "Decision" to Fight On in 1940: Right Policy, Wrong Reasons', in Richard Langhorne (ed), *Diplomacy and Intelligence During the Second World War* (Cambridge, 1985), 147–67.

10   See Russell F. Weigley, *The American Way of War: A History of United States Military Strategy and Policy* (New York, 1963).

11   Carl Van Doren, *Benjamin Franklin* (Garden City, NY, 1941), 551–2; Danchev and Todman, *Alanbrooke War Diaries*, 680.

12   Churchill, *The Grand Alliance*, 664–5, emphasis in original.

13   *Foreign Relations: Washington and Casablanca*, 92–3.

14   Ibid., 92–3; Forrest C. Pogue, *George C. Marshall*, vol. 2: *Ordeal and Hope, 1939–1942* (New York, 1966), 280; Larry I. Bland (ed), *George C. Marshall: Interviews and Reminiscences for Forrest C. Pogue* (Lexington, VA, 1991), 358.

15   See Chapter 4 for details.

16   *Foreign Relations: Washington and Casablanca*, 93.

17   Theodore A. Wilson *et al.*, 'Coalition: Structure, Strategy, and Statecraft', in David Reynolds, Warren F. Kimball and A.O. Chubarian (eds), *Allies at War: The Soviet, American, and British Experience, 1939–1945* (New York, 1994), 86–8.

18   Richard Overy *et al.*, 'Co-operation: Trade, Aid, and Technology', in ibid., 202–32. See also William H. McNeill, *America, Britain and Russia: Their Cooperation and Conflict, 1941–1946* (New York, 1953, 1970), 129–37.

19   Richard Overy, *Why the Allies Won* (New York, 1995), 192; Allan R. Millett and Peter Maslowski, *For the Common Defense: A Military History of the United States of America* rev. expanded edn (New York, 1994), 408–12; Allan R. Millett, 'The United States Armed Forces in the Second World War', in Allan R. Millett and Williamson Murray (eds) *Military Effectiveness*, (Boston, 1988), 3: 47–52. See also John Ellis, *World War II: A Statistical Survey* (New York, 1993), 273–81.

20   Richard M. Leighton, 'The American Arsenal Policy in World War II: A Retrospective View', in Daniel Beaver (ed.), *Some Pathways in Twentieth-Century History: Essays in Honor of Reginald Charles McGrane* (Detroit, 1969), 251–2.

21   David Reynolds, *From Munich to Pearl Harbor: Roosevelt's America and the Origins of the Second World War* (Chicago, 2001), 114; Overy *et al.*, 'Co-operation: Trade, Aid and Technology', 209–11.

22   Gerhard Weinberg, *A World at Arms: A Global History of World War II, 2nd edn* (Cambridge, 2005), 471–2 ff. and 645; Williamson Murray and Allan R. Millett, *A War to Be Won: Fighting the Second World War* (Cambridge, MA, 2000), 535; Overy,

Notes

Why the Allies Won, 180–207; and R. Overy 'Mobilization for Total War in Germany, 1939–41', *English Historical Review,* 103 (1988), reproduced in Gordon Martel (ed.), *The World War II Reader* (New York, 2004), 40–64. In a revision of the standard approach, Overy concludes that Germany was indeed preparing for total war in the 1930s but that its preparations were far from complete when the war began in 1939.

23 Wilson, 'Coalition', 85, 89–90.

24 Richard Rhodes, *The Making of the Atomic Bomb* (New York, 1986), 368–79.

25 Kimball, *Churchill & Roosevelt,* vol. 1, 249.

26 *Foreign Relations: Washington and Casablanca,* 63, 432; Winston Churchill, *The Second World War,* vol. 4: *The Hinge of Fate* (Boston, 1950), 379–81. For the 1943 and 1944 agreements, see below, Chapters 7, p. 126; 8, p. 170; and 9, p. 184. See also Robin Edmonds, *The Big Three: Churchill, Roosevelt and Stalin in Peace and War* (New York, 1991), 395–402. Churchill may have confused his 1941–42 visits to the United States with his 1943–44 visits.

27 See F.H. Hinsley, *British Intelligence in the Second World War: Its Influence on Strategy and Operations* (New York, 1979, 1981), vols 1, 311–14, and 2, 55.

28 Carl Boyd, *Hitler's Japanese Confidant: General Oshima Hiroshi and MAGIC Intelligence, 1941–1945* (Lawrence, KS, 1993), 1 and ff. For Midway, see below, Chapter 4, pp. 64–6.

29 Bradley F. Smith, *The Ultra-Magic Deals: And the Most Secret Special Relationship* (Novato, CA, 1993), 157; Hinsley, *British Intelligence in the Second World War,* vol. 2, 41–58.

30 Eric Larrabee, *Commander in Chief: Franklin Delano Roosevelt, His Lieutenants, and Their War* (New York, 1987), 155.

31 The title is taken from Warren Kimball's article, published in *Prologue* 6 (Fall, 1974): 169–82.

32 See Doris Kearns Goodwin, *No Ordinary Time: Franklin and Eleanor Roosevelt: The Home Front in World War II* (New York, 1994).

33 For different versions of this famous story, see Robert Sherwood, *Roosevelt and Hopkins: An Intimate History,* rev. edn (New York, 1950), 442–3; Martin Gilbert, *Winston S. Churchill, 7: Road to Victory, 1941–1945* (Boston, 1986), 28, and Warren F. Kimball, *Forged in War: Roosevelt, Churchill and the Second World War* (New York, 1997), 132 and 359, n. 31.

34 Kimball, *Churchill & Roosevelt,* 1: 337.

35 Kimball, *Forged in War,* 22–3; *The Juggler* (Princeton, NJ, 1991), 225–6; and 'Like Goldfish in a Bowl: Churchill and Alcohol', lecture before Churchill Society for the Advancement of Parliamentary Democracy, 8 November 2004.

36 Henry L. Stimson Diary, June 22, 1942, Yale University, New Haven, CT; Danchev and Todman (eds), *War Diaries,* 590; Harry C. Butcher, *My Three Years with Eisenhower* (New York, 1946), 8.

37 For a recent and ringing defence of Churchill's behaviour in this regard, both practically and as a model of appropriate civil-military relations, see Eliot Cohen, *Supreme Command: Soldiers, Statesmen, and Leadership in Wartime* (New York, 2002), 95–132.

38 Reynolds, *From Munich to Pearl Harbor,* 170.

39 Churchill, *The Grand Alliance,* 695–6.

40 Reynolds, *From Munich to Pearl Harbor,* 119.

41 Robert M. Hathaway, *Ambiguous Partnership: Britain and America, 1944–1947* (New York, 1981), 16–21.

42 Kimball, *Churchill & Roosevelt,* vol. 1: 357–8; *The Juggler,* 48–60. esp. 58–9. See also Elliot Roosevelt, *As He Saw It* (New York, 1946), 35–6; Lloyd C. Gardner, *Architects of Illusion: Men and Ideas in American Foreign Policy, 1941–1949* (Chicago, 1970), 113–19;

Peter Calvocoressi, Guy Wint and John Pritchard, *Total War: The Causes and Courses of the Second World War*, rev. second edn (New York, 1989), vol. 1, 447–8; and below, Chapter 9.

43 Steven Merritt Miner, *Between Churchill and Stalin: The Soviet Union, Great Britain, and the Origins of the Grand Alliance* (Chapel Hill, NC, 1988), 199; Hathaway, *Ambiguous Partnership*, 45; Terry H. Anderson, *The United States, Great Britain and the Cold War 1944–1947* (Columbia, MO, 1981), 4.

44 Churchill, *The Grand Alliance.*, 671–2; Gilbert, *Churchill*, 7: 27, 29.

4 Military disasters and disputes over grand strategy, December 1941–July/August 1942

1 John W. Dower, *War Without Mercy: Race and Power in the Pacific War* (New York, 1986).

2 Barbara Tuchman, *Stilwell and the American Experience in China, 1911–45* (New York, 1970), 300.

3 See Evan Mawdsley, *Thunder in the East: The Nazi-Soviet War, 1941–1945* (London, 2005).

4 Richard Overy, *Why the Allies Won* (New York. 1990), 28–9.

5 Quotes from memos, King to Knox, 8 Feb. 1942, and King to Roosevelt, 5 Mar. 1942, King Papers, Navy Historical Center, Washington, DC, latter reproduced in Thomas Buell, *Master of Seapower: A Biography of Fleet Admiral Ernest J. King* (New York, 1980), 531–3. See also memos, King to Marshall, 18 Feb. and 29 Mar. 1942 in ibid.; memo by A.S. McDill, 'Initiation of Operations Leading to Guadalcanal', 19 Sept. 1945, SPD, serial 3, box 48, Guadalcanal, ibid.; Maurice Matloff and Edwin Snell, *Strategic Planning for Coalition Warfare, 1941–1942* (Washington DC, 1953), 154–6, 211; and George C. Dyer, *The Amphibians Came to Conquer: The Story of Admiral Richmond Kelly Turner* (Washington, DC, 1969), 230–45.

6 Alfred D. Chandler, Jr. (ed.), *The Papers of Dwight David Eisenhower: The War Years* (Baltimore, MD, 1970), vol. 1, 66, 112.

7 The US Army General Staff underwent a major reorganization in March, with the new Operations Division replacing the old War Plans Division and serving as the army's key planning organization for the duration of the war.

8 Hastings, Lionel Ismay, *The Memoirs of General Lord Ismay* (New York, 1960), 226.

9 Chandler, *Eisenhower Papers*, vol. 1, 118.

10 A. Danchev and D. Todman (eds), *War Diaries, 1939–1945: Field Marshal Lord Alanbrooke* (Berkeley, CA, 2001), 246–50.

11 Ibid., 246.

12 See above, Chapter 3, pp. 39–40, 53–4.

13 Robert Sherwood, *Roosevelt and Hopkins* (New York, 1950) 561–3, 577; *Foreign Relations, 1942* (Washington, DC), vol. 3, 575–7, 587, 593–4. For the Soviet documents, see Oleg A. Rzheshevsky, *War and Diplomacy: The Making of the Grand Alliance; Documents from Stalin's Archives* (Amsterdam, 1996), 170–261.

14 Warren F. Kimball (ed.), *Churchill & Roosevelt: The Complete Correspondence* (Princeton, NJ, 1984), vol. 1, 494.

15 Winston S. Churchill, *The Second World War,* vol. 4: *The Hinge of Fate* (Boston, 1950), 383.

16 *Foreign Relations of the United States: The Conferences at Washington, 1941–1942, and Casablanca, 1943* (Washington, DC, 1968), 465–7.

17 Ibid., 434–5, 468–9, 478–9; J.R.M. Butler and J.M.A. Gwyer, *History of the Second World War: Grand Strategy,* vol. 3: *June, 1941–August, 1942* (London, 1964), 627.

18 Kimball, *Churchill & Roosevelt,* vol. 1, 520–1.

19 John Colville, *The Fringes of Power: 10 Downing Street Diaries, 1939–1945* (New York, 1985), 624.

20 Memo, Marshall and King to President, 'Latest British Proposals Relative to BOLERO and GYMNAST', 10 July 1942, OPD 381 Gen. (sec. 2), 73, Record Group 165, National Archives, Washington, DC.

21 Mark Stoler, *Allies and Adversaries: The Joint Chiefs of Staff, the Grand Alliance, and U.S. Strategy in World War II* (Chapel Hill, NC, 2000), 79–83, and 'The Pacific-First Alternative in American World War II Strategy', *International History Review* 2 (July 1980): 432–52.

22 Roosevelt handwritten messages, Roosevelt Papers, Map Room File, Box 7-A, Folder 2, Roosevelt Library, Hyde Park, NY; tel., Roosevelt to Marshall, 14 July 1942, WDCSA BOLERO, Super Secret, Round Group 165, National Archives; Stimson Diary, 15 July 1942; memo, Marshall to King, 15 July 1942, in Larry I. Bland (ed.), *The Papers of George Catlett Marshall, 3* (Baltimore, MD, 1991), 276.

23 Larry I. Bland (ed.) *George C. Marshall: Interviews and Reminiscences for Forrest C. Pogue* (Lexington, VA, 1991), 622.

24 Sherwood, *Roosevelt and Hopkins*, 602–5.

25 Churchill, *The Hinge of Fate*, 481; *Foreign Relations, 1942,* vol. 3, 619.

26 Bland, *Marshall Papers*, vol. 3, 278–80: Thorne, *Allies of a Kind: The United States, Britain, and the War against Japan* (New York, 1978), 136; Thorne, minutes, CCS 32nd meeting, 24 July 1942, CCS 334 (26 May 1942) Record Group 218, National Archives; Butler and Gwyer, *Grand Strategy*, 3, part 2, 635–6, 684–5; Forrest C. Pogue, *George C. Marshall,* vol. 2: *Ordeal and Hope, 1939–1942* (New York, 1966), 346–8.

27 Kimball, *Churchill & Roosevelt*, vol. 1, 591–2.

5 Turning the tide, July/August 1942–January 1943

1 Williamson Murray and Allan R. Millett, *A War to Be Won: Fighting the Second World War* (Cambridge, MA, 2000), 270.

2 Ibid., 271.

3 See above, Chapter 4, p. 67.

4 See above, Chapter 4, pp. 3, 50, and below, Chapter 6, pp. 101–2.

5 Murray and Millett, *A War to Be Won*, 300.

6 Charles L. Bolte Interview, 9 December 1971, p. 77, US Army Military History Research Collection, Senior Officers Debriefing Program, US Army Military History Institute, Carlisle, PA; also cited in David Reynolds, *Rich Relations: The American Occupation of Britain, 1942–1945* (New York, 1995), 93–4.

7 Hastings Lionel Ismay, *The Memoirs of General Lord Ismay* (New York, 1960), 262–3; Stephen E. Ambrose, *Eisenhower: Soldier, General of the Army, President-Elect, 1890–1952* (New York, 1983), 186.

8 See Arthur L. Funk, *The Politics of TORCH: The Allied Landings and the Algiers Putsch, 1942* (Lawrence, KS, 1974).

9 Alfred D. Chandler (ed.), *The Papers of Dwight David Eisenhower* (Baltimore, MD, 1970), vol. 2, 811.

10 See Rick Atkinson, *An Army at Dawn: The War in North Africa, 1942–1943* (New York, 2002), 163–262.

11 See above, Chapter 3, p. 45.

12 Ronald Spector, *Eagle Against the Sun: The American War with Japan* (New York, 1985), 216.

13 See Evan Mawdsley, *Thunder in the East: The Nazi-Soviet War, 1941–1945* (London, 2005).

14 Richard M. Leighton and Robert W. Coakley, *Global Logistics and Strategy*, 1 (Washington, 1955), 662 in United States Army in World War II. See also Maurice Matloff and Edwin Snell, *Strategic Planning for Coalition Warfare, 1941–1942* (Washington, DC, 1953), 389–95 in same series.

15 Winston S. Churchill, *The Second World War*, vol. 4: *The Hinge of Fate* (Boston, 1950), 651.

16 Reynolds, *Rich Relations*, 101.

17 Richard Overy, *Why the Allies Won* (New York, 1990), 48.

18 US State Department, *Foreign Relations of the United States: The Conferences at Washington, 1941–1942, and Casablanca, 1943* (Washington, DC, 1968), 774.

19 Ibid., 509.

20 Ibid., 511.

21 Minutes, JCS 52nd meeting, 16 Jan. 1943, CCS 334 (1–14–43), Record Group 218, National Archives; *Foreign Relations: Washington and Casablanca*, 601–4, 614–22, 774–5.

22 Notes dictated by Hopkins. 23 Jan. 1943, Harry L. Hopkins Papers, Sherwood Collection, Box 137, Casablanca Folder, Franklin D. Roosevelt Library, Hyde Park, NY.

23 Ministry of Foreign Affairs of the USSR, *Correspondence Between the Chairman of the Council of Ministers of the U.S.S.R. and the Presidents of the U.S.A. and the Prime Ministers of Great Britain During the Great Patriotic War of 1941–1945* (hereafter cited as *Stalin's Correspondence*) (Moscow, 1957), vol. 2, 50.

24 *Foreign Relations: Washington and Casablanca*, 631, 805–7.

25 Ibid., 727.

26 For a classic early statement of this view, see Hanson W. Baldwin, *Great Mistakes of the War* (New York, 1949), 14–24.

27 *Foreign Relations: Washington and Casablanca*, 727.

28 See below, Chapter 10.

29 Elliot Roosevelt, *As He Saw It* (New York, 1946), 117.

30 See Raymond G. O'Connor, *Diplomacy for Victory: FDR and Unconditional Surrender* (New York, 1971).

31 Letter, Wedemeyer to Handy, 22 Jan. 1943, OPD Exec. 3, Item 1a, Paper 5, Record Group 165, National Archives.

32 Chandler, *Eisenhower Papers*, vol. 2, 927–9.

6 Aspects and impacts of total war: the irregular, intelligence, naval and air wars

1 See above, Chapter 3.

2 See below, Chapter 9, pp. 185, 188.

3 See Evan Mawdsley, *Thunder in the East: The Nazi-Soviet War, 1941–1945* (London, 2005).

4 See above, Chapter 5, pp. 77–8, 89.

5 See, for example, Milton Viorst, *Hostile Allies: FDR and Charles de Gaulle* (New York, 1965); and Dorothy S. White, *Seeds of Discord: De Gaulle, Free France, and the Allies* (Syracuse, NY, 1964), as well as Julian G. Hurstfield's *America and the French Nation* (Chapel Hill, NC, 1986).

6 See below, Chapter 7, pp. 121–3, 127–9.

7 See Peter Hoffman, *The History of the German Resistance, 1933–1945* (Cambridge, 1977).

8 JCS 506, 'Instructions concerning Duty as a Military Observer at American-British-Soviet Conference', CCS 337 (9–12–43), Section 1, Record Group 218, National Archives.

9   See Archimedes L.A. Patti, *Why Vietnam? Prelude to America's Albatross* (Berkeley, CA, 1980); and David G. Marr, *Vietnam, 1945: The Quest for Power* (Berkeley, CA, 1995).

10 See also below, Chapter 9, pp. 181–3.

11 Michael Schaller, *The U.S. Crusade in China, 1938–1945* (New York, 1979), 231–50; Ronald H. Spector, *Eagle Against the Sun: The American War with Japan* (New York, 1985), 461–3.

12 Gordon Wright, *The Ordeal of Total War, 1939–1945* (New York, 1968), 79–106. See also R.V. Jones, *The Wizard War: British Scientific Intelligence, 1939–1945* (New York, 1978).

13 See above, Chapter 3, p. 50.

14 For a brief and clear description of how the machine worked by a Bletchley Park cryptologist and historian, see Peter Calvocoressi, *Top Secret Ultra* (New York, 1980), 23–9.

15 The claim was first made in F.W. Winterbotham's *The Ultra Secret* (New York, 1974), the first volume to reveal the secret.

16 See below, Chapter 9, pp. 171–7; and Williamson Murray, 'Ultra: Some Thoughts on Its Impact on the Second World War', *Air University Review* 35 (July–Aug. 1984): 52–64.

17 See above, Chapter 3, p. 50; Chapter 4, pp. 63–6; and Chapter 5, pp. 72–5.

18 Winston S. Churchill, *The Second World War*, vol. 3: *The Grand Alliance* (Boston, 1950), 111–55.

19 Richard Overy, *Why the Allies Won* (New York, 1996), 28–9.

20 Churchill, *The Grand Alliance*, 111–12.

21 US State Department, *Foreign Relations of the United States: The Conferences at Washington, 1941–1942, and Casablanca, 1943* (Washington, DC, 1968), 774.

22 Winston S. Churchill, *The Second World War*, vol. 2: *Their Finest Hour* (Boston, 1949), 598.

23 Alfred Thayer Mahan, *The Influence of Seapower Upon History, 1660–1783* (Boston, 1890).

24 Henry L. Stimson and McGeorge Bundy, *On Active Service in Peace and War* (New York, 1948), 506.

25 Overy, *Why the Allies Won*, 31.

26 Different sources give the exact number of sinkings as 23 out of 36 and 26 out of 39.

27 Overy, *Why the Allies Won*, 193–4.

28 John Ellis, *World War II: A Statistical Survey: The Essential Facts and Figures for All the Combatants* (New York, 1993), 267.

29 James L. Stokesbury, *A Short History of World War II* (New York, 1980), 129.

30 Different sources list the May U-boat losses as 37, 41, and 47. I have used the middle figure in the text.

31 Overy, *Why the Allies Won*, 53–62; Michael J. Lyons, *World War II: A Short History*, 4th edn (Upper Saddle River, NJ, 2004), 225; John Buckley, *Airpower in the Age of Total War* (London, 1999), 136.

32 Ibid., 136; and Buckley, 'Atlantic Airpower Cooperation, 1941–1945', in John Gooch (ed.), *Airpower: Theory and Practice* (London, 1995), 175–97.

33 See below, Chapter 1, p. 7.

34 Tami Davis Biddle, 'Bombing by the Square Yard: Sir Arthur Harris at War, 1942–1945', *The International History Review* 21 (Sept. 1999): 634.

35 Ibid., 629.

36 *Foreign Relations: Washington and Casablanca*, 774, 781–2.

37 US Department of State, *Foreign Relations, 1942*, vol. 3 (Washington, DC), 619.

38 Tami Davis Biddle, *Rhetoric and Reality in Air Warfare: The Evolution of British and American Ideas About Strategic Bombing, 1914–1945* (Princeton, NJ, 2002), 215.

39 *Foreign Relations: Washington and Casablanca*, 781–2.

40 Sir Charles Webster and Noble Frankland, *The Strategic Air Offensive Against Germany* (London, 1961), vol. 2, 5.

41 USTAAF included the 8th Air Force in England under Major General James Doolittle and the 15th Air Force in Italy under Major General Nathan Twining. Eaker at the end of 1943 became Commander-in-Chief of Allied Air Forces in the Mediterranean. He and Spaatz were both promoted to Lieutenant General in 1943.

42 See below, Chapter 8, pp. 154–5.

43 Willliamson Murray, 'Strategic Bombing', lecture to US Military Academy ROTC Fellowship, 22 June 1992, West Point, New York. See also Williamson Murray, *Strategy for Defeat: The Luftwaffe, 1933–1945* (Washington, DC, 1983, 1996), 303.

44 Reproduced in Conrad C. Crane, *Bombs, Cities and Civilians: American Airpower Strategy in World War II* (Lawrence, KS, 1993), 163–4.

45 Lyons, *World War II*, 235; Overy, *Why the Allies Won*, 128; Murray, *Strategy for Defeat*, 303. For the bombing of Japan, see below, Chapter 10, p. 205.

7 Seizing the initiative and redefining the coalition, January–November 1943

1 See Evan Mawdsley, *Thunder in the East: The Nazi-Soviet War, 1941–1945* (London, 2005).

2 See above, Chapter 5, pp. 72–9.

3 US Department of State, *Foreign Relations: The Conferences at Washington and Quebec, 1943* (Washington, DC 1970), 25–7.

4 Ibid., 43–4.

5 Hastings Lionel Ismay, *The Memoirs of General Lord Ismay* (New York, 1960), 296.

6 *Foreign Relations: Washington and Quebec*, 346–51.

7 Ibid., 193–5; Winston S. Churchill, *The Second World War*, vol. 4. *The Hinge of Fate* (Boston, 1950), 810. Quotes from Charles Wilson (Lord Moran), *Churchill: Taken from the Diaries of Lord Moran; The Struggle for Survival, 1940–1965* (Boston, 1966), 104; and Stimson Diary, 17 and 25 May 1943.

8 Minutes of meetings at Eisenhower's villa, May 29, 31 and June 3, 1943, CCS 381 (4–23–43), Sec. 1, Record Group 218, National Archives; Churchill, *The Hinge of Fate*, 816–30; Moran, *Churchill*, 109–12; Maurice Matloff and Edwin Snell, *Strategic Planning for Coalition Warfare, 1943–1944* (Washington, DC, 1959), 153–5, in United States Army in World War II.

9 Ewen Montagu, *The Man Who Never Was* (Philadelphia, PA, 1954).

10 *Foreign Relations: Washington and Quebec*, 488–96.

11 See above, Chapter 6, p. 101.

12 Quote from Henry H. Arnold, *Global Mission* (New York, 1949), 444. See also Ernest J. King and Walter M. Whitehill, *Fleet Admiral King: A Naval Record* (New York, 1952), 486–7; and Winston Churchill, *The Second World War*, vol. 5: *Closing the Ring* (Boston, 1951), 90–1.

13 Alex Danchev and Daniel Todman (eds), *War Diaries, 1939–1945: Field Marshal Lord Alanbrooke* (Berkeley, CA, 2001), 441; Churchill, *Closing the Ring*, 85.

14 Danchev and Todman, *War Diaries*, 187.

15 See Brian Loring Villa, 'The Atomic Bomb and the Normandy Invasion', *Perspectives in American History* 11 (1977–78): 461–502.

16 Churchill, *The Hinge of Fate*, 478; US Dept. of State, *Foreign Relations, 1942*, (Washington, DC), vol. 3, 619.

17 *Stalin's Correspondence* (Moscow, 1957) vol. 2, 73–6 see p. 000, n. 23.

18 Mark A. Stoler, *The Politics of the Second Front: American Military Planning and Diplomacy in Coalition Warfare, 1941–1943* (Westport, CT, 1977), 104–6, 116–18.

19 Ibid., 118–23.

20 *Foreign Relations: Washington and Quebec*, 940, 942, 1010–18; Stoler, *Politics of the Second Front*, 123.

21 *Foreign Relations: Washington and Quebec*, 638, 894, 1117–18; Martin J. Sherwin, *A World Destroyed: The Atomic Bomb and the Grand Alliance* (Stanford, CA, 2000), 71–89; Robin Edmonds, *The Big Three: Churchill, Roosevelt and Stalin in Peace and War* (New York, 1991), 399–402, 487–9.

22 Harold Macmillan, *The Blast of War* (New York, 1967), 308; and *War Diaries: Politics and War in the Mediterranean, January 1943–May 1945* (New York, 1984), 167. I am deeply indebted to Warren Kimball for bringing this priceless quote to my attention.

23 Danchev and Todman, *Alanbrooke War Diaries*, 459.

24 *Foreign Relations, 1943*, vol. 1, 534–6, 583–4, 771–81. See also Keith Sainsbury, *The Turning Point: Roosevelt, Stalin, Churchill, and Chiang Kai-Shek, 1943; The Moscow, Cairo and Teheran Conferences* (New York, 1986), 53–109.

25 W. Averell Harriman and E. Abel, *Special Envoy to Churchill and Stalin, 1941–1946* (New York, 1975), 244.

26 See below, p. 134 and note 27 directly below.

27 Letter, MacArthur to Gen. A.C. Smith, Chief of Military History, 'General MacArthur's Answer to Questionnaire Submitted by Dr. Louis Morton', 5 Mar. 1953, OCMH Collection, Personal Papers, Douglas MacArthur 1953 Response folder, Military History Institute.

28 See Chapter 4, p. 65.

29 Herbert Feis, *The China Tangle: The American Effort in China from Pearl Harbor to the Marshall Mission* (Princeton, NJ, 1953).

30 Jack Belden, *Retreat with Stilwell* (Garden City, NY, 1943), 32.

31 Barbara Tuchman, *Stilwell and the American Experience in China, 1911–1945* (New York, 1970), 383, 321; 190–91; quotes on British from unpublished Stilwell Diary at Hoover Institute, Stanford, CA, as quoted in Alex Danchev, *Very Special Relationship: Field-Marshal Sir John Dill and the Anglo-American Alliance, 1941–1944* (London, 1986), 73.

32 Larry I. Bland (ed.), *George C. Marshall: Interviews and Reminiscences for Forrest C. Pogue* (Lexington, VA, 1991), 622; Forrest C. Pogue, *George C. Marshall* (New York, 1963–1987), vol. 3, 306–7.

33 Theodore H. White (ed.), *The Stilwell Papers* (New York, 1948), 245.

34 Warren F. Kimball (ed.), *Churchill & Roosevelt: The Complete Correspondence* (Princeton, NJ, 1984), vol. 1, 421.

35 US Dept. of State, *Foreign Relations of the United States: The Conferences at Cairo and Tehran, 1943* (Washington, DC, 1961), 3–12; Warren Kimball, *Forged in War: Roosevelt, Churchill adn the Second World War* (New York, 1997), 215–16; Robert Dallek, *Franklin D. Roosevelt and American Foreign Policy, 1932–1945* (New York, 1979), 401–2.

36 *Foreign Relations: Cairo and Tehran*, 533–52 (Stalin quote on p. 539), 553–5.

37 Ibid., 553–5; Churchill, *Closing the Ring*, 373–4.

38 *Foreign Relations: Cairo and Tehran*, 582.

39 See below, Chapter 10, pp. 190–7.

40 David Dilks (ed.), *The Diaries of Sir Alexander Cadogan, 1938–1945* (New York, 1972), 582.

41 Frances Perkins, *The Roosevelt I Knew* (New York, 1946), 84.

8 Military successes and early post-war planning, December 1943–September 1944

1 US Dept. of State, *Foreign Relations of the United States: The Conferences at Cairo and Tehran, 1943* (Washington, DC, 1961), 796.

2 Ibid., 541.

3 John Ehrman, *Grand Strategy, 6: October 1944–August 1945* (London, 1956), 342.

4 Ibid., 342–3; Forrest C. Pogue, *George C. Marshall* (New York, 1963–1987), vol. 3, 585; Charles Wilson, *Churchill: Taken from the Diaries of Lord Moran: The Struggle for Survival, 1940–1965* (Boston, 1966), 292.

5 Robert Sherwood, *Roosevelt and Hopkins: An Intimate History* (New York, 1950), 803.

6 Winston S. Churchill, *The Second World War, Closing the Ring* (Boston, 1951), 513–14. For Marshall quote, see *Foreign Relations: Cairo and Tehran*, 528.

7 *Foreign Relations: Cairo and Tehran*, 796.

8 Ronald Spector, *Eagle Against the Sun: The American War with Japan* (New York, 1985), 354.

9 William D. Leahy, *I Was There: The Personal Story of the Chief of Staff to Presidents Roosevelt and Truman Based on his Notes and Diaries Made at the Time* (New York, 1950), 213–14.

10 Churchill, *Closing the Ring*, 488.

11 Stimson Diary, 21 June 1944; Mark A. Stoler, *Allies and Adversaries: The Joint Chiefs of Staff, the Grand Alliance, and U.S. Strategy in World War II* (Chapel Hill, NC, 2000), 171–4.

12 Alex Danchev and Daniel Todman (eds), *War Diaries, 1939–1945: Field Marshal Lord Alanbrooke* (Berkeley, CA, 2001), 541.

13 Pogue, *Marshall*, vol. 3, 413.

14 J.F.C. Fuller, *The Second World War, 1939–1945: A Strategical and Tactical History* (London, 1948), 268.

15 See below, pp. 157–60 and Chapter 9, pp. 171–2.

16 Larry Bland (ed.), *George C. Marshall* (Lexington, VA, 1991), 612.

17 *Foreign Relations: Cairo and Tehran*, 489, 526–8.

18 David Reynolds, *Rich Relations: The American Occupation of Britain, 1942–1945* (New York, 1995), 127–40. See also Brian Villa, *Unauthorized Action: Mountbatten and the Dieppe Raid* (Toronto, 1990).

19 *Foreign Relations of the United States: The Conferences at Washington and Quebec, 1943* (Washington, DC, 1970), 488–96.

20 Smith lecture, 'Problems at an Integrated Headquarters', from *Journal of the Royal United Service Institution*, XL (Feb. to Nov. 1945): 462; Charles H. Bonesteel II, Oral History Transcript, p. 127, Senior Officer Debriefing Program, Military History Institute.

21 See above, Chapter 5, p. 76.

22 That is the subtitle of Reynolds' *Rich Relations*.

23 Reynolds, *Rich Relations*, xxiii and 143. Reynolds deals extensively with both the problems and the efforts to minimize them.

24 Churchill, *Closing the Ring*, 383.

25 Richard Overy, *Why the Allies Won* (New York, 1995), 151. FORTITUDE NORTH was the deception plan for the Norway attack.

26 *Foreign Relations: Washington and Quebec*, 488–96.

27 See Chapter 6, pp. 114–15.

28 Reynolds, *Rich Relations*, 301, 359.

29 Overy, *Why the Allies Won*, 148–50.

30 See Alfred D. Chandler (ed.), *The Papers of Dwight David Eisenhower* (Baltimore, MD, 1970), vol. 3, 1908.

31 Ibid., vol. 3, 1837–41, 1846–47.

32 Williamson Murray and Allan R. Millett, *A War to Be Won: Fighting the Second World War* (Cambridge, MA, 2000), 417–18.

33 See Chapter 6, pp. 96–7.

34 See Evan Mawdsley, *Thunder in the East: The Nazi-Soviet War, 1941–1945* (London, 2005).

35 See Chapter 7, pp. 131–3.

36 I.C.B. Dear (ed.), *The Oxford Companion to World War II* (New York, 1995), 703.

37 For Leyte Gulf, see below, Chapter 9, pp. 178–81. For Guadalcanal, see above, Chapter 5, pp. 82–4.

38 Maurice Matloff and Edwin Snell, *Strategic Planning for Coalition Warfare, 1943–44*, (Washington, DC, 1959), 491, in *United States Army in World War II*; Warren F. Kimball (ed.), *Churchill & Roosevelt: The Complete Correspondence* (Princeton, NJ, 1984), vol. 2, 766–7.

39 See above, Chapter 3, pp. 54–55.

40 Robert M. Hathaway, *Ambiguous Partnership: Britain and America, 1944–1947* (New York, 1981), 16–35; Randall B. Woods, *A Changing of the Guard: Anglo-American Relations, 1941–1946* (Chapel Hill, NC, 1990), 115–48.

41 See below, Chapter 9, p. 84.

42 *Foreign Relations: The Conference at Quebec, 1944* (Washington, DC, 1972), 313.

43 Arthur Bryant, *Triumph in the West: A History of the War Years Based on the Diaries of Field Marshal Lord Alanbrooke, Chief of the Imperial General Staff* (Garden City, NY, 1959), 120–4, Kimball, *Churchill & Roosevelt* vol. 3, 38–40.

44 *Foreign Relations: Quebec*, 315–16; Danchev and Todman, *War Diaries*, 590–2.

45 *Foreign Relations: Quebec*, 316.

46 Ibid., 334; Andrew B. Cunningham, *A Sailor's Odyssey: The Autobiography of Admiral of the Fleet Viscount Cunningham of Hyndhope* (New York, 1951), 612.

47 *Foreign Relations: Quebec*, 326, 348. For the atomic sharing agreement, see below, Chapter 9, p. 186 and Chapter 10, p. 196.

48 Terry Anderson, *United States, Great Britain and the Cold War, 1944–1947* (Columbia, MO, 1981), 12; Forrest C. Pogue, *The Supreme Command*, in *United States Army in World War II* (Washington, DC, 1954), 543.

9 Alliance problems and the deferral of victory, September 1944–January 1945

1 Williamson Murray and Allan R. Millett, *A War to Be Won: Fighting the Second World War* (Cambridge, MA, 2000), 444.

2 Alex Danchev and Daniel Todman (eds), *War Diaries, 1939–1945: Field Marshal Lord Alanbrooke* (Berkeley, CA, 2001), 365.

3 As quoted in David Reynolds, *Rich Relations: The American Occupation of Britain, 1942–1945* (New York, 1995), 343–4.

4 Made famous by Cornelius Ryan's popular history, *A Bridge Too Far* (New York, 1974), as well as the ensuing movie of the same name.

5 David M. Kennedy, *Freedom from Fear: The American People in Depression and War, 1929–1945* (New York, 1999), 740–1.

6 Winston S. Churchill, *The Second World War* vol. 6: *Triumph and Tragedy*, (Boston, 1953), 278–80.

7 Steven E. Ambrose, *Eisenhower*, (New York, 1983), vol. 1,379. Patton responded by

publicly blaming Montgomery, whom he called 'a tired little fart', for allowing the German Army to escape from the Bulge. Ibid., 379–80.

8   See above, Chapter 8, p. 168.

9   See below, pp. 178–81.

10 See above, Chapter 7, p. 135.

11 Barbara Tuchman, *Stillwell and the American Experience in China, 1911–1945* (New York, 1970), 349–53; Michael Schaller, *The US Crusade in China, 1938–1945* (New York, 1978), 119–20.

12 Theodore White (ed.), *The Stilwell Papers* (New York, 1948), 333–4.

13 See above, Chapter 8, pp. 165–70.

14 Robert M. Hathaway, *Ambiguous Partnership: Britain and America, 1944–1947* (New York, 1981), 68–9.

15 US Dept. of State, *Foreign Relations of the United States: The Conference at Quebec, 1944* (Washington, DC, 1972), 327; David Marr, *Vietnam, 1945* (Berkeley, CA, 1995), 268.

16 Warren F. Kimball (ed.), *Churchill & Roosevelt: The Complete Correspondence* (Princeton, NJ, 1984), vol. 3: 407–8, 419–21; Hathaway, *Ambiguous Partnership*, 70–85.

17 *Foreign Relations, 1944,* vol. 3, 1376; vol. 4, 988–98; W.A. Harriman and E. Abel, *Special Envoy to Churchill and Stalin, 1941–1946* (New York, 1975), 340–9.

18 JCS 838/1 'Disposition of Italian Overseas Territory', 6 May 1944, ABC 092 Italy (27 Apr. 44), Record Group 165, National Archives; and JCS 973, 'Fundamental Military Factors in Relations to Discussions concerning Territorial Trusteeships and Settlements', 28 July 1944, CCS 092 (-7–27–44), Record Group 218, National Archives. These are partially reproduced in the following *Foreign Relations* volumes: *Quebec,* 190–2; *The Conferences at Malta and Yalta, 1945,* 106–7; *1944,* 1: 699–703; and *The Conference of Berlin (Potsdam),* 264–6. See also Mark A. Stoler, *Allies and Adversaries: The Joint Chiefs of Staff, the Grand Alliance, and U.S. Strategy in World War II* (Chapel Hill, NC, 2000), 171–90.

19 Terry Anderson, *The United States, Great Britain, and the Cold War* (Columbia, MO, 1981), 12–13; Anthony Sampson, *Macmillan: A Study of Ambiguity* (London, 1967), 61.

20 *Foreign Relations: Quebec,* 314.

21 Ibid., 492–3; Martin J. Sherwin, *A World Destroyed: The Atomic Bomb and the Grand Alliance,* 3rd edn (Stanford, CA, 2000), 108–14, 284.

22 Churchill, *Triumph and Tragedy,* 227–8.

23 Anderson, *The United States, Great Britain, and the Cold War,* 24–5; Hathaway, *Ambiguous Partnership,* 97–8.

24 Kimball, *Churchill & Roosevelt,* vol. 3, 436–40; Anderson, *The United States, Great Britain, and the Cold War,* 1.

10   Final victory and the changing of the guard, February–September 1945

1   John Lukacs, *1945: Year Zero* (Garden City, NY, 1978).

2   Robert Sherwood, *Roosevelt and Hopkins: An Intimate History,* rev. edn (New York, 1950), 847.

3   Ehrman, *Grand Strategy* (London) 6: 96–104. See also below, pp. 198–200.

4   See above, Chapter 8, pp. 167, 170.

5   The full and final Yalta Protocol is in US Dept. of State, *Foreign Relations of the United States: The Conferences at Malta and Yalta, 1945* (Washington, DC, 1955), 975–82.

6   Ibid., 984–5.

7   Mark A. Stoler, *Allies and Adversaries: The Joint Chiefs of Staff, the Grand Alliance, and U.S. Strategy in World War II* (Chapel Hill, NC, 2000), 226.

8   Sherwood, *Roosevelt and Hopkins,* 870.

9   See above, Chapter 8, p. 70.

10 Winston S. Churchill, *The Second World War,* vol. 6: *Triumph and Tragedy* (Boston, 1953). 365.

11 US Dept. of State, *Foreign Relations: Malta and Yalta,* 668–9.

12 Ibid., 854.

13 William D. Leahy, *I Was There: The Personal Story of the Chief of Staff to Presidents Roosevelt and Truman Based on his Notes and Diaries Made at the Time* (New York, 1950), 315–16.

14 Warren Kimball, *The Juggler: Franklin Roosevelt as Wartime Statesman* (Princeton, NJ, 1991), 173 and 268 (n. 29); and *Forged in War* (New York, 1997), 318.

15 David Dimbleby and David Reynolds, *An Ocean Apart: The Relationship between Britain and America in the Twentieth Century* (New York, 1988), 174.

16 See above, Chapter 8, p. 170, and Chapter 9, p. 186.

17 See Diane Shaver Clemens, *Yalta* (New York, 1970), 85–95.

18 Walter LaFeber, 'Roosevelt, Churchill, and Indochina: 1942–1945', *American Historical Review* 80 (Dec. 1975): 1277–95; Robert Dallek, *Franklin D. Roosevelt and American Foreign Policy* (New York, 1979, 1995), 511–13; Christopher Thorne, *Allies of a Kind* (New York, 1978), 628–31.

19 See Clemens, *Yalta,* 267–91; and Melvyn P. Leffler, 'Adherence to Agreements: Yalta and the Experiences of the Early Cold War', *International Security* 11: 1 (1986): 88–123.

20 Charles E. Bohlen, *Witness to History, 1929–1969,* 209; *Foreign Relations, 1945,* vol. 3, 745–6.

21 Alfred Chandler, *The Papers of Dwight David Eisenhower* (Baltimore, MD, 1970), vol. 4, 2551–2, 2432–3.

22 See Steven Ambrose, *Eisenhower and Berlin, 1945: The Decision to Halt at the Elbe* (New York, 1967).

23 Warren F. Kimball (ed.), *Churchill and Roosevelt: The Complete Correspondence* (Princeton, NJ, 1984), vol. 3, 613.

24 Ibid., 3: 607–9, 617, 630.

25 Churchill, *The Second World War,* vol. 6: *Triumph and Tragedy* (Boston, 1953), 429, 471, 478.

26 Hans-Adolf Jacobsen and Arthur L. Smith, Jr., *World War II Policy and Strategy: Selected Documents with Commentary* (Santa Barbara, CA, 1979), 324–30.

27 See above, Chapter 8, pp. 164–5.

28 Ronald Spector, *Eagle Against the Sun: The American War with Japan* (New York, 1985), 371–92.

29 Ibid., 518.

30 Ibid., 524–8.

31 See above, Chapter 8, pp. 169–70.

32 Spector, *Eagle Against the Sun,* 532, 537–8; I.C.B. Dear (ed.) *The Oxford Companion to World War II* (New York, 1945), 836, 1104.

33 Harry S. Truman, *Memoirs, 1: Year of Decisions* (Garden City, NY, 1955), 5, 19.

34 Ibid., 82. See also *Foreign Relations, 1945,* vol. 5, 253, 256–8.

35 Robert M. Hathaway, *Ambiguous Partnership Britain and America, 1944–1947* (New York, 1981), 142–7, 172–5, 178; *Foreign Relations: The Conference of Berlin,* vol. 2, (Washington, DC, 1960). 1202–3.

36 Memorandum, Groves to Secretary of War, 'The Test', 18 July 1945, Manhattan Engineer District Records, National Archives, reproduced in Michael B. Stoff,

Jonathan F. Fanton and R. Hal Williams (eds), *The Manhattan Project: A Documentary Introduction to the Atomic Age* (New York, 1991), 188–91.

37 Truman, *Memoirs*, vol. 1, 10–11.

38 A.H. Compton, *et al.*, 'Recommendation on the Immediate Use of Nuclear Weapons', 16 June 1945, reproduced in Stoff, *et al.*, *The Manhattan Project*, 149–50.

39 *Foreign Relations: Berlin*, vol. 2, 1474–6.

40 Ibid., vol. 2, 225, 378–79; Truman, *Memoirs*, vol. 1, 416; Martin J. Sherwin, *A World Destroyed: The Atomic Bomb and the Grand Alliance*, 3rd edn (Stanford, CA, 2000), 224, 227.

41 See David Holloway, *Stalin and the Bomb: The Soviet Union and Atomic Energy, 1939–1956* (New Haven, CT, 1994), 116–18, 129–33.

42 *Foreign Relations: Berlin*, vol. 2, 1293.

43 See, for example, Gar Alperovitz, *The Decision to Use the Bomb and the Architecture of an American Myth* (New York, 1995) vs Robert P. Newman, *Truman and the Hiroshima Cult* (East Lansing, MI, 1995).

44 See above, Chapter 1, p. 7, and Chapter 6, pp. 109–16.

45 Barton J. Bernstein, 'Roosevelt, Truman, and the Atomic Bomb, 1941–1945: A Reinterpretation', *Political Science Quarterly* 90 (Spring 1975), 23–69; Sherwin, *A World Destroyed*.

46 Hadley Cantril (ed.), *Public Opinion, 1935–1946* (Princeton, NJ, 1951), 23.

47 Barton J. Bernstein, 'Understanding the Atomic Bomb and the Japanese Surrender: Missed Opportunities, Little-Known Disasters, and Modern Memory', *Diplomatic History* 19 (Spring 1995): 227–73.

48 *Foreign Relations: Berlin*, vol. 225.

11 Aftermath, consequences and conclusions

1 Gerhard Weinberg, *A World at Arms: A Global History of World War II*, 2nd edn (Cambridge, 2005), 894.

2 James L. Stokesbury, *A Short History of World War II* (New York, 1980), 377.

3 Telford Taylor, *Nuremberg and Vietnam: An American Tragedy* (New York, 1971), 53, 91–2, 181–2; Richard A. Falk, Gabriel Kolko and Robert J. Lifton (eds), *Crimes of War: A Legal, Political Documentary, and Psychological Inquiry into the Responsibility of Leaders, Citizens, and Soldiers for Criminal Acts in Wars* (New York, 1971), 141–61, 224–5.

4 See above, Chapter 9, pp. 186 and 244, note 18.

5 Jonathan R. Adelman, *Prelude to the Cold War: The Tsarist, Soviet, and U.S. Armies in the Two World Wars* (Boulder, CO, 1988), 128; John Ellis, *Brute Force: Allied Strategy and Tactics in the Second World War* (New York, 1990), 128–30 and tables 35–36; Russell D. Buhite, *Decisions at Yalta: An Appraisal of Summit Diplomacy* (Wilmington, DE, 1986), xv–xvi. Weinberg, *A World at Arms*, 264, notes that 'more people fought and died' on the Eastern Front 'than on all other fronts of the war around the globe put together'.

6 Milovan Djilas, *Conversations with Stalin* (New York, 1962), 114.

7 Weinberg, *A World at Arms*, 894. The British figure includes civilian deaths. The American figure includes non-combat deaths for those in uniform; US combat dead totalled approximately 294,000.

8 Adelman, *Prelude to the Cold War*, 128–9.

9 David Reynolds, *Rich Relations: The American Occupation of Britain, 1942–1945* (New York, 1995), 384.

10 See in this regard the numerous works by David Glantz as well as Evan Mawdsley,

      Thunder in the East: The Nazi-Soviet War, 1941–1945 (London, 2005).

11   Mark A. Stoler, *Allies and Adversaries: The Joint Chiefs of Staff, the Grand Alliance, and U.S. Strategy in World War II* (Chapel Hill, NC, 2000), 211–64.

12   David Kennedy, *Freedom from Fear: The American People in Depression and War* (New York, 1999, 854.

13   Douglas, quoted in Lloyd C. Gardner, *Architects of Illusion: Men and Ideas in American Foreign Policy, 1941–49* (Chicago, 1970), 316; Churchill, in Fraser J. Harbutt, *The Iron Curtain: Churchill, America, and the Origins of the Cold War* (New York, 1986), 186.

14   'X' (George F. Kennan), 'The Sources of Soviet Conduct', *Foreign Affairs* 25 (July, 1947): 566–82.

15   Walter Lippman, *U.S. Foreign Policy: Shield of the Republic* (Boston, 1943).

16   *Public Papers of the Presidents of the United States: Harry S. Truman, 1947* (Washington, DC, 1963), 176–80.

17   State Department *Bulletin*, 16 (15 June 1947): 1159–60.

18   See Michael J. Hogan, *The Marshall Plan, 1947–1952* (New York, 1987), 1–25.

19   John Lewis Gaddis, *The Long Peace: An Inquiry into the History of the Cold War* (New York, 1987).

20   Thomas G. Paterson, J. Garry Clifford, Shane J. Maddock, Deborah Kisatsky and Kenneth J. Hagan, *American Foreign Relations: A History*, 6th edn (Boston, 2005), 247.

21   See above, Chapter 6, pp. 98–100.

22   As quoted and analysed in John Spanier, *The Truman-MacArthur Controversy and the Korean War* (New York, 1965), 214–54.

23   See Lloyd C. Gardner, *Approaching Vietnam: From World War II through Dienbienphu* (New York, 1988); and George Herring, *America's Longest War: The United States and Vietnam, 1950–1975*, 4th edn (New York, 1996), esp. 3–45.

24   Kennedy, *Freedom From Fear*, 856–7.

25   Alan Brinkley, 'World War II and American Liberalism', in Lewis A. Erenberg and Susan E. Hirsch (eds), *The War in American Culture: Society and Consciousness* (Chicago, 1996), 314–27.

26   See above, Chapter 9, p. 186.

27   David Reynolds, 'Roosevelt, Churchill, and the Wartime Anglo-American Alliance': Towards a New Synthesis', in William Roger Louis and Hedley Bull (eds) *The 'Special Relationship': Anglo-American Relations since 1945* (Oxford, 1986), 38.

28   Quote from Randall B. Woods, *A Changing of the Guard: Anglo-American Relations, 1941–1946* (Chapel Hill, NC, 1990), 301. See also 212–43, 274–407; Robert M. Hathaway, *Ambiguous Partnership: Britain and America, 1944–1947* (New York, 1981), 182 ff. (especially 182–216 and 260–3); and Louis and Bull (eds), *The Special Relationship*, especially the chapters by Bradford Perkins, 'Unequal Partners: The Truman Administration and Great Britain', and Margaret Gowing, 'Nuclear Weapons and the "Special Relationship"', 43–64 and 117–28.

29   Smith lecture, 'Problems at an Integrated Headquarters' from *Journal of the Royal United Service Institution*, XL (Feb. to Nov. 1945), 455.

30   Ibid., 461.

31   Reynolds, 'The Wartime Anglo-American Alliance', 38–40.

SELECT BIBLIOGRAPHY

In 1989, more than 70,000 volumes on World War II had already been published.[1] That number has only increased over the past 15 years. Consequently what follows is by necessity highly limited and incomplete. For that very reason it begins with a listing of some of the more important guides to additional World War II literature.

Guides

Janet Ziegler (ed.) *World War II: Books in English, 1945–1965* (Stanford, CA: Hoover Institution Press, 1971) has been updated by Arthur L. Funk, *et al.* (eds) in *A Select Bibliography of Books on the Second World War in English, Published in the United States, 1966–1975* (Gainesville, FL: American Committee on the History of the Second World War, 1975), and Arthur L. Funk (ed.), *The Second World War: A Select Bibliography of Books in English Published Since 1975* (Claremont, CA: Regina Books, 1985). Updates continue in the quarterly newsletter of the World War Two Studies Association. See also A.G.S. Enser (ed.), *A Subject Bibliography of the Second World War, and Aftermath, Books in English, 1939–1974* (Boulder, CO: Westview Press, 1977) and Enser's update for *1975–1987* (Brookfield, VT: Gower, 1990); ABC-CLIO Information Services, *World War II from an American Perspective: An Annotated Bibliography* (Santa Barbara, CA: ABC-CLIO, 1983); Gwyn M. Bayliss (ed.), *Guide to the Two World Wars: An Annotated Survey of English Language Reference Materials* (New York: Bowker, 1977); and Marty Bloomberg and Hans H. Weber (eds), *World War II and its Origins: A Selected Annotated Bibliography of Books in English* (Littleton, CO: Libraries Unlimited, 1975). For extensive bibliographies on specific World War II theatres and topics, see John J. Sbrega (ed.), *The War Against Japan, 1941–1945: An Annotated Bibliography* (New York: Garland, 1989); Donal J. Sexton, Jr, *Signals Intelligence in World War II: A Research Guide* (Westport, CT: Greenwood, 1996); Myron J. Smith, Jr (ed.), *Air War Bibliography, 1939–1945*, 5 vols (Manhattan, KS: Aerospace History, 1977–1982), his *World War II at Sea: A Bibliography of Sources in English*, 3 vols (Metuchen, NJ: Scarecrow, 1976), and his *World War II: The European and Mediterranean Theaters: An Annotated Bibliography* (New York: Garland, 1984). For Churchill, see Eugene L. Rasor's *Winston S. Churchill, 1874–1965: A Comprehensive Historiography and Annotated Bibliography* (Westport, CT: Greenwood, 2000). See also Chapters 17 and 18 in Robert L. Beisner (ed.), *American Foreign Relations Since 1600: A Guide to the Literature*, 2 vols (Denver: ABC-CLIO, 2003); and Colin F. Baxter, *The Normandy Campaign: A Selected Bibliography*: *The War in North Africa, 1940–1943: A Selected Bibliography*; and *Field Marshal Bernard Law Montgomery: A Selected Bibliography* (Westport, CT: Greenwood, 1992, 1996, 1999).

As valuable as these bibliographies are the numerous historiographical essays available on specific World War II issues. The most recent and comprehensive collection is Loyd Lee's two edited volumes, *World War II in Europe, Africa, and the Americas, with General Sources: A Handbook of Literature and Research*, and *World War II in Asia and the Pacific and the War's Aftermath, with General Themes: A Handbook of Literature and Research* (Westport, CT: Greenwood, 1997, 1998), which includes essays on 58 different World War II topics. See also the extensive historiographical essays in Baxter's three bibliographies cited above.

Documents and official histories

The unpublished documentary record of World War II is enormous. US Army files alone weigh 17,120 tons and fill 188 miles of filing cases.[2] After the war, both the British and the US Governments sponsored massive, multivolume histories of the war based on these documents. Many of the ensuing histories took decades to complete. They provide excellent coverage, and they should be consulted both for detailed information on specific topics and before plunging into the unpublished records themselves. Some of the documents have also been published in both official and unofficial volumes.

Most official British diplomatic and military records for the war years are housed in the National Archives (formerly the Public Records Office) in Kew, England. The Churchill Archive at Churchill College, Cambridge, also contains such records, as well as important World War II manuscript collections. Additional important collections are housed at the Liddell Hart Centre at King's College, London; the Library at the London School of Economics; and the University of Edinburgh. Most official American diplomatic and military records are in the US National Archives in Washington, DC, and College Park, MD. Additional important material can be found in the military service archives, most notably the US Army's Military History Institute in Carlisle, PA, and the Naval Historical Center in Washington, DC. The Franklin D. Roosevelt and Harry S. Truman Presidential Libraries in Hyde Park, NY, and Independence, MO, also contain a great deal of important official records, as well as the manuscript collections of the presidents and many of their high-level advisers. Many other officials deposited their papers with the Library of Congress in Washington, DC, or in university libraries around the country. Special libraries in Lexington and Norfolk, VA, house the papers of Generals Marshall and MacArthur as well as their associates.

Numerous multivolume official British military histories have been published under overall editorship of J.R.M. Butler and the general title *History of the Second World War: United Kingdom Military Series* (London: Her Majesty's Stationery Office). In preparing this book, the most important volumes consulted within the series were the six-volume *Grand Strategy* sub-series, also under the editorship of Butler. See also the multivolume sets by Stephen Roskill, *The War at Sea, 1939–1945*, 3 vols (1954–1961); C.K. Webster and Noble Frankland, *The Strategic Air Offensive Against Germany, 1939–1945*, 4 vols (1961); I.S.O. Playfair *et al.*, *The Mediterranean and the Middle East*, 6 vols (1954–1987); S. Woodburn Kirby *et al.*, *The War Against Japan*, 5 vols (1957–1969); and L.F. Ellis, *Victory in the West*, 2 vols (1962, 1968). Single volumes within the series include Basil Collier, *The Defence of the United Kingdom* (1957); T.K. Derry, *The Campaign in Norway* (1952); F.S.V. Donnison, *Civil Affairs and Military Government, North-West Europe, 1944–1946* (1961); L.F. Ellis, *The War in France and Flanders, 1939–1940* (1953); and C.R.S. Harris, *Allied Military Administration of Italy, 1943–1945* (1957).

Each branch of the US military services published separate, multivolume histories of the war. The largest and most comprehensive is the 79-volume *United States Army in World War II* (Washington, DC: US Government Printing Office, 1947–1998). For a guide to this enormous series, see Richard D. Adamczyk and Morris J. MacGregor (eds), *United States Army in World War II: Reader's Guide* (Washington, DC: US Government Printing Office, 1992). A summary of some of the most important conclusions reached by individual authors in the series can be found in the brief volume by former army chief historian, Kent Roberts Greenfield, *American Strategy in World War II: A Reconsideration* (Baltimore, MD: The Johns Hopkins University Press, 1963), and his edited collection, *Command Decisions* (Washington, DC: US Government Printing Office, 1960). The most valuable volumes in the full army series for the preparation of this book were in *The War Department* sub-series, particularly the two volumes by Maurice Matloff and Edwin Snell, *Strategic Planning for Coalition Warfare*, that parallel the British *Grand Strategy* volumes in their coverage. A multivolume official history of the JCS was written after the war, but only one of the volumes has been published: Grace Person Hayes's *The History of the Joint Chiefs of Staff in World War II: The War Against Japan* (Annapolis, MD: US Naval Institute Press, 1982). The others, on the war against Germany and an administrative history of the organization, are available in unpublished form in the National Archives and on microfilm.

Whereas each volume in the US Army series was written by a separate author, the 15 volumes in the US Navy official history, *History of United States Naval Operations in World War II* (Boston: Little, Brown, 1947–1962) were all written by Samuel Eliot Morison, one of the most prominent American historians of his generation; a one-volume summary was also published as *The Two Ocean War* (Boston: Little, Brown, 1963). See also Wesley Frank Craven and James Lea Cate (eds), *The Army Air Forces in World War II*, 7 vols (Chicago: University of Chicago Press, 1948–1958), and *History of U.S. Marine Corps Operations in World War II*, 5 vols (Washington, DC: Historical Branch, G-3, US Marine Corps, 1958–1968).

The official British diplomatic history is Sir Ernest Llewellyn Woodward, *British Foreign Policy in the Second World War*, published first as a single volume and then in five volumes (London: Her Majesty's Stationery Office, 1962, 1970–76). No similar official volumes analyse US diplomacy during the war, though wartime State Department official Harley A. Notter did publish the more limited *Post-war Foreign Policy Preparation, 1939–1945* (Washington, DC: US Government Printing Office, 1949), an indispensable source on mid-level State Department wartime thinking about the post-war world. The State Department has also published two very extensive and important collections of wartime documents within its ongoing series, *Foreign Relations of the United States*: the annual volumes for the war years; and the special volumes on the wartime summit conferences, which include critical military as well as diplomatic documents (Washington, DC: US Government Printing Office, 1956–1972). The British Foreign Office has not published any World War II document collections, but see Thomas E. Hachey (ed.), *Confidential Dispatches: Analyses of America by the British Ambassador, 1939–1945* (Evanston, IL: New University Press, 1974), and H.G. Nicholas (ed.), *Washington Despatches 1941–1945: Weekly Political Reports from the British Embassy* (Chicago: University of Chicago Press, 1981). See also Graham Ross (ed.), *The Foreign Office and the Kremlin: British Documents on Anglo-Soviet Relations, 1941–1945* (New York: Cambridge University Press, 1984); and Oleg A. Rzheshevsky (ed.), *War and Diplomacy: The Making of the Grand Alliance: Documents from Stalin's Archives*, 2 vols (Amsterdam: Harwood Academic Publishers, 1996), which contains numerous Russian documents relating to Eden's 1941 visit to Moscow and Molotov's 1942 visits to London and Washington.

Additional US diplomatic, military and presidential documents have been produced in microfilm editions by Scholarly Resources (SR) (Wilmington, DE), and LexisNexis Academic and Library Solutions (LN) (Bethesda, MD). The most important microfilm collections for subjects covered in this volume are the Roosevelt and Truman Map Room Messages (LN, 1980–81, 1990); the Wartime Conferences of the Combined Chiefs of Staff

(SR, 1982); Records of the Joint Chiefs of Staff (LN, 1980); OSS/State Department Intelligence and Research Reports (LN, 1977–80); and the MAGIC Documents (LN, 1980). Harley Notter's files are also available on microfilm (LN, 1987), as are portions of the State Department Decimal File and other State Department records (SR, 1981). See also the numerous commercially published collections of selected World War II documents and essays, such as Russell A. Buchanan (ed.), *The United States and World War II: Military and Diplomatic Documents* (Columbia: University of South Carolina Press, 1972); Hans-Adolf-Jacobsen and Arthur L. Smith, Jr, *World War II: Policy and Strategy: Selected Documents with Commentary* (Santa Barbara, CA: Clio Books, 1979); Donald S. Detwiler and Charles Burton Burdick (eds), *War in Asia and the Pacific, 1937–1949: A Fifteen Volume Collection* (New York: Garland, 1980); Mark A. Stoler and Melanie S. Gustafson, (eds), *Major Problems in the History of World War II* (Boston: Houghton Mifflin, 2003); Theodore A. Wilson (ed.), *WW 2: Readings on Critical Issues* (New York: Charles Scribner's Sons, 1974) and *America and World War II: Critical Issues* (Dubuque, IA: Kendall/Hunt, 2005); and the specific document collections listed below under both civilian and military memoirs, published papers and biographies.

Encyclopedias and dictionaries

Baudot, Marcel, *et al.* (eds), *The Historical Encyclopedia of World War II* (New York: Facts on File, 1980).
Boatner, Mark. M. (ed.), *Biographical Dictionary of World War II* (Novato, CA: Presidio Press, 1996).
Chant, Christopher (ed.), *The Encyclopedia of Codenames of World War II* (London: Routledge and Kegan Paul, 1986).
Dear, I.C.B. (ed.), *The Oxford Companion to World War II* (New York: Oxford University Press, 1995).
Ellis, John, *World War II: A Statistical Survey: The Essential Facts and Figures for All the Combatants* (New York: Facts on File, 1993).
Goralski, Robert (ed.), *World War II Almanac, 1931–1945: A Political and Military Record* (New York: Putnam, 1981).
Keegan, John (ed.), *Rand McNally Encyclopedia of World War II* (New York: Rand McNally, 1995).
Keegan, John, *Who's Who in World War II* (New York: Oxford University Press, 1995).
Parrish, Thomas (ed.), *The Simon and Schuster Encyclopedia of World War II* (New York: Simon and Schuster, 1978).
Sandler, Stanley (ed.), *World War II in the Pacific: An Encyclopedia* (New York: Garland, 2001).
Snyder, Louis L., *Louis L. Snyder's Guide to World War II* (Westport, CT: Greenwood, 1982).
Wells, Anne Sharp (ed.), *Historical Dictionary of World War II: The War Against Japan* (Lanham, MD: Scarecrow, 1999).
Wheal, Elizabeth-Anne, Pope, Stephen and Taylor, James (eds), *A Dictionary of the Second World War* (New York: Peter Bedrick, 1990).
Zabecki, David, *et al.* (eds), *World War II in Europe: An Encyclopedia*, 2 vols (New York: Garland, 1999).

General World War II histories

Calvocoressi, Peter, Wint, Guy and Pritchard, John, *The Penguin History of the Second World War* (New York: Penguin Books, 2001), previously published as *Total War: Causes and Courses of the Second World War*, 2 vols, rev. 2nd edn (New York: Pantheon, 1989).

Ellis, John, *Brute Force: Allied Strategy and Tactics of the Second World War* (New York: Viking, 1990).

Fuller, J.F.C., *The Second World War: A Strategical and Tactical History* (London: Eyre and Spottiswoode, 1948).

Gilbert, Martin, *The Second World War: A Complete History* (New York: Henry Holt, 1989).

Keegan, John, *The Second World War* (New York: Penguin, 1990).

Kitchen, Martin, *A World in Flames: A Short History of the Second World War in Europe and Asia, 1939–1945* (New York: Longman, 1990).

Leckie, Robert, *Delivered from Evil: The Saga of World War II* (New York: Harper and Row, 1987).

Lee, Loyd, *The War Years: A Global History of the Second World War* (New York: Unwin Hyman, 1989).

Leopard, Donald D., *World War II: A Concise History* (Prospect Heights, IL: Waveland, 1992).

Liddell-Hart B.H., *History of the Second World War* (New York: Putnam, 1970, reprinted 1982).

Louis, Roger, and Bull, Hedley (eds), *The Special Relationship: Anglo-American Relations since 1945* (Oxford: Clarendon Press, 1989).

Lyons, Michael J., *World War II: A Short History*, 4th edn (Upper Saddle River, NJ: Prentice Hall, 2004).

Maddox, Robert J., *The United States and World War II* (Boulder, CO: Westview, 1992).

Mawdsley, Evan, *Thunder in the East: The Nazi-Soviet War, 1941–1945* (London: Arnold, 2005).

Michel, Henri, *The Second World War*, trans. Douglas Parmee (New York: Praeger, 1975).

Murray, Williamson and Millett, Allan R., *A War to Be Won: Fighting the Second World War* (Cambridge, MA: Harvard University Press, 2000).

Overy, Richard, *Why the Allies Won* (New York: Norton, 1996).

Parker, R.A.C., *The Second World War: A Short History*, rev. edn (New York: Oxford University Press, 1997).

Purdue, A.W., *The Second World War* (New York: St Martin's Press, 1999).

Stokesbury, James L., *A Short History of World War II* (New York: Morrow, 1980).

Weinberg, Gerhard L., *A World at Arms: A Global History of World War II*, 2nd edn (New York: Cambridge University Press, 2005).

Willmott, H.P. *The Great Crusade: A New Complete History of the Second World War* (New York: Free Press, 1990).

Wright, Gordon, *The Ordeal of Total War, 1939–1945* (New York, Harper, 1966).

Civilian memoirs, published papers, and biographies

Abramson, Rudy, *Spanning the Century: The Life of W. Averell Harriman, 1891–1986* (New York: William Morrow, 1992).

Barker, Elisabeth, *Churchill and Eden at War* (New York: St Martin's Press, 1978).

Ben-Moshe, Tuvia, *Churchill, Strategy and History* (Boulder, CO: Lynne Rienner, 1992).

Bird, Kai, *The Chairman: John J. McCloy and the Making of the American Establishment* (New York: Simon & Schuster, 1992).

Blum, John Morton, *From the Morgenthau Diaries*, 3 vols (Boston: Houghton Mifflin, 1959–1967).

Bohlen, Charles E., *Witness to History, 1929–1969* (New York: W.W. Norton, 1973).

Buhite, Russell D. and Levy, David W. (eds), *FDR's Fireside Chats* (Norman, OK: University of Oklahoma Press, 1992).

Burns, James M, *Roosevelt: The Soldier of Freedom* (New York: Harcourt, Brace, Jovanovich, 1970).

Callahan, Raymond, *Churchill: Retreat from Empire* (Wilmington, DE: Scholarly Resources, 1984).

Campbell, Thomas M. and Herring, George C., *The Diaries of Edward R. Stettinius, Jr., 1943–1946* (New York: New Viewpoints, 1975).

Carlton, David, *Anthony Eden: A Biography* (London: Allen & Unwin, 1981, 1984).

Charmley, John, *Churchill, The End of Glory: A Political Biography* (New York: Harcourt Brace, 1993).

Charmley, John, *Churchill's Grand Alliance: The Anglo-American Special Relationship, 1940–1957* (New York: Harcourt Brace, 1995).

Churchill, Winston S., *The Second World War*, 6 vols (Boston: Houghton Mifflin, 1948–1953).

Cohen, Eliot, 'Churchill and Coalition Strategy in World War II', in Paul Kennedy (ed.), *Grand Strategies in War and Peace*, (New Haven, CT: Yale University Press, 1991), 43–67.

Colville, John, *The Fringes of Power: 10 Downing Street Diaries, 1939–1945* (New York: Norton, 1985).

Dallek, Robert, *Franklin D. Roosevelt and American Foreign Policy, 1932–1945* (New York: Oxford University Press, 1979).

Davis, Kenneth S., *FDR*, 5 vols (New York: Random House, 1985–2000).

Dilks, David, (ed.), *The Diaries of Sir Alexander Cadogan, O.M., 1939–1945* (New York: Putnam, 1972).

Dutton, David, *Anthony Eden: A Life and Reputation* (London: Arnold, 1997).

Eden, Anthony, *The Reckoning: The Memoirs of Anthony Eden, Earl of Avon* (Boston: Houghton Mifflin, 1965).

Emerson, William, 'FDR as Commander-in-Chief in World War II', in *Military Affairs* 22 (Winter 1958–1959): 181–207.

Ferrell, Robert H. (ed.), *Off the Record: The Private Papers of Harry S. Truman* (New York: Harper and Row, 1980).

Freidel, Frank, *Franklin D. Roosevelt: A Rendezvous with Destiny* (Boston: Little, Brown, 1990).

Gardner, Lloyd C., *Architects of Illusion: Men and Ideas in American Foreign Policy, 1941–1947* (Chicago: Quadrangle, 1970).

Gellman, Irwin F., *Secret Affairs: Franklin D. Roosevelt. Cordell Hull, and Sumner Welles* (Baltimore, MD: The Johns Hopkins University Press, 1995).

Gilbert, Martin S., *Winston S. Churchill, vols. 6 and 7: Finest Hour, 1939–1941* and *Road to Victory, 1941–1945* (Boston: Houghton Mifflin, 1983, 1986).

Graff, Frank Warren, *Strategy of Involvement: A Diplomatic Biography of Sumner Welles* (New York: Garland, 1988).

Halifax, Edward Frederick Lindley Wood (Lord), *Fullness of Days* (London: Dodd, Mead 1957).

Harper, John Lamberton, *American Visions of Europe: Franklin D. Roosevelt, George F. Kennan, and Dean G. Acheson* (New York: Cambridge University Press, 1994).

Harriman, W. Averell and Abel, Elie, *Special Envoy to Churchill and Stalin, 1941–1946* (New York: Random House, 1975).

Hassett, William D., *Off the Record with F.D.R., 1942–1945* (New Brunswick, NJ: Rutgers University Press, 1958).

Hodgson, Geoffrey, *The Colonel: The Life and Wars of Henry Stimson, 1867–1950* (New York: Alfred A. Knopf, 1990).

Hull, Cordell, *The Memoirs of Cordell Hull*, 2 vols (New York: Macmillan, 1948).

James, Robert Rhodes, *Anthony Eden* (London: Weidenfeld and Nicolson, 1986).

Kimball, Warren F. (ed.), *Churchill & Roosevelt: The Complete Correspondence*, 3 vols (Princeton, NJ: Princeton University Press, 1984).

Kimball, Warren F. *The Juggler: Franklin Roosevelt as Wartime Statesman* (Princeton, NJ: Princeton University Press, 1991).

Kimball, Warren F., *Forged in War: Roosevelt, Churchill, and the Second World War* (New York: William Morrow, 1997).

Lash, Joseph P., *Roosevelt and Churchill, 1939–1941: The Partnership that Saved the West* (New York: Norton, 1976).

Lowenheim, Francis L., Langley, Harold D. and Jonas, Manfred (eds), *Roosevelt and Churchill: Their Secret Wartime Correspondence* (New York: Saturday Review Press, 1975).

Macmillan, Harold, *The Blast of War, 1939–1945* (New York: Harper and Row, 1968).

Macmillan, Harold, *War Diaries: Politics and War in the Mediterranean, January 1943–May 1945* (New York: St Martin's Press, 1984).

Maney, Patrick, *The Roosevelt Presence* (New York: Twayne, 1992).

Marks, Frederick W., *Wind Over Sand: The Diplomacy of Franklin Roosevelt* (Athens, GA: University of Georgia Press, 1988).

McJimsey, George T., *Harry Hopkins: Ally of the Poor and Defender of Democracy* (Cambridge, MA: Harvard University Press, 1987).

Morison, Elting E., *Turmoil and Tradition: A Study of the Life and Times of Henry L. Stimson* (Boston: Houghton Mifflin, 1960).

Murphy, Robert, *Diplomat Among Warriors* (Garden City, NY: Doubleday, 1964).

Nicolson, Nigel (ed.), *Diaries and Letters [by] Harold Nicolson, Vol. 2: The War Years, 1939–1945* (New York: Atheneum, 1967).

Pratt, Julius, *Cordell Hull*, in Samuel Flagg Bemis and Robert H. Ferrell (series eds), *The American Secretaries of State and Their Diplomacy* series, vols 12–13 (New York: Cooper Square, 1964).

Resis, Albert (ed.), *Molotov Remembers: Inside Kremlin Politics; Conversations with Felix Chuev* (Chicago: Ivan R. Dee, 1993).

Roosevelt, Elliot, *As He Saw It* (New York: Duell, Sloan and Pearce, 1946).

Roosevelt, Elliot (ed.) *F.D.R.: His Personal Letters*, 4 vols (New York: Duell, Sloan and Pearce, 1947–50).

Roosevelt, Franklin D., *The Complete Presidential Press Conferences of Franklin Delano Roosevelt* (New York: DaCapo Press, 1972).

Rosenman, Samuel I., *Public Papers and Addresses of Franklin D. Roosevelt*, 13 vols (New York: Random House, 1938–1950).

Sainsbury, Keith, *Churchill and Roosevelt at War: The War They Fought and the Peace They Hoped to Make* (Washington Square, NY: New York University Press, 1994).

Schewe, Donald B. (ed.), *Franklin D. Roosevelt and Foreign Affairs, January 1937–August 1939*, 11 vols (New York: Garland, 1979–1980).

Schmitz, David F., *Henry L. Stimson: The First Wise Man* (Wilmington, DE: Scholarly Resources, 2001).

Sherwood, Robert E., *Roosevelt and Hopkins: An Intimate History*, rev. edn (New York: Harper, 1950).

Smith, Frederick W.F. (Lord Birkenhead), *Halifax: The Life of Lord Halifax* (London: Hamish Hamilton, 1965).

Stimson, Henry L. and Bundy, McGeorge, *On Active Service in Peace and War* (New York: Harper, 1948).

Truman, Harry S., *Memoirs, 1: Year of Decision* (Garden City, NY: Doubleday, 1955).

Tuttle, Dwight W., *Harry L. Hopkins and Anglo-American-Soviet Relations, 1941–1945* (New York: Garland, 1983).

USSR Ministry of Foreign Affairs, *Correspondence between the Chairman of the Council of Ministers of the U.S.S.R. and the Presidents of the U.S.A. and the Prime Ministers of Great*

Britain during the Great Patriotic War of 1941–1945, 2 vols (Moscow: Foreign Languages Publishing House, 1957).

Walker, Richard L., 'E.R. Stettinius, Jr.', in Samuel Flagg Bemis and Robert H. Ferrell (series eds), *The American Secretaries of State and Their Diplomacy*, Vol. 14 (New York: Cooper Square, 1965).

Ward, Geoffrey C. Ward, *Closest Companion: The Unknown Story of the Intimate Friendship between Franklin Roosevelt and Margaret Suckley* (Boston: Houghton Mifflin, 1995).

Welles, Benjamin, *Sumner Welles: FDR's Global Strategist: A Biography* (New York: St Martin's Press, 1997).

Welles, Sumner, *The Time for Decision* (New York: Harper, 1944).

Welles, Sumner, *Seven Decisions That Shaped History* (New York: Harper, 1951).

Wills, Matthew B., *Wartime Missions of Harry L. Hopkins* (Raleigh, NC: Pentland, 1996).

Wilson, Charles, *Churchill: Taken from the Diaries of Lord Moran: The Struggle for Survival, 1940–1965* (Boston: Houghton Mifflin, 1966).

Military memoirs, published papers and biographies

Adams, Henry H., *Witness to Power: The Life of Fleet Admiral William D. Leahy* (Annapolis, MD: Naval Institute Press, 1985).

Alexander, Field-Marshal Sir Harold, Earl of Tunis, *The Alexander Memoirs, 1940–1945* (ed.), John North (London: Cassell, 1962).

Ambrose, Steven E., *The Supreme Commander: The War Years of General Dwight D. Eisenhower* (Garden City, NY: Doubleday 1970; reprinted by University of Mississippi Press, 1999).

Ambrose, Steven E., *Eisenhower, Volume I: Soldier, General of the Army, President-Elect, 1890–1952* (New York: Simon & Schuster, 1983).

Arnold, Henry H., *Global Mission* (New York: Harper, 1949).

Barnett, Correlli, *The Desert Generals*, 2nd edn (Bloomington, IN: Indiana University Press, 1982).

Bland, Larry I. (ed.), *George C. Marshall: Interviews and Reminiscences for Forrest C. Pogue* (Lexington, VA: George C. Marshall Research Foundation, 1991).

Bland, Larry I. (ed.), *The Papers of George Catlett Marshall*, 5 vols to date (Baltimore, MD: Johns Hopkins University Press, 1981–2003).

Blumenson, Martin (ed.), *The Patton Papers, 1885–1940*, 2 vols (Boston: Houghton Mifflin, 1972–74).

Blumenson, Martin, *Mark Clark* (New York: Congdon and Weed, 1984).

Blumenson, Martin, *Patton: The Man Behind the Legend* (New York: Morrow, 1985).

Bradley, Omar N., *A Soldier's Story* (New York: Holt, 1951).

Bradley, Omar N. and Blair, Clay, *A General's Life: An Autobiography* (New York: Simon & Schuster, 1983).

Bryant, Arthur, *The Turn of the Tide: A History of the War Years Based on the Diaries of Field-Marshal Lord Alanbrooke, Chief of the Imperial General Staff* (Garden City, NY: Doubleday, 1957).

Bryant, Arthur, *Triumph in the West: A History of the War Years Based on the Diaries of Field-Marshal Lord Alanbrooke, Chief of the Imperial General Staff* (Garden City, NY: Doubleday, 1959).

Buell, Thomas B., *The Quiet Warrior: A Biography of Admiral Raymond A. Spruance* (Boston: Little, Brown, 1974).

Buell, Thomas B., *Master of Sea Power: A Biography of Fleet Admiral Ernest J. King* (Boston: Little, Brown, 1980).

Butcher, Harry C., *My Three Years with Eisenhower: The Personal Diary of Captain Harry*

C. Butcher, USNR, Naval Aide to General Eisenhower, 1942–1945 (New York: Simon & Schuster, 1946).

Chandler, Alfred D., Jr, The Papers of Dwight David Eisenhower: The War Years, 1941–1945, 5 vols (Baltimore, MD: Johns Hopkins University Press, 1970).

Clark, Mark, Calculated Risk (New York: Harper, 1950).

Coffey, Thomas M., HAP: Military Aviator: The Story of the US Air Force and the Man Who Built It, General Henry H. 'Hap' Arnold (New York: Viking, 1982).

Connell, John, Auchinleck: A Biography of Field-Marshal Sir Claude Auchinleck (London: Cassell, 1959).

Connell, John, Wavell: Scholar and Soldier (London: Collins, 1964).

Cray, Ed, General of the Army: George C. Marshall, Soldier and Statesman (New York: Norton, 1990).

Crosswell, D.K.R., The Chief of Staff: The Military Career of General Walter Bedell Smith (New York: Greenwood, 1991).

Cunningham, Andrew Browne, A Sailor's Odyssey: The Autobiography of Admiral of the Fleet, Viscount Cunningham of Hyndhope (New York: Dutton, 1951).

D'Este, Carlo, Patton: A Genius for War (New York: HarperCollins, 1995).

D'Este, Carlo, Eisenhower: A Soldier's Life (New York: Henry Holt, 2002).

Danchev, Alex, Very Special Relationship: Field-Marshal Sir John Dill and the Anglo-American Alliance, 1941–1944 (Washington, DC: Brassey's, 1986).

Danchev, Alex (ed.), Establishing the Anglo-American Alliance: The Second World War Diaries of Brigadier Vivian Dykes (Washington, DC: Brassey's, 1990).

Danchev, Alex and Todman Daniel, (eds), War Diaries, 1939–1945: Field Marshal Lord Alanbrooke (Berkeley, CA: University of California Press, 2001).

Daso, Dik Alan, Hap Arnold and the Evolution of American Airpower (Washington, DC: Smithsonian Institution Press, 2000).

Davis, Richard G., Carl A. Spaatz and the Air War in Europe (Washington, DC: Center for Air Force History, 1993).

De Guingaud, Francis, Operation Victory (New York: Charles Scribner's Sons, 1947).

Dyer, George C., The Amphibians Came to Conquer: The Story of Admiral Richmond Kelly Turner, 2 vols (Washington, DC: US Government Printing Office, 1969).

Eiler, Keith, Wedemeyer on War and Peace (Stanford, CA: Hoover Institution Press, 1987).

Eisenhower, David, Eisenhower at War, 1943–1945 (New York: Random House, 1986).

Eisenhower, Dwight D., At Ease: Stories I Tell to Friends (Garden City, NY: Doubleday, 1967).

Eisenhower, Dwight D., Crusade in Europe (Garden City, NY: Doubleday, 1948; reprinted by DaCapo, 1988).

Ferrell, Robert H. (ed.), The Eisenhower Diaries (New York: Norton, 1981).

Fraser, David, Alanbrooke (New York: Atheneum, 1982).

Halsey, Willam F. and Bryan, Joseph, Admiral Halsey's Story (New York: Whittlesey House, 1947).

Hamilton, Nigel, Monty, 3 vols (London and New York: McGraw-Hill, 1981–86).

Harris, Arthur, Bomber Offensive (New York: Collins, 1947).

Hobbs, Joseph P., Dear General: Eisenhower's Wartime Letters to Marshall (Baltimore, MD: Johns Hopkins University Press, 1970).

Ismay, Hastings Lionel, The Memoirs of General Lord Ismay (New York: Viking, 1960).

James, D. Clayton, The Years of MacArthur, 3 vols (Boston: Houghton Mifflin, 1970–1985).

James, D. Clayton and Wells, Anne Sharp, A Time for Giants: Politics of the American High Command in World War II (New York: Franklin Watts, 1987).

Keegan, John (ed.), Churchill's Generals (London: Weidenfeld, 1991).

Kennedy, Sir John, The Business of War: The War Narrative of John Kennedy (New York: Morrow, 1958).

Kenney, George C., *General Kenney Reports: A Personal History of the Pacific War* (New York: Duell, 1949).

King, Ernest J. and Whitehill, Walter M., *Fleet Admiral King: A Naval Record* (New York: Norton, 1952).

Larrabee, Eric, *Commander in Chief: Franklin Delano Roosevelt, His Lieutenants, and Their War* (New York: Harper & Row, 1987).

Leahy, William D., *I Was There: The Personal Story of the Chief of Staff to Presidents Roosevelt and Truman Based on his Notes and Diaries Made at the Time* (New York: Whittlesey House, 1950).

Leasor, James and Leslie Hollis, *War at the Top: Based on the Experiences of General Sir Leslie Hollis* (London: Michael Joseph, 1959).

LeMay, Curtis, with MacKinlay Kantor, *Mission with LeMay: My Story* (Garden City, NY: Doubleday, 1965).

Lewin, Ronald, *Slim: The Standard-bearer* (London: Leo Cooper, 1976).

Lewin, Ronald, *The Chief: Field Marshal Lord Wavell, Commander-in-Chief and Viceroy, 1939–1947* (London: Hutchinson, 1980).

MacArthur, Douglas, *Reminiscences* (New York: McGraw-Hill, 1964).

Metz, David R., *Master of Airpower: General Carl A. Spaatz* (Novato, CA: Presidio, 1988).

Montgomery, Bernard Law, *Normandy to the Baltic* (London: Hutchinson, 1947).

Montgomery, Bernard Law, *The Memoirs of Field-Marshal the Viscount Montgomery of Alamein* (London: Collins, 1958).

Morgan, Sir Frederick E., *Overture to Overlord* (Garden City, NY: Doubleday, 1950).

Mountbatten, Louis, *Personal Diary of Admiral the Lord Louis Mountbatten, Supreme Allied Commander, South-East Asia, 1943–1946* (London: Collins, 1988).

Neilland, Robin, *The Bomber War: Arthur Harris and the Allied Bomber Offensive, 1939–1945* (London: Murray, 2001).

Nicolson, N. Alex, *The Life of Field Marshal Earl Alexander of Tunis* (London: Weidenfeld and Nicolson, 1973).

Parrish, Thomas, *Roosevelt and Marshall: Partners in Politics and War* (New York: Morrow, 1989).

Parton, James, *'Air Force Spoken Here': General Ira Eaker and the Command of the Air* (Bethesda, MD: Adler & Adler, 1986).

Patton, George S. *War as I Knew It* (Boston: Houghton Mifflin, 1947, 1975).

Perret, Geoffrey, *Old Soldiers Never Die: The Life of Douglas MacArthur* (New York: Random House, 1996).

Perry, Glen C.H., *'Dear Bart': Washington Views of World War II* (Westport, CT: Greenwood, 1982).

Petillo, Carol Morris, *Douglas MacArthur: The Philippine Years* (Bloomington, IN: Indiana University Press, 1981).

Pogue, Forrest C., *George C. Marshall*, 4 vols (New York: Viking Press, 1963–1987).

Potter, E.B., *Nimitz* (Annapolis, MD: Naval Institute Press, 1976).

Potter, E.B., *Bull Halsey* (Annapolis, MD: Naval Institute Press, 1985).

Richards, Denis, *Portal of Hungerford: the Life of Marshal of the Royal Air Force, Viscount Portal of Hungerford* (London: Heinemann, 1977).

Richardson, Charles, *From Churchill's Secret Circle to the BBC: The Biography of Lieutenant General Sir Ian Jacob* (Washington, DC: Brassey's, 1991).

Rogers, Paul P., *The Bitter Years: MacArthur and Sutherland* (Westport, CT: Greenwood, 1990a).

Rogers, Paul P., *The Good Years: MacArthur and Sutherland* (Westport, CT: Praeger, 1990b).

Schaller, Michael, *Douglas MacArthur: The Far Eastern General* (New York: Oxford University Press, 1989).

Simpson, B. Mitchell, III, *Admiral Harold R. Stark: Architect of Victory, 1939–1945* (Columbia, SC: University of South Carolina Press, 1989).

Simpson, Michael, *The Cunningham Papers: Selections from the Private and Official Correspondence of Admiral of the Fleet Viscount Cunningham of Hyndhope, Vol. 1: The Mediterranean Fleet, 1939–1942* (Brookfield, VT: Ashgate for the Navy Records Society, 1999).

Slessor, John, *The Central Blue: Recollections and Reflections* (London: Cassell, 1957).

Slim, William J., *Defeat into Victory* (New York: D. McKay, 1961).

Smith, Walter Bedell, *Eisenhower's Six Great Decisions* (New York: Longmans, Green, 1956).

Stoler, Mark A., *George C. Marshall: Soldier-Statesman of the American Century* (Boston: Twayne, 1989).

Strong, Kenneth, *Intelligence at the Top: The Recollections of an Intelligence Officer* (Garden City, NY: Doubleday, 1967).

Sunderland, Riley and Romanus, Charles F. (eds), *Stilwell's Personal File: China, Burma, India, 1942–1944*, 5 vols (Wilmington, DE: Scholarly Resources, 1976).

Tedder, Arthur William, *With Prejudice: The War Memoirs of Marshal of the Royal Air Force, Lord Tedder* (Boston: Little, Brown, 1967).

Terraine, John, *The Life and Times of Lord Mountbatten* (London: Hutchinson, 1968).

Tuchman, Barbara, *Stilwell and the American Experience in China, 1911–1945* (New York: Macmillan, 1970).

Wedemeyer, Albert C., *Wedemeyer Reports!* (New York: Holt, 1958).

White, Theodore H. (ed.), *The Stilwell Papers* (New York: W. Sloan Associates, 1948).

Wilson, Henry Maitland, *Eight Years Overseas, 1939–1947* (New York: Hutchinson, 1950).

Ziegler, Philip, *Mountbatten* (New York: Alfred A. Knopf, 1985).

US entry into the war and Anglo-American wartime relations

Abbazia, Patrick, *Mr. Roosevelt's Navy: The Private War of the U.S. Atlantic Fleet, 1939–1942* (Annapolis, MD: Naval Institute Press, 1975).

Bailey, Thomas A. and Ryan, Paul B., *Hitler vs. Roosevelt: The Undeclared Naval War* (New York: Free Press, 1979).

Borg, Dorothy and Okamoto, Shumpei (eds), *Pearl Harbor as History: Japanese-American Relations, 1931–1941* (New York: Columbia University Press, 1973).

Brinkley, Douglas and Facey-Crowther, David R. (eds), *The Atlantic Charter* (New York: St Martin's Press, 1994).

Clarke, Richard, *Anglo-American Economic Collaboration in War and Peace, 1942–1944* (New York: Oxford University Press, 1982).

Compton, James V., *The Swastika and the Eagle: Hitler, the United States and the Origins of World War II* (Boston: Houghton Mifflin, 1967).

Conroy, Hilary and Wray, Harry (eds), *Pearl Harbor Reexamined: Prologue to the Pacific War* (Honolulu: University of Hawaii Press, 1990).

Danchev, Alex, *On Specialness: Essays on Anglo-American Relations* (New York: St Martin's Press, 1998).

Dimbleby, David and Reynolds, David, *An Ocean Apart: The Relationship Between Britain and America in the Twentieth Century* (New York: Random House, 1988).

Divine, Robert A., *The Illusion of Neutrality* (Chicago: University of Chicago Press, 1962).

Divine, Robert A., *The Reluctant Belligerent*, 2nd edn (New York: Wiley, 1979).

Dobson, Alan P., *US Wartime Aid to Britain, 1940–1946* (New York: St Martin's Press, 1986).

Dobson, Alan P., *The Politics of the Anglo-American Economic Special Relationship, 1940–1987* (New York: St Martin's Press, 1987).

Dobson, Alan P., *Peaceful Air Warfare: The Politics of International Aviation* (New York: Oxford University Press, 1991).

Dobson, Alan P., *Anglo-American Relations in the Twentieth Century: of Friendship, Conflict, and the Rise and Decline of Superpowers* (New York: Routledge, 1995).

Dunn, Walter Scott, Jr., *Second Front Now, 1943* (University, AL: University of Alabama Press, 1980).

Eisenhower, John D., *Allies: Pearl Harbor to D-Day* (Garden City, NY: Doubleday, 1982).

Farrell, Brian P., *The Basis and Making of British Grand Strategy, 1940–1943: Was There a Plan?* 2 vols (Lewiston, NY: Edwin Mellen, 1998).

Feis, Herbert, *The Road to Pearl Harbor: The Coming of War between the United States and Japan* (Princeton, NJ: Princeton University Press, 1950).

Friendlander, Saul, *Prelude to Downfall: Hitler and the United States, 1939–1941* (New York: Alfred A. Knopf, 1967).

Goodhart, Philip, *Fifty Ships That Saved the World: The Foundation of the Anglo-American Alliance* (Garden City, NY: Doubleday, 1965).

Grigg, John, *1943, The Victory That Never Was* (New York: Hill and Wang, 1980).

Hathaway, Robert M., *Ambiguous Partnership: Britain and America, 1944–1947* (New York: Columbia University Press, 1981).

Hearden, Patrick J., *Roosevelt Confronts Hitler: America's Entry into World War II* (DeKalb, IL: Northern Illinois University Press, 1987).

Heinrichs, Waldo, *Threshold of War: Franklin D. Roosevelt and American Entry into World War II* (New York: Oxford University Press, 1988).

Hess, Gary R., *America Encounters India, 1941–1947* (Baltimore, MD: Johns Hopkins University Press, 1971).

Higgins, Trumbull, *Winston Churchill and the Second Front, 1940–1943* (New York: Oxford University Press, 1957).

Higgins, Trumbull, *Soft Underbelly: The Anglo-American Controversy over the Italian Campaign, 1943–1945* (New York: Macmillan, 1968).

Howard, Michael, *The Mediterranean Strategy in the Second World War* (New York: Praeger, 1968).

Iriye, Akira, *The Origins of the Second World War: Asia and the Pacific* (London: Longman, 1987).

Jones, Matthew, *Britain, the United States and the Mediterranean War, 1942–1944* (New York: St Martin's Press, 1996).

Kimball, Warren F., *The Most Unsordid Act: Lend-Lease, 1939–1941* (Baltimore, MD: Johns Hopkins University Press, 1969).

LaFeber, Walter, *The Clash: U.S.-Japanese Relations Throughout History* (New York: Norton, 1997).

Langer, William L. and Gleason, S. Everett, *The World Crisis of 1937 and American Foreign Policy, Vol. 1: The Challenge to Isolation, 1937–1940* and *Vol. 2: The Undeclared War, 1940–1941* (New York: 1952–53, Peter Smith reprint, 1970).

Leutze, James R., *Bargaining for Supremacy: Anglo-American Naval Collaboration, 1937–1941* (Chapel Hill, NC: University of North Carolina Press, 1977).

Louis, William Roger, *Imperialism at Bay: The United States and the Decolonization of the British Empire, 1941–1945* (New York: Oxford University Press, 1978).

Lowenthal, Mark M., *Leadership and Indecision: American War Planning and Policy Process, 1937–1942*, 2 vols (New York: Garland, 1988).

Lukacs, John, *Five Days in London, May 1940* (New Haven, CT: Yale University Press, 1999).

Moser, John E., *Twisting the Lion's Tail: American Anglophobia between the World Wars* (New York: New York University Press, 1999).

Nicholas, H.G., *The United States and Britain* (Chicago: University of Chicago Press, 1975).

Offner, Arnold A., *The Origins of the Second World War: American Foreign Policy and World Politics, 1917–1941* (New York: Praeger, 1975).

Prange, Gordon W., *At Dawn We Slept: The Untold Story of Pearl Harbor* (New York: McGraw-Hill, 1981).

Prange, Gordon W., *Pearl Harbor: The Verdict of History* (New York: McGraw-Hill, 1986).

Renwick, Robin, *Fighting with Allies: America and Britain in Peace and at War* (New York: Times Books, 1996).

Reynolds, David, *The Creation of the Anglo-American Alliance, 1937–1941: A Study in Competitive Co-operation* (Chapel Hill, NC: University of North Carolina Press, 1981).

Reynolds, David, 'Roosevelt, Churchill, and the Wartime Anglo-American Alliance, 1939–1945', in William Roger Louis and Hedley Bull (eds), *The Special Relationship: Anglo-American Relations Since 1945*, (New York: Oxford University Press, 1986), 17–41.

Reynolds, David, *From Munich to Pearl Harbor: Roosevelt's America and the Origins of the Second World War* (Chicago: Ivan R. Dee, 2001).

Rock, William R., *Chamberlain and Roosevelt* (Columbus, OH: Ohio State University Press, 1988).

Ross, Steven T. (ed.), *American War Plans, 1919–1941* 5 vols (New York: Garland, 1992).

Ross, Steven T. (ed.), *US War Plans, 1938–1945* (Boulder, CO: Lynne Rienner, 2002).

Sainsbury, Keith, *The North African Landings, 1942: A Strategic Decision* (London: Davis-Poynter, 1976).

Schroeder, Paul W., *The Axis Alliance and Japanese-American Relations, 1941* (Ithaca, NY: Cornell University Press, 1958).

Shogan, Robert, *Hard Bargain: How FDR Twisted Churchill's Arm, Evaded the Law, and Changed the Role of the American Presidency* (New York: Scribner, 1995).

Smith, Kevin, *Conflict over Convoys: Anglo-American Logistics Diplomacy in the Second World War* (New York: Cambridge University Press, 1996).

Steele, Richard W., *The First Offensive 1942: Roosevelt, Marshall and the Making of American Strategy* (Bloomington, IN: Indiana University Press, 1973).

Stoler, Mark A., *The Politics of the Second Front: American Military Planning and Diplomacy in Coalition Warfare, 1941–1943* (Westport, CT: Greenwood, 1977).

Stoler, Mark A., *Allies and Adversaries: The Joint Chiefs of Staff, the Grand Alliance, and U.S. Strategy in World War II* (Chapel Hill, NC: University of North Carolina Press, 2000).

Thorne, Christopher, *Allies of a Kind: The United States, Britain, and the War Against Japan* (New York: Oxford University Press, 1978).

Trefousse, Hans L., *Germany and American Neutrality, 1939–1941* (New York: Bookman, 1951).

Utley, Jonathan, *Going to War with Japan* (Knoxville, TN: University of Tennessee Press, 1985).

Watt, Donald Cameron, *Succeeding John Bull: America in Britain's Place, 1900–1975: A Study of the Anglo-American Relationship and World Politics in the Context of British and American Foreign-Policy-Making in the Twentieth Century* (New York: Cambridge University Press, 1984).

Weiss, Steve, *Allies in Conflict: Anglo-American Strategic Negotiations, 1938–1944* (New York: St Martin's Press, 1996).

Wilmot, Chester, *The Struggle for Europe* (New York: Harper, 1952).

Wilson, Theodore A., *The First Summit: Roosevelt and Churchill at Placentia Bay, 1941* 2nd edn (Lawrence, KS: University Press of Kansas, 1991).

Woods, Randall B., *A Changing of the Guard: Anglo-American Relations, 1941–1946* (Chapel Hill, NC: University of North Carolina Press, 1990).

The Grand Alliance, Allied conferences and post-war planning

Anderson, Terry H., *The United States, Great Britain, and the Cold War, 1944–1947* (Columbia, MO: University of Missouri Press, 1981).

Beitzell, Robert, *The Uneasy Alliance: America, Britain, and Russia, 1941–1943* (New York: Alfred A. Knopf, 1972).

Buhite, Russell D., *Decisions at Yalta: An Appraisal of Summit Diplomacy* (Wilmington, DE: Scholarly Resources, 1986).

Campbell, Thomas M., *Masquerade Peace: America's UN Policy, 1944–1945* (Tallahassee, FL: Florida State University Press, 1973).

Clemens, Diane Shaver, *Yalta* (New York: Oxford University Press, 1970).

Dormael, Armand van, *Bretton Woods: Birth of a Monetary System* (New York: Holmes and Meier, 1978).

Eckes, Alfred, *A Search for Solvency: Bretton Woods and the International Monetary System, 1941–1971* (Austin, TX: University of Texas Press, 1975).

Edmonds, Robin, *The Big Three: Churchill, Roosevelt, and Stalin in Peace and War* (New York: Norton, 1991).

Eubank, Keith, *Summit at Teheran* (New York: Morrow, 1985).

Feis, Herbert, *Churchill, Roosevelt, Stalin: The War They Waged and the Peace They Sought* (Princeton, NJ: Princeton University Press, 1957).

Feis, Herbert, *Between War and Peace: The Potsdam Conference* (Princeton, NJ: Princeton University Press, 1960).

Gardner, Lloyd C., *Spheres of Influence: The Great Powers Partition Europe, from Munich to Yalta* (Chicago, Ivan R. Dee, 1993).

Gardner, Richard N., *Sterling Dollar Diplomacy: Anglo-American Collaboration in the Reconstruction of Multilateral Trade,* rev. edn (New York: Mc-Graw Hill, 1956, 1969); (new expanded edn, New York: Columbia University Press, 1980, under new title of *Sterling Dollar Diplomacy in Current Perspective: The Origins and Prospects of Our International Economic Order*).

Harbutt, Fraser, *The Iron Curtain: Churchill, America, and the Origins of the Cold War* (New York: Oxford University Press, 1986).

Hearden, Patrick, *Architects of Globalism: Building a New World Order During World War II* (Fayetteville, AK: University of Arkansas Press, 2002).

Herring, George C., *Aid to Russia: Strategy, Diplomacy and the Origins of the Cold War* (New York: Columbia University Press, 1973).

Hilderbrand, Robert C., *Dumbarton Oaks: The Origins of the United Nations and the Search for Post-war Security* (Chapel Hill, NC: University of North Carolina Press, 1990).

Hoopes, Townsend and Brinkley, Douglas, *FDR and the Creation of the U.N.* (New Haven, CT: Yale University Press, 1997).

Kimball, Warren F. (ed.), *Swords or Ploughshares? The Morgenthau Plan for Defeated Nazi Germany, 1943–1946* (Philadelphia, PA: Lippincott, 1976).

King, F.P., *The New Internationalism: Allied Policy and the European Peace, 1939–1945* (Hamden, CT: Archon Books, 1973).

Kolko, Gabriel, *The Politics of War: The World and United States Foreign Policy, 1943–1945* (New York: Random House, 1968).

Lane, Ann and Temperly, Howard (eds), *The Rise and Fall of the Grand Alliance, 1941–1945* (New York: St Martin's Press, 1995).

Lukacs, John, *1945: Year Zero* (Garden City, NY: Doubleday, 1978).

Mastny, Vojtech, *Russia's Road to the Cold War: Diplomacy, Warfare, and the Politics of Communism, 1941–1945* (New York: Columbia University Press, 1979).

Mayle, Paul D., *Eureka Summit: Agreement in Principle and the Big Three at Teheran, 1943* (Newark, DE: University of Delaware Press, 1987).

McNeill, William H., *America, Britain and Russia: Their Cooperation and Conflict, 1941–1946* (New York: Oxford University Press, 1953).

Mee, Charles L., *Meeting at Potsdam* (New York: M. Evans, 1975).

Nadeau, Remi, *Stalin, Churchill and Roosevelt Divide Europe* (New York: Praeger, 1990).

Neumann, William L., *After Victory: Churchill, Roosevelt, Stalin and the Making of the Peace* (New York: Harper and Row, 1967).

O'Connor, Raymond G., *Diplomacy for Victory: FDR and Unconditional Surrender* (New York: Norton, 1971).

Offner, Arnold A. and Wilson, Theodore A. (eds), *Victory in Europe 1945: From World War to Cold War* (Lawrence, KS: University Press of Kansas, 2000).

Olla, Paola Brundu (ed.), *Yalta* (Rome: Edizioni dell'Ateneo Provincia di Cagliari, 1988).

Reynolds, David, Kimball, Warren F. and Chubarian, A.O., *Allies at War: The Soviet, American and British Experience, 1939–1945* (New York: St Martin's Press, 1994).

Russell, Ruth B., *A History of the United Nations Charter: The Role of the United States, 1940–1945* (Washington, DC: Brookings Institution, 1958).

Sainsbury, Keith, *The Turning Point: Roosevelt, Stalin, Churchill, and Chiang Kai-shek, 1943: The Moscow, Cairo and Teheran Conferences* (Oxford: Oxford University Press, 1985).

Schaller, Michael, *The U.S. Crusade in China, 1938–1945* (New York: Columbia University Press, 1978).

Schild, Georg, *Bretton Woods and Dumbarton Oaks: American Economic and Political Post-war Planning in the Summer of 1944* (New York: St Martin's Press, 1995).

Smith, Gaddis, *American Diplomacy during the Second World War*, 2nd edn (New York: McGraw-Hill, 1985).

Snell, John, *Illusion and Necessity: The Diplomacy of Global War, 1939–1945* (Boston: Houghton Mifflin, 1963).

Snell, John L., *et al.*, *The Meaning of Yalta: Big Three Diplomacy and the Balance of Power* (Baton Rouge, LA: Louisiana State University Press, 1956).

Theoharis, Athan, *The Yalta Myths: An Issue in U.S. Politics, 1945–1955* (Columbia, MO: University of Missouri Press, 1970).

Watt, Donald Cameron, 'Britain and the Historiography of the Yalta Conference and the Cold War', *Diplomatic History* 13 (Winter 1989): 67–98.

Wheeler-Bennett, John, and Nichols, Anthony, *The Semblance of Peace: The Political Settlement after the Second World War* (New York: St Martin's Press, 1972).

Woolner, David B. (ed.), *The Second Quebec Conference Revisited: Waging War, Formulating Peace: Canada, Great Britain and the United States, 1944–1945* (New York: St Martin's Press, 1988).

Economic mobilization and the home fronts

Addison, Paul, *The Road to 1945: British Politics and the Second World War* (London: Quartet, 1975).

Blum, John Morton, *V Was for Victory: Politics and American Culture during World War II* (New York: Harcourt Brace Jovanovich, 1976).

Calder, Angus, *The People's War: Britain, 1939–1945* (New York: Pantheon, 1969).

Catton, Bruce, *The War Lords of Washington* (New York: Harcourt, Brace, 1948).

Eiler, Keith, *Mobilizing America: Robert P. Patterson and the War Effort, 1940–1945* (Ithaca, NY: Cornell University Press, 1997).

Goodwin, Doris Kearns, *No Ordinary Time: Franklin and Eleanor Roosevelt: The Home Front* (New York: Simon and Schuster, 1994).

Hancock, W.K. and Gowing, M.M., *The British War Economy* (London: His Majesty's Stationery Office, 1949).

Harrison, Mark (ed.), *The Economics of World War II: Six Great Powers in International Comparison* (Cambridge: Cambridge University Press, 1998).

Janeway, Eliot, *The Struggle for Survival* (New York: Weybright and Tauey, 1951).

Jeffries, Kevin, *The Churchill Coalition and Wartime Politics* (New York: St Martin's Press, 1991).

Kennedy, David, *Freedom from Fear: The American People in Depression and War* (New York: Oxford University Press, 1999).

Lingemann, Richard, *Don't You Know There's a War On? The American Home Front, 1941–1945* (New York: Putnam, 1970).

Marwick, Arthur, *The Home Front: The British and the Second World War* (London: Thames and Hudson, 1976).

Milward, Alan S., *War, Economy and Society, 1939–1945* (Berkeley, CA: University of California Press, 1977).

Nelson, Donald, *Arsenal of Democracy: The Story of American War Production* (New York: Harcourt Brace Jovanovich, 1946).

O'Neill, William, *A Democracy at War: America's Fight at Home and Abroad in World War II* (New York: Free Press, 1993).

Perrett, Geoffrey, *Days of Sadness, Years of Triumph: The American People, 1939–1945* (New York: Coward, McCann and Geoghegan, 1973).

Polenberg, Richard, *War and Society: The United States 1941–1945* (Philadelphia, PA: Lippincott, 1972).

Postan, Michael M., *British War Production* (London: Her Majesty's Stationery Office, 1952).

Reynolds, David, *Rich Relations: The American Occupation of Britain, 1942–1945* (New York: Random House, 1995).

Smith, Harold (ed.), *War and Social Change: British Society in the Second World War* (New York: St Martin's Press, 1986).

Vatter, Harold G., *The U.S. Economy in World War II* (New York: Columbia University Press, 1985).

Winkler, Allan, *Home Front USA: America during World War II*, 2nd edn (Arlington Heights, IL: Harlan-Davidson, 2000).

The scientific and intelligence revolutions

Aldrich, Richard J., *Intelligence and the War Against Japan: Britain, America and the Politics of Secret Service* (New York: Cambridge University Press, 2000).

Alvarez, David J. (ed.), *Allied and Axis Signals Intelligence in World War II* (Portland, OR: Frank Cass, 1999).

Alvarez, David J., *Secret Messages: Codebreaking and American Diplomacy, 1930–1945* (Lawrence, KS: University Press of Kansas, 2000).

Ambrose, Steven E., with Richard H. Immerman, *Ike's Spies: Eisenhower and the Espionage Establishment* (Garden City, NY: Doubleday, 1981).

Bath, Alan Harris, *Tracking the Axis Enemy: The Triumph of Anglo-American Naval Intelligence* (Lawrence, KS: University Press of Kansas, 1998).

Bennett, Ralph, *Ultra in the West: The Normandy Campaign, 1944–45* (New York: Scribner, 1979).

Bennett, Ralph, *Ultra and Mediterranean Strategy* (New York: Morrow, 1989).

Boyd, Carl, *Hitler's Japanese Confidant: General Oshima Hiroshi and Magic Intelligence, 1941–1945* (Lawrence, KS: University Press of Kansas, 1993).

Budiansky, Stephen, *Battle of Wits: The Complete Story of Codebreaking in World War II* (New York: Free Press, 2000).

Calvocoressi, Peter, *Top Secret Ultra* (New York: Pantheon, 1980).

Cave-Brown, Anthony, *Bodyguard of Lies* (New York: Harper & Row, 1975).

Chalou, George C. (ed.), *The Secrets War: The Office of Strategic Services in World War II* (Washington, DC: National Archives and Records Administration, 1992).

Clark, Richard W., *The Man Who Broke Purple: The Life of Colonel William F. Friedman, Who Deciphered the Japanese Code in World War II* (Boston: Little, Brown, 1977).

Cochran, Alexander S., Jr, *The MAGIC Diplomatic Summaries: A Chronological Finding Aid* (New York: Garland, 1982).

Drea, Edward, *MacArthur's ULTRA: Code-breaking and the War Against Japan* (Lawrence, KS: University Press of Kansas, 1992).

Dulles, Alan, *The Secret Surrender* (New York: Harper & Row, 1966).

Foot, M.R.D., *SOE in France* (London: Her Majesty's Stationery Office, 1966).

Foot, M.R.D., *SOE: An Outline History of the Special Operations Executive, 1940–1946* (London: BBC, 1984).

Gardner, W.J.R., *Decoding History: The Battle of the Atlantic and Ultra* (Annapolis, MD: Naval Institute Press, 1999).

Handel, Michael I. (ed.), *Strategic and Operational Deception in the Second World War* (Totowa, NJ: Frank Cass, 1987).

Handel, Michael I. (ed.), *Leaders and Intelligence* (London: Frank Cass, 1989).

Handel, Michael I. (ed.), *Intelligence and Military Operations* (Portland, OR: Frank Cass, 1990).

Hinsley, F.H., *British Intelligence during the Second World War*, 5 vols in 6 (New York: Cambridge University Press, 1979–1990) and one-volume abridgement (1993).

Hinsley, Francis H. and Stripp Alan, (eds), *Codebreakers: The Inside Story of Bletchley Park* (Oxford: Oxford University Press, 1993).

Holt, Thaddeus, *The Deceivers: Allied Military Intelligence in the Second World War* (New York: Scribner, 2004).

Jakub, Jay, *Spies and Saboteurs: Anglo-American Collaboration and Rivalry in Human Intelligence Collection and Special Operations, 1940–45* (New York: St Martin's Press, 1999).

Jones, R.V., *The Wizard War: British Scientific Intelligence, 1939–1945* (New York: Coward, McCann, and Geoghegan, 1978).

Kahn, David, *Seizing the Enigma: The Race to Break the German U-Boat Codes, 1939–1943* (Boston: Houghton Mifflin, 1991).

Kahn, David, *The Codebreakers: The Story of Secret Writing*, rev. edn (New York: Scribner, 1996).

Langhorne, Richard (ed.), *Diplomacy and Intelligence during the Second World War: Essays in Honor of F.H. Hinsley* (New York: Cambridge University Press, 1985).

Lewin, Ronald, *Ultra Goes to War: The First Account of World War II's Greatest Secret Based on Official Documents* (New York: McGraw-Hill, 1978).

Lewin, Ronald, *The American Magic: Codes, Ciphers and the Defeat of Japan* (New York: Farrar Straus Giroux, 1982).

Masterman, J.C., *The Double-Cross System in the War of 1939 to 1945* (New Haven, CT: Yale University Press, 1972).

Montagu, Ewen, *The Man Who Never Was* (New York: Lippincott, 1954).

Parrish, Thomas, *The Ultra Americans: The US Role in Ultra* (Chelsea, MI: Scarborough House, 1991).

Persico, Joseph E., *Roosevelt's Secret War: FDR and World War II Espionage* (New York: Random House, 2001).

Prados, John, *Combined Fleet Decoded: The Secret History of American Intelligence and the Japanese Navy in World War II* (New York: Random House, 1995).

Smith, Michael, *The Emperor's Codes: The Breaking of Japan's Secret Ciphers* (New York: Arcade, 2001).

Smith, Bradley F., *The Ultra-Magic Deals and the Most Secret Special Relationship, 1940–1946* (Novato, CA: Presidio, 1993).

Smith, Bradley F., *Sharing Secrets with Stalin: How the Allies Traded Intelligence, 1941–1945* (Lawrence, KS: University Press of Kansas, 1996).

Smith, R. Harris, *OSS: The Secret History of America's First Central Intelligence Agency* (Berkeley, CA: University of California Press, 1972).

Stafford, David, *Britain and European Resistance, 1940–1945: A Survey of the SOE* (London: Macmillan, 1980).

Stafford, David, *Camp X* (New York: Dodd, Mead, 1986).

Stafford, David, *Roosevelt and Churchill: Men of Secrets* (New York: Overlook Press, 2000).

Stephenson, William S. (ed.), *British Security Coordination: The Secret History of British Intelligence in the Americas, 1940–1945* (New York: Fromm International, 1999).

Stevenson, William, *A Man Called Intrepid* (New York: Harcourt Brace Jovanovich, 1976).

West, Nigel, *MI5, British Security Operations, 1909–1945* (London: Bodley Head, 1981).

West, Nigel, *MI6, British Secret Intelligence Service Operations, 1909–1945* (New York: Random House, 1984).

Winston, John, *ULTRA at Sea: How Breaking the Nazi Code Affected Allied Naval Strategy* (New York: Morrow, 1988).

Winterbotham, F.W., *The Ultra Secret* (New York: Harper & Row, 1974).

Wohlstetter, Roberta, *Pearl Harbor: Warning and Decision* (Stanford, CA: Stanford University Press, 1962).

Campaigns and operations: Europe, the Mediterranean and the Atlantic

Ambrose, Steven, *D-Day, June 6, 1944: The Climactic Battle of World War II* (New York: Simon & Schuster, 1994).

Ambrose, Steven, *Citizen Soldiers: The US Army from the Normandy Beaches to the Bulge to the Surrender of Germany, June 7, 1977–May 7, 1945* (New York: Simon & Schuster, 1997).

Astor, Gerald, *The Bloody Forest: Battle for the Huertgen: September 1944–1945* (Novato, CA: Presidio, 2000).

Atkinson, Rick, *An Army at Dawn: The War in North Africa, 1942–1943* (New York: Henry Holt, 2002).

Biddle, Tami Davis, *Rhetoric and Reality in Air Warfare: The Evolution of British and American Ideas About Strategic Bombing, 1914–1945* (Princeton, NJ: Princeton University Press, 2002).

Blumenson, Martin, *The Battle of the Generals: The Untold Story of the Falaise Pocket – The Campaign That Should Have Won World War II* (New York: Morrow, 1993).

Boog, Horst (ed.), *The Conduct of the Air War in the Second World War: An International Comparison* (New York: Oxford University Press, 1992).

Botjer, George F., *The Sideshow War: The Italian Campaign, 1943–1945* (College Station, TX: Texas A&M University Press, 1996).

Brower, Charles F., IV (ed.), *World War II: The Final Years* (New York: St Martin's Press, 1998).

Bungay, Stephen, *The Most Dangerous Enemy* (London: Aurum, 2000).

Carver, Michael, *Dilemmas of the Desert War: A New Look at the Libyan Campaign, 1940–1942* (Bloomington, IN: Indiana University Press, 1986).

Copp, DeWitt S., *Forged in Fire: Strategy and Decisions in the Air War over Europe, 1940–1945* (Garden City, NY: Doubleday, 1982).

Crane, Conrad C., *Bombs, Cities and Civilians: American Airpower Strategy in World War II* (Lawrence, KS: University Press of Kansas, 1993).

D'Este, Carlo, *World War II in the Mediterranean, 1942–1945* (Chapel Hill, NC: Algonquin, 1990).

D'Este, Carlo, *Decision in Normandy* (New York: Dutton, 1994).

Doubler, Michael, *Closing with the Enemy: How GIs Fought the War in Europe, 1944–1945* (Lawrence, KS: University Press of Kansas, 1994).

Dulles, Allen, *The Secret Surrender* (New York: Harper & Row, 1966).

Dupuy, Trevor N., Bongard, David L., and Anderson, Richard C., *Hitler's Last Gamble: The Battle of the Bulge, December 1944–January 1945* (New York: HarperCollins, 1994).

Funk, Arthur L., *The Politics of TORCH: The Allied Landings and the Algiers Putsch, 1942* (Lawrence, KS: University Press of Kansas, 1974).

Gannon, Michael, *Operation Drumbeat* (New York: Harper & Row, 1990).

Garrett, Stephen A., *Ethics and Airpower in World War II: The British Bombing of German Cities* (New York: St Martin's Press, 1993).

Gelb, Norman, *Desperate Venture: The Story of Operation Torch, the Allied Invasion of North Africa* (New York: Morrow, 1992).

Gentile, Gian P., *How Effective in Strategic Bombing? Lessons Learned from World War II to Kosovo* (New York: New York University Press, 2001).

Graham, Dominick and Bidwell, Sheldon *Tug of War: The Battle for Italy, 1943–1945* (New York: St Martin's Press, 1986).

Hapgood, David and Richardson, David, *Monte Cassino* (New York: Congdon & Weed, 1984).

Hart, Russell A., *Clash of Arms: How the Allies Won in Normandy* (Boulder, CO: Lynne Rienner, 2001).

Harvey, A.D., *Arnhem* (London: Cassell, 2001).

Hastings, Max, *Bomber Command* (New York: Dial Press, 1979).

Hastings, Max, *Overlord: D-Day and the Climactic Battle for Normandy* (New York: Simon & Schuster, 1984).

Holland, Jeffrey, *The Aegean Mission: Allied Operations in the Dodecanese, 1943* (New York: Greenwood, 1988).

Hughes, Thomas, *Overlord: General Pete Quesada and the Triumph of Tactical Airpower in World War II* (New York: Free Press, 1995).

Keegan, John, *Six Armies at Normandy* (New York: Viking, 1982).

Lamb, Richard, *War in Italy, 1943–1945: A Brutal Story* (New York: St Martin's Press, 1993).

Levine, Alan J., *The Strategic Bombing of Germany, 1940–1945* (New York, Praeger, 1992).

Levine, Alan J., *From the Normandy Beaches to the Baltic Sea: The Northwest Europe Campaign, 1944–1945* (Westport, CT: Praeger/Greenwood, 2000).

Lewis, Adrian R., *Omaha Beach: A Flawed Victory* (Chapel Hill, NC: University of North Carolina Press, 2001).

Lucas, James, *War in the Desert: The Eighth Army at El Alamein* (New York: Beaufort, 1983).

MacDonald, Charles B., *Mighty Endeavor: The American War in Europe* (New York: Oxford University Press, 1969).

MacIsaac, David, *Strategic Bombing in World War II: The Story of the Strategic Bombing Survey* (New York: Garland, 1976a).

MacIsaac, David, *The United States Strategic Bombing Survey*, 10 vols (New York: Garland, 1976b).

Mansour, Peter R., *The GI Offensive in Europe: The Triumph of American Infantry Divisions, 1941–1945* (Lawrence, KS: University Press of Kansas, 1999).

May, Ernest R., *Strange Victory: Hitler's Conquest of France* (New York: Hill and Wang, 2000).

McFarland, Stephen L. and Newton, Wesley Phillips, *To Command the Sky: The Battle for Air Superiority over Germany, 1942–1944* (Washington, DC: Smithsonian Institution Press, 1991).

McKee, Alexander, *Caen: Anvil of Victory* (London: Souvenir, 1964).

Messenger, Charles, *'Bomber' Harris and the Strategic Bombing Offensive, 1939–1945* (New York: St Martin's Press, 1984).

Messenger, Charles, *The Tunisian Campaign* (London: Ian Allen, 1982).

Messenger, Charles, *The Second World War in the West* (London: Cassell, 1999).

Middlebrook, Martin, *Arnhem 1944: The Airborne Battle, 17–26 September* (Boulder, CO: Westview, 1994).

Miller, Nathan, *War at Sea: A Naval History of World War II* (New York: Oxford University Press, 1995).

Morris, Eric, *Circles of Hell: The War in Italy, 1943–1945* (New York: Crown, 1993).

Murray, Patrick G.E., *Eisenhower versus Montgomery: The Continuing Debate* (Westport, CT: Praeger/Greenwood, 1996).

Murray, Williamson, *Strategy for Defeat: The Luftwaffe, 1933–1945* (Maxwell, AL: Air University Press, 1983).

Overy, Richard J., *The Air War, 1939–1945* (New York: Stein and Day, 1980).

Overy, Richard J., *The Battle of Britain: The Myth and the Reality* (New York: W.W. Norton, 2001).

Parish, Michael W., *Aegean Adventures, 1940–1943: And the End of Churchill's Dream* (Sussex: Book Guild, 1993).

Ray, John, *The Battle of Britain: New Perspectives* (London: Arms and Armour, 1994).

Runyan, Timothy J. and Capes Jan M. (eds), *To Die Gallantly: The Battle of the Atlantic* (Boulder, CO: Westview Press, 1994).

Ryan, Cornelius, *The Longest Day* (New York: Simon & Schuster, 1959).

Ryan, Cornelius, *A Bridge Too Far* (New York: Simon & Schuster, 1974).

Schaffer, Ronald, *Wings of Judgment: American Bombing in World War II* (New York: Oxford University Press, 1985).

Sheehan, Fred, *Anzio: Epic of Bravery* (Norman, OK: University of Oklahoma Press, 1994).

Shennan, Andrew, *The Fall of France, 1940* (London: Longman, 2000).

Sherry, Michael S., *The Rise of American Airpower: The Creation of Armaggedon* (New Haven, CT: Yale University Press, 1987).

Smith, Bradley F. and Rossi, Elena Aga, *Operation Sunrise: The Secret Surrender* (New York: Basic Books, 1979).

Syrett, David, *The Defeat of the German U-Boats: The Battle of the Atlantic* (Columbia: University of South Carolina Press, 1994).

Taylor, Telford, *March of Conquest: The German Victories in Western Europe, 1940* (New York: Simon & Schuster, 1958).

Terraine, John, *A Time for Courage: The Royal Air Force in the European War, 1939–1945* (New York: Macmillan, 1985).

Terraine, John, *The U-Boat War, 1916–1945* (New York: Putnam, 1989).

Tomblin, Barbara Brooks, *With Utmost Spirit: Allied Naval Operations in the Mediterranean, 1942–1945* (Lexington, KY: University Press of Kentucky, 2004).

Van der Vat, Dan, *The Atlantic Campaign: World War II's Great Struggle at Sea* (New York: Harper & Row, 1988).

Villa, Brian Loring, *Unauthorized Action: Mountbatten and the Dieppe* Raid (New York: Oxford University Press, 1989).

Waddell, Steve R., *United States Army Logistics: The Normandy Campaign, 1944* (Westport, CT: Greenwood, 1994).

Weigley, Russell F., *Eisenhower's Lieutenants: The Campaigns of France and Germany, 1944–1945* (Bloomington, IN: Indiana University Press, 1981).

Wilson, Theodore A. (ed.), *D-Day 1944* (Lawrence, KS: University Press of Kansas, 1994).

Wilt, Alan F., *The French Riviera Campaign of August 1944* (Carbondale, IL: Southern Illinois University Press, 1981).

Wright, Robin, *Dowding and the Battle of Britain* (London: MacDonald, 1969).

Asia and the Pacific

Alexander, John H., *Utmost Savagery: The Three Days at Tarawa* (Annapolis, MD: Naval Institute Press, 1995).

Allen, Louis, *Burma: The Longest War, 1941–1945* (New York: St Martin's Press, 1984).

Allen, Louis, *Singapore, 1941–42* (London: Cass, 1993).

Allen, Thomas B. and Polmar, Norman, *Code-Name Downfall: The Secret Plan to Invade Japan and Why Truman Dropped the Bomb* (New York: Simon & Schuster, 1995).

Alperowitz, Gar, *Atomic Diplomacy: Hiroshima and Potsdam: The Uses of the Atomic Bomb and the American Confrontation with Soviet Power* (New York: Vintage, 1965, 1985).

Alperowitz, Gar, *The Decision to Use the Atomic Bomb and the Architecture of an American Myth* (New York: Knopf, 1995).

Belote, James and Belote, William, *Typhoon of Steel: The Batttle for Okinawa* (New York: Harper & Row, 1970).

Belote, James and Belote, William, *Titans of the Seas: The Development and Operation of American Carrier Task Forces during World War II* (New York: Harper & Row, 1975).

Bergerud, Eric, *Touched with Fire: The Land War in the South Pacific* (New York: Viking, 1996).

Bernstein, Barton J., 'Roosevelt, Truman, and the Atomic Bomb, 1941–1945: A Reinterpretation', *Political Science Quarterly* 90 (Spring 1975): 23–69.

Bernstein, Barton J., 'The Uneasy Alliance: Roosevelt, Churchill, and the Atomic Bomb, 1940–1945', *Western Political Quarterly* 29:2 (1976): 202–30.

Bernstein, Baron J., 'Understanding the Atomic Bomb and the Japanese Surrender: Missed Opportunities, Little-Known Disasters, and Modern Memory', *Diplomatic History* 19 (Spring 1995): 227–73.

Blair, Clay, Jr, *Silent Victory: The U.S. Submarine War Against Japan* (Philadelphia, PA: Lippincott, 1975).

Brett-James, Anthony and Evans, G.C., *Imphal* (London: Macmillan, 1962).

Butow, Robert J.C., *Japan's Decision to Surrender* (Stanford, CA: Stanford University Press, 1954).

Callahan, Raymond, *The Worst Disaster: The Fall of Singapore* (Newark, DE: University of Delaware Press, 1977).

Callahan, Raymond, *Burma, 1942–1945* (London: Davis-Poynter, 1978).

Campbell, A.F., *The Siege: A Story from Kohima* (London: Allen, 1956).

Connaughton, Richard, *MacArthur and Defeat in the Philippines* (Woodstock, NY: Overlook, 2001).

Costello, John, *The Pacific War 1941–1945* (New York: Rawson, 1981).

Cutler, Thomas J., *The Battle of Leyte Gulf: 23–26 October 1944* (New York: HarperCollins, 1994).

DeRose, James, *Unrestricted Warfare: How a New Breed of Officers Led the Submarine Force to Victory in World War II* (New York: Wiley, 2000).

Dower, John, *War Without Mercy: Race and Power in the Pacific War* (New York: Pantheon, 1986).

Dunnigan, James F., *Victory at Sea: World War II in the Pacific* (New York: Morrow, 1995).

Falk, Stanley L., *Seventy Days to Singapore: The Malayan Campaign, 1941–1942* (New York: G.P. Putnam's Sons, 1975).

Frank, Richard B., *Guadalcanal: The Definitive Account of the Landmark Battle* (New York: Random House, 1990).

Frank, Richard B., *Downfall: The End of the Imperial Japanese Empire* (New York: Random House, 1999).

Friedman, Kenneth J., *Afternoon of the Rising Sun: The Battle of Leyte Gulf* (Novato, CA: Presidio, 2001).

Gailey, Harry A., *The War in the Pacific: From Pearl Harbor to Tokyo Bay* (Novato, CA: Presidio, 1995).

Gowing, Margaret, *Britain and Atomic Energy, 1939–1945* (New York: St Martin's Press, 1964).

Groves, Leslie R., *Now It Can Be Told: The Story of the Manhattan Project* (New York: DaCapo, 1983).

Hallas, James H., *The Devil's Anvil: The Assault on Peleliu* (Westport, CT: Praeger, 1994).

Hewlett, Richard B. and Anderson, Jr, Oscar E., *A History of the Atomic Energy Commission, Vol. 1: The New World, 1939–1946* (University Park, PA: Pennsylvania State University Press, 1962).

Hogan, Michael J. (ed.), *Hiroshima in History and Memory* (Cambridge: Cambridge University Press, 1996).

Hoyt, Edwin Palmer, *The Battle of Leyte Gulf: The Death Knell of the Japanese Fleet* (New York: Weybright & Talley, 1972).

Hoyt, Edwin Palmer, *Blue Skies and Blood: The Battle of the Coral Sea* (New York: Eriksson, 1975).

Iriye, Akira, *Power and Culture: The Japanese-American War, 1941–1945* (Cambridge, MA: Harvard University Press, 1981).

Iriye, Akira and Cohen, Waren, (eds), *American, Chinese and Japanese Perspectives on Wartime Asia, 1931–1945* (Wilmington, DE: Scholarly Resources, 1990).

Kerr, Bartlett E., *Flames Over Tokyo: The U.S. Army Air Forces' Incendiary Campaign Against Japan, 1944–1945* (New York: Donald I. Fine, 1991).

Koburger, Charles W., *Pacific Turning Point: The Solomons Campaign, 1942–1943* (Westport, CT: Praeger, 1995).

Leckie, Robert, *Okinawa: The Last Battle of World War II* (New York: Viking, 1995).

Levine, Alan J., *The Pacific War: Japan Versus the Allies* (Westport, CT: Praeger, 1995).

Maddox, Robert, *Weapons for Victory: The Hiroshima Decision Fifty Years Later* (Columbia, MO: University of Missouri Press, 1995).

Matthews, G.F., *Reconquest of Burma, 1943–1945* (Aldershot: Gale, 1966).

Mayo, Lida, *Bloody Buna* (Garden City, NY: Doubleday, 1975).

Newcomb, Richard F., *Iwo Jima* (New York: Holt, Rinehart & Winston, 1965).

Newman, Robert P., *Truman and the Hiroshima Cult* (East Lansing, MI: Michigan State University Press, 1995).

Ogburn, Charlton, *The Marauders* (New York: Harper & Row, 1959).

Parillo, Mark P., *The Japanese Merchant Marine in World War II* (Annapolis, MD: Naval Institute Press, 1993).

Prange, Gordon W., *Miracle at Midway* (New York: Penguin, 1982).

Prefer, Nathan N., *Vinegar Joe's War: Stilwell's Campaigns for Burma* (Novato, CA: Presidio, 2000).

Renzi, William A. and Roehrs, Mark D., *Never Look Back: A History of World War II in the Pacific* (Armonk, NY: Sharpe, 1991).

Reynolds, Clark G., *The Fast Carriers: The Forging of an Air Navy* (New York: McGraw-Hill, 1968).

Rhodes, Richard, *The Making of the Atomic Bomb* (New York: Simon & Schuster, 1986).

Rooney, David, *Wingate and the Chindits: Redressing the Balance* (London: Arms & Armour Press, 1994).

Sherwin, Martin J., *A World Destroyed: The Atomic Bomb and the Grand Alliance*, 3rd edn (Stanford, CA: Stanford University Press, 2000).

Sigal, Leon V., *Fighting to a Finish: The Politics of War Termination in the United States and Japan, 1945* (Ithaca, NY: Cornell University Press, 1988).

Skates, Roy, *The Invasion of Japan: Alternative to the Bomb* (Columbia: University of South Carolina Press, 1994).

Spector, Ronald, *Eagle Against the Sun: The American War with Japan* (New York: Macmillan, 1985).

Taaffe, Stephen R., *MacArthur's Jungle War: The 1944 New Guinea Campaign* (Lawrence, KS: University Press of Kansas, 1998).

Thorne, Christopher, *The Issue of War: States, Societies, and the Far Eastern Conflict* (New York: Oxford University Press, 1985).

Walker, Samuel J., *Prompt and Utter Destruction: Truman and the Use of the Atomic Bombs against Japan* rev. edn (Chapel Hill, NC: University of North Carolina Press, 2004).

Werrell, Kenneth P., *Blankets of Fire: U.S. Bombers Over Japan during World War II* (Washington, DC: Smithsonian Institution Press, 1996).

Willmott, H.P., *Empires in the Balance: Japanese and Allied Strategies to April 1942* (Annapolis, MD: Naval Institute Press, 1982).

Willmott, H.P. *The Barrier and the Javelin: Japanese and Allied Strategies, February to June 1942* (Annapolis, MD: Naval Institute Press, 1983).

Willmott, H.P., *The War with Japan: The Period of Balance, May 1942–October 1943* (Wilmington, DE: Scholarly Resources, 2002).

Y'Blood, William T., *Red Sun Setting: The Battle of the Philippine Sea* (Annapolis, MD: Naval Institute Press, 1980).

Young, Donald J., *The Battle for Bataan* (Jefferson, NC: McFarland, 1992).

Notes

1 Michael J. Lyons, *World War II: A Short History*, 4th edn (Upper Saddle River, NJ, 2004), xi.
2 Kent R. Greenfield, *The Historian and the Army* (New Brunswick, NJ, 1954).

INDEX

Illustrations are denoted by page numbers in *italic*.

Index

Index